Ellen Waugh, Mór Jókai

Freedom Under the Snow

A Novel

Ellen Waugh, Mór Jókai

Freedom Under the Snow
A Novel

ISBN/EAN: 9783337029623

Printed in Europe, USA, Canada, Australia, Japan

Cover: Foto ©Thomas Meinert / pixelio.de

More available books at **www.hansebooks.com**

MAURUS JOKAI

THE GREEN BOOK

OR

FREEDOM UNDER THE SNOW

𝔄 𝔑ovel

TRANSLATED BY

MRS. WAUGH

NEW YORK AND LONDON
HARPER & BROTHERS PUBLISHERS
1898

THE GREEN BOOK

OR

FREEDOM UNDER THE SNOW

CONTENTS

THE GREEN BOOK

CHAPTER I

SNOW ROSES

A BLIZZARD is covering the roads with a thick coating of snow. The horses are up to their fetlocks in it. The dark-green firs bend beneath its weight, and what has melted in the midday sun already hangs from the slender branches of the undergrowth in thick masses of icicles; and as the wind sweeps through the forest the ice-covered leaves and branches ring and jingle like fairy bells.

Ever and anon the moon shines out from amid the fast-flying clouds; then, as though it has seen enough, hides itself again under the ghostly mist. The sighing of the wind through the forest is like the trembling of fever-stricken nature. In the stillness of night, through the pathless forest, rides a troop of horsemen. Their little long-maned horses sniff their way with low, sunk necks; by the shaggy fur caps of their riders, and their long lances hanging far back at their sides, they are to be recognized as a party of Don Cossacks.

They ride in battle array. In the van a picket with drawn carbines; next to them a detachment; then a cannon drawn by six horses. After that follow a large body of men; then, again, a mounted gun and artillery-

I

men. Behind these another troop of mounted horsemen, and another gun-carriage drawn by six horses.
But to this the cannon is wanting. In its stead a human
form lies bound. The head hangs down over the back
of the rattling carriage, and as the moon ever and anon
peeps out from between the clouds, it discloses a face
distorted with agony, from which all trace of hair on
head or beard has been cut away—perhaps dragged out.
The eyes and mouth are wide open. A coarse horse-
cloth covering is fastened underneath the man. A corner of it drags along the snow-covered ground. From
it every now and then a drop of blood falls—a sign that,
in bleeding, the man still lives. The drops of blood in
the snow fantastically change, as they fall, into roses.
Red flowers on the white snow-field! The ghost-like
procession disappears in the mist.

Keeping carefully to one side, but ever following
closely on the track of the soldiers, is a horseman, also
mounted on a long-maned, broad-headed pony. He
wears a thick fur coat; a fur-bordered czamarka is on
his head; icicles hang from his long beard. He rides
slowly and cautiously, his horse taking long strides, as
though its master were seeking something on the ground.
Then, as often as he sees a red rose upon the snow, he
dismounts, kneels, and with a golden spoon he takes up
the crystallized token and places it in an enamelled reliquary, then rides on to the next.

The way leads without interruption through a primeval forest. It is the forest of Bjelostok. Only there, in
all Europe, are bisons to be met with. There no sound
of axe is ever heard; storms alone bring down the giant
trees. One forest arises out of the decay of the former.
Beeches, oaks, limes, vie in height with tall pines. In
the dead of night resound the shriek of the lynx, and

the roar of the female bison anxiously calling for its sucking calf. But no human sound is to be heard. No human dwelling is near. Had not the path through the forest been a highway, undergrowth had long since made it impenetrable.

The fallen drops of blood lead the rider on farther and farther. Now they appear at longer intervals. At length the last rose is reached; the track left by the wheels of the gun carriage is now his only guide. The horseman continues to follow it. The man bound to the gun-carriage is assuredly dead by this time. If dead, they will as surely bury him somewhere.

Upon the endless solitary forest follow towns equally void of human beings. On the banks of a great river stand two towns facing one another, marked upon maps of a former century as still fortified places, but now only to be classed among ruins. At that time they were specified by name, Kazimir and Ivanowicze, I believe. Now their very names are lost to history. Fallen walls, heaps of bricks and stones everywhere. Nettles grow rank in the snow-covered squares and streets; castles, churches, and temples are overgrown with briers to the very roofs. The broad river is frozen over; from out the ice rise the piles of a half-burned draw-bridge, near to which stretches a track across the snow. The solitary horseman follows the traces. In the middle of the river his scrutinizing search is suddenly brought to a halt by a newly made gap in the ice.

That it is newly made is shown by the broken ice lying about, upon which no fresh layer of snow has had time to form. The shape of the gap is oblong—like an open grave. Close round it are traces of many feet upon the snow; not far away the smooth surface shows the pressure of a human form, which must have lain

there face downwards.   Here, without a doubt, has
been the place of burial.   They had lowered the body
under the ice (a secure burial-place, indeed) ; the current would then convey it gently to the sea.

The horseman dismounts, kneeling down beside the
open space and baring his head.   He murmurs something—perhaps a prayer.   Into the water beneath there
drops something—perhaps a tear.

At that instant the moon shines out resplendent.
The man's head is distinctly visible—a head once seen
not easily forgotten.   A high forehead ; the hair of reddish hue, but already tinged with gray, growing low
upon it ; the face thin, nervous ; cheek-bones and
chin prominent ; nose aquiline ; deep-set eyes ; the
towsled beard brushed forward ; the character of the
whole face was one of suppressed suffering, of silent woe.
The moon has again disappeared under the clouds.   A
thick, heavy mist falls around.   Primeval forest and
ruins alike fade ; the figure of the horseman grows more
and more shadowy.

Through the thick mist, in the dead stillness of black
night, is a weird sound of sighing and moaning.   Perhaps it is the she-bison calling her young—perhaps it is
the voice of one singing " Boze cos Polske."

CHAPTER II

MIST SHADOWS

At the same time that the wanderer on the rough path
of Bjelostok forest was gathering up its snow roses,
another man on the far-off shores of the Black Sea was
preparing for a long, distant, and hurried journey. The

two men hasten to the same goal. They had never seen one another, had never heard the other's name, had never corresponded. Yet each is aware of the other's existence; aware that they are to meet, and that this meeting must take place on a given day. The first has, perhaps, the shorter road to take, but he can only ride slowly; he has to avoid inhabited towns, to utilize night for his progress, to pass the days in isolated csards.

The second has the longer and more difficult way; but the only battle he has to fight is with the elements of earth, water, fire, and wind, and these he can conquer. The fifth obstacle—man—places himself obsequiously at his service. This traveller wears the uniform of a colonel. Short of stature, he gains in height by the singular erectness of his head and the elasticity of his walk. By that walk he can be detected under any disguise. His closely cropped hair displays a broad, high brow; his eager eyes dance in his head as he speaks. He has an expressive face—one from which it is easy to read his thoughts, even when his lips are silent —a face in which every muscle moves with his words; one in strongest contrast to that of the other man. He can hide his every feeling under an immovable countenance; this one betrays beforehand his every thought. During his five minutes' colloquy with the jemsik, he has exhausted a whole gamut of expressions, from flattery to rage, as if playing upon the strings of a violin. He gesticulates violently with his hands; now his five fingers are under the peasant's nose; then they strike him on the shoulder, punch him in the ribs, seize him by the lappet of his coat; now shake, then embrace him. He kisses him, strokes his beard with coaxing action, then tugs at it, pushes him roughly away, finally reaching him

his flask for a drink ; and perhaps his only object has
been to find out whether the road to Jekaseviroslaw is
passable or not.

For while the snow still lies deep in the forest of Bjelostok, and gun-carriages may yet drive across the ice-covered Niemen, thaw has already set in along the valleys
of the Dnieper and the Don, and the whole plain is a
sea, from out which the rush huts, with their surrounding plantations of reeds, stand out like solitary islands.
To every hut a boat made of willow is secured; this
boat is the one and only mode of locomotion, albeit a
dangerous one, whereby in the spring season the inhabitants can convey themselves to the pasture-land to look
after their cattle and horses.

As far as eye can reach stretches out the endless red-
dish-brown plain.   Rushes, reeds, and other water-plants
not yet freed from their dried-up winter clothing, lend a
deep-red shimmer to the landscape, to which the sprout-
ing willows, now illumined by the light of the setting
sun, add their tinge of color.   The storm-portending
evening glow tinges the fleecy clouds flame color, causing
the rest of the sky to appear topaz green.   Myriads of
water-birds whirl restlessly through the air, filling the
plain with their cries.   In the far distance swim a flock
of swans, tinged golden in the setting sun, which, half-
sunken beneath the horizon, sends out its last rays
across the changing clouds, like a departing sovereign
clothed in gold and purple.

Across the great, never-ending plain there is but one
path, laid bridge - like with willow stems.   Over this
the traveller must needs make his way—there is no alternative.   The river banks passed, further sign of human habitation ceases.   The smithy of a gypsy colony, which has established itself on the side of a hill,

alone sends its light far out into the evening mist. Soon
that, too, will be lost in the gathering gloom ; then the
traveller's three-horsed car must jolt along by the fitful
light of the moon. An occasional kurgan rising up here
and there in the Steppe is the sole sign that it was once
inhabited by a people. Those tschudas upon the brow
of the hill were their gods. Blocks of stone, with roughly
carved human heads, proclaim afar, even to the banks
of the Amur, the former abiding-place of a race which
has not left even a name behind, only its gods, which
later races have called tschudas (from the Hungarian
word *csuda*, signifying " miracle ").

The traveller will find shelter for the night with a
Czaban, who has chanced to dig himself a cave near
the wayside, and lives there, surrounded by his numer-
ous herds of sheep. The Colonel remarks in his note-
book that the shepherds living in the neighborhood of
the kurgans are a stupid, squalid set, who smell of cheese.

Next morning the chariot with its ringing bells proceeds ever farther and farther, until the inundated banks
of the Dnieper oblige it to halt. Here the traveller has
no resource but to take to a boat. Luckily the stream
is sufficiently swollen to enable his boat successfully to
navigate the famous Falls of Herodotus without striking on the rocks. Only of the last does the ferryman
warn him. It is the Nyenaschiketz (the Insatiable).
There it is not advisable to tempt one's fate by evening light.

" But I must go on," says the traveller, imperiously.
He is in haste. That alters the case. His imperious
" must" knows no hindrances. Upon it follows the
only answer, " Seisas" (Immediately). This one word
characterizes the whole people. It even bridges over
the " Insatiable." The boat goes to pieces, but boat-

man and traveller swim safely to shore. The remainder of the night is passed in a fisherman's hut. The traveller here remarks in his note-book that the boatmen and fisher-folk who live on the banks of the Dnieper are a stupid, squalid set, who smell of fish.

The opposite bank is inhabited by the Zaporogenes, who take their name from the falls "zaporagi"—people who live beside waterfalls. Here it is only possible to proceed on horseback. By nightfall the traveller has reached Szetsa, a so-called village. The houses are earthen caves, thatched with grass, called "kurenyi." The traveller, after having sung and drunk with the Zaporogenes, observes in his note-book that the dwellers in "kurenyi" are a stupid, squalid set, smelling of coach-grease.

The first work of a Zaporagen is to soak his new garments in tar, to make them durable. Among that people are to be found the first indistinct traces of a longing after freedom, primitive, but still existent. This instinct reaches its culminating-point in the propensity to rob their neighbors; turn their wives out of doors when tired of them, and take to themselves a fresh one, who may please them better.

On, on, in the saddle, until the ancient city of the Steppe looms in the horizon, "the Mother of Cities." It is Kiev, the so often razed and rebuilt Jerusalem of the Scythians, with its catacombs and remains of Sarmatic saints. In the distance a deceptive Fata Morgana, looking with its gilded cupolas like a city of churches, from out which the mighty tower of Lavra rises like a giant.

The traveller avoids alike the Beresztovo, the most inhabited quarter, and the barracks; nor does he avail himself of the hospitable shelter of the Lavra monastery, but seeks the Jewish quarter, and there in a poor-looking Jewish hovel passes the night, taking counsel with soldiers who, as though informed beforehand of his coming, have entered one by one through the low entrance-door, to disappear in like manner by the opposite one.

The traveller remarks in his note-book that the Jews are a stupid, squalid set, who smell of anise-seed.

The way lies ever northwards. Spring-time vanishes from the earth; the glow of evening from the sky; a canopy of gloomy gray mist overspreads the firmament: the pale disk of the sun is like a medal upon a ragged soldier's cloak. Even the waning moon only rises late of nights. The nights grow longer, and the flames of the rush-heaps burning in the fields impede the way. The traveller is often obliged to turn back to the houses which border the pine forests. They are well-ordered, pretty domiciles, inhabited by apostates who have taken refuge from their pursuers in the woods.

There, too, sounds an occasional chord of yearning after freedom. They are prepared to endure, to make a firm stand, one and the other, in order to be allowed to write the name of Jesus ("Jhsus"). This is something for a beginning!

The traveller records in his note-book that the Raskolniks are stupid and unhappy, and smell of leather.

Still farther northwards. Upon the plains green with young wheat follow again expanses of snow; instead of flocks of swans and cranes, swarms of ravens and Arctic birds are to be seen thickening the air. This time the traveller passes the night in the Sloboden, where all sorts and conditions of men congregate—men from the most remote parts in search of work, offering their pair of hands for any description of labor. Hither each brings his misery, his ignorance, and—foul odors. The misery and ignorance are one and the same, but the foul odors are diverse : by these they distinguish one from another, through these they fall into broils. No sooner do they perceive the alien smell than they come to blows.

Time presses with the traveller. Now he has reached the land of sledges.

Thick mists and snow-storms are his companions. There come days in which there is no morning or noon-day; the snow-drifts change the world around him into a prison-house. Such terrific snow-storms are only known in those parts; they are "pad," the terror of travellers. The night frosts have become insupportable in their severity; the mile-stones lie hidden under the snow; the north wind has swept it into hillocks in many places; then, again, into deep holes, in which the sledge sinks axle-deep: a chorus of wolves howl in the woods. By morning the door of the csárda is snowed up; the only mode of egress is to crawl through the hole in the roof, where the jemsik, his sledge already horsed, is in waiting, leaning against the chimney. He calls laugh-ingly to his fare :

"It is cold enough for a couple of fur coats, sir !"

The north wind has chased away the clouds over night; the sky is the color of steel. In the gray lilac-tinted horizon a red glowing fire-ball is rising—it is the sun, which, running its orbit, scarce rises over the earth; even at mid-day it gives out no warmth. The king-dom of winter reigns. And now the way becomes more peopled. Life seems bright and stirring in this king-dom of winter. Whole strings of sledges, laden high with wares, move onwards in the one direction; well-appointed equipages, steering clear of the heavily laden freight, pass them by. It is the last day of the journey.

Along the horizon a shining streak grows visible—the frozen ocean. The streak grows broader and broader, and as the sun goes down the rays of the aurora borealis stretch up over the starry sky to its very zenith; and, illuminated by this magic sea of rosy light, there arises from out the expanse of snow a giant city, with the white roofs of its palaces, the cupolas of its churches, the bastions of its fortresses, cupolas and bastions alike of dazzling whiteness, as though it were the ghost of a city, painted white upon white; above it the rosy northern light, behind it the bluish-leaden veil of mist.

The traveller has reached his goal. But the other—is he here too?

CHAPTER III

COMME LE MONDE S'AMUSE

It is the last day of "Butter-week." Despite the excessive cold, the streets of St. Petersburg are thronged with a tumultuous crowd. To-day meat may still be eaten, to-morrow the great fast begins; every butcher's shop will be shut; for seven whole weeks oil is in the ascendant. Every one is in haste to make a good meal to-day.

The great Haymarket, the "Szenaja Plostadt," is the attraction to the hungry throng. There, in long rows before the butchers' booths, stand on their four feet frozen oxen, bucks, and wild boars, with heads outstretched, the butcher either sawing or chopping off the desired joint for his customers; his knife would make no impression upon the hard-frozen meat. Quantities of small game — hares, partridges, pheasants, and black-

cock—from other countries, preserved by the icy atmosphere, hang in festoons from the booths. The venders
of bear's flesh have their separate quarter; the centre of the square is taken up by the fish shops, where
great heaps of bemaned sea-lions are offered as del-
icacies. Purchasers in tens of thousands pass before
the booths, some on foot, others in sleighs with bells
jingling, the greater part of them women, while the sell-
ers are all men. No women hawkers are to be found
here. Even the special delicacy of Butter-week, the
"blinnis," are made by men bakers; these are om-
elets soaked in butter and spread with caviare. Then
there are the Raznocsiks, tall young fellows, their fur
coats fastened with a girdle round their waists, who,
with baskets on their heads piled high with every kind
of eatable, go in and out of the crowd with untiring cry,
" Come, buy pirogo ! saikis ! kwast !" The venders of
tea are keeping it boiling hot in their great samovars;
the doors of the spirit-booths are forever on the swing.
Pirog especially disposes to a good drink. It is a flat
cake, composed of chopped fish, meat, and coarse vege-
tables — a choice morsel — and this is the last day on
which it may be enjoyed; to-morrow it may not even be
thought of. All St. Petersburg is in the streets. It is a
lovely day in March; not a day of spring and violets,
but of frost and icicles. The north wind of yesterday
has sent down the thermometer fourteen degrees. Splendid weather !

At midday, just as the great clock of Isaac Church
begins to strike, a fresh hubbub arises among the noisy
throng. Down the long, straight street, called Czarskoje
Zelo Prospect, a party of huntsmen were seen coming
along in full pursuit of a magnificent twelve-antlered
stag. A stag-hunt at that season of the year is forbid-

den by the common laws of hunting. The new antlers are not yet grown ; they are but knots grown over with tender hide. No less is it permitted to follow a hunt through the streets of a city, more especially of St. Petersburg during Maflicza week. But this distinguished party does not seem bound by ordinary laws.

The hunting-party consists of some twelve men and three of the opposite sex, not counting about fifty huntsmen and packs of hounds. They send the people flying the whole length of the street before them.

It may have been that the start had been in Czarskoje Zelo Deer Park, that the stag had broken away and had taken his course towards the town, the huntsmen after him. A huntsman's zeal does not stop to inquire which way is permitted or which prohibited.

The stag dashes across Fontankabridge. In vain the toll-keepers put up the barrier, it clears it at a bound. Then, seeing the hunting-party in pursuit, the terrified toll-keepers prepare to reopen the passage. "Leave it alone !" shouts the foremost, and the company, following the example of the stag, clears it. Mr. Stag has meanwhile reached one of the principal streets, the hounds on his track ; the gaping country bumpkins at the street corners rush back in panic as the huntsmen dash past them.

At the entrance to the barracks of the Imperial Cadet Corps stands a grenadier on guard. If he has any sense he will shoot down the approaching stag, that it may not injure the crowd in its mad career. But military etiquette goes before common-sense. The soldier on guard, recognizing his superior in command, lowers his gun and presents arms. The rebellious stag meanwhile, knowing no such etiquette, springs upon the guard, and, catching him on its antlers, tosses him into the air.

The guard on reaching the ground again will probably present arms once more from that lowly position. The stag, by this time, has reached a cross street. This is one of the most frequented promenades in the imperial city. The loungers rush away in all directions, women screaming, men swearing, dogs barking—one runs against and upsets the other — sledges overturn upon fallen foot - passengers. The stag and hunting-party spring over outstretched bodies and overturned sledges alike. It is capital sport—no one can take any hurt, the snow lies too thick. Now the stag, reaching the Haymarket, seems somewhat bewildered. For one second it stands affrighted, the dense throng blocking up the great square. The next something attracts its attention. It is the row of stags, which it takes for a herd, standing up before the game-dealers' booths. Now the instinct of all hunted animals is to seek refuge in a herd if they come upon one. So away into the thick of the throng! Now the roar, the screams, and curses become a very pandemonium. Booths and butchers' stalls overturned bear witness to the creature's wild career; but no sooner has it reached its lifeless fellows and, with quick instinct, scented blood, than, maddened with fury and with antlers lowered, it forces itself a passage back into the Garten Strasse, and tears off panting and snorting towards the Costinoi Dwor. This is one of the curiosities of St. Petersburg—the great bazaar.

The Costinoi Dwor is a distinct quarter in itself, where everything of most costly nature, from Persian carpets to diamond necklaces, is to be bought. Here the stag evidently thinks to find shelter. All the doors stand open. From among the thousand shops he must needs select that of a Venetian glass-dealer, huntsmen and hounds in hot pursuit. In the vast apartment,

supported by pillars, are massed crystal ornaments,
amounting in value to hundreds of thousands of rubles,
artistically piled into pyramids of fairy - like elegance,
the walls hung with Venetian mirrors reaching from
floor to ceiling. The unhappy Italian proclaims himself bankrupt as he sees the stag make for his shop,
containing such costly and perishable wares, and it is'
a comical sight to see the poor signor and his *fauteuil*
fall back head over heels when the crash comes. But
no sooner does the stag see an innumerable number of
its fellows reflected in the mirrors all around him, hounds
upon them, closely followed by galloping huntsmen, than
it completely loses the little remnant of wits it had retained, and, turning its back on the raving Italian, it
dashes through the ranks of its pursuers towards the
Appraxin Dwor, where Turks, Jews, Armenians, Per-
sians, brokers, second-hand dealers, Little and Great
Russians, Copts, and Raskolniks, Gruses, and Finlanders
abound, their stalls crammed with old rubbish from every
quarter of the globe, and they themselves standing out in
the middle of the street to better attract the passers-by,
two or three seizing the unwary customer by the arm at
the same time, crying up their own wares, depreciating
those of their neighbors, squabbling among themselves,
vociferating oaths, lying, cheating, bargaining—playing
the rogue in every barbaric language under the sun. And
to them, in their very midst, the excited, maddened stag!
Now the real fun begins.   It was a sight to see the terrified peddlers scattered right and left among their heaps of
rubbish, to hear their agonized adjurations to all the powers of heaven and earth ; to see them crawl on all fours,
frog-like, into their holes, as the huntsmen and hounds
went galloping in full course over their fallen bodies;
and to watch the angry company, after the wild hunt

had passed, streaming back again to their desecrated
wares with loud laments, proclaiming that the world was
coming to an end. The stag simply flew over the heads
of the densely packed throng; the hunt could not follow
up so rapidly; it required the huntsmen's whips to keep
the dogs together in such a bewildering crowd. Thus
it gained a certain advantage, and, reaching the Boule-
vard of the Fontana Canal, dashed across the frozen
stream to the opposite bank, and sped down the Goron-
schaja Street before its pursuers came up with it. [At
the time of our story (1825) a palace, surrounded by a
large park, the Bulasky Gardens, stood there. The
great fire of 1862 has since laid it, as well as the whole
Appraxin Dwor, in ruins; the railway-station of Czarskoje Zelo now occupies the site.]

The park is surrounded by a high gilded railing,
through which sprigs of vine-covered firs push their way.
Perhaps the stag takes it for its native home. Close by
palace and park lies the great Obuchow Hospital; some
five hundred patients, men and women (most of them
epileptics) are just coming down the opposite street, returning from Trinity Church, where they have been attending mass. Should the affrighted creature rush in
among the panic-stricken crowd, there would be no escape for them—their crippled, infirm forms, their en-
feebled brains, would render it impossible. The very
fright alone might kill them, deadened as are their
senses. Now a chorus of horror arises from the procession of imbeciles, who, as if under a spell, come to a halt,
helplessly awaiting the attack of the incomprehensible
foe. Infirmity has not crippled their feet alone, but
their thinking powers also. Nothing intervenes to stop
the approaching stag. As it flies in full career past the
principal gate of the Bulasky Gardens a shot resounds in

the air.   The stag makes a side spring, throws back its
head, sinks down, struggles up again, plunges its bleeding nose into the snow, then stretches itself out, resting
its stately antlered head on the threshold of the gate,
as though in gratitude to him whose well-directed aim
has released it from its pursuers.

Sport was spoiled.

CHAPTER IV

NO RIVAL

WHAT unheard-of audacity, to spoil the sport of such
an aristocratic hunting-party !

"Who fired that shot?" cried the foremost of the
huntsmen, with a threatening crack of his whip.

The hounds dashed furiously on towards the open
gate, their sense of the dignity of the hunt equally insulted.

The question had been put in Russian ; and the action was in accord with the speech, although the speaker's face was close shaven in the French style, while the
other members of the hunt all wore short whiskers.

"I took that liberty!" returned a woman's voice ;
and from under the fir-trees, whose branches overhung
the gate, appeared a woman's form, slender as one of
the Amazons of the "Kalevala" Saga, her pale oval
face surrounded by loose-falling hair of reddish gold,
like a lion's mane ; the nose, straight and delicate, and
full lips recalling the Niobe group ; while at sight of the
great flashing eyes, instinct with magic beauty, one was
irresistibly reminded of a peri from the "Sakuntala."
A very fairy, who united in herself the threefold myths.

2

" I dared do it !" she said, coming forward alone, unattended. And carelessly dispersing the excited dogs
with one hand, she raised the pistol she held in the other,
and, pointing it at her interlocutor, continued : " And
there is another shot in it for you if you do not instantly
lower your whip."

The hounds were cringingly snuffing about her whom
the moment before they had been ready to tear in
pieces; the huntsman, too, was not less susceptible to
the charm than was the pack. Raising his whip, he
touched his cap courteously with it, and addressed her
in French, the language of Russian society:

" It were unnecessary, madame, that you should use
firearms, possessing as you do in your eyes such powerful weapons."

By this speech the huntsman betrayed the school of
Versailles, where men were accustomed to carry on war
with compliments, and to mask retreat with gallant
words.

Meanwhile the rest of the hunting-party had come up
to the gates. The gentlemen, seeing with whom their
comrade was in conversation, held in their horses, as
though not wishing to take part in it; only an older
man, wearing an order set in diamonds on his fur-lined
coat, approached nearer ; and one of the ladies, galloping
straight up to the gate, pulled up her horse at its threshold, the body of the dead stag alone separating her
from the other woman.

The huntswoman wore a blue, fur-bordered jacket,
with hunting-cap to match, under which her fair hair
hung in ringlets to the shoulders. Her face was
crimsoned with eagerness and the extreme cold, giving to her somewhat prominent eyes a still more dazzling brilliancy than they were wont to have ; her thin,

delicately shaped lips were half open; the blue veil falling over her forehead, and the blue band she wore under
her chin as a protection from the cold, did not allow
more of her face to be seen. But as she drew up close
beside the other lady she pushed back the chin band,
perhaps in order to speak more freely, thereby displaying a pretty, rosy chin, divided by charming dimples.

"How dared you shoot that stag?" she cried to the
other lady. "Did you not know it was an imperial
one?"

"How dared you chase that stag to the very gates of
the hospital? Did you not know that it is a hospital for
cripples?"

"I hope you recognize that the Czar is the first gentleman in Russia."

"Throughout the whole world the first gentlefolks are
the sick."

"You are foolhardy, madame."

"That I admit."

Now the huntswoman lifted her veil. She was heated.
She toyed impatiently with the riding-whip in her hand.

"Why am I not a man?" she muttered, between her
pearly teeth.

The huntsman with the clean-shaven face, reading
from his companion's working features and piercing eyes
that there was something more in dispute than the shot
stag, now bending towards her, addressed her audibly
enough in German. For though the French language
—that of the best-beloved enemy—is the language of
society in the Russian capital, German — that of the
most hated friend — is only spoken by the exclusive.
German is therefore spoken when the servants are not
desired to understand.

"A rival, eh?" asked the clean-shaven one.

The huntswoman projected her lips scornfully, and, knitting her brows, answered aloud in German :

"Neither rival nor ———"

The lady standing by had distinctly heard the short colloquy, and was perfectly aware that she had another charge in her pistol.

The speaker had turned pale as she spoke, like a duellist who, having fired his shot and wounded his adversary, now awaits the other's fire.

The owner of the park did not do this, however. There are words, looks, and gestures which can strike deeper than the most deadly weapon. Placing one foot on the crowned antlers of the stag lying prone before her, she smiled full in the face of her adversary; and, as though to emphasize the insulting challenge, raising her pistol, she fired the remaining shot into the air. For an insult loses its sting if directed by an armed person against one unarmed. Now once more she stood conqueror.

The huntswoman's face flamed with fury. She twisted her riding-whip in her hands like a serpent, as though inwardly debating whether to strike it across the other's face, and thus wipe away the irritating smile.

One of the other two ladies was young, little more than a child. Her face a perfect oval, with exquisitely formed chin, a little rosebud mouth, large, deep-blue eyes, looking black in the distance, dark, finely pencilled eyebrows, and hair hanging in soft, shining plaits down her back.

Her whole face wore the astounded expression of a school-girl. The strangest thing about her was that she rode a gentleman's saddle, with which her costume was in keeping—the Circassian beshmet, the broad, white salavár, high boots, and flowing cashmere, with hanging

kindzsál.   Every one but she knew what the two women
were saying to each other.   He who happened to be ignorant of the language could understand the gestures,
the contemptuous expression of the features, the cross-
fire of eyes.   The young girl did not understand even
that.   She merely looked on in amazement.   That the
two ladies were angry with each other she saw—and
about a stag's antlers!   The riding-whip was twisted
about in the huntswoman's nervous fingers until it
snapped.   She made use of another weapon.

"Bethsaba!" she exclaimed, turning to the girl, and
speaking to her in a language unknown to any of their
auditors—possibly Circassian; but the expression on
the speaker's face, and the terror-stricken, pallid look
on that of the young girl, said as plainly as words:

"You have asked me what the devil looks like? Look
at that woman; there you have the fiend in human form."

The girl, bending her head, crossed herself as she cast a
frightened side glance at the dreadful woman, who was the
embodiment of his Satanic Majesty.   Then the Amazon,
turning her own horse, and at the same time seizing the
reins of that upon which the young girl was mounted, galloped back the way she had come, huntsmen and hounds
following.   The stag remained where it had fallen.

CHAPTER V

PLAN OF WAR AGAINST A WOMAN

On the way back to Ghedimin Palace naturally nothing was spoken of by the members of the hunt but the
exciting scene to which they had just been witness.

"*Parole d'honneur*," said the clean-shaven horseman,

as he struck his riding-boot with his whip, "the whole
world is turned upside down ! In the time of the Empress Elizabeth, if any woman had allowed herself to
insult a Princess Ghedimin in that manner, she would
have had her tongue cut out and have been punished
with the knout."

"This is what we have to thank exaggerated philan-
thropy for ! It was never created for us. Voltairian-
ism will be the ruin of the nation. How can Araktseieff suffer it ?"

" The woman is no Russian ?"

" Perhaps some English or German here to spite us,
and who has placed herself under the protection of the
Embassy ? By Jove ! in 1816, when I was last at home,
such a thing would not have been permitted !"

"These cursed foreigners ! Anyway, if the president
of the police does not take the matter in hand, we will
administer the knout ourselves. I swear your presence
alone withheld me just now, Princess Maria Alexievna !"

"Indeed ! You do not know who the woman is."

" What does it matter who she is ? She may even be
a princess."

" She is more than that."

"Then some expatriated queen, perhaps from Georgia."

" Silence !" said the lady, as she gave a warning look
in the direction of the girl riding at her other side.

" She does not understand German. So the woman
is really a queen ?"

At this question the lady laughed heartily.

" Really a queen ! A true queen ! A reigning queen
—an absolute monarch ! We all are her slaves ; you,
I, even Alexis Maximovitch. A queen who is not to

be driven out of her kingdom by means of cannon, but
with this !" and she held out to her companion the
whistle of her shattered riding-whip.

"What ! an actress ?"

" Of course.   What else should she be ?"

" Ha, ha, ha !   To whom the whistle means a revolution ; whose throne is upset by hisses !   Ah, Maria
Alexievna, present me with this whistle.   With it I will
fight for you, as a knight *sans peur et sans reproche.*"

The lady resigned the fatal weapon, so efficacious in
the downfall of stage potentates, to her cavalier, as the
latter lifted her out of her saddle in the portico of the
Ghedimin Palace.

He then kissed her hand.   She kissed him on the
cheek, and, taking the young girl by the hand, she
passed through a treble glass door and ascended the
broad frescoed staircase within.

Here the hunting-party broke up, making rendezvous
at the opera that evening.

Now the silent, bestarred gentleman, who had hitherto
not mixed in the conversation, slapping the clean-shorn
one on the back with the flat of his hand, said :

" Nicholas Sergievitch, a word with you.   Come along
with me."

" At your service, Alexis Maximovitch."

And together they rode off to the Araktseieff Palace.

There are no old palaces in St. Petersburg.   The
whole city only dates back a century and a half.   The
palace of the favorite official of the Czar is situated
on the Nevski Prospect, and is built more for comfort
than for elegance.   During the winter the whole building is heated throughout with hot-air pipes ; every window has treble cases ; the floors of the rooms are of
parquetry.

The two huntsmen said nothing until they had re-
freshed themselves with hot tea seasoned with arak and
a curious compound of cayenne and cantharides. A
tiny portion on the point of a knife of this latter warms
one's frozen limbs. In any other climate it were poison.

The great man whom we now recognize from the
name of his palace, Araktseieff, first locking the door of
the room they were in, pushed up a rocking-chair to the
fireplace for his guest, gave him a chibouque, and himself took up his station before the fire.

" Hark ye, Nicholas Sergievitch, put the whistle you
received from the Princess just now among your treasures, and when you want to blow it go out into the
woods. That is my advice to you. For if you carry
out what you have sworn to the Princess you will find
yourself next day on the road to Irkutsk, and, by Heaven!
I can't say when you will be coming back."

" The devil!"

" You see, the Czar is of opinion that he can create a
hundred noblemen such as you in an hour; but singers
such as Zeneida Ilmarine are to be met with but once in
the century."

" Ah! So this mysterious stranger is Zeneida Ilmarine, the far-famed Simarosa heroine? All honor to
her! I take my pipe out of my mouth as I speak her
revered name! When I made my promise to Princess
Ghedimin, I had no idea whom it concerned. This ab-
solves me from my oath. Against the ' divine ' Zeneida
one may not revolt, even to please the ' angelic ' Maria
Alexievna. Rather raise the standard against the whole
army of legitimate rulers! What a fool I was! The excessive cold must have frozen my wits like quicksilver
in a thermometer. Of course, I had heard abroad that
the *diva* was a *protégée* of the Czar and Czarina, and,

moreover, the beloved of the brave Ivan Maximovitch. From the dialogue in which the two ladies indulged, I might have gathered that it was a meeting between wife and lady-love."

" Now you must devise a way to find favor with both. Favor with the wife, as with the sweetheart."

" Easy as kiss your hand. I have only to tell one about the other."

" That may succeed with the wife, for she is outspoken, straightforward, and passionate. With the favorite, however, it may be more difficult; for she understands how to play as many parts in real life as on the stage. And your office it will be to find out which is the real one."

" That I will do—as sure as my name is Galban."

" Well, Chevalier Galban, you may imagine that it is a matter of some importance which has induced us to call you back from Versailles, where you were to us as eyes and ears are to man. You have there learned, in masterly fashion, how to unravel the most secret diplomatic webs by means of a woman's heart, yourself the while remaining unscathed. Now you must carry out your masterwork at home."

" What, Holy Russia has secrets which her police and the priests are unable to fathom?"

" My dear Chevalier Galban, our good Chulkin has enough to do to catch thieves, and is not too successful in that department. I counsel you, if your sledge be stopped on the way home from the club at night, give the thief your purse quietly, for if you call the watch the soldiers will ease you of your fur coat into the bargain. If, on the other hand, you fall into the hands of a policeman, he will not only clear you out, but the thief too. As for the priests, they count for nothing to our people, who are atheists."

"Have we come to that?"

"Yes; to that. General Kutusoff did well to say, when our forces came back from the French War, 'The best thing the Czar could do would be to drown the whole expedition in the Baltic.' They were all indoctrinated to a man with liberalism, and have infected the entire army. I assure you that many a young officer carries 'The Catechism of a Free Man' and 'A Scheme of Constitutional Monarchy' about with him in his coat-pocket."

"How do they get hold of them?"

"They must have a secret press."

"They have been allowed to play with freedom too long."

"That were the least danger. As long as we allowed them the game of freemasonry, all was open and above board. At the court balls they would talk in the presence of the Czar himself of freedom, and debate over the rights of the people and the emancipation of serfs. That was all academical discussion. But when the masonic lodges were closed, and the insignia sold by auction in the Jews' market on the Appraxin Dwor, the secret evil grew worse and worse. The freemasonry of Mamonoff, of a sudden, took five or six different forms. One called itself a 'General Betterment Society,' Orloff at its head. Another was 'Szojus Spacinia,' a third 'The Confederation of Patriots,' a fourth 'Szojus Blagadenstoiga.' There is another constituted under the title of 'Republic of the Eight Slav Races'; its members wear an eight-pointed star as a token, the inscription on one of the points being Hungary. They grow like mushrooms."

"Ridiculous! Even in my time there were clubs where secret meetings were held. But there was no talk then of danger to the State. If certain much-wronged

husbands had no complaint to make, the police might
let us go scot-free."

"That is not the case now," answered Araktseieff, impatiently. (It was his habit, when receiving secret visits
in his own house, to keep a sword-stick in his hand, with
which he would incessantly prod screens, walls, and hangings, as though ever suspecting listeners; and did he perceive that his visitor had a bulging pocket-handkerchief
or note-book, he would prod that, too, to discover what
was there.) "They are about everywhere, and yet nowhere to be traced. They give each other rendezvous at
balls, concerts, wine-parties, etc., and so contrive to give
our spies the slip. Why, they actually keep a register, a
sort of parliamentary hand-book, in which the confer-
ences of every distant province are entered concerning
the organizing of a systematic revolution throughout Russia; the best form of constitution; what is to become
of the dynasty; how the empire is to be partitioned,
and whether to be represented by landed proprietors
or the people. And this protocol it is which contains
a fully named register of the conspirators, those who
hold the threads of the net in their hands throughout
the whole land, from the shores of the Black Sea to the
Arctic Pole. Among themselves they call it 'the green
book.' Now, where is this book? That is the question."

"To which I reply by a counter-question. But do
not keep on so incessantly prodding my coat-pockets
with that sharp stiletto of yours. Has any one seen
this book—and, if seen, why has he not said where he
has seen it?"

"That I will tell you, too. The conspirators are divided into three classes. The first are 'Brethren.' To
this community any one may belong, on his introducer
making himself responsible for him; they know nothing

beyond the fact that they are members of a conspiracy,
and have the right to attend meetings. The second class
are called 'Men.' They are trusty people, who, on a certain watchword being given them, are authorized to act.
You may reckon one-third of the officers in the army as
belonging to this class. They cannot betray anything
beyond their own individual names and the work given
them to do. Then we come to the third class, the 'Bojars,' and leaders of the whole affair. It is extremely
difficult to get in among them; and those who do belong
to them do not betray one iota."

"Are they married men? Have they no wives—no
mistresses?"

"That question occurred to me long ago. It is no new
discovery that women are the best mediums for discovering secrets. Bright eyes and diamonds can cast light into
many a dark corner—that is an old story! That 'the
green book' is in the custody of some woman is un-
questionable; but, so far, with all our espionage, we
have reached no further. We were informed that Orloff's mistress was the possessor of 'the green book,'
and paid down enormous sums for the information.
And what did we find? A pack of scandalous anecdotes of St. Petersburg society, all of which, moreover,
were known to us before. Then we got on another
scent. 'The green book' was in the keeping of the
'Martinists,' whose president had a lady-love—faithfulness itself. In her case all our bribes were useless.
So one night we had her surprised in her room, bound,
the boards of the floor raised, and actually there was
found a 'green book.' But it contained nothing but
atheistic theses. What was the use of them? People
may rebel against the Deity, but not against the Czar!
At length we received secret information that the heart

of the conspiracy is that league which calls itself 'The Northern Union'—its head Prince Ghedimin."

" The devil !"

" Yes, my friend ; the next in succession to the throne ! He it is who must hold possession of 'the green book,' or who has had it in his keeping. To whom should a man confide so dangerous a treasure but to his own wife ? But the husband, we are told, always wore the key of the iron chest in which the book was guarded round his neck. Father Hilary attacked the Princess on the religious side, and persuaded her to remove the key from her husband's neck when he lay unconscious in typhus fever. She must have had many sins to atone for. Anyway, she did commit the small piece of treachery, and I passed a whole night studying 'the green book' obtained from Ghedimin."

" Well ?"

" Well, having carefully gone through it, I flung it to the other end of the room. The book was filled with dangerous doctrines—nothing more. Pure abstract reasoning, philosophical treatises, and the like, but no single name of any member. What care I for the utterances of Seneca, Rousseau, Saint-Just ? What I want to know is what the Muravieffs and Turgenieffs are talking about. That, too, was a mere piece of trickery. That cunning Ghedimin did not trust his wife. He gave her a book to keep which the Censor—had she betrayed him—would readily have condemned to be burned, but for which the President of Secret Police would have grudged the oil consumed in the reading."

" Then, if the real 'green book' is not to be found in his wife's keeping, it must be in that of his lady-love —and that lady-love is Zeneida?"

" Right."

"Is she a foreigner?"

"No; a subject. A Finnish girl from Helsingfors; and especially favored by'the Czar, because she has triumphed over the pride of the Empire—Catalani. The Czarina, too, is very gracious to her. You know that the Czar is a great music-lover, and will not suffer the school of Cimarosa and Paisiello to be set aside by the modern school of Rossini. Zeneida Ilmarine does not sing a note of Rossini. At all hours she is admitted to the imperial family. How often have I—ay, and even the Grand Duke Nicholas—had to kick our heels in the antechamber while she was having audience? At the court soirées she is treated like any reigning princess; she alone is privileged to wear in her hair a white rose, the Czarina's favorite flower. It is entirely due to the magic of her voice that the Finnish students of Helsingfors escaped being sent off in a body to Kiew after the rebellion; for she can intercede as effectually as she can sing. The Czar would have raised her to the rank of a duchess, but what do you think the spoiled *diva* said? 'Would your Majesty wish to degrade me?'"

"And is this the woman who could take part in a conspiracy against the Czar?"

"Why not? if the leader of that conspiracy be sweet upon her, a Prince Ghedimin, the most powerful among Russia's twelve ruling families, the number of whose serfs and estates more than equals the whole kingdom of Würtemberg. Do not forget, moreover, that she is a 'Kalevaine.'"

"What are the proofs of this suspicion?"

"I have already told you that the conspirators are marvellously clever in eluding detection. It is not their way to creep into obscure corners or subterranean caves; they rather hold their meetings in the midst of crowds and in public places. This is a wrinkle they have learned from the Poles, among whom the 'Phila-retes' and 'Vendita' usually meet at their yearly fairs. Now the fast is at hand. For seven weeks every public amusement is forbidden, that the people may see that great folks do penance as well as themselves. High and low must attend the services of the Church. But no one asks what takes place o' nights behind closed doors. This is the harvest-time for secret meetings. The invited guests have no political proclivities; they have no wish to found constitutions; their sole idea is to enjoy a good dinner—'Anti-fasters' they call themselves. Surprised by the police, all that would be discovered would probably be a table spread with appetizing game or steaming roast-beef, and, maybe, a few guests the worse for liquor. The 'sinners' would, of course, be fined, but no one would be the wiser of what was taking place in the more private apartments. And here our prima donna has peculiar advantages. The stage, as you know, makes its own laws. Who in the world expects to find strict morality among actresses and ballet-dancers? The police wisely shut their eyes to much that goes on among them. He who is lucky enough to be an invited guest to one of Zeneida Ilmarine's exclusive Carême soirées will find all the frivolous beauties of the opera and ballet, all the *jeunesse dorée* of St. Petersburg, assembled, and will have no need to complain of either the lack of fiery eyes or fiery wines. Many a man has been singed by them. But if he be wise enough to keep his head in the midst of the tumult, he will observe a certain portion of the company disappear gradually and noiselessly from the reception-rooms."

"There may be other reasons for such disappearance."

"Certainly. For instance, roulette may be carried on in those private apartments. Now, the Czar has issued a severe prohibition against roulette‑playing— any one caught in the act is sent straight off to Siberia, without possibility of remission of sentence. It is a fact that Zeneida's calumniators, especially among the women who are envious of her, have circulated the report that she keeps a roulette bank, which enables her to indulge in all her lavish luxury. I hold a different opinion."

"Upon what grounds?"

"That Michael Turgenieff is a constant guest at these theatrical soirées, and is one of those who at midnight disappear into the inner apartments. Now, Michael Turgenieff is a philosopher and a puritan."

"Even philosophers have their lucid intervals, induced by combined charms of pretty women and good wine."

"We know Michael better. I have had my eye upon him ever since his Demi-Decemvir. He was the only one among his young companions who did not give way to any of the modern forms of debauchery. In his travels through England, France, and Germany, he only sought out great writers and men of mind and genius; he was never to be found in fashionable or vicious haunts. Not even in Paris, where vice and pleasure reign supreme. What, then, should possess him to se-cretly worship here at the altar of false gods? No; the presence of this one man alone is sufficient to betray that those closed doors conceal other than Eleusinian mysteries."

"And it has, so far, been impossible to discover them?"

"No sooner does Zeneida, taking the Duke's arm, leave the company than it assumes the aspect of a revel. Beauty and folly take possession of men's

senses, and next day not one of them can recall anything but that they have had a jolly evening. If a
'Brother' try to follow a 'Bojar' in his retreat, he is
surrounded by sirens, who lure him back by a conspiracy of charms. In order to let diamond cut diamond,
and so conquer the high-priestess of the mysteries
herself, it needs just such a conquering hero as you
are."

"Very flattering for me! When shall I make a beginning?"

"This very night. It is the last day of Maslica week,
the last night of the opera. Zeneida is to sing in Cimarosa's *Secret Marriage.* The streets will be thronged.
At the stroke of midnight the bells of all the churches
will proclaim the beginning of Lent. Every one goes to
confession. In the opera queen's kingdom, however, the
revel begins. Prince Carnival, with his merry company,
will make his joyous procession through the brilliantly
lighted saloons, through whose fast-closed windows no ray
of light, no sound of music, may penetrate. You must
manage to procure an invitation to the entertainment."

"After the insult of to-day?"

"You are master in the art of intrigue."

"I have given my promise to Princess Ghedimin to
hiss her rival off the stage to-night."

"You have given me your promise to win her to-night."

"The time is too short."

"But the opportunity favorable. I am informed that
yesterday two men arrived in the capital who are rarely
seen here. The one is Krizsanowski, from Poland; the
other, Colonel Pestel, of the Southern Army. Both have
already received invitations to Zeneida's so-called dance.
Only there can you come across them; and you must
find out from them what has brought them here."

3

"I will be there."

"How will you manage it?"

"As we men begin all love affairs—by means of presents."

"Ah! this nymph is richer than you, my dear fellow. She makes her forty thousand rubles in a single concert. If her mood is for diamonds, she chooses out the most costly; if for something better than diamonds, she divides her night's earnings among the poor. It may happen that you receive back your presents twofold."

"I will make her a present which will command her favor—an eight-in-hand."

"Ah! such as the Czar alone possesses?"

"Such as not even the Czar possesses! You shall see, with this eight-in-hand, I will force open the gates of the fairy castle. Leave the rest to me. If a 'green book' be in existence, I will know its contents."

CHAPTER VI

OLD AGE

PRINCE GHEDIMIN was dining that day with his wife. Both he and the Princess studiously avoided mention of the affair which so abruptly ended the hunt. Yet it was unlikely that the news of it should not have spread throughout the city. The police alone appeared ignorant of it, the shot stag remaining on the spot where it fell. Was it the intention to remove it at nightfall, when no one could see who took it away?

"Shall I meet you at the opera to-night?" asked the Princess.

"I am not sure if I can be there."

"It would be a pity to remain away. Fräulein Ilmarine sings in the *Secret Marriage* for the last time this season. She will have a great ovation."

The Princess firmly believed that Zeneida would be hissed off the stage; and what could be better than that the Prince should have the pleasure of witnessing her humiliation from his wife's box?

"I am awfully sorry that I cannot engage to be there, my dear. As you are aware, it is my night to visit my grandmother, and when once I am there the dear old lady is sure not to let me come away. She has so much to ask about every one, and at the stroke of midnight she will expect me to take the organ in the chapel adjoining the apartment and sing through the penitential mass; and I cannot refuse her. But if you wish that we should spend the evening together, why not come with me?"

"Oh, many thanks. I do not sing in masses."

"But you have not once been to see the grandmother since our marriage."

"I think you know that I shrink from dead people."

"But the poor old soul is still living."

"So much the worse—a living death! It makes me shudder to look at a mummy, and to think that some day I too shall appear like one!"

"Ah, well! A pleasant evening to you, my love."

"Edifying devotions, your Excellency."

The Prince withdrew. The Princess sent her dwarf after him, that—hidden among the orange-trees in the conservatory—he might find out whether the Prince had actually gone to his grandmother's apartments, and how long he stayed there.

Ivan Maximovitch Ghedimin really did pass through the corridor into his grandmother's apartments. The old lady inhabited the central block of the palace, its windows, on both sides, looking on to the court-yard.

It is twenty years since Anna Feodorovna has left her apartments. Even in the sultry summer heat, a time when all the aristocrats of the capital take refuge in the islands of the Neva, she passes it among her fur-hung walls.

Since the spring of 1804, when she had a critical nervous illness, she has spent her days in a wheel-chair, the being wheeled from the dinner to the card-table and back again her only exercise. She dreads fresh air.

At first she had some society. Three old ladies of her own age used to come to play whist and gossip with her. Gradually they left off coming; first one, then two, at length all three. No one dared to tell her that they were dead; she was told that they found it difficult to mount the stairs. Since then she had played her game of whist alone.

The old lady still wears the old-fashioned cotton costume which was so fashionable in 1803, when the Czar Alexander had forbidden the importation of foreign woollen stuffs. She thinks that every lady in society still wears it, and with it a cap and feather, closely resembling a turban.

It is now twelve years since the last of her contemporaries visited her. All have now been gathered to their fathers. But Anna Feodorovna must not know this. All are living, and on every great occasion send her their messages and congratulations, exchange consecrated cakes with her, and colored Easter eggs; and on Easter morning she always finds on her table their illuminated visiting-cards, with the inscription in letters of gold, "Christos wosskresz."

History for her has stopped with the signing of peace

between the Emperors Napoleon I. and Alexander I.; and the appointment, at that date, by the Czar, of her only son, Maxim Wassilovitch, to the command of the new Georgian regiment of Lancers. Georgia had just been incorporated into Russia, and Anna Feodorovna tells proudly to this day how, on one occasion, she had the honor of a conversation with Heraclius, the deposed Emperor of Georgia; how her beloved son, Maxim, brought his Majesty up to her, and although she did not understand what he said to her—for his ex-Majesty only spoke Persian, which was not at all like either Russian or French—they had had a most interesting conversation.

From that period in history it had been the endeavor of the family that no rumors of the world and its events should disturb the quiet of that revered member. A daily paper was published separately for her, from which every war detail was scrupulously expunged. The reigning sovereigns did nothing in the world but give or take a princess in marriage, magnanimously yield each other territory, distinguish their generals for no reason whatever; and, that the century might not pass over without some blood-shedding, the unbelievers on the far-off island of Tenedos were occasionally slaughtered; a revolt of the Kurds on the boundaries of Persia would be suppressed from time to time; or Belgrade be conquered by Csernyi-Gyurka. Anna Feodorovna knew nothing of the terrible French invasion, nor of the burning of Moscow; nor that her only son, Maxim, had fallen in the battle of Borodino. Her paper, on the contrary, stated that Maxim Wassilovitch had been appointed Governor of Georgia, and had at once proceeded there without furlough. From that time news had regularly come to her from him, and he had sent letters, which her man-servant was obliged to read to

her, for her eyes were not capable now of deciphering
handwriting. The good son who never forgot his old
mother! Her man-servant, faithful Ihuasko, is everything to her—cook, house-maid, reader. He, too, must
be some seventy-five years old; thus fifteen years
younger than his mistress. No other serving-man would
have held on as he had done, no other have submitted
to put a seal to his lips, and have observed silence as
to all that was passing without. Even among us men
there are few Ihnaskos. And on a fête day, such as this,
it is especially difficult, when Anna Feodorovna does not
play cards—for card-playing is sinful—and there being
no whist, she questions the more.

Fortunately for her she has a good appetite, and can
enjoy all the varieties of cakes sent her by "her friends"
on this last Maslica day.

"Ihnasko, I cannot believe that Sofia Ivanovna prepared these cakes herself. She always stones the raisins
so carefully. Try this one."

"You are right, your Highness. But then the poor
lady's eyesight is not so good as it was."

"Oh yes; she grows old, like me. Reason enough to
see nothing."

(The main reason, however, is that six feet of earth
lie between her and the world.)

"And the little princess, and the brunette countess,
have they sent their usual congratulations to-day? And
the Lieutenant-General's wife, who is so hard of hearing?"

"The cards are all laid on the silver table, your Highness."

"And you have acknowledged them in the customary
manner?"

"At once, your Highness."

" You should have written in very large characters to
the Lieutenant-General's lady, for she is so hard of hearing. Has the old beggar-woman come for the warm
clothing? Was she glad to have it? Did she not prophesy good luck for this year? Is it not to be a comet
year? Ah, there is no chance of that! Have you taken
the grand duchesses their bouquets?"

" I took them. They return their thanks."

" Are neither of them married yet? Dear me! They
must be of marriageable age now."

(Both are long married—in their girlhood—to the
white bridegroom, Death; but no one has ever told
Anna Feodorovna this.)

" How is the old man?"

" As usual."

" Does he make use of the Elizabeth pills I sent him
against gout?"

" Constantly."

" Can he sleep at night?"

" Sometimes, yes; sometimes, no."

" Does he not grumble when it is new moon, or the
wind blows?"

" At times. But he soon calms down."

"Of course, he always has that horrid pipe in his
mouth, and sits in clouds of smoke like a charcoal-
burner."

" What else should he do?"

" Wait a minute. Just take him these warm night-
caps. I knitted them with red wool for the old man
myself. He has always liked red caps. Tell him that
I think of him, though he does not think of me. But
what could he send me—tobacco ashes?"

(Alas! the *old man* has long become dust and ashes
himself. He was Anna Feodorovna's husband, a martyr

to gout, who did not see his wife once in a year, although
they lived in the same house.   Neither would visit the
other.   She could not endure a pipe ; he could not live
without it.   One day he, too, found that his mausoleum
in the Alexander Nevski Cathedral was a more peaceful
resting-place than his bed ; but he was interred so silently
that his old wife did not know of his death, and continued
to knit him his red night-caps.)

"Where can Boysie be so long?   My boy is surely not
ill?   It would be a fine thing if Boysie forgot me !   I will
give him a downright scolding for this."

Hereupon Ihnasko had to calm his old mistress by
telling her that "Boysie" had been called upon to attend
an important council held by his Imperial Majesty the
Czar.   Most probably concerning some new grant of
territory.

That was quite another thing !

Of course, Boysie was a grown-up man now—a man of
thirty, and the owner of many an order set in brilliants.
It is her grandson, the haughty, powerful Prince Ivan
Maximovitch Ghedimin, whom his old grandmother still
calls the "Boy."

The lamp has long been lighted ; indeed, for days together it is not extinguished.   At the least current of air
the windows are closely curtained, and three or four days
may pass before daylight is again admitted.   It matters
little to the owner of the apartment whether it be day or
night; she neither rises nor goes to bed.   She lives in
her arm-chair.   If she is sleepy, she goes to sleep ; when
she awakes she is ready for her food, and with good appetite.   Every Sunday her maid washes and dresses her,
and that function lasts for the week.   When the bells of
the Isaac Cathedral begin their midnight peal she knows
that Sunday has come round again ; when her newspaper

is brought to her she knows that it must be Friday.
Sometimes the two, Ihnasko and she, quarrel about politics.

Just now there are strained relations between mistress
and man. A paragraph in the newspaper has stated
that "the heroic George Csernyi has taken the fortress
of Belgrade from the Turks."

The mistress chooses to understand by this that Csernyi had stormed the fortress and massacred the unbelievers; the man, on the contrary, takes it literally, that
he had bought the fortress from the Turks for sterling
cash.

Over this they quarrel hotly.

"When Ivan comes, he shall decide it; and if you
are right, you shall have a brand-new coat trimmed with
fox; if I am right, you shall get five-and-twenty lashes
with this rod from my own hands!"

From her hands, who had not the strength to kill a
fly! But the old woman is vindictive, and has already,
for the third time, ordered him to lay out the new coat
and the courbash on two chairs, so that the instant
Ivan comes he shall get either the one or the other.
And yet she forgets all about her anger, Belgrade, and
George Csernyi the moment "Boysie" appears on the
scene.

He comes in so gently at the tapestried door that she
only perceives him when he stands before her.

Her Boysie is the handsomest man in the whole capital; he is as tall as the Czar.

His languishing gray eyes wear an earnest, thoughtful
expression.

"Now, you bad boy—to come so late! Is school but
just over? Are you not afraid that I shall make you
kneel to ask my pardon?"

He is already kneeling before her ; and the old grandmother passes her thin, wrinkled hand over his face as
he bows his head on her lap.   Laughing, she playfully
ruffles his hair.

"This naughty Boysie!   He knows how to coax his
old grandmother, like any kitten.   All right ; you shall
have no blows this time.   I forgive you ; so no need to
cry.   He has just the same shaped head as my Maxi- .
milian ; only Maximilian loves me best, for he writes to
me every month ; and yet he is a great man.   At your
age two orders of merit already decorated his breast.
But what have you done?   Have you fought yet for the
honor of your country?   Are you following in your
father's footsteps?"

The old woman's hands feel over the young man's
breast until they rest upon the diamond star of the
Alexander Nevski order, upon which she cries, joyfully :

"This is no cross ; it is a star !   And set in brilliants !
You have robbed your father, for this order would have
sat well upon him.   He is a hero, a great man ; the diamond star would well have become him.   But he, too,
has already obtained the first grade of the order, has he
not?   And set with diamonds as fine as these?"   (Ah
yes — ah yes ! he has received it set with glistening
pebbles in the cool sands of the Muscovite soil.)   "But
now stand up.   You are a grown-up man, and what
would the Czar say if he were to know that his privy-
councillor still knelt, like a boy, at his grandmother's
knee?   Stand up, my dear boy, and tell me about matters of State.   I know how to talk about them.   Oh, in
Czar Paul's time I was up in everything.   It was I who
kept the old man back from joining in Count Paklem's
conspiracy, or he would be even now in Siberia.   Eh,
my boy, you love the Czar?   That's right.   How many

a time has Czar Paul bastinadoed your grandfather! And he never complained. But now there are no conspiracies throughout the whole land against the Czar."

"None, dear granny."

"If at any time you should hear of plots, mind you tell it at once to headquarters. If you knew there was a thief lurking under your grandmother's bed, would you not straightway drag him out by the legs? Much more is it your sacred duty to destroy all conspiracies against the Czar's Majesty. He who works against the Czar will be punished, but he who serves him will be richly rewarded. How was it with Kutusoff? Did not the Czar take the finest jewel from his crown to present to him, and had a golden leaf set in the empty space with 'Kutusoff' inscribed upon it? The family of the Ghedimins is not inferior to that of the Kutusoffs."

Ivan turned pale. The family name, "Ghedimin," and the Czar's crown? One was a part of the other. The topic was a dangerous one. High-treason might be named in the next breath.

"My whole life I have consecrated to the Czar, granny." And then he blushed at his own words, for he had spoken falsely. He neither can nor dare tell the truth to living soul. His old grandmother is the only being on earth he really loves; and her, too, he must deceive. From morning to night his life is a lie; he must look men in the face and lie; must lie to baffle the spies ever on his track, so that at night he dare not offer up the prayer, "Incline thine ear to me, O God," for dread lest he must lie even to his God.

"I have been waiting for you ever so long. I have had a sharp dispute with Ihnasko, and you must be the arbiter;" and she related the subject of their dispute. "So now, who is in the right?"

Ivan laughed.

"As far as experience goes, you were right, grandmother; for fortresses, as a rule, are taken by force. But in this case Ihnasko was right, for George Csernyi really did buy Belgrade for good coin of the realm. So give the good fellow the coat, and not the whip."

The old lady nodded to her man-servant.

"Do you hear, Ihnasko? Thus should a just judge decide. Like Prince Ivan, he should give the servant right over the master, if need be, even if it be over his own grandmother. Rejoice, ye people, that your fate will rest in the hands of a man whose lips only know the truth!"

Ivan turned away.

"But now come nearer, sit down by me, and make your confession. When are you going to marry? It is high time. Have you not made your choice yet?"

And Ivan had to answer, "No."

He could not tell her that he had been already married three years to a woman who was so utterly heartless that she would not be presented to his old grandmother because she was afraid of her age and wrinkles—so he had answered, "No."

"Now you are telling me a fib. Let me feel your pulse. Of course, it was a fib! And why should you not have fallen in love? Look! in this drawer I am keeping a diadem for your bride; it is the same diadem I wore when your grandfather led me to the altar. Then Moscow was the capital of the empire. Where this fine palace stands were nothing but clumps of willows. Now, your bride shall adorn herself with this diadem. Take it; I give it you. You best know who is to wear it. The girl you love shall be my very dear granddaughter."

But Ivan, in truth, did not know to whom to give the diadem. He had a wife who had no love for him, and he loved a woman who could never be his wife. Thus to neither could he give it.

"I will take care of it, dear granny, until the right one comes."

"But now you will stay to supper with me, will you not, that we may eat the last Butter-night meal together? You are not going to be off to any bachelor drinking-party—to get into all sorts of wild company? You will stay, like a good son, with the old grandmother."

And so Ivan stayed to supper, and had to declare how much he was enjoying it, when he had dined but so short a time before, and knew all the while that in Zeneida's palace a Lucullus-like feast awaited him. If his digestion rebelled against the sacrifice, his heart made it a thousand times heavier.

Oh, the unspeakable agony that overpowered him as he thought how at that very time his affronted wife would be venting her whole vengeance upon that other woman who the world knew had thrown her soft shackles over him, and whom he dared not openly protect, least of all against this aggressor, his own wife! Had the Czar been in St. Petersburg, she would not have dared to molest her; but, in his absence, his powerful favorite, Araktseieff, was supreme.

To tell the truth, Ivan was glad that his absence was compulsory. A warm, tender-hearted man, of weak will, he was unequal to the situation. Taller by a head than most other men, he had been chosen as a leader among them; but the position oppressed him, for, capable as he was in all else, he lacked the necessary courage and decision for the post.

What he would most gladly have done would have

been to say adieu one fine day to all his palaces, possessions, confederates, and to Russia, and to go out
with Zeneida into the wide world to sing tenor to her
soprano. Perhaps, too, it might have come about, had
Zeneida been an ordinary artist and nothing more. But
the disquieting thought is there — what may happen
to-night on that other stage? Perhaps she is destined
to mortification on the one; but on the other? On those
boards the blood of the actors is wont to flow.

And all this time his fond grandmother could not press
him enough to eat, as she asked news of Maria Louisa
and the great Napoleon, of the little King of Rome, and
many another who had long passed away; to many of
which questions Ivan returned such mixed answers that
the good Ihnasko was constantly exercised to set him
right, being far better informed through his newspapers of all these things than was the absent-minded
Prince.

At the first sound of the bells the old lady conscien-
tiously lays down her knife and fork; and Ihnasko, without awaiting orders, proceeds to clear the table, and
spreads another silken cover over it.

It was Lent.

"Let us draw near to our heavenly Father!" whispers
the pious old lady.

Ivan kisses her cheeks, and she his.

There was a small door opening out from her bedchamber into the chapel. Opening this, Prince Ghedimin went in; and while his old grandmother, rosary in
hand, began telling her beads, the tones of the organ
were heard, and a man's clear voice began chanting the
penitential psalm.

"What a good son and a good Christian is my Ivan
Maximovitch!" murmured Anna Feodorovna, amid her

prayers. "And what a lovely voice he has! He might be one of the Czar's choristers."

And amid the sounds of pealing organ and penitential psalm she reverently thanked the Lord, and, praying for the living and the faithful dead, fell into peaceful slumber in her arm-chair.

The organ still continues to peal, and penitential psalms ascend, for Ivan Maximovitch—Prince Ghedimin—is a good man, and a tender, loving son.

And yet this again is a fresh lie; for, as Ivan entered the chapel from his grandmother's room, one of the Czar's choirmen, who had been admitted by a secret door, was already in waiting there, and his task it was to sing on and play the organ until the old woman had fallen asleep.

Prince Ghedimin, meanwhile, hastily descended the secret staircase and passed into a masked corridor leading from his palace into the next house. There, quickly assuming a disguise, he jumped into a sledge awaiting him in the courtyard, and gave the coachman directions where to drive.

Upon the Princess's return from the opera she was informed, both by his Highness's coachman and her dwarf, that the Prince was still at home, and had not yet left his grandmother's apartments.

CHAPTER VII

THE EIGHT-IN-HAND

PRINCE GHEDIMIN left his secret domicile in a simply appointed sledge, without crest, his coachman wearing no livery. He ordered his man to drive to the opera.

At that time the capital possessed but one large,

newly built theatre—the opera-house. Here representations of the drama, comedy, and opera were given, and
often on one and the same evening, the performances
lasting, as a rule, from early evening to midnight.

It was just the period when Russians had conceived a
passion for the drama. One theatre no longer sufficed
them. It had become the fashion for the wealthy princes
of the blood to have stages erected in their own palaces,
and to have representations given by their own private
companies of Shakespeare and Molière. Even in the
Czar's two palaces—the Winter Palace and Hermitage—
there were theatres, where the court actors and actresses
made their début. One leader of fashion carried the
theatrical mania so far that he never travelled to his
country-seat without taking his troop with him ; but, the
main difficulty there being to find the audience, he had
a collection of wax figures made—generals, statesmen,
and elegant women — and with these figures he filled
his stalls, to give the illusion of a full house.   If we add
that this theatrical company was largely recruited from
the retainers and serfs of the said magnate, there is
nothing improbable in the story that went about of him
that one night, as Othello was in the very act of throt-
tling his Desdemona, my lord in his box was seized with
a fit of sneezing, which resounded through the house ;
whereupon the dark-skinned tyrant, instantly abandon-
ing his murderous design, advanced to the front of the
stage, humbly uttered the Russian form, " God bless
your Grace," and then retreated, to proceed with Shakespeare's ghastly deed.

Hence we may imagine the enthusiasm excited by so
extraordinary an artistic genius as was Zeneida, a child
of the people—since Finland was *born* to Russia on the
day of Zeneida's birth.

Zeneida was a more powerful factor than a cabinet minister. Even in Catharine II.'s time a prima donna, on the Czarina's representing to her that she was drawing as heavy pay as the most renowned of her generals, had presumed to say flatly to her, " Then, your Majesty, bid your generals sing to you."

Prince Ghedimin's great source of anxiety was not that Zeneida might be exposed to some insult or humiliation at the hands of a wounded rival ; much more, knowing her spirit, he dreaded lest she, at first sound of a hiss, should rush forward to the footlights and begin singing the *Marseillaise*, and that if rotten eggs were thrown one moment, in the next men's heads would be flying. It needed so tiny a spark to fire the whole mine.

His heart was beating violently as he neared the opera-house. The clang of bells from a hundred clock-towers drowned all other sounds ; but as they ceased a roar rose in the long street into which his sledge had turned. The stately avenue was simply filled with a moving mass of people surging in his direction. What could it be ? A revolt, or a triumphal procession ? Hundreds and hundreds of torches cast their lurid light over the heads of the throng.

His heart beat faster and faster. He was not a lover of revolutions ; not one of those who grow drunk with enthusiasm when they hear the leonine roar of an insurgent mass. On the contrary, his soul shuddered within him at the thought. But he was a brave man—a man who, although heart and spirit might shrink, would know how to die with those to whom he had sworn fidelity; who, although his soul might faint within him, would walk with firm step to the scaffold for the great aspirations with which that soul was fired. More than one man has proved himself a hero whose soul has

4

quailed within him before the beginning of the fight.
Prince Ivan, ordering his coachman to stop, awaited the
throng.

And presently a strange sight met his gaze. In the
very midst of the torch-lit crowd came a golden sledge,
shaped like a swan. It was Zeneida's well-known sledge.
In it was sitting the prima donna (wrapped in her costly
sables, and literally covered with bouquets, the flowers
of which were beginning to sparkle with the night frost),
drawn by a team of eight—such a team as the Czar
himself had never been drawn by, since it was composed
of eight young noblemen, the cream of Russia's *jeunesse
dorée*. On the coachman's box sat Chevalier Galban in
person.

Prince Ghedimin, springing from his sledge, joined
the procession. Among the crowd a man was pressing
and forcing his way. In him the Prince recognized one
of his wife's lackeys. Reaching Zeneida's sledge, the
man handed up to Chevalier Galban an enormous bouquet of hyacinths, whispering a few words as he did so.
The Chevalier, straightway standing up, called out with
stentorian voice :

" Ho, ho, gentlemen ! Noble team of teams ! halt an
instant ! Look at this brilliant trophy ! See these flowers with their diamond-set bouquet-holder—'With the
expression of her admiration for our divine Zeneida—
from Princess Ghedimin !' "

A thousand hurrahs resounded through the icy air,
thickened for an instant with the breath from many
vociferous lungs.

"*Allons!* forward, my noble steeds !" And the eight-
in-hand proceeded on its way.

A young man was standing at the back of the sledge.
As Zeneida leaned forward to take the flowers, he reached

over her so that his face, bent downward, nearly touched
hers.   In such a position even a well-known face is hard
to recognize.   The man thus standing whispered to her:

" Timeo Danaos et dona ferentes."

" I do not understand Latin," she answered.   " Trans-
late it into some other language for me."

And he at once, converting it into faultless hexame-
ter, said, in their own tongue:

" Ever I fear the Russian, even when with gifts he
comes."

" Thanks, Pushkin."

The members of the "Northern Confederation " called
each other by their family names, in contradistinction to
the old Russian usage, which is to call every one by
their Christian names, adding to a man that of his father,
to a woman that of her mother.

So this young man was to become the renowned Pushkin.   At that time he had no such claim; at that time
he was a nobody.

CHAPTER VIII

AN ORGY OVER A VOLCANO

It needed a well-seasoned head to keep his wits about
him when, on entering Zeneida's palace, a man found
himself suddenly plunged into the fairy-like pell-mell,
such as is usually only to be seen at a masked ball at
the opera.

Hundreds of guests, invited and uninvited, thronged
the brilliantly lighted reception-rooms.   Zeneida to-night
had been acting in the last scene of *Semiramide*, and it
suited her mood to carry on the part of the all-conquer-

ing queen off the stage; to see her admirers, her slaves, and those she fooled, at her feet.

The whole *corps de ballet* were here assembled in the dresses in which they had appeared on the stage; the chorus and singers wearing their rich costumes of Persian and Median nobles. The male aristocracy of St. Petersburg, young and old, were there assembled. As the hostess appeared in the ballroom, leaning on Chevalier Galban's arm, the band, concealed behind the balcony of the gallery, struck up a welcoming overture; the guests cheered, and those nearest pressed round to kiss her hands.

However, things were not long destined to proceed so smoothly.

In the middle of the ballroom was standing a police-agent in full uniform, his helmet on his head. Going forward to meet the hostess and her cavalier, and bowing stiffly, he made a hissing sound which was supposed to stand for *Sudar* and *Sudarinja* ("Monsieur" and "Madame").

"His Excellency the President of Police bids you take notice that at the stroke of twelve to-night the great fast has begun, and all dancing, music, and entertainments of every description are in consequence prohibited. Such being the case, monsieur and madame's guests are to return forthwith to their own houses, and monsieur and madame, the host and hostess, to retire to their apartments. Monsieur and madame—"

Here Zeneida burst into a merry laugh; while Galban inwardly cursed the Minister of Police, who by his clumsy zeal was in danger of spoiling the excellent plan he and Araktseieff had together made out.

Zeneida drawing three golden-shaped arrows from her hair, handed them to the sergeant of police.

"Go back to your chief and show him these symbols. From them he will recognize that Assyria's queen challenges the Prince of Sarmatia to combat."

The words were over the head of the agent of police, but he took the golden arrows.

"Then I shall be compelled to take your names. Yours, sir, is—"

"Caracalla," replied Galban, readily, "and this lady is my wife."

The police-agent duly entered in his book, "Herr Caracallus and Madame Caracalla"; then turned to a gentleman who had just entered, Prince Ghedimin. "And what is your name?"

"Rainbow. Here is my card."

It may be mentioned that hundred-ruble notes are called "rainbows" on account of their gay coloring. The name pleased the agent of police so well that he evinced no further curiosity. With obsequious bow he wished the company a pleasant evening, drank a bottle of champagne on his way out, pinched the cheek of a pretty ballet-girl, then hastened back to make his truthful report to the President of Police that all was quiet and dark at Palace Ilmarinen as in a church, and not a soul waking save the house porter.

But this was not the sole interruption that night. Scarce had the agent of police taken his departure before the organist and chaplain of the Protestant church appeared. The chaplain began a honeyed speech, probably to the effect that he hoped the lady of the house, as a good Protestant, would not give cause of offence to the faithful of the State religion by desecrating the first night of so holy a fast by entertaining so motley a crew of the worshippers of Baal.

But Zeneida did not suffer him to proceed.

"Go back and tell your superintendent, my dear sir," said Zeneida, "that I am holding the rehearsal of a grand concert, which I intended to give during Lent in aid of the building of the Protestant church-tower."

Chaplain and organist were fully pacified. Going back they announced that the zealous and religious lady had begun the great fast with a good work for the benefit of the Church.

And now, at length, the doors could be shut; now there would be no further interruptions from without, and those present would not be leaving until to-morrow night had set in.

Chevalier Galban judged it advisable to resign the lady of the house to Prince Ghedimin.

"Allow me to introduce myself, Prince — Chevalier Galban."

"A name world-renowned. And one all-powerful among the ladies."

"I may perhaps claim in that respect to have kept up my reputation to-day. See, Prince, the bracelet round this bouquet. Do you not recognize it? And this?" And he drew forth from his waistcoat-pocket the silver whistle which had formed the handle of Princess Ghedimin's riding-whip.

Ivan recognized his own crest upon it.

"These are the two conflicting *souvenirs* of this morning's stag-hunt and to-night's triumph."

"And it is you who have formed the connecting link."

Prince Ghedimin was on the point of shaking hands with the Chevalier for having made conquest of his wife, and thus enabling his beloved to go scot-free; but in this he was prevented by the young man we have heard called Pushkin, who, pressing in between the Prince and

Galban, intercepted the intended hand-shake by a demonstrative embrace.

"Zdravtvujtjé Galban! I am Pushkin!"

"Ah, Pushkin! Bravo! I have heard of you. You are a Russian edition of a perfected Paris *bon vivant.*"

"Proud of the title!" None the less, he was anything but proud of it. You cannot offer a poet a worse insult than to credit him with a quality which has no relation to Parnassus. Still, Galban was no censor; he could not know how many of the bard's great works were lying low, massacred under the murderous red pencil. "Proud, my dear fellow, to act Rinaldo to the St. Petersburg dare-devils, and in that capacity your modest Epigon. Permit me, without delay, to make you known to some of the prettiest girls of our party to-night."

So saying, he passed his arm under that of Galban, and in rollicking fashion led him into the thick of the throng.

The Chevalier was content. It was his immediate task to make as many acquaintances as possible among the malcontents here assembled. To this end the guidance of so open-hearted and loquacious a comrade was highly acceptable. All the same, he soon had reason to find he had been a little mistaken in him.

The first individual with whom Pushkin made Chevalier Galban acquainted was the English ambassador, Mr. Black.

Mr. Black had only one leg; his other was an artificial one, which, however, in no wise prevented his taking part in every country dance to the very end of the programme. Moreover, all his movements were as automatic as if head and arms were on springs, and as if he took himself to pieces every night before going to bed."

"Mr. Black, the best fellow in the world! He neither

understands French, German, Greek, nor Russian. In fact, he only speaks English; and that we none of us know, so he is dumb to us. All the same, he is jolly as a sand-boy. A year or two ago he had one man about him with whom he could converse, his secretary. Unfortunately he took the poor devil with him one day in December, when it was atrociously cold, to the Alexander Nevski church-yard, to see the fine show of tombstones. A granite obelisk took the secretary's fancy uncommonly. On the way home my fine fellow partook somewhat too plentifully of brandy, to keep the cold out, and froze to death. Mr. Black carted him off to the stone-mason, then and there, and bought for him an obelisk like the one he had admired so much."

The ambassador, guessing that his praises were being sung, duly put in motion that part of his mechanism necessary for bringing a smile to his face; then shook the Chevalier's hand violently, and without more ado took possession of Galban's other arm. And now both men towed their victim along, until they came face to face with a third man, whom Pushkin introduced to the Chevalier with the words—

"Sergius Sumikoff Alexievitsch."

"Ah, the renowned conjuror! I have heard of your fame far and wide."

The very word "conjuring," and, above all, the notion of befooling others for the general amusement, had just then become the fashion, in Paris especially—of course to be readily imitated in St. Petersburg.

"But you have not heard his latest," broke in Pushkin, "the story about the negro? I must tell it you; it is such a joke. Sumikoff painted his face jet black, and gave himself out to be Prince Milinkoff's black slave. We were all in the fun, save Count Petroniefsky; he was to be fooled. Mungo played the piano and guitar, spoke Greek, Latin, declaimed Schiller, uncommonly rare acquirements in a negro slave. Moreover, he had all kinds of interesting details to tell, among others, how, when king in his native land, he had had his prime-minister, convicted of theft, crushed to death in a mortar. Petroniefsky, awfully taken with the fellow, goes to Milinkoff, and offers to purchase him. Milinkoff at first refuses; he is his favorite slave, can't part with him, etc. At length they settle the matter for six thousand rubles. On receiving the purchase-money Milinkoff gives his friend a hint to keep a sharp eye on the fellow, as he is deucedly fond of giving his owner the slip. The count answers, he'll see to that. Of course, the very first night Sumikoff washes off his Chinese black, and quietly takes himself off, without any concealment, through the open palace gates. We ordered a jolly supper for the six thousand rubles, and Petroniefsky has no idea to this day that it was he who paid the piper. He still daily routs up the unlucky police officials to bring him back his negro."

Every one laughed, Galban, with the others, all the time thinking, "Does my new friend really think with such worn-out anecdotes to keep me in pawn, and prevent my seeing that for which I came?"

And he did see it. He was an adept in the art of recognizing people from description, and amidst the noisiest surroundings to find that of which he was in search.

First among the crowded rooms, he made out the man described to him as Krizsanowski, and soon after the man called Pestel. He seemed to be all eyes for the conjuror's clever doings, the while he was closely watching the two men to see if they accosted each other.

Would they approach Prince Ghedimin and Zeneida?
Neither of these things took place. Did they acciden-
tally come across each other, they simply passed each
other by without even a look ; on the whole, they seemed
rather to avoid Zeneida. In between the crowd of
merry, noisy dancers he perceived many a striking face,
yet none of them seemed to have anything in common
one with another. Now Pushkin made a proposition.

"Why should not we four have a game of *ombre ?*"

Chevalier Galban saw through it. Not a bad dodge
to pin him to a card-table in some dark corner for the
remainder of the night.

"Thanks. I only play hazard."

"Humph! Strictly forbidden here."

"As is ball-giving in Lent," returned Galban, laughing.

Now a fresh procession riveted the general attention.
"The gypsies!" went from mouth to mouth.

In Russia, as in Hungary, the gypsy is the minstrel
of national song. It is curious that in Hungary instru-
mental music is the gypsies' art, while in Russia it is
singing. Troops of them go from town to town as choral
societies, and never fail at entertainments given at the
houses of the great.

The group of some four-and-twenty men and women,
clad in their picturesque Oriental costume, formed themselves into a circle in the ballroom, and began their
songs of wood and valley, while one of them, a girl, represented in her dance the subject of thei, song.

"By Jove! come and look at our black pearl," said
Pushkin, by the aid of his friend drawing Galban into
the circle. "Bravo, Diabolka! Show yourself worthy
of your name. Look how supple she is! she is a very
devil! Every one of her gestures is enticement. See

how her eyes sparkle! All the fires of hell are burning in
them! Enviable they who do penance there. And when,
with downcast eyes, she casts you a melancholy glance
from beneath those long silken lashes, you think she
must be on the verge of swooning. But, beware, the
tiger can bite."

The wild gypsy girl, suddenly starting from her lifeless
statuesque posture, here sprang upon Chevalier Galban,
and threw her arms around him.

"By Jove! the comedy is well planned," thought Chevalier Galban to himself. "Here am I fast bound in the
arms of this gypsy. My friends, the conspirators, know
how to set about things."

"Bravo, Diabolka!" applauded Pushkin; and in a
trice the three gentlemen had disappeared from Galban's
side; it was unnecessary to watch him longer. Once
Diabolka's net was spun about him, he was caught and
meshed.

Chevalier Galban saw through this also. Yet he was
too much a man of the world, and appreciated pretty
women too keenly, to turn from the offered cup. Accepting the situation, he led her to the buffet, to the ballroom,
to the palm-grove, everywhere, in fact, as faithful cavalier,
keeping the two men, however, always in sight. He began to observe that they whom he thus watched were also
watching him, and to feel convinced that they would not
leave the noisy, overflowing reception-rooms as long as
they saw him there. He planned a stratagem.

As he made the tour of the rooms for the second time
with Diabolka he promised to marry her, and in sign of
the betrothal drew off a ring and placed it on her finger.
The girl forgot to ask him his name; but she well knew
the name of the stone that flashed in the ring. It was
a diamond.

"And when you are my husband will you come with
me to our encampment where we mend pots and kettles,
and feast on the sheep we have stolen?"

"Not so. When you are my wife you shall come with
me into my castle. There you shall dress yourself in
new dresses five times a day, and eat off silver dishes as
if every day were our wedding-day."

"I will tell your fortune with cards; then we will see
which is the true prophecy. Come! Let us hide away
in some corner, where no one can see us."

Diabolka, it appeared, was perfectly at home. She
knew exactly where to press the spring in the wainscot
which should open a secret door. Within this door was a
tempting hiding-place, roomy enough for a cooing pair.
The door closed after them. In the crowded rooms one
couple was not missed. In the middle of the little retreat was a round table. On giving this table a twist it
sank, to come up again spread with a tempting refec-
tion, among which champagne, cooled in ice, was not
wanting.

Chevalier Galban smiled. So this was the idea. And
to make it more secure they had shut the cat in with
the mouse. Poor fools! They think to catch a serpent in a mouse-trap! Meanwhile, why not amuse
himself? The enemy must be allowed time to get into
battle-array. They believe him disposed of already.
And now, safe from his sharp eyes, the initiated will
be betaking themselves to the place of meeting. But
where is this place of meeting? In what hidden
portion of this mysterious building? These and like
thoughts rush through his brain. Tschirr! a sound
of shattered glass falling in a thousand pieces on the
table.

"When I am by your side, I forbid you to think of

anything else. When you can look into my eyes, do not
stare out into the wide world. Or are you afraid of me?
Don't you drink?"

Galban soon proved to her that he was not afraid of
her, and that he did drink. Seizing the bottle, he
drank. He may have had his reasons for thus drinking
direct out of the bottle. No sleeping potion can be
mixed with a bottle of champagne, for, once opened, it
forces its way out; while a drug can be easily conveyed
into a glass.

Chevalier Galban's suspicion that they might seek to
disarm him by means of a narcotic is the more easily explained in that he himself was carrying a similar medium
in his waistcoat-pocket, with the idea of ridding himself of any inconvenient obstacle did it come in his
way.

But one cannot listen to two things at a time, the
beating of one's heart and the tick of the clock. Galban knew this from experience. He must rid himself
betimes of the dark beauty. They were drinking by turns
from the bottle. One such bottle must do the work for
her. Four-fifths of a champagne bottle standing in ice
is frozen; the sleeping powder shaken into it can only
mix with that which remains fluid. The first who drinks
receives the opiate; the next one, drinking the wine as
it melts, takes no harm.

Diabolka's wild abandonment suddenly seemed to
give place to a certain exhaustion; her arms sank weari-
ly to her side; she began to yawn; her head fell back.
For an instant she pulled herself together as though
shaking off the inertia. She must not sleep now when
some great danger might be threatening without. She
reached out her hand for the water-jug. But the potion had been too powerful. Going a step or two, she

staggered; in the act of pressing her hand to her head she fell into a deep sleep. " Chain up the bear," she stammered. She was already dreaming of the forest. Then she fell full length on to the ground.

Galban, lifting her on to the couch, pressed the spring. The secret door opened to his touch, and he found himself once more in the palm-grove. This was an amphitheatre, some six fathoms high, massed with the rarest palms from India and Senegal, which in an atmosphere of artificial heat and sunshine were being coaxed into flourishing in a land where winter reigns nine months in the year.

Hidden behind a giant cactus, Chevalier Galban peered into the adjacent apartment, intent upon discovering whether the men he had previously marked were taking part in the Eleusinian mysteries. None were visible. It was in truth a *masked* ball; the ball was the mask, and they who wore the mask were no longer present.

Where were they then ?

All had disappeared, even Pushkin, the head and front of the revels.

He resolved to go in search of them. It was a difficult and dangerous undertaking. It meant beginning a search in a vast place, utterly strange to him, to which he had no clew; it meant avoiding any he might meet, deceiving those who noticed him by simulated intoxication—a drunken man, not knowing whither he was going; it meant the risk of being kicked out from intrusive disturbance of flirting couples. And even if at length he find the spot whither the conspirators had retired, it is only too probable that some watch would be kept to warn them of the approach of a suspected person. This watchman he must murder, his pistol at his breast; for

where a guard is necessary, a conspiracy lurks behind
the portal. Then to force his way in. If the doors be
closed, suspicion is well founded. Then is the palace
doomed; if need be, razed to the last stone. If the
doors stand open, then to enter with the words, " In the
name of the Czar, you are my prisoners !" Possible
that they may overpower him, but far more likely that
they will not. A detected conspiracy is demoralizing;
to say, " If I do not return to Araktseieff by to-morrow
morning, all who are here to-night will fall into the
hands of justice," will be to lame them and bring them
to his feet. Moreover, it is his profession. One man
dies in one way, one in another. The soldier knows
the enemy will fire upon him, yet he goes forward; the
sailor knows the sea is treacherous, yet he trusts himself to it. One man bows his head to the executioner's
axe, another bares his breast to the dagger. In both it
is heroism.

And suppose he should find the missing guests round
the board of green cloth, instead of round "the green
book," staking their money at the prohibited roulette-
table ? *Eh bien !* then he would join them, and say
nothing to Araktseieff. It would not be a gentleman-
like thing to tell upon them.

In his search he had, in a measure, an Ariadne clew,
like that strewn sand which, according to the fable,
served to guide the lost child out of the wood.

Zeneida had returned from the opera in her costume
as Semiramide, her wealth of reddish golden hair inter-
woven with real pearls. When Chevalier Galban, on
her triumphal return to the palace, had assisted the *diva*
to remove the bashlik from her head, he had, unseen
and purposely, severed one of the strings of pearls in
her hair. For a time the thick masses of hair might

hold them together, but it was unlikely that in moving hither and thither one should not occasionally fall to the ground.

He had already picked up one in the palm-grove; she had, therefore, passed through there. The second he found in a corridor; a third betrayed to him the threshold of the apartments into which she had disappeared. Where she is, there must the others be.

CHAPTER IX

THE BOARD OF GREEN CLOTH AND THE GREEN BOOK

THE room in which the "Confederation of the North" held its meetings was provided with double doors—a circumstance by no means uncommon in Russian palaces, in order that there should be no spying through keyholes, no listening at doors.

The centre of the room was taken up by a massive table, or rather a great chest, the upper part of which formed a roulette-table.

The rolls of gold—probably sovereigns (bank-notes are not used in roulette)—are laid out in rows, beside which is placed the croupier's long scoop. Each newcomer, as he enters, takes his seat at the table and puts down his purse before him. But there is no play—in fact, it is a mere sham. At each arrival the opening of the outer door sets the table in motion, the noise of the rotary ball calling the attention of those present to the fact that some one is coming. Thus there is no fear of surprises.

The introductions are performed by the lady of the house—a necessary ceremony, for on this occasion there

are people who have never met before — accredited
agents, representatives of secret societies which have
been formed in the remotest corners of the Russian do-
minion. The president and keeper of the privy seal of
the Northern Confederation is Prince Ghedimin; the
secretary, Ryleieff, is a young poet, and agent of the
American corn trade.

Of the three brothers Turgenieff, Nicholas, the his-
torian, is present; as well as Colonel Lunin, the proprietor of the secret press; Bestuseff, Kuchelbäcker,
Commandant of Artillery. There are also Vaskofsky,
Chief of the "Welfare Union"; Muravieff, the represent-
ative of the "United Slavs"; and Orloff, the life and soul
of the "Patriots." All are distinct secret societies; yet
all are united in one aim, "Freedom" (freedom under
the snow) -- their mode of procedure, action, the instru-
ments employed, wholly diverse. For this reason they
have arranged the present meeting, in order to unite the
various opposing plans into one common form of action.
To this conference they have called the president of the
"Southern Confederation," Colonel Pestel, from the far-off
shores of the Black Sea, and the still more distant chief
of the Caucasian "Barbarians," Jakuskin. But of all, he
who has come from the remotest part (for he had had to
wade through the sea of blood which separates the two
countries) was the spokesman of the Polish "Kosinyery,"
Krizsanowski. All these men wear uniforms, save Ryleieff, who is of the burgher class, and who wears a modern
blue frock-coat with gold buttons; all are beardless, with
clean-shaven faces; only the Pole preserves the national
type; and Jakuskin, whose shaggy eyebrows join his
tousled beard, represents the wild Cossack, and seems,
by his rough, neglected exterior, to bid defiance to the
civilized world.

5

There is something written on the foreheads of all these
men.

Zeneida stands by the door to receive the new-comers,
until the room fills up.   Conversation is not loud ; each
seems to be conferring with the spirit which has led him
hither.

The rolling of the roulette ball is heard yet again.

" Who can still be coming ?" asks Zeneida.

Pushkin appears on the threshold.

Zeneida's countenance involuntarily assumes an expression of alarm.

" Why do you come here ?" she whispers, excitedly, to
him.

" Is it not permitted ?"

" Did I not commission you to watch Galban, that he
might not take us by surprise ?"

" I found a better guardian for him.   Diabolka has
got him in the mouse-trap."

" But your responsibility remains."

" I will go back as soon as I can do so without exciting attention.   At present, I stay here.   Introduce
me !"

" What a child you are !   Are you not consumed with
curiosity to know what we are about here ?"

" I wish to take my part in it."

" What wilfulness !   Of course you imagine lives are
going to be risked, and must needs stake yours for sake
of the glory.   Well, stay here.   You shall see.   Herr
Pushkin !"   And she turned her back upon him, as if
in anger, while making the introduction.

Zeneida was the accredited agent of the whole union.
Whom she invited to her palace was received as a
" Brother "; to whom she confided any work was ranked
among the " Men "; but to take part in secret confer-

ences and to be promoted to be a "Bojar" required a further recommendation.

"Who else stands security for him?" asked Prince Ghedimin.

"I," answered Ryleieff.

Upon which room was at once made for Pushkin at the table.

His was a fine head. The curly hair and form of the nose recalled the African blood which ran in his veins, one of his forefathers having taken to wife a daughter of Hannibal, the negro slave promoted by Peter the Great to be a general. His eyes were dark and deep-set, yet, despite the irregular features, one could trace in the expression a resemblance to Byron. Pushkin was in love with Zeneida—that is, he raved about her. Zeneida was deeply in love with Pushkin, therefore she did not want him really to love her.

A word will clear up this seeming paradox. Zeneida knew too well that he who united his fate to hers must inevitably meet some dark doom, in the background of which loomed the scaffold. Finland had been reduced to subjection by the same power against which these secret societies were waging war, and Zeneida could still remember her mother's tears, and the plain black coffin brought by stealth to her home one dark night, wherein lay the corpse of a headless man for whom they dared not even mourn. Only when she was grown up had she learned that that man was her father. She loved Pushkin far too dearly to lead him on that perilous path on which men risk their heads. She had dreamed of a happier, sunnier lot for him. She had long detected in the wild, restless youth that genius that had not been given him to make the lion of a lady's boudoir—a genius which belonged, not to Russia only, but to the whole

world. A poet was not thus to be wasted. Why load
the gun with a charge of diamonds when common lead
would answer the purpose equally well, nay, better!

"Gentlemen," said Zeneida, addressing those assembled. "I will first request our brother Ryleieff to read
to us the verses we are to spread among the people. To
prepare the minds of the people is, indeed, the main object." (General applause.)

Ryleieff, the poet, a fair, slim, handsome young man,
here rising, produced the verses he had written.

It was a fine, noble-toned poem, perfectly rhythmical,
and true to every rule of composition. The rhetorical
warmth rising gradually to an impassioned climax, the
under - current expressing that deep spirit of yearning
melancholy which harmonizes so entirely with the spirit
of the people.

The poem recited, all united to congratulate the
youthful Tyrtæus; while Zeneida, with eyes filled with
tears, kissed him on both cheeks.

Pushkin, annoyed, looked away. For a woman to
kiss a man is the accepted custom in Russian society.
Ghedimin scarcely heeded Zeneida's action, and he certainly had the best right to demur; but Pushkin was
plainly annoyed by it. He envied Ryleieff: envied him
the kiss; how much more the poem which answered its
purpose—*faute de mieux!*

"The verses are splendid!" exclaimed Prince Ghedimin. "We will have a million copies of them struck
off in Lunin's press, and distributed among the peasants."

"You forget, Prince," put in Zeneida, "that our peasants cannot read. I would suggest it were more prac-
tical to have the poem set to music, that it might be
diffused more rapidly among them. In that way it

would pass from field to field; mowers, reapers, wag-
oners, would carry it from village to village, and what is
once sung among them never dies out. In our Finnish
Volkslieder has lived the history of the nation, the tradi-
tions of its historical life, its freedom. These no man
can take away. The *Marseillaise* alone raised an army
in France."

" But to whom confide the setting of it to music ?"
asked the Prince.

" Here is Herr Pushkin," said Zeneida. " He com-
poses charming melodies."

Pushkin felt as if stung by a tarantula.

He compose the melody to Ryleieff's song of freedom ! Subordination can be carried to a nicety of perfection. A state councillor, when he puts on the uniform
of a private of volunteers, may find he has to obey the
orders of his own chancery clerk and corporal; or a
duke, if he become a freemason, have to make obei-
sance to a bootmaker, as master of the lodge; but for
one poet to be called upon to write the music to another
poet's effusion, when he feels himself to be Cæsar and
the other man Pompey, is a sheer impossibility.

Pushkin's face crimsoned.

" To the best of my belief, the words and air of the
Marseillaise were composed at one and the same time.
Rouget de l'Isle wrote them together. Nor can it be
otherwise. The poet alone can find the fitting inspiration. Ryleieff's poem is fine, very fine, but it does not
inflame and excite one. To such an end the fire of enthusiasm is a necessity." And unconsciously he slapped
his breast, as though to say; " And it is here."

" Do you know, Pushkin," said Zeneida, " if you are
really feeling the poetic ardor of which you speak—if
you think you can compose something better than we

have here, you could not do better than to retire into
this little side chamber; there you will find piano and
writing-table. Give us something better suited to our
purpose!"

Pushkin was caught.

"Why not? I will write you a song which the peasant
will not need to take first to the priest to have its meaning explained to him."

And with that he looked straight into Zeneida's eyes,
with a look which said, "If you can bestow a kiss for
Ryleieff's rhymes, what will you give me when I put on
paper the words that burn in my heart?"

Rising, he repaired to the inner room. Soon the
sound of chords showed him to be deep in poetic creation. When once thus absorbed, a man does not lightly
break off.

Zeneida had no better wish for him.

As Pushkin left the room Zeneida turned the roulette-
board. The ball stopped at Nicholas Turgenieff. He
was thus made President of the Council that day, and ac-
cordingly took the chair—made to resemble that of the
banker of a roulette-table.

And now Prince Ghedimin, drawing out a delicate
little polished key, which fitted into a keyhole revealed
by pushing aside a brass button, handed it to the President, who turned it twice in the lock. Hereupon the
copper slab, upon which the roulette-board was fixed,
slid to the other end of the long table, disclosing, in the
part thus laid open, "the green book." One single lamp
hanging from the ceiling illuminated the figures of those
sitting there, looking, by its light, like statues in a mu-
seum; every feature seemed to gain in sharpness of outline; their immobility lending character and determination to their faces; so many historical subjects destined

either to rise to eminence, the idols of the people, or to fall under the hand of the executioner. In those few moments, devoted to silent reflection, in which each man seemed to be engaged in studying his neighbor, many were looking upon the other for the first time, and appeared to be mentally comparing the reality with the ideal previously formed. The members of the Southern Confederation had never before met their Polish brother. Many of them had seen Jakuskin ten years before, but then he was a merry youth with clean-shaven face. That has all disappeared. He is now a wild man of the woods, who only smiles when he speaks of murder. Leaning against the President's chair is Zeneida; attitude and figure alike recall statues of the "Republic," only that instead of a dagger she holds a bouquet in her hand sent her by her rival. A dagger in disguise. Besides those we have already named, the following historical personages were present : the three brothers Bestuseff, Prince Trubetzkoi Obolensky, Korsofski, Urbuseff, Peslien, Orloff, Konovitzin, Odojefski, Setkof, Sutsin, Battenkoff, Rostopschin, Rosen, Steinkal, Arsibuseff, Annenkoff, Oustofski, and Muravieff Apostol, all representatives of the many wide-spread secret societies.

Ryleieff, the secretary, opened "the green book."

The President desired him to read out the business done during the last sitting.

It concerned the working out of a plan of constitutional government for the whole Russian empire; its title—"Ruskaja Pravda." It was a republic in which every province that the Russian despot had annexed to form one vast empire was to arise as an independent state under its individual president—Great Russia, Little Russia, Finland, Poland, Livland, Kasan, Siberia, the Crimea, the Caucasus ; nine republics with one govern-

ment and one army, under the control of one Director-
ate, to hold its sittings at Moscow.

The Republic needed no St. Petersburg. Neither the
"Saint," nor the "Peter," nor the "burg" (city).

The device upon the plan was—

Question : "Will Europe in fifty years' time be republican or Russian ?"

To which the answer was—"Both."

This plan of constitution was painted with the colors
of a glowing fancy. First, to free every people, and
then to unite all free peoples! None to be oppressed
by the other. Each to be left to choose his own way to
prosperity, speak his own tongue, cultivate his own land.
No more hatred or jealousy among nations.

So it stood in "the green book."

Prince Ghedimin was the first to speak.

"It is a grand idea; but the greatest obstacle in the
way of freeing the people is that the people are unconscious of their servitude. Let it be our part to make it
clear to them. Let us flood the land with catechisms of
the 'free man'; let us study the special grievances of
every race in the provinces; learn to know their want
and misery, and win them to the cause of freedom by
promising them redress. A people suffers when it is
hungry; has to submit to blows; has its sons taken off
to be soldiers; but it is ignorant of the yoke that is
bowing down its neck.

Pestel waited impatiently until he could speak.

"My dear Prince, your plan may be very good for
such as can afford to wait fifty years and build card
houses, which fall to pieces at every current of air. We
have not the time to devote to philosophical theories.
We count upon the army and the aristocracy. The power
once in our hands, we can take our measures to secure

the education of the masses. A revolution left in their hands would lead to another Pugatsef revolt."

"And would that be a bad thing?" asked Jakuskin, in a hoarse voice, advancing to them from the corner where he was seated.

"It would be bad because there could be no organization. He who would carry out our scheme must be master of the situation. In Russia, the successful leader of an insurgent movement would only be another tyrant. Our scheme must be carried out simultaneously, at the word of command, throughout all Russia. No sooner that done than every secret society is abandoned, and we suppress all conspiracies; and, hateful as is now the system of police detectives, it must, in future, be raised to an honorable calling. Every man of mind, every free man, and every patriot must be proud to make himself a police-agent of a free country. All this must come about at the stroke of a magic wand."

"And what do you propose to do under the stroke of the magic wand with the Czar and the Grand Dukes?" asked Jakuskin, with chilling irony.

"Make them prisoners, convey them on board a man-of-war, and ship them off to the New World."

"Humph! to the other world! In Charon's boat," hissed out the Caucasian soldier; and, going up to the table, he struck it with his clinched fist. "Hark ye, envoys of the North and South, members of your various virtuous and benevolent societies, you are all on a wrong tack, you deceive yourselves. There is but one answer to the question I put to you: scatter their ashes to the four winds. I am no puling child, such as you are. I have not covered two thousand versts to come here and hear you thresh out your philosophical theses; I am here to act."

Ryleieff here interrupted the speaker with quiet dignity.

"Quite right. But you will act as the majority decide."

At this call to order the vehement Caucasian's blood boiled within him.

"Once I was young like you, Ryleieff; but that is long past. Once I, too, believed that one only needed to be a good man one's self to make the world better. I, too, had then as young and lovely a betrothed as you now have; I was an officer in the guards, and at twenty had distinguished myself in ten battles. And do you know what happened to me? The evening before my wedding-day, Araktseieff's son, a worthless fellow who did not even know how to buckle on his sword, and who had been made colonel over me, stole away my bride. I challenged him in mortal combat, and the dastardly coward, instead of accepting my challenge, denounced me to the Czar, and I was exiled to the Caucasus. As, with hell in my heart, I was taking my leave of the city, the last thing that met my eyes was the body of a drowned girl brought to me. It was my bride. I kissed her. I still feel the chill of that kiss upon my lips, and I shall feel it until the blood wipes it out, for which I long as keenly as any cannibal. When you are in Czarskoje Zelo look at a certain finely painted battle-piece. Close behind the Czar you will see a youth on a rearing horse, a youth wielding his sword high in air, his face beaming with triumph and loyalty. That youth was I! Years have quenched my enthusiasm; but my sword still swings over his head."

"And so I trust it may remain, ever wielded on high as in the picture."

"But that it will not!" cried Jakuskin, vehemently. "I

swear it by the devil they sent into my heart as its constant indweller, I will listen to naught else but my eternal vengeance! You may fill your 'green book' with
resolutions—this is my determination!" And as he
waved his arm aloft, he extracted a hidden dagger from
his coat-sleeve, and displayed its glittering surface to
the company.

Horrified, Ryleieff, springing up, drew forth a pistol
from a side-pocket and levelled it at Jakuskin's breast.

"And I swear that I will shoot you down on the
spot if you venture to assert yourself against our rules."

"Very well, then, shoot me down! Fire away, boy!"
growled Jakuskin, tearing open his coat and presenting
his bare breast to the mouth of the pistol. "And learn
from me how to die."

"Obey the rules, Jakuskin! Take back your word!"
shouted several, as they rushed up to pacify the infuriated man.

"I will not withdraw it! You are cowards, all! He
shall fire!" he shouted back, roughly pushing them
away.

"Gentlemen!" exclaimed Krizsanowski, the Pole,
rising.

"Shoot me down!" roared Jakuskin, continuing to
wave his dagger.

Then it was that Zeneida, drawing a hyacinth from
out her bouquet, aimed it at the raging man's forehead.
And the seasoned man, who had never known what it
was to shrink from a bullet, was so confused by this
playful projectile that, letting fall the dagger from his
hand, he put his hand to his brow.

A quiet smile passed over the faces of those present,
and before the Caucasian could recover his dagger,
Zeneida was beside him, had picked it up from the

ground, restored it to him, and was stroking his beard with caressing action.

"Dear friend, be courteous. Our guest Krizsanowski, the delegate of the Polish 'Kosyniery,' wishes to speak. Let us listen to him, and put this shaving apparatus away!"

Jakuskin calmed down. This delicate woman had more than once stepped in to spread oil on the waves of the most impassioned debates when, dagger or pistol in hand, the disputants seemed bent on doing one another a violence.

And now Krizsanowski, hat in hand, began:

"Gentlemen, I wish to bid farewell to you. I will not enter upon the subject under discussion with you, nor have I any desire to await the resolution arrived at. I will not listen to the question of murdering the Czar, still less will I submit to be bound by your decisions. There is not one among you who has endured such wrongs; not one among you who carries such grief in his heart as I. What did your sovereign, as its king, do with your country? He freed it from foreign conquest, made it great and powerful, added new territory to it. What did he do with your people? He gave them prosperity and knowledge, and erected a school in every one of your villages. What is your ruler? A noble mind in a noble body—'the handsomest man in all Europe,' as Napoleon said of him—and with heart as good as he looks. And the most remarkable thing about him is that, in every fault, in every feeling, he is a Russian to the backbone. His only crime in your eyes is that he is the Czar. And to you that is crime enough to make him die. And what is my ruler, the Czar's brother, Constantine? A monster, in whose very face nature has curiously wedded the hideous with the ridiculous; and his hideous features are a true mirror of the hideous promptings of his soul. He is what he seems to be—cruel and contemptible. In the whole extent of my poor, unhappy nation there is not one feeling heart which he has not trampled upon; no article of value, no relic, no Church money, he has not appropriated to himself. But a Pole would see in that no cause to treacherously murder his king. A Pole's hand is accustomed to the sword; it knows not the use of a dagger. Let me take leave of you; I would go back to my people. I came hither in the belief that I should find here brave men ready for battle; who, at the appointed hour, would range themselves in fighting order, and declare war upon their oppressors as do we, who fight in open battle—as do we who, in open and honorable warfare, settle on whose side is the right. Such I thought to find here. On my journey hither, on the way from Warsaw to the Niemen, my predecessor, glorious Valerian Lukasinski, was being conveyed before me—he whom treachery had given over to the authorities. He was my relative, friend, and leader—trebly dear to me. He had been subjected to every species of physical and mental torture in order to make him reveal the aims of and participators in the conspiracy. They had not succeeded in drawing a word out of him. Constantine himself took the knout from the executioner's hands, and taught him how to use the agonizing implement. When Lukasinski was wellnigh flayed to death, no sign of humanity left in him, only one mass of bleeding flesh and bones and gaping wounds, the viceroy had him laid bound on a gun-carriage, and had this still breathing, bleeding mass dragged to his captivity through the rigor of mid-winter. I followed his track guided by the drops of blood which fell on the snow. Those frozen drops I gathered up one by one

on the way, and placed them in a reliquary.   Heaven
had compassion on the sufferer; he died on the road.
They made a hole in the ice of the river Niemen, and
threw the body in ; the current carried it off to the sea.
I know that I shall follow him, and that my end will be
like his.   Still that knowledge neither moves me from
fear or revengeful feeling to lie in ambush and murder-
ously strike my ruler in the back at any time, when he
may be sleeping, or kneeling in prayer !   Our God was
never a God of murder.   The dagger which struck down
Cæsar but opened the door to Caligula and Heliogaba-
lus.   While William Tell told Gessler to his face, 'With
this arrow I will kill you.   Defend yourself as best you
can !'   I do likewise.   When the time comes I will declare war upon my enemies, and if God is with me, I
shall destroy them ; but as long as I do not feel myself
strong enough to engage in open warfare, no oppression,
no cruelty, and no fantastic ravings shall lead me, by
any untimely revolt, to draw the cord tighter, which I
fain would loose.   Your plans are untimely, unripe,
without sufficient basis ; they destroy, but do not build
up again.   I know them, and will not unite our cause to
yours.   Let me go."

Pestel, seizing the Pole by the hand, held him back.

" You cannot go yet ; you have learned nothing of our
intentions.   What you have heard hitherto was only a
weak, academical discussion.   The words this madman
said were only the ravings of his mad passion.   I, too,
do not inscribe upon my shield, ' Strew their ashes to the
winds'; not because my soul would shrink from it, but
because such a dictum would scatter our several societies
like shots among a flock of birds.   The people themselves would turn against us.   To the masses the prayer
for Czar and Grand Dukes is a necessity, and were the

priest ever to leave it out, they would hang him for a
heretic.   If I were to ask my soldiers, 'Do you want a
republic?' they would straightway answer, 'Yes, if the
Czar commands.'   We must begin at the beginning; we
must not startle any one.   The first step is the difficulty;
the others will follow of themselves.   Thus let us go
back to the point where Jakuskin interrupted us.   And
you, Krizsanowski, resume your seat.   The question is
the removal of the Czar and Grand Dukes—their removal
only.   Let them go to America, by all means.   There
Russia has noble possessions; there they can reign.
But to this end you Poles must lend us a helping hand.
For what use would it be to us to ship off the three
brothers, when the fourth, Constantine, who by fundamental law is next after Alexander in succession to the
throne, remains at large in Warsaw?"

"Let us clearly understand one another, Pestel," replied Krizsanowski.   "We Poles have ever been, since
our first existence as a nation, ready to shed our blood for
the benefit of others.   Tell me, what is to become of us
if we succeed in freeing ourselves from the Romanoffs?"

"Form Poland into a republic."

"But your Polish republic will still be a part of the
vast Russian dominions, just as Livland and Little Russia will be; and over us there will be some one—a chief,
who is lord over the nine republics, although I know not
what title or what amount of power he will possess.   And
I swear to you I do not wish for a freedom that shall be
the downfall of my country."

The deep silence which ensued proved that the Pole
had hit the right nail upon the head.   There was an expression of uneasy conviction on all faces.

Then Nicholas Turgenieff, the president, rose to speak.

"Take comfort, Krizsanowski.   The chief of the re-

public, he who will be head of the nine republics, will
be no autocrat, no tyrant under any other name."

" What, then ?"

"That which he must of necessity be—*un président
sans phrases.*"

The conversation had taken place in French.   These
four words had nearly cost Turgenieff his estates and
his head.

The words were scarce spoken, when the roulette-
board suddenly slipped back into its place, effectually
concealing "the green book," and the door opened.
Copper-plate and door were an ingeniously constructed
piece of machinery.   If "the green book" were exposed to view, and any one opened the outer door, the
roulette slid back instantly into its place.

Chevalier Galban, entering, only heard Nicholas Turgenieff's four last words, and saw nothing but a gambling-
table.

The banker repeated—

" Je suis un président sans phrases.   Messieurs, faites
vos jeux !"

One of the men playing—the Pole—rose from his
seat with a disturbed look—

"Merci, monsieurs, c'en était assez !"

Another, Jakuskin, drying the sweat from his brow,
struck his hand on the table—

" J'ai tout perdu !"

All as if it were a real roulette-table.

The others continued cold-bloodedly to lay their par-
cels of gold on the numbers, seeming unaware of the
new-comer's arrival.

The hostess only advanced quickly to greet him.

" I was certain that you would find out our den ; I
kept this seat for you."

"You honor me too much, *diva.* I ought to have good luck in play to-night, as I have just had the opposite fate in love."

" How is that ? Did the pretty Gitanitza escape you ?"

"*Au contraire*, she fell asleep. A checkmate such as never happened to me before !"

Zeneida gave a merry laugh. No one could have divined under its mask the agitation she was feeling. She knew that a sleeping-draught had been given to Diabolka.

" Come along ! let us be partners for gain or loss."

Chevalier Galban, accepting, took the seat allotted to him ; Zeneida seated herself on the arm of his chair.

So it is a roulette-table pure and simple, and the party assembled gamblers. There is no "green book." A thickness of half an inch lay between him and it—his arm rested on it.

Merely contravention of a police regulation—a thing winked at by the authorities. Suppressed inclinations will find a vent—far better it should be on moral than political domains. Nor is it any matter for wonder that Nicholas Turgenieff should be the roulette banker. A man may be a *bel esprit*, a great author, philosopher, philanthropist, and yet have a passion for play. Even Napoleon was a gambler.

As the game was in full swing, Pushkin suddenly entered to them from a side room with flushed cheeks, crying, in a tone of triumph :

" The song is ready."

The gamblers looked askance at him.

Now he would betray all.

Lucky for them all that his eyes had mechanically sought Zeneida's.

6

She, still sitting on the arm of Galban's chair, glanced significantly at the Chevalier.

Pushkin saw him.

"Let us hear it," said Galban, toying with his pile of gold pieces.

Pushkin changed color for an instant as he stared at him, then plunged his hand into his breast-pocket. All followed his movements anxiously. What would he bring out? Perhaps the song of freedom, just composed; and would he declaim or sing it, for Chevalier Galban's edification? Or would he draw that which every conspirator carried, dancing or drinking, a pointed stiletto to strike down the traitor then and there?

He drew out a packet of papers, smiling the while.

"Here is what I promised you, *The Romance of the Lovely Gypsy Girl.* Shall I read it?"

A romance instead of a song of freedom? Why not? in order to cover an untimely appearance, the wisest thing for a poet to do was to read or recite something, no matter what, so that the others meanwhile could recover their self-possession.

But this was no mere rhyming jingle. No sooner had he begun than the attention of all was riveted on his verses. The poetic form was striking and brilliant, the thought original, the conception fine; there were fire, passion, audacity, and beauty of expression in it, united to a natural grace and simplicity.

No one had heard the lines before. As he finished, Zeneida, hurrying up to him, pressed both his hands in hers. She did not kiss him as she had kissed Ryleieff, but the tears which flowed from her eyes were a higher recompense. A kiss is cheap. Tears are costly.

The whole company of conspirators, forgetting alike "green book" and reorganization, hastened to congratulate the poet, who suddenly, like a comet from before which the wind has chased the clouds, found himself revealed in all his glory.

Chevalier Galban was now convinced that this was no gathering of conspirators, but merely a select assemblage who met for games of chance and intellectual and literary interchange of thought—both prohibited, it is true, in Russia—for which reason they were obliged to meet in secret.

Par exemple, such verses would be public property in any other country, and half the world would be running after the poet.

" Bah !" returned Pushkin, excited by the applause he had created. " Do you not know that feebleness is the goddess we worship, and the priest of her altar is called the 'Censor'?"

General laughter broke out at these cutting words. The Censor is as stereotyped a marionette in Russia as in other countries. Galban seized the opportunity to bring his talents as *agent provocateur* into the field.

" Yes, indeed, ladies and gentlemen, the Censor is a necessary evil among us. You are aware that the Czarina Catherine II. once, at the instance of her men of letters, commanded full freedom of the press in Russia for—three days ! It would be seen then what fruit the tree would bear. It would have been thought that those three days would have proved a harvest-time for songs of freedom, prohibited pamphlets, and philosophical treatises to crawl out of their hiding-places, but the result was only an avalanche of low slander and scurrilous anecdotes. The press was flooded with a stream of scandalous personalities, directed against well-known families and personages ; so that already on the second day of the freedom of the press the Czarina was besieged with petitions to countermand the third day and reinstate the censure."

No one save Pushkin deemed it advisable to accept the proffered challenge; but he, as a poet, could not suffer the liberty of the press to be a mark for ridicule.

"Come, I say, Galban, if I were to tell a man who had never tasted wine that he might drink what ran out from the bung-hole of a cask the third day after the vintage, that man would swear that there was no such disgusting stuff as wine in the world."

"Messieurs, je suis un président sans phrases. Le dernier jeu!" broke in the banker's voice, interrupting the dangerous turn the conversation had taken.

It was time, moreover, to finish the game; for if by five o'clock Chevalier Galban had not left the palace, the police would have broken open the doors, and every one in it have been arrested. The roulette was turned for the last time. Chevalier Galban had won six thousand four hundred rubles, which he gallantly shared with Zeneida. Then, with the customary forms of good society, he took his leave.

The remaining company looked at one another. Every one well knew that roulette was a mere farce among them. It was alike Zeneida's money which furnished bank and players. Hence the general smile which went round on Galban's winning a pile of his hostess's money and then courteously sharing it with her.

But there was a glow of triumph on Zeneida's countenance, as, raising the bouquet with its diamond-set holder in her hand, she murmured, in a tone of angry satisfaction:

"Je le payais!"

Chevalier Galban had received back the price of his diamonds, without ever suspecting that it had, so to speak, been thrown after him.

CHAPTER X

FROM SCENT OF MUSK TO REEKING TAR

WHEN those assembled were assured of Galban's departure, Pestel began :

" My lords and gentlemen, that was very fine—I mean the romance ; but it seems to me we have met to discuss other matters.   Is it not so, Cousin Krizsanowski ?"

The Polish noble shrugged his shoulders.

" I have nothing more to say."   At the same time, drawing from his pocket the inevitable meerschaum and tobacco - pouch, he slowly filled and lighted his pipe, which in the Eastern " language of tobacco " implies, " I should have plenty to say, if I could only smoke out from here certain folk who seem suspicious to me."

Zeneida, understanding his meaning, whispered something in Ryleieff's ear.

" All right," returned Ryleieff, " let us hear our Pushkin's song of liberty.   True, the fine romance you read us entitles us to name you our Tyrtæus.   Never, since Byron—"

Pushkin did not allow him to finish the sentence. His praises excited him to fury.   A schoolboy may win with pride the prize for the best verses, and carry it home in triumph to his parents, but your true poet cannot brook being praised to his face.   He feels that he has constrained your praises.   Thus, if you be a woman, throw him a flower ; if a man, give him a shake of the

hand; but never tell him face to face that he has composed a fine poem; by so doing you repel him. And
worse than all is it for another poet to praise his work.
" *Genus irritabile vatum.*"

"No, no, gentlemen," he cried, in wrathful voice.
"My poem is not for your ears. It is not meant for
musk-scented atmospheres, but for such as reek with
tar and tobacco. Come, Jakuskin, let us go off to some
beer-shop; that's the right place for it."

Springing up, Jakuskin held out his hand to him.

"All right, let us go to the Bear's Paw."

"Very well."

No one attempted to detain them. Between the two
doors the rest of their conversation was heard.

"Shall we take Diabolka with us?" said Jakuskin.

"All right. Let's look for her."

"She must have fallen asleep somewhere. I will soon
wake her to life again."

In this unceremonious fashion did the guests take
their leave of their hostess. Zeneida, however, following them, left the room.

"Now you can talk out," exclaimed Pestel, hurriedly,
to Krizsanowski. "Perhaps Zeneida's presence has ham-
pered you. Have you anything to make known to us?"

"Yes," replied the Pole. "But it was not her presence which deterred me. Far from it. Women, when
they are in a conspiracy, know well how to keep secrets.
Laena bit out her tongue on the wheel of torture that
she might not betray her colleagues. Ever since then
the tongueless lioness has been the emblem of silence.
Oh, I reckon greatly upon our women. I would even
rather await Zeneida's return before speaking, were I
assured that she would not bring back the other two
with her."

" You mistrust them ?"

" No, but I do not like them. In conspiracies it is
not the absolute traitors who are the most to be feared.
There are three classes I dread more—cowards, self-
willed and fantastic persons. The last is the most
dangerous of all, for he deceives himself, and reports
falsely. If he hear a drunken peasant swear, he reports the existence of a revolutionary spirit; if he see
a solitary deserter, he distorts him into a whole regiment. He believes just what his fancy paints. If he
has filled his head with revolutionary writings he
conceives himself to be a Robespierre, and every St.
Petersburg mujik is a Paris *sans culotte* to him. To
the working out of a conspiracy we want no fantastic
notions; but, on the contrary, common-sense and judgment. With those two men I prefer not to discuss
matters; the one is a fool, the other a poet."

Pestel hastily pulled the Pole's long hanging sleeve.

" Do not affront Ryleieff," he said.

" Oh, Ryleieff is different. He can write any number
of correct verses—faultless as to rhyme ; he measures
his thoughts into iambics and trochees, like a corn
merchant does his wheat into bushels and sacks. He
is master of his imagination — imagination does not
master him."

Ryleieff was manager of the American Corn Company,
and being, in truth, more business man than poet, received this doubtful compliment with an acquiescent
smile.

The party, meanwhile, had risen from the table, and
was standing about in little groups, awaiting Zeneida's
return.

Ryleieff and Krizsanowski retired together into a
corner. The Pole, smoking furiously, blew thick clouds

of smoke about him, as though considering his rigid features a too transparent mask, likely to betray him. And in order not to be questioned, he began to question.

"There are one or two points I should be glad to have cleared up. The first spring of every great aim proceeds from selfish motives. Freedom—well, yes, is the sun ; private aims are earth. We are upon the earth. From mere abstract motives a new era has never been started. My private motives require no explanation ; they are expressed in two words — I am a Pole. That is sufficient ground for me to stand upon. Fräulein Ilmarinen is a Finn. I take it that is sufficient reason for her action. I have no fear that she will be dazzled by the pinnacle she stands on, encircled with wreaths and diamonds. I can also understand your moving spring. You love your own race ; you see how it has remained behind other nations, and would raise it to their level. Pestel's motives also I can grasp. He has immense ambition. He would fain be the head of a newly formed state. The basis is broad enough ; his foot rests on a sure pedestal. The rest are shifting, unstable, attracted to the movement by the hope of playing some brilliant part in it. Then we have Apostol Muravieff. He, too, is constrained to it by a paternal heritage, from which he cannot free himself. Pushkin is in love with Zeneida ; that, too, is sure ground enough. That madman Jakuskin is actuated by revenge ; another safe passion on which one may rely. His sense of puritanical integrity binds that fine fellow Turgenieff to us. From earliest youth he has ever been in the advance guard of freedom, first in the first rank. Such iron rectitude can be recast in no other form, rather it would break than yield. Now there is but one man

here whose presence I cannot understand : that is Duke
Ghedimin. A member of one of the twelve old Russian
dynastic families, his possessions so immense that he is
simply unable to expend his yearly income on Russian
soil, holding the highest grade at Court, himself an
accomplished, brilliant, sought-after aristocrat, who by
any changes you may effect has everything to lose,
nothing to gain — what does he seek here ?   What
is his interest in making himself one of this conspiracy ?"

"He is the very one, among us all, who has the
weightiest reason : the recollection of an irreconcilable
affront, for it was a personal one.   You know the Czar.
You know that, as a man, no one is his enemy.   Even
Jakuskin merely hates in him the Czar, not the man.
Duke Ghedimin is the sole one who stands opposed to
him, as man to man.   The Czar wås married very
young, to a delicate wife ; his children died early.   He
grew cold towards his wife, and sought compensation in
a new passion.   The only daughter of one of our first
families, renowned far and wide for her great beauty,
was willing to console him.   The illicit connection had
consequences—a daughter.   The affair was kept strictly
secret.   The young duchess journeyed to Italy as an un-
married girl, and returned from there the same.   Soon
after she married Duke Ghedimin.   Meanwhile a young
girl was growing up in Italy who went by the name of
Princess Sophie Narishkin, and who, in her fourteenth
year, was brought to St. Petersburg.   It was her father,
not her mother, who brought her here.   The girl resides
in a house surrounded by a garden in the outskirts of
the capital, where her father visits her constantly, her
mother never.   The father worships the child, who,
moreover, is terribly delicate.   The mother simply hates

her. Her father is the Czar, her mother, Princess
Ghedimin. Now do you see what brings Prince Ghedimin among us?"

"Yes, yes. But does he know the secret of the girl's
birth?"

"Know it? We all do."

"Still, no reason why the husband should. Think a
moment. What human being is there who could go to
a man like Prince Ghedimin and breathe to him such
a foul statement about his own wife? At the least
whisper of such a slander an inferior would receive the
knout, an equal be shot. A shopkeeper may denounce
his wife; no gentleman does such a thing. Who could
have made this known to Ghedimin?"

"Who other than his sweetheart! Is not Zeneida
Prince Ghedimin's sweetheart, and has she not a thousand reasons to enlighten him upon his wife's shame?"

"Do not believe a word of it! She has not done it.
You do not know Fräulein Zeneida; I do. First of all,
I do not believe she is Ghedimin's sweetheart; or, if she
love him, it is with a real love, not that of a *Ninon de
l'Enclos.* But my belief is that she is in love with some
one else; and I believe, moreover, that she controls
that love. She is a woman capable of defying the scorn
of the whole world, but not of doing anything to merit
her own self-contempt. And for a woman who loves a
man to denounce his own wife to him is a piece of vile-
ness only fit for the lowest of the low. You do not
know with whom you have to deal. Zeneida is playing
some far-seeing game with you. You are mere chessmen in her hands; one may be a castle, another a
bishop, the third a knight. Possibly Ghedimin may be
your king of chess, but she is not the queen. She is
playing the game."

" And you have confidence enough in her to consent to this ?"

" Yes ; because I am her partner."

The roulette ball spun round. Some one was coming. All hurriedly returned to their places. Krizsanowski did not deserve the scornful smile with which Ryleieff had silently received his great utterance—for, indeed, it was a great utterance—"You others are only the chessmen ; we two are the players." But so it was. The others only saw single moves ; these two saw the whole game.

Krizsanowski had also plainly observed—although he made as if he saw nothing—with what painful anxiety Zeneida was moved to keep Pushkin away from the dangerous chess-board. Such a head is too costly for a " pawn "; perhaps too precious to be staked for a whole nation—the whole world—certainly in her estimation.

She had chased him away as if he were the evil one; now she had hastened after him to prevent his coming back. She knew that the heads of all those taking part in the conspiracy would fall prey to the executioner did it not succeed, and Pushkin's must not be among them. And yet poets have their whims. Should Jakuskin on the way reveal anything of the fateful conference which had taken place round Zeneida's roulette-table, the very charm of danger would bring Pushkin back. If he learned that it was no mere academical discussion, but a council of war, which was being held, he would break open her doors to take his share in it.

Pushkin was still in the sulks. While Jakuskin hastened from one cabinet to another in search of Diabolka, he had thrown himself upon a sofa in the palm-grove, replying to all the blandishments of passing fair ones.

" Leave me alone. I don't want you."

"Nor me either?" asked a well-known voice, at sound
of which another, fairer, world seemed to open to him.
And Zeneida, seating herself beside him on the couch,
asked, "Are you angry with me?"

"Confess. It was you who put Ryleieff up to insulting me?"

"In what way, dear friend?"

"I will not submit to be called Byron! I am Pushkin, or no one. Men may say that my verses are common Russian brandy which gets into the head, but no
one shall presume to call them the dregs of an English
teapot. I may be only a hillock, but I will not pose as
a miniature Chimborazo. And it was your whisper to
Ryleieff that did it."

"Yes; so it was."

"To drive me away?"

"To drive you away."

"I am not worthy, then, to join the society of the
Bojars!"

"What care I for the Bojars and the whole Szojusz
Blagadenztoiga? I give them shelter—and *basta!*"

"And am I not worthy to singe my wings in the fire
of your eyes?"

"It would convert you to ice."

"Are you so cold, then?"

"Cold as the northern light."

"Have you no heart?"

"According to anatomy I have such a thing; but it
has other functions than those ascribed to it by poets.
That of which you speak has, Gall tells us, its seat in
the skull, in No. 27 portion of the brain, and is not de·
veloped in my organization."

"Do not kill me with your phrenology. You know
what love is—"

" I know. The compact of a tyrant with a slave."

" Be you the tyrant; I will be the slave."

" With these words as many women have been deceived as there are grains of sand on the sea-shore."

" I swear to you, my life, my very soul, are yours."

" By whom do you swear? By Venus, so inconstant; by Allah, who denies that women have souls, and divides the heart of man in four parts; by Brahma, who burns the widow on the funereal pyre; or by the great Cosmos?"

" There is nothing so formidable as a woman who takes to philosophizing!"

" That is why I do so."

" You kill every iota of poetry with it."

" Then speak prose."

" Well, then, I ask nothing of you—I give. I give you my soul, my hand, my name!"

" Ah, your name! That is a gift. A woman like me has diamonds, horses, houses, given her; but he who would offer her his name is indeed rare to meet with. And yet a name is the most precious ornament. Without such a name, I am nobody. Were I to marry my groom of the chambers to-morrow, I should be a woman of respectability. My poor good Bogumil never dreams that in his fur-lined gloves, besides his own red hands, lies my reputation! So you would give me your name? —a name which, so far, has been written on nothing else than overdue bills and ale-house doors. You silly boy! Why, people would not call me 'Frau Pushkin,' but you 'Herr Ilmarinen.' But once let your name be written in the fiery letters of fame, instead of chalked on innkeepers' slates, would you then unite it to another whose every letter is besmeared with—"

" With calumny!" broke in Pushkin, vehemently.

"It is but just. There is nothing so bad that can be said of me that I cannot fill in. I am selfish, unfeeling; I have no faith in religion, nor in honor. Both are sophistries, contradicting each other, according as the ethnographical relations change about. The only good is, what benefits mankind. Virtue is folly. The sole use of good men is to be the tools of their more clever fellows."

"Do not say such things," cried Pushkin. "When I hear you speak so, you seem to me as if you had smeared your face with hideous colors."

Was it not her calling to do so?

Zeneida drew her wrap about her shoulders.

"You will not see me such as I am. I am sorry for it; but I cannot deceive. Have you no eyes for the magnificence which surrounds me? Do you know whence it all comes? Would you have me forsake it all—for what?"

"For another world before whose splendor all you see around you must fall into dust. The world into which I would lead you is filled with more magnificent palaces than even yours, Zeneida. It is Paradise!"

"Find yourself another Eve. Did I love you, I should kill you with *my* jealousy; did I not love you, with *yours*. To-day with one, to-morrow with another, for my caprices are boundless. I know no law, no oath, no shame. Go; save yourself from me! Now you are but ice, do not wait until you are aflame. I can be his only who loves me not!"

"Your words are mere falsehoods from beginning to end. You wish to drive me from you that I may not take part in the conspiracy! I am not worthy, in your eyes, to share the dangers my more distinguished friends are running. Let me go back to them!"

"What conspiracy?" exclaimed Zeneida, feigning astonishment. "Our friends are now debating how to introduce the American form of 'Temperance Associations' into Russia in order to put an end to the enormous consumption of brandy now going on. There is no talk of upsetting dynasties in my house. Do you suppose that the 'court singer' of the Czar, the court favorite, did she hear of any conspiracy against his Majesty, would not at once hasten to smooth her own way to a coronet by its disclosure?"

"A way marked out by the skulls of her best friends?"

"Well, yes."

"No. You would not do it."

"Who knows? I have no soul, and do not believe in the souls of others. I have no faith in a future world, therefore I use this world so that things may go well with me in it."

"And supposing it were to happen for a change that things did not go well with you?"

"Then I would give back to earth what is earth's. The fable of the Phœnix has a deep-set meaning. When he feels that his plumage is worn out, he changes into ashes. Of all creatures man has the greatest right to decide the term of his life."

Pushkin sought in the face which knew so well how to keep its secrets what there was of truth in all this.

A sound of laughter and oaths behind the jasmine bush betokened the approach of some noisy revellers. Zeneida sprang up from Pushkin's side. Laying her hand upon his shoulder, she whispered to him, in a voice made tender by deep feeling:

"Avoid me, and seek her who is worthy of you and truly loves you, your Muse, and be faithful to her!"

And, like a phantom, she disappeared.

Jakuskin came forcing his way through the jasmine bower, Diabolka with him.

"Come, let's be off to the Bear's Paw."

Pushkin sprang defiantly to his feet, and said, with a laugh.

"By Jove! here is my Muse! Come along; we'll go where we are understood."

And the three made their noisy way through the still thronged ballroom.

It was Zeneida whose reappearance the whirling roulette-ball had announced. A look from her told that the two had taken their departure.

Krizsanowski, removing the pipe from his mouth, put it in his pocket.

"Now we are among ourselves. Let us continue."

Pestel asked permission to speak.

"In order to disperse friend Krizsanowski's fears, let me first of all state that we look upon Jakuskin as a fool; and that not a man of us endorses his mad views of a *Cæsaricidium;* in fact, there is not a man among us who would not prevent it. Our plan is this: In the coming spring there is to be a great concentration of troops in the Government of Minsk. The Ninth Army Corps will march to the fortress of Bobrinszk on the Beresina; the Czar and the Grand Dukes will themselves lead the manœuvres, returning at night to the fortress, which fortress will be guarded by the Saratoff regiment of infantry, the colonel of which, Bojar Sveikofsky, is a member of the 'Szojusz Blagadenztoiga.' All the officers of the Saratoff regiment belong to our Union. At night a patrol of officers, disguised as privates, commanded by Apostol Muravieff and Corporal Bestuseff, will relieve the guard outside the Czar's pavilion. They will promptly take the Czar, the Grand Dukes, and Com-

mandant Diebitsh prisoners, proclaim a constitution,
institute a provisionary government, and proceed straightway, at the head of the whole army corps, on the road
to Moscow. On their way they will gain over all the
troops they come across. At news of their success Moscow will yield; and from thence St. Petersburg can be
compelled to surrender. The men and officers of the
fleet, anchored off Cronstadt, are fully informed of our
plan. A man-of-war is in waiting to convey the entire
imperial family to England. The revolution will be accomplished without the shedding of one drop of blood.
What do you say to it, friend Krizsanowski?"

"That your plan is too complicated; has too much
romance about it ; and that the miscarriage of any minor
detail would throw your whole reckoning into confusion.
However, I do not look upon a successful issue as wholly
impossible. The thing has already been achieved in
Russia. Now, I will tell you what I bring, and which
will serve to perfect your plan. Do you not agree
with me that its success were highly problematical if,
after the kidnapping of the Czar, a Czarevitch were remaining, who, by right of succession to the throne, could
at the head of a whole army enter Russia to test the
power of a republican government by the loyalty of
the people to throne and army?"

"That, in truth, is the rock on which we may be
wrecked."

"Then, you may set yourselves at ease in that par-
ticular. I can promise you my head in pledge of my
words that the Czarevitch will very shortly resign his
rights of succession; and resign after a fashion which
will make it impossible for him to recall the step, even
did he himself desire to do so. Ay, even were he the
sole remaining member of the Romanoff dynasty; and

7

were the whole nation, senate, and peerage to press him
to ascend the throne, it would be an impossibility to
him.".

"And is this no romancing?" cried Ryleieff.

"No. Positive knowledge; psychological necessity;
logical sequence."

"Devil take me! If that is not a greater riddle than
the Sphinx!" growled Pestel.

"I have said what I know. Whether you like to believe it or not, is your affair."

So saying the Polish magnate rose, and thrust his
pipe between his teeth, which was as much as to say
that he had said his say, and was intent on seeing that
his pipe drew well.

But Zeneida, approaching him, whispered:

"Is not the key to this riddle called 'Johanna'?"

A nervous contraction passed over his set face at the
mention of the name.

"If you have guessed it, tell it no further," he muttered under his mustache.

"I?"

"True. You are the 'tongueless lioness!'" returned
the Pole, with a smile.

At that period lanterns were a luxury known but in
few streets of the imperial city; and where a lantern
did exist was posted a guard to watch that it was not
stolen. Therefore, in the courtyards of great palaces
huge fires were blazing, in order to give light to the
guests' sledges, and that the jemsiks might protect themselves against the bitter night cold. These fires gave
out warmth and light at one and the same time.

With some difficulty Jakuskin found his sledge among
the lines of others. Placing Diabolka between them,

the two men wrapped her in their furs. She was too heedless ever to think of bringing her own. The jemsik, made loquacious by oft recurrence to his brandy bottle, told them that the distinguished gentleman who had driven the eight-in-hand into the courtyard had but just gone off in his sledge, and had given his man orders to drive to Araktseieff Palace.

That was a piece of intelligence worth having.

Jakuskin told his jemsik to drive to the Bear's Paw.

"Never fear, children," returned the man; "I'll drive you safely through side streets, that you may not be robbed."

"None of your side streets," said Jakuskin, "but just you drive along the Prospect and over the Fontanka Ringstrasse, where the patrols are. Don't be afraid about us, my man; we have our pistols."

"Ah, there's no use in that, children. The robbers might let you pass scot-free when they saw your pistols; but the guards have no fear of firearms, and they would plunder you."

And the jemsik was by no means joking. Under the police presidency not only the soldiers managed to slip out of barracks to act the light-fingered gentry, but the patrols shared in the spoil, and commissioners of police were the most reliable of accomplices. Great folk only ventured out at night with mounted escorts; their palace-doors were strengthened with iron bars.

As they drove along the two men began scolding Diabolka for letting Chevalier Galban escape her, telling her how they had had to get rid of him at the cost of some thousands of rubles.

Just as the sledge turned off from the broad Prospect into Fontanka Ringstrasse, five armed men suddenly sprang out upon it. Two seized the horses' bridles, one levelled his weapon at the coachman's head, the two others fell upon the occupants of the sledge. All were armed with swords and pistols, their faces concealed by masks; long sheep-skins covered their persons from head to foot; their tall, pointed fur caps alone betraying them to be not only soldiers but grenadiers. One of them, speaking in French (consequently an officer), ejaculated:

"La bourse ou la vie, messieurs!"

On which Diabolka, suddenly springing up, jerked the pistol directed at Pushkin's head out of the assailant's hand, and, throwing both arms round his neck, began, coaxingly:

"Ei, ei, sweetheart, cousin! would you plunder poor folk like us? Don't you know us, then? Look! this is the brave Jakuskin, a captain on half-pay; this, Pushkin, who has more creditors on his heels than kopecs in his pocket. I am Diabolka, who pays, and is paid, in kisses. Here are a few — on your cheeks, eyes, lips. There, take as many as there is room for. But if you are wise, and want to make money, there's a rich gentle-man just now on his way home from Araktseieff Pal-ace, who has just pocketed thirteen thousand rubles at roulette. If you are quick you'll catch him up on the ice, crossing the Fontanka. He is wearing a red fox coat, trimmed with white bear-skin."

Her words were as magic. With one accord the four thieves, deserting sledge and their leader, took to their heels in the direction of the Fontanka, as if they were possessed. The officer, too, seeing himself thus left alone, endeavored to free himself from Diabolka's em-brace. But that was not so easy.

"Stop! just one kiss on the tip of your nose."

Then he, too, was suffered to follow his companions. Diabolka laughed unrestrainedly.

"Ha, ha, ha! what good the consciousness of a meri-
torious action does one! They are safe to clear out
Chevalier Galban."

"But you might have let the fellow off the last kiss,"
growled Jakuskin. "On the tip of his nose, too! As
though he could feel it through his mask!"

"But those kisses were useful," returned the girl, with
a sly wink. "While kissing him, I was spying what the
dear youth was wearing upon his breast, and this is
what I found." And she held up a star set with diamonds.

"Eh, the devil! Why, it is a Vladimir order of the
first class," exclaimed Jakuskin.

"Our Rinaldo is high up in the army." .

"A Vladimir order set with brilliants! Eh, jemsik,
hold hard, and strike a light. The names of owners,
as a rule, are usually written in gold inside the ribbons
of the orders."

The jemsik, taking out his flint and steel, struck a
light, and while Diabolka puffed at it with distended
cheeks, the two men simultaneously read out the name
engraven on the ribbon—"Jevgen Araktseieff."

"By Jove! The son of our trusty Araktseieff, too,
plies the trade," cried Jakuskin.

"He is a known *mauvais sujet.*"

"Well, Diabolka, this is a fine catch. For this you
may claim to-morrow every penny Jevgen has robbed
overnight."

"And next day I should be as poor as ever," laughed
the girl.

"If you chose, this order might make you Jevgen's
wife—a real countess," put in Pushkin.

"What would be the good of that? In a week after
I should be going back to the gypsies."

"Do you mean to expose him—to have him hanged?"

"I am not such a fool; they would hang me beside him. Leave it to me. I know what to do with my prize."

Jakuskin said to Pushkin, in German, that Diabolka might not understand:

"That man wrecked my whole life; and I had him at my pistol's mouth but now! But the ball is destined for another now. You see, I did not even break out into fury when I read his name. When we are on the watch for bears we can afford to let foxes go. The huntsman's spear is on his neck. He is in Diabolka's clutches. Come, let us go to the Bear's Paw, and hear Germain's new effusion, *The Song of the Knife.*"

CHAPTER XI

THE HUNTED STAG

NEXT morning the Office of the Great Fast was initiated in Isaac Cathedral by the court singers—a celebrated choir of men and boys, who possessed the finest voices in the whole empire, and who were maintained at great cost.

Contemporary accounts extol these services beyond anything ever produced by human voices. In his riper years the Czar could endure no other music than the sound of harps and mystic sacred song. It was on that account that Zeneida Ilmarinen, the church singer, was so great a favorite of the Czar. He never went to a theatre. Did he desire music his favorite artiste was commanded to the Winter Palace or the Hermitage. During the fasts, however, he went daily to church to hear the boys sing.

On such occasions it was considered the correct thing by the aristocracy also to go to church, and in order to appear still more devotional, great ladies made a point of wearing no rouge, only powder.

In the row next the high altar sat Prince Ghedimin, Muravieff, Orloff, Trúbetzkoi, all of whom had inscribed their names in "the green book"; after them, those officers of the guards who had deliberated the previous night whether the Czar should die, or be merely banished. There they stood in two rows, erect, with military bearing, holding their drawn swords in their hands.

The heads of all were bowed so low that perhaps none remarked that the husband and wife, the rulers of all the Russias, only extended a finger to each other as they passed up the aisle, deigned no look at one another as the service proceeded, and exchanged no word together as they took the holy-water.

Zeneida also was among the congregation. As she left church an officer bowed to her. It was Pushkin.

"Madame, you have been weeping—your cheeks are wet. Was *some one*, then, in church?"

"There is no *some one*," returned Zeneida; "but the music tells on one's nerves. We are but animals; even dogs howl when they hear music."

"Did you observe with what devotion the Czarina kissed the crucifix? Did you not know what was her petition?"

"I neither know, nor did I remark anything."

It was late before the church service had ended. The congregation quickly dispersed and hastened home. The streets were deserted. On the first day of Lent every family man makes a point of supping at home. And as among the poorer classes in St. Petersburg only about every seventh man is blessed with a wife, others join together and get some female of their own class in life to prepare the Lenten soup for them. This is seen on every table, rich and poor, whether in hardware vessel or delicate china tureen. Even upon the Czar's table it may not be absent; the imperial cook prepares it according to time-honored formula.

This soup every head of the family is expected to partake of in his own home. Time was when even in the Winter Palace the custom was observed. Time was! The table was laid for two covers only; no guests were invited. The many dishes, all prepared with oil and honey, were served for the two alone. Then came a day when the imperial wife awaited her husband in vain at the Lenten meal. He came not. And yet she waited and waited; the supper waited also. Some untoward circumstance had come between them. First the meats grew cold, then their hearts. Yet all the same, year after year, the wife had two covers laid on the first evening in Lent, and waited on and on, until the dishes grew cold, and still she did not touch them. She was waiting for him. Hours would pass, the imperial wife sitting lonely, waiting, listening for the slightest sound, wondering whether it were not her husband's footstep outside the tapestried door which connected the corridor of their apartments—that door, at the opening of which her heart had formerly overflowed with earthly bliss. Alas! now the lock had long grown stiff and rusty. Suddenly the clock began to strike—a mechanical clock which Araktseieff had had made in Paris. The piece it plays is the National Anthem; it plays it but once in the twenty-four hours—at one o'clock in the morning—the hour at which Czar Paul had been murdered by his generals and nobles in his bedchamber.

The son of the murdered man, who had ascended the

throne over his father's dead body, had, at the turn of
the year, listened for many an anniversary to the solemn strain, kneeling low, bedewing his *prie dieu* with his
tears; and one being there was who fully shared the
sorrow of his heart. With every fibre that heart of his
vibrated to the sad notes, a truer timepiece than the
clock: it attuned its note to the triumphant strains of
victory, as to the undertone of sadness when it re-
proached him that his father's corpse had been his
stepping-stone to the throne, threatening that his body,
likewise, should be the stepping-stone to his successor.
This was the great trouble of his life; the ever-present
torture of his soul. To no one had he confided it save
to his wife. No one had ever comforted him in the
hours of his agonized wrestling with that burden of
grief save his wife. Now that is all over. The soul-
destroying blue eyes, in whose depths he had sought a
new heaven, gave him for heaven the cold, blue ether
eternally separating earth from heaven for him. The
Czar of all the Russias has no one in whom he can
trust. The mightiest of the mighty has no place where
he may sleep in peace. The most forlorn pilgrim of the
desert is not so utterly alone as is he.

When the last notes of the hymn has died away, and
the husband, so long waited for, has not returned, the
wife, rising, fetches a portrait of him painted upon ivory,
and places it upon the table by the place he should have
occupied. It is the portrait of a proud, heroic man, with
smiling lip and unclouded brow—such as he was as a
bridegroom. She gazes at it long, so long that her eyes
are suffused with tears. Nothing is left to her of him
but this portrait. He whom it represents has long ceased
to smile.

Two sledges, already horsed, are drawn up before the

colonnade of the Winter Palace. One is harnessed
with six horses, the other with three. Both are closed
carriages with drawn blinds. The coachman and footmen belonging to the six-in-hand wear the livery of the
Czar; those of the three-horsed sledge that of the Grand
Duke. But, on getting into them, the Czar takes the
Grand Duke's sledge, the Grand Duke that of the Czar;
and as they pass out of the gates, with jingling of bells,
the one sledge turns to the right, the other to the left.
The six-horsed sledge is followed by an escort of the
guards; where it halts, there halts the escort. The
three-horsed sledge skims along the road unattended.
It is known that the Grand Duke drives home direct;
he is a domesticated man. But of the Czar none knows
whither he will take his way in the course of the long
night; and nowadays it behooves one to be careful; an
escort has become a necessity!

Araktseieff had had a sharp tussle that very morning
with Chulkin, Chief of Police, and the governor of the
city, Miloradovics. There were three sets of police on
active duty—military, civil, and secret police. And instead of playing into each other's hands, their sole study
seemed to be for each to set the other's regulations at
naught. Araktseieff was furious at Chulkin because
Chevalier Galban had been set upon and robbed the
previous night, not only of his money, but of his papers
—papers, among which were many important state secrets. To which Chulkin had retorted that the soldiers
on patrol had been the thieves. Hereupon Araktseieff's
wrath was turned upon Miloradovics, and he demanded
that the officer in command, who had had the inspection on the night past, be sternly reprimanded for lack
of supervision. To which the governor returned that
the said officer in command was no other than young

Araktseieff, his hopeful son. Hereupon Araktseieff waxed still more wroth; but with whom? He fully believed that his son had been Chevalier Galban's plunderer, well knowing him to be capable of the act.

He made no further official inquiry into the matter, merely adding that in future the Household Regiment of Hussars, under his own immediate command, were to accompany the Czar, at a distance, whenever he left the palace. No reliance, evidently, was to be placed on either infantry or police.

Araktseieff possessed a sure instinct which warned him of conspiracies against the Czar, even when he failed to obtain any certain clew. His was the sole and ever-watchful eye that guarded the person of the Czar. He gathered upon his head the detestation of a whole nation in order to protect the head of the one man in whom his entire individuality was merged.

But the pursued knew how to elude protector as efficiently as pursuer. Whilst thus secretly escorted, the six-horsed sledge proceeded from barrack to barrack, the Grand Duke probably holding an inspection to satisfy himself that the officers on guard had not removed their tight stocks; the three-horsed sledge glided along the banks of the Moika Canal, drawing up, at length, before a long walled-in enclosure set with iron spikes. Alighting from his sledge the Czar took from his breast-pocket a key, opened the gate, and entered unattended, the unlit path marked by a line of oak-trees. No footprint was to be seen on the fresh-fallen snow. The path was unused by any but himself. In among the trees with their crows' nests an old-fashioned house was visible, its wooden steps leading to a low oaken door. The solitary man has with him a key to this door also; he opens it, and enters. Here it is so dark he has to take a lantern from his pocket in order to find the stairs leading to the story above. Having ascended the stairs, he proceeds on tiptoe down a long corridor. There is not even a dog to bark at him. As he opens a door two persons, engaged in conversation, look round in startled fear. They are an old man and woman. The old woman screams; the old man throws himself at the Czar's feet.

"Who is this man, Helenka?"

"My old man, my husband. Hold up your ugly pate, Ihnasko, that the Czar may see who you are."

"You never told me you had a husband."

"Why should one tell of the gout one is plagued with, or any other ugly thing one would rather forget?"

"Well, what does he want here?"

Here the old woman, covering half her mouth with her hand, whispers:

"He has brought the king's daughter here."

At these words the icy look melts from the Czar's severe features.

"What! Bethsaba here?"

"Yes; and she is to stay the night. They are playing draughts together."

"How is Sophie?" The inquirer's voice falters.

"Fairly well. She slept well last night, and took her chocolate this morning. She has not been so cross as usual to-day, since the doctor told her that giving way to temper was bad for her."

"Has she followed the doctor's directions?"

"Rather too closely. If I am a second after time in giving her her medicine, she rings for me."

"Did the doctor say anything about diet?"

"Yes; he said her Highness was not to observe the fast, but to eat meat and eggs daily; and that will

strengthen her. But the Princess gave it him soundly.
What was he thinking of? Did he mean to endanger
her soul for sake of her body? And she has ordered
me to pay no attention to what he said, and has threatened me with blows if I attempt to deceive her."

"Indeed! And the doctor said that the observance
of strict fast would be injurious to her health?"

"Certainly. He said she wanted blood, she was
anæmic, and that beans cooked in oil did not make
blood."

"What have you prepared for her supper to-night?"

"The usual soup for the fast."

"Just oblige me, my good Helenka. I have brought
something with me which will do our invalid good. I
have had it over expressly from a celebrated physician
in England. Give her a spoonful of it daily in her soup."

"Of course I will do what you command, sire. But
tell me first, is it prepared from the flesh of any animal?
For if the dear soul were to find out that I had mixed
any meat preparation in her soup during the fast, she
would cry and rage to that extent that she would make
herself ill again."

"Do not be afraid, good Helenka. It is a remedy
composed of palm-root, which takes the place of meat."

"And I shall not endanger my own soul by using it?"

"No, no; have no fear. I will take all responsibility
upon myself."

And yet were it an unpardonable sin to eat meat during Quadragesima the Czar had laid a great burden
upon his soul, for his remedy was no other than extract
of beef, at that time the patent of an English chemist.
But the Czar was a philosopher and—a father.

"Go in and tell her I am here, that she may not be
startled at my coming."

By a lamp, whose light was tempered by a lace shade,
sat two young girls playing draughts.

The one we have already seen at the noteworthy stag-
hunt; and now we know her to be a "king's daughter."

As the Czar entered the Princess's room, and Ihnasko
was alone with his wife, he could not refrain from asking—

"What did you mean by 'king's daughter'?"

"Slow coach! Don't you know that yet? She has
lived the last eight years in your house without your
knowing that she is the daughter of a Circassian king.
Her father was once a mighty ruler there, where the
currants and olives grow; he was killed by the Turks,
and the Queen brought her crown and her little
daughter, and fled to us for protection. She was a
wonderfully handsome woman. I saw her once in all
her national costume at a New-year's review. I did
not wonder at what had happened. It was General
Lazaroff who had received orders to bring her from
her own country to Russia. The General was a man
of amorous nature. On one occasion the wine he
drunk flew to his head, and he forgot that he was es-
corting a queen, and only saw the lovely woman.
But the Circassian butterflies have stings as sharp as
any bee. The Queen drove her kindzal into his heart,
and he fell down dead at her feet. Not much was
made of the affair; it was hushed up. The Queen was
put into a convent, where she has always been treated
with royal honors. But she is not allowed to leave
it. Only on New-year's day she takes her place
with the widowed Queens of Imeritia and Mingrelia
on the steps of the throne. As for her little six-
year-old daughter, she was taken from her, that her
royal mother might not teach her to follow her ways.

Why, there would not be a man left in St. Petersburg!
The child was intrusted to Princess Ghedimin's care,
who has not the blessing of a child of her own."

"What child?" blurted out Ihnasko.

"Oh, you goose! What a question to ask! What
child? None at all, seeing she hasn't got one. Don't
wink at me, or you'll get a cuff in the face. So the
king's daughter was brought to Ghedimin Palace, and is
now a member of the family. Forgetting her own mother, she looks upon the Princess as one."

"I should just like to know why the Princess sends
her here to visit your sick princess?"

"That's nothing to do with your thick skull."

The other draught-player is Sophie Narishkin, a tall,
delicate-looking girl with straw-colored hair. It is well
that she is kept in strict retirement, for in face she is
the image of what Princess Ghedimin was at that age.
There is an expression of premature wisdom in her countenance blended with that of superstitious fear. Her
eyes wear a softer look than those of her prototype; instead of Princess Ghedimin's haughty, contemptuous expression, hers are dreamy and melancholy.

What can be a maiden's dreams who knows nothing
of the world? The world, peopled with mankind. She
may dream of lovely landscapes, of rocks, woods, waterfalls. But of the beings who people the world she
knows none save her nurse, to whose fairy tales she listens so eagerly, and her governesses, who had vainly
striven to indoctrinate her into the sciences and fine arts.

All spoiled, no one loved, her.

All around were traces of work or play, begun and
left unfinished — draught-board, cards, chessmen, patience, embroidery, drawings, patterns. She is sitting, in

a white embroidered dressing-gown, upon a wide divan,
both feet drawn up under her.   Beside her sits the Circassian Princess on a low stool.

His Imperial Majesty is received ungraciously.   Evidently he has interrupted the two girls in some amusement.   And yet he seems to have the right to go up to
Sophie and, taking her face between both hands, to im-
print a hearty kiss upon her cheek—a kiss the traces of
which the girl, with childlike coquetry, instantly tries to
remove by means of the sleeve of her dress, which has
the effect of making the offending cheek as red as a
rose.

"How are you feeling, my Madonna?"

"Oh, now you have come and interrupted the lovely
story Bethsaba was telling me!"

"She shall go on with it.   I will listen too."

"How can you, when you were not here at the beginning?"

"I know Bethsaba will not mind beginning it again."

The Princess nodded acquiescently, while Sophie, with
a look, directed her father to take a seat at the other end
of the divan.   The Czar, understanding the look, did
as he was bid; and, taking one of the girl's delicate,
transparent hands in his, stroked it, and, as he did so,
succeeded in feeling the pulse, to assure himself that
there was still hope for her.   He wanted to put a
question, but the delicately pencilled eyebrows commanded silence, and the Ruler of All the Russias was
obedient.

"Once upon a time," began the king's daughter, "there
lived on the Caspian Sea a mighty king who took a lovely
woman to wife, not knowing, when he did so, that she
was a fire-worshipper.   Now, fire-worshippers are in
league with the Jinn (spirit), and the queen had prom-

ised the Jinn that if she married and bore a daughter
she would give her to him when grown up. No sooner
had the child become a maiden than the Jinn came and
knocked at the king's door to claim her. The poor
king was terribly frightened when he was told that the
spirit had come to fetch away his daughter—"

"If he was a king, why could he not command the
spirit to obey him?" broke in the sick girl, angrily.

"Ah, my dearest, the spirit is so powerful that no king
can control him."

"And no *emperor?*"

"No, not even emperor. No one has power over
him; but he has power over every one. There is no
locking him up or shutting him out, for he can penetrate
everywhere. He has no material weight, yet can suffo-
cate; carries no sword, yet can kill."

"What a good thing that the spirits only live on the
Caspian Sea!"

"When the king heard this he began to entreat the
spirit not to take his beloved daughter from him so soon;
to grant her to him yet another year. 'Very well,' said
the spirit, 'I will leave you your daughter a year longer
if you will promise to give me your thumb in exchange.'
The king cared nothing about his thumb, so he promised, and the spirit took his departure. At the lapse of a
year the spirit came again either to take the princess or
the king's thumb. The king loved his daughter very
dearly, but he also valued his thumb, for without it he
would not be able to draw a bow. So again he entreated
the spirit that he might grant her to him only one year
more. 'Be it so,' returned the spirit, 'I will leave her to
you another year, but then either I will take her away
or you will give me your right hand.' And the king
again closed the bargain. A year passed, and the spirit

8

came a third time. The king would neither give up his child, nor would he part from his right hand. Thereupon the spirit demanded the king's whole arm as forfeit."

"But, then, do the spirits never die?" asked Sophie.

"No, darling, the spirits live forever. Well, the king promised him his arm—if by that means he might save his child—and his hand. And from year to year the spirit came back, demanding ever more and more as forfeit-money. At last he obtained promise of the king's head and heart. And when the king's whole body belonged to him he said, 'This is the last year. Now I shall either carry off your daughter or you must promise me your shadow.' Upon which the king replied, 'No; I will give you no more. Take what is yours; but neither my daughter nor my shadow shall you have.' Thereupon the spirit left him amid loud claps of thunder. The next day was fine and sunny, and the king set out for a pleasure sail upon the sea. Suddenly a violent storm arose, and engulfed both ship and king in the waves. His body was never found. His daughter still lived on; and every evening, when the sun was going down, she saw a shadow draw near to her—the shadow of a man with a kingly crown upon his head; and as the shadow glided past her it seemed to her as if she felt a kiss upon her cheek, and as if her cheek became rosy red."

The Czar had grown thoughtful. That king, whose shadow alone wandered upon the face of the earth, was so like to himself. And Sophie, too, thought that she was like the king's daughter—kissed every evening by a kingly shadow.

Bethsaba, however, added, playfully, "We have so many such legends with us. I could tell you more than a hundred."

"It is a very sad story, my dear child," said the Czar.

"I like stories that have a sad ending," said Princess Sophie. "Those that end, 'And if they are not dead, they are alive to this day,' I cannot endure. I like books, too, to end badly; but the doctor says I must not read. But little Bethsie knows such a lot of nice stories."

"Have in your supper now. Are you not hungry?"

"Oh, who wants to be always thinking of eating? Besides, we are eating all day long." And Sophie pointed to a box of bonbons, from which a few had been taken.

"But you ought to eat nourishing things, to make you strong."

"Who says I am ill? Give me my hand-mirror. Have I not color enough?"

"Yes, you have a good color. You are really looking well to-day."

"Phew, phew!" she exclaimed, spitting twice behind her. "One should never tell anybody they look well; it is unlucky. Now let us lay the table for supper."

The mighty ruler was quite ready to act the lackey to the pale child with the weary eyes, in whom his whole soul was concentrated. But, with the best of will, he did it awkwardly; it was plain he was not learned in the art. And Sophie scolded him roundly.

"See how badly you are holding that plate! Did one ever hear of placing the spoon betwixt knife and fork like that? No, the salt must be turned out upon the table; it is not to be put on the table in the salt-cellar; for if the salt-cellar should happen to be upset it is unlucky. You must not stick in the point of the knife when you are cutting bread! First make the sign of the cross over it, or Heaven will be angry. To think that such a big man should be so clumsy!"

Meanwhile Helenka had brought in the Lenten soup. Sophie tasted it, then laid her spoon down.

"There is something different about it. You have smuggled some meat into it. I will not eat it! You wanted to deceive me! You wanted to make me eat meat soup!"

The Czar, tasting the soup, assured her that it had no taste of meat. But the sick girl, angry at the mere suspicion of being tricked, sent all away untouched, and vowed she would eat nothing but sweets. The Czar implored her not to spoil her digestion with such trash; whereupon, bursting into tears, she complained that they would let her die of hunger. At length the Czar, sending for the samovar, made her some tea with his own hands, and, breaking some biscuit into it, begged her to try it. And great was his joy when she said it was "very nice." She ate a whole biscuit; dipped another in it, ate a piece of it, and gave the rest to the Czar for him to taste how good it was. Then, letting him take her upon his knee, she laid her head upon his shoulder, and seemed inclined to sleep. Soon she asked him to carry her to bed and unplait her hair; then, winding her fingers in the Czar's, she said her evening prayer; and when it came to "Amen" her virgin soul seemed to breathe itself away upon the Czar's lips.

She was the sole being in the world he could call his own! Among his forty millions of subjects she alone belonged exclusively to him.

The Czar of All the Russias found so many little things still to do for his sick child. There was a cushion to be warmed to be placed at her feet; orange-flower water to be prepared for her night drink. He pushed a branch of consecrated palm under her pillow to chase away bad dreams — he, a philosopher, believing in the efficacy of a consecrated palm branch! But philosophy is nowhere by the sick-bed of one's child.

"Now, you go home," whispered Sophie; "Bethsaba is to sleep with me. Good-night. I know I shall have no bad dreams."

"Lay your hand upon my head, that I, too, may sleep well. Good-night."

They called one another by no endearing names, though they knew that in the whole wide world they had no one but each other.

It was past midnight when the Czar went back to his sledge—too early to go home.

"Drive along Newski Prospect," said the Czar.

The coachman understood the command. Upon Newski Prospect there is a two-storied house with "Severin" upon the door. Here the coachman drew up. The windows of the first story were lighted. On ringing the bell, men-servants with lamps promptly appeared, who led the great Czar to the master of the house. Herr Severin was a simple paper-maker and printer, carrying on his business with his sons and sons-in-law, who, with their families, lived here with him. Upon great festivals it was the Czar's custom to indulge himself for an hour or two with the sight of their simple family life and joys—such joys as were denied to him. The tiny children recite their verses to grandpapa, who rides them upon his knee; converting them into generals by dint of paper hats and wooden swords. The Czar has no such generals! Then five or six of them, forming into a circle, dance round, and sing the story of the "Ashimashi Beggars," each striking up in a different key. No such choir does the Czar possess! At supper every dish is so well cleared out that it would be a puzzle to say what it had contained. Such a feast the Czar cannot give! And supper over, the favorite game of " Clock and Hammer " is brought out. They play for high stakes—nuts ; and the stakes are eaten while the game is played. The Czar has no such national coin!

So he sits among them until the little ones, growing sleepy, are carried off to bed by their nurses ; first kissing everybody—even the Czar. No such thing happens in the Winter Palace!

When that is all over, the distinguished guest has a long talk with the old man over the good old times. He listens to all the joys and sorrows of his host's every-day life. The samovar is emptied and filled again. The Czar cannot tell what does him so much good— whether the tea, the cakes, or the good old man's integrity—his honest, straightforward spirit. No such tea does the Czar taste in his own house!

Without, on the snow-covered roads, gallop the escort of the guards, while stealthy conspirators peer out from dark doorways, and look after the six - horsed sledge, pistol and knife in hand.

The hunted stag knows nothing of all this!

None may tell whither he has wandered through the long hours of the night, nor who it is that so persistently tracks him.

CHAPTER XII

HOW A FORTRESS WAS TAKEN

" Lock and bolt the doors, and see that you let no one in! To him who doubts that I am not at home, say I am dead!"

" And suppose it's some one to bring you money?"

"There's no man living who would do that."

"And if it's a love-letter?"

"Let him push it under the door; but don't let him in! For it might prove to be some rascal of a creditor."

Unnecessary to state that this dialogue took place between a young officer and his servant. It may, however, be as well to add that the said young officer was Pushkin.

With heavy head and light pockets he had reached home in the small hours, and, dressed as he was, had thrown himself on his bed, feeling as if each individual hair in his head were being torn out by a devil with red-hot pincers.

Suddenly he was aroused from his uneasy slumbers by a hideous noise of scuffling and quarrelling in the street. A man beneath his windows, seemingly set upon by ruffians, was screaming loudly for help, and no one going to his aid. Why should they—when the police did not trouble themselves about private disturbances?

Pushkin could stand it no longer; going to his window, he breathed upon the frozen pane to clear a space, and looked out. Two men were belaboring a third, who was vainly endeavoring to defend himself, his face covered with blood. One of his assailants gave a tug at the long beard, worn divided in the middle, plucking out a handful. That was too much for Pushkin; the sight of such brutality made his blood boil. Snatching his dog-whip from the wall, he tore down into the street. In vain his man cried after him, "Don't open the door, sir;" he was out like a shot, and, plunging into the middle of the trio, began laying his whip upon the two offenders right merrily, upon which they quickly took to their heels; and Pushkin, raising in his arms the injured, groaning victim of their brutality, carried him into his house. Reaching his room, he sent for cold water and a basin, that the poor fellow might bathe his face. This he proceeded to do so effectually that not only the vermilion dye stained the water deep red, but also the beard, which was only stuck on, entirely disappeared from his face. Drying his face, he turned with a smile to Pushkin, drew out a folded paper from the sleeve of his caftan, and said :

" Very glad to have the opportunity of speaking to you again. Will you not pay me this little account ?"

And now, for the first time, did Pushkin perceive that it was his worst creditor, the usurer Zsabakoff, who stood before him.

" Was it the devil brought you here ?"

" No, sir, you brought me yourself."

His servant interposed—

" Didn't I tell you, sir, not to open the door ?"

" But they were pulling out his beard."

" It was only stuck on," confessed Zsabakoff, with a grin.

" And the two men who were laying their sticks about you ?"

" Are my two brothers-in-law. That was all a prearranged thing. I knew that you were too much a gentleman to see a man ill-treated before your very door. There seemed no other way of getting at you."

Pushkin saw that he had been thoroughly sold, and that it was best to put a good face on it."

" Well, and what's your business ?"

" Only humbly to ask you, sir, to pay this miserable one thousand rubles. You know how long they have been owing."

" Yes, I have already paid them twice over in interest.

"Ah, if it were my own money! But I had to borrow it, in order to lend it to you; and the horse-leech from whom I borrowed it has put on the screw each time you renewed it, so that I have had to pay him the same rate of interest that you have been paying me. And now he swears he will grant me no more time; that he will have the caftan off my back if I do not raise the thousand rubles. And here, in the depths of winter, shall I have to go about in shirt-sleeves, and my seven children—beautiful as angels—will have no bread! To pay your debts the very pillow under their heads will be taken from them. I shall have nothing left; everything I had I have turned into money to satisfy those blood-sucking usurers; even my wife's last gown has been pawned in Appraxin-Dwor. What will become of me, miserable man that I am?" And the usurer wept like a water-spout.

"But I cannot help you," said Pushkin, irritably. "Where the devil am I to get the money from? I do not coin bank-notes."

"When will you pay me?"

"I am no prophet."

"But what is a poor devil like me to do, then?" said the usurer, trembling.

"County court me."

"Ah, dear, kind sir, don't make a joke of it. I should only be thrown into prison for lending money to an officer in the army. Have pity on me! Nine people will pray daily for your soul's good if you will only pay me."

"Where am I to get the money from, if I have none?"

"Just reflect a little, sir. You have some wealthy aunts—one of them may make you her heir. There are no end of rich, beautiful princesses in St. Petersburg who would be only too glad to help such a brave gentle-

man did they but know that he was in temporary difficulty. I could tell you this moment of an excellent
match—a good, handsome, well-behaved young lady, with
half a million rubles for her dowry. I will undertake
the affair for you, if you wish it. Then you have such
a fine estate at Pleskow. There are plenty of honest
bankers here who, not knowing that your property is
confiscated by the Crown, would lend you money on it.
Such a man is rolling in gold, he would not miss it; and,
of course, you would give back his money when you got
back your lands, and that would be sure to be the case
when you have done some brave soldiering, and the Czar
rewards you for it."

Pushkin held his sides with laughing as he listened to
this view of his affairs.

Zsabakoff grew desperate at the way Pushkin took his
suggestions.

"Do not make light of it, sir," cried he. "I assure
you, it is a matter of life and death with me. If I have
to go home like this to those angels who are crying out
for bread, I will take a razor and cut their seven throats,
then their mother's, and then my own. That I have made
up my mind to. You may depend, if you go on laughing at me, I will prepare you a comedy that will turn
your laughter into something very different. A desperate man sticks at nothing. When you have it on your
conscience that a father of seven hanged himself, before
your very eyes, upon your window-frame—"

"Try it," said Pushkin, laughing; "but be quick
about it, for it's uncommonly late, and I want to go to
sleep." And with these words he threw himself upon
his camp-bedstead.

"Well, then, you shall see, before you have time to
sleep."

And the money-lender, dragging a chair to the window, got on it, made a noose of his scarf, fastened it to the window-frame, passed his head through it, and kicked away the chair. And suddenly Pushkin saw his creditor struggling in the air, his eyes starting out of his head.

So then it was more than a joke! Springing from his bed, he snatched up his dagger to cut the noose; then saw that his would-be suicide was wearing a kind of cravat of stout leather under his shirt, which effectually prevented any possibility of strangulation. Furious at the deception, he threatened the man with a sound thrashing.

"Thrash as hard as you like, but pay. I would willingly sacrifice my life to get back my thousand rubles. Don't tell me you have no money. I know you have. Did you not pay back Nyemozsin, that shameless usurer, last week? He's a thorough horse-leech! Takes two hundred per cent. And yet you could pay him, though he held no written acknowledgment of yours."

"Just why I did pay him. It was a debt of honor."

Zsabakoff, as he heard this, took his I.O.U. and tore it into shreds.

"Now I have no written security either—and mine is a debt of honor!" he said, placing both hands in his girdle.

This was too much for Pushkin.

"Devil take you!" he cried. "Here is my pocket-book. What you find in it you may take."

And the money-lender did find something in it — a poem called *The Gypsy Girl*. He began to dance round with glee, now stopping, now starting off afresh, like a merry Cossack.

"Ho, ho, what a find! *The Gypsy Girl!* Heaven bless you for it! I am off with it."

"Where to?"

"To Severin. He was only just telling me how all the world of fashion was besieging his doors to know when Pushkin's poem of *The Gypsy Girl*, that he had read at Fräulein Ilmarinen's, was coming out. He said he would give any amount for it. So my thousand rubles are safe. If I can, I will squeeze something more out of him, and honorably share the surplus with you. I kiss your hand, sir. Pardon any annoyance I may have caused you. Command me when you are in want of more money. I shall be only too happy to be at your service."

The money-lender had said the half of this speech as he looked back on the threshold. Pushkin thought the man had gone mad. Angrily throwing himself back on his bed, he forbade his man-servant to admit the fellow again; then slept till noon. When he awoke he rang for his man.

"That fellow came again, sir."

"But you did not let him in?"

"No. But he pushed this packet under the door. Shall I throw it into the fire, sir?"

"No. Give it me."

And, opening the packet, Pushkin found in it a copy of his romance, *The Gypsy Girl*, two bank-notes for one hundred rubles each, and a letter from the publisher, Severin, informing him that he had bought his poem for twelve hundred rubles, of which he herewith enclosed two hundred, and had paid the rest to the person who brought the manuscript. He forwarded a copy to Pushkin that he might obtain the necessary permission to publish.

It was a queer story; and especially that he should have made money for what he had merely scribbled down for his own amusement. Absurd! A gambler had more right to the accumulated gains of a gambling club than a man to extort money from the multitude for permission to read what he had written! An author's fee! Surely a hybrid betwixt the degrading and the ridiculous! Did it most savor of theft or deception? or was it but a loan?

These thoughts passed through Pushkin's head as he read the letter. Now he had to go to the Censor—he, a military man, to humiliate himself to a scurvy civil official, and acknowledge him to be his judge and superior! In all else the army has its own court-martial. Poetry is truly an unsavory implement when it so demeans a smart officer to defer to a civilian. Pushkin decided to make this sacrifice to Apollo.

CHAPTER XIII

A CANNIBAL

THE devourer of human flesh is called a cannibal, but what shall we call him who feeds upon the souls of men? —who breakfasts off flights of youthful imagination, dines off great thoughts, and sups on the heart's blood of genius—what shall we call such an one? A censor? A man who sits in judgment on the gods!

At that period there were certain especially renowned censors in St. Petersburg, at the head of whom was Magnitsky, Araktseieff's right hand, if one may use the word *right* to either of his hands.

Certain anecdotes which have gone the round about these men insure them immortality.

Herr Sujukin revised Homer's *Iliad*, made Venus

into an irreproachable lady and Mars an officer of un-
questionable morality, and changed the capital letters
of all the false gods into small type.   Only Mars was
permitted to retain the capital M, out of respect to the
Czar, who was also the god of war.

He struck out "unknown heaven" from the works of
a poet, because there is but one heaven where the saints
dwell; consequently it is not unknown.   From another
he struck out the passage, "I despise the world!"   It
is a treasonable offence to despise the world in which
Czar and Grand Dukes, foreign rulers and their ministers, delight to dwell.

In the love sonnets of a third, beginning, "Worshipped
being, creator of my bliss!" the solitary word "being"
alone found grace in the eyes of the arbitrary Censor.
We may only "worship" Divinity; there is but one
Creator.   "Bliss" is only to be known in eternity for
such as have ended their lives as true Christians.   Thus
the adjuration "being" was accounted fully sufficient
for the lady of the poet's thoughts.

And this was the man to whose tender mercies Pushkin must perforce commit his poem!   Knocking at his
door, he courteously requested him to do him the favor
of first reading through his poem, which request was as
courteously conceded, a holy Friday being the day appointed for the next interview.

Never yet had the youth looked forward to a meeting
with his lady-love so ardently as he did to this appointment.   He knew his man, and that he should have
a hard fight for it—for there was no forgetting that
though there were many censors there was no possibility of choice.   Each had his special province: one
the press, another religion, the third education, the
fourth advertisements, the fifth theatrical programmes

and announcements, and, lastly, the sixth, poetical effusions.

Herr Sujukin, who represented the earthly providence of the poetical world, had exercised that function in Czar Paul's time. He was now an aged man, with perfectly bald head, and, his face being also clean-shaven, he looked for all the world like a death's-head, only that his skull was still provided with every imaginable expression of torture; his contemptuous grimaces could galvanize the luckless poet standing before him; and many a one felt a death sentence passed upon him as he encountered the glare of those little red eyes, fixed upon him from out their wrinkled sockets.

"Well, dear son Pushkin!" Every poet was "son" to him. "I have read your papers through from beginning to end. I am truly sorry for you. What has induced you to mix with the lower orders and select a pack of gypsies for the subject of your poetical labors? Have you no higher associates? Are you desirous to bring shame on your noble father by this versifying of gypsydom?"

Here Pushkin calmed him by informing him that his father was dead long ago—which, be it known, was not strictly in accordance with the truth; but it is not necessary to tell the truth to a censor.

"Then you have certainly noble relatives who will feel ashamed as they read these lines! Why, they will think you have become a gypsy yourself! Now, if you had at least idealized gypsy life! But you have drawn them true to nature, thus sinning against the first rules of poetry. Nor is this your grossest fault. But, in the name of all the poets, what versification is this? The like I have never come across before! Virgilius Mars wrote in hexameters; Horatius Flaccus in alcaic, sapphic, and anapestic verse. But what do you call yours? There is no rhythm, the lines rhyme in all directions, as if the smith had three hammers working together on his anvil; one line is too long, another too short! That I could not allow; where I have found a line too short I have lengthened it with an interjection: because; namely; but; however." And the death's-head beamed with self-satisfaction. "Yes, yes, my son, I have helped out many a poet. Derschavin owes the greater part of his fame to me; and I shall make something out of you!"

"All right, make what you like out of me, but not one iota do you add to my verses! Your office is to cut out what does not please you."

"Now, don't flare up, my child. You will have no need to complain of want of cutting. Do you see this red pencil in my hand? It is historical. It has never been pointed; that is done effectually by the constant striking out it performs. Since the year 1796—before you were born—I have been engaged, with this very pencil, striking out words, lines—ay, whole pages! And what it has struck out has been condemned to eternal death!"

"By Jove! that pencil, then, is a very guillotine."

"Eh, eh! A young man such as you should not pronounce the word 'guillotine!' This red lead, my son, preserves society from degeneration, conspiracies, epidemics. It is more precious than the philosopher's stone; more powerful than a marshal's staff. It is the pillar on which rests the peace of the whole land."

"Just let me hear what miracles your enchanted wand has effected on my poor verses?"

"It has done its duty. Do you suppose that lines like 'Men enclosed within narrow walls are ashamed to love one another' may see the light? Humph! to love in the sense of your fine heroes one might well be ashamed! Running after gypsy girls, without the sanction of a priest, without wedlock — all unfettered — a pretty incentive to the young who would read it!"

"But, my dear sir, that is not my intention. As the dramatic development proceeds, I purpose to show up my hero's wrong-doing, for which he has to atone."

The death's-head was discomfited. He was not prepared for this reply.

"Oh, so they are the adventurer's opinions? Then you should have made a foot-note stating that they are not the author's views, and that the offender will atone for them later on. But listen again: 'He' (that is, the citizen) 'basely sells his freedom, bows his head to the dust before his fetich, and by his importunity wrests from it gold and fetters!' Now, is it permissible to put this in black and white? What 'freedom' does he sell? and to whom does he sell it? No one in Russia has freedom; consequently neither can he sell it to any one! It is a revolutionary appeal. An incitement to anarchy! A proclamation! And then, 'bows his head to the dust before his fetich.' Who is this fetich? The Czar or the holy images? Do you want to provoke the people to iconoclasm? But it is worse than blasphemy. In former times you would have had your tongue torn out for such words. And again: 'By importunity wrests gold and fetters.' A calumny upon our thirteen official grades! Fetters! Thorough Jacobin heresy! So the fetters offend you? Without them you were wolves and no men! Nor do you need to importune for them; they are conceded without it, of grace! You must have fetters — *must*, I say! It is in vain to versify against them! Did not my red pencil strike out those three

9

lines, I should deserve to have it bored through my nose !"

And, upon this awful possibility, he began applying the said fateful pencil with dire force to expunge the offending lines.

" But I do not permit you to strike those lines out of my poem. I would rather withdraw it from publication."

" But I will not give it back !" returned the death's-head, placing a hand upon the manuscript. " What is once presented to my censure can no more be withdrawn !   It must receive the deserved castigation !"

" And I protest against the striking out of any single letter of it !   The manuscript is mine; it is as much my individual property as is that red pencil yours.   You are at liberty to reject my writings, but not to deface them with your confounded chalk !"

" Deface ! Confounded chalk !" screamed the death's-head, rigid with horror.   " Audacity like this has no superlative."

" By heavens, it has !" shouted Pushkin, on his side; and to substantiate his words, snatching the red pencil from the Censor's hand he threw it so violently to the ground that the precious relic was shattered to a thousand pieces; at which awful result Pushkin himself was so terrified that he took to flight, leaving the terrible man alone with the pieces.

The Censor was aghast with rage and horror at the deed.   His all-powerful pencil shattered to atoms !   He could scarce believe it.   Such a thing had never before happened in civilized Europe.   What would men leave sacred and untouched in future, when even that hallowed implement could be dashed to the ground ?

Herr Sujukin did not call his servant, but himself,

kneeling down, began collecting the precious fragments, weeping so bitterly as he did so that his chin trembled.

"My faithful—my treasure—pride of my life—thou art no more!" He endeavored to fasten the larger portions together, but in vain.

Such an offence needed a special punishment.

The aggrieved Censor, wrapping the *corpus delicti* in a paper, rolled Pushkin's poem round it, and hastened off to Araktseieff's Palace, mentally conning the speech the while with which he should make his patron acquainted with the abominable assault.

Araktseieff's palace was just then being decorated with those historic frescos by which the celebrated Doyen perpetuated the deeds of Czar Alexander. The master was even then himself at work on the immense circle which formed the cupola of the domed reception-room, and in which the Czar appears in the midst of his generals and surrounded by mythological and allegorical figures.

The furious Censor had to pass through this saloon. He glanced up at the master, who, astride on the plank, was touching up the figures, already designed, with color. It was just what he wanted. He would let off some of his rage upon him.

"Is it Master Doyen, or one of his assistants, who is painting up there?" asked he.

To this singular question the artist made reply:

"And pray what may be your business down there?"

"I have no 'business,' but am Vasul Sujukin Sergievitch, Counsellor of Enlightenment to his Majesty." Such was the Censor's title.

"A jolly good thing you have come. There is precious little light in this city with its confounded fogs."

"Learn, sir, that this is no 'confounded' fog. A St.

Petersburg fog is purer than that of any other city. We allow no complaints of our skies. But, look! who is that woman up there in the picture, standing close to the Czar, with leg bared to the knee?"

"It is Fame, the goddess of novelty."

"But what indecency for any one to stand in proximity to the Czar in such a costume!"

"Ha, my friend, in the period of Roman-Greek mythology stockings were not in fashion."

"But we are in Russia, where ladies who have been presented do not go about barefoot. I forbid you to bring women in such *negligée* in contact with the person of the Czar!"

"All right! I will give her sandals."

"And let down her dress!"

"It is going to have a border to it."

"Mind, then, that it is a broad one that covers the knee. And who is that with a roll of papers in his hand?"

"General Kutusoff."

"Why is his right arm shorter than the left?"

"It is not shorter; only his position makes it appear so. We call that *scorzo* in Italian."

"*Scorzo* here, *scorzo* there! We are not Italians! Here we call a man who has one arm shorter than the other deformed!"

"But I cannot paint my characters with stretched-out arms as if they were on a crucifix!"

"I don't see why not."

The artist here, giving up the discussion, began touching up the face of the Czar.

"What is that black you are smearing over the countenance of the Czar?"

"*Terra di Siena.* It gives the shadows."

"But there must be no shadow on the countenance of the Czar! It must shine, be radiant, brilliant. And then, look here, one-half of the imperial face is broader than the other."

"Of course it is; because it is taken in three-quarter profile."

"But why do you take the Czar in three-quarter profile?"

"Because he could not otherwise be looking straight at Kutusoff."

"Then turn Kutusoff's head so that the Czar may look at him in full face."

The artist was nigh to springing off his plank with brush and palette, and alighting on the head of the dictatorial Counsellor of Enlightenment. But, controlling himself, he took up a large brush and began painting in the clouds in the background. This thoroughly provoked the Censor's severity.

"Halt! What are you doing? What is that?"

"A cloud."

"I can under no conditions permit you to paint clouds behind the person of the Czar. It might seem to some to have an allegorical meaning, as though our political horizon were threatened with dark clouds."

"But, my dear sir, clouds are necessary to make the figure stand out."

"The Czar stands out by himself! You must paint in a twilight sky for your background."

"Impossible! Light is thrown on to the figures from the other side, where the sun is shining."

"Where is the sun? How are you going to paint it —in what colors? With us the sun shines far more brilliantly than in any other country."

The artist looked round to see which paint-pot he

could aim at the Enlightened Counsellor's head. Then a better idea struck him.

"Stop a bit, Herr Counsellor! Here at the feet of the Czar is to be a figure, 'Death Conquered.' Your head will make a capital model. Just let me jot down a sketch of it."

The Counsellor of Enlightenment once more felt his reason staggered. He could not at the moment decide whether it were a compliment or an impertinence that his physiognomy should be perpetuated on one canvas with that of the Czar as "Death Conquered." But his brutish instincts whispered him that it would be doing the Frenchman a service to stand as his model; so he did not do it. Leaving him in the lurch, he passed on to his patron's apartments.

CHAPTER XIV

THE YOUNG HOPEFUL

·THE Counsellor of Public Enlightenment was just by way of detailing at large to Araktseieff Pushkin's un-heard-of outrage upon the censorial red pencil, with all its aggravations, when a young man, unceremoniously bursting open the door of the reception-room of the dread President of Police, appeared upon the scene. The intruder seemed privileged to break in upon ·him unannounced, whoever might be having audience of the all-powerful statesman. The new-comer was a man of some thirty years of age; his dress the uniform of a colonel in the Life Guards. His features were pleasing and regular, but the expression uneasy, shifty; he never looked the person to whom he was speaking full in the face.

It was Junker Jevgen, Araktseieff's son and young hopeful.

"Ah!" cried his father, "you have got into some other ugly scrape, sir!"

"*Au contraire*, governor! Mistaken for once."

"Your appearance rarely means anything else. Have you anything of importance to say to me?"

"Oh, nothing of a nature that I cannot say before Herr Sujukin."

"I suppose some pressing money difficulty?"

"*Au contraire*," returned the young man, carelessly throwing himself back upon a couch, and ostentatiously drawing out a handful of gold from his pocket. "You see it is not that which brought me."

"By Jove! you have lined your pockets well. May I inquire the source of this plenty?"

"Why not? No need to conceal it from Herr Sujukin. I won it a night or two ago at rouge-et-noir."

"So! At nights, when you are intrusted with the inspection, you can manage to find time for the faro-bank?"

"I only just happened in *en passant*. I just hazarded a couple of sovereigns; seven times, one after another, I won. I had deuced good-luck; red always turned up. And I left off playing while the vein was on."

"And you come to tell me the good news?"

"Oh no! On the contrary, I come to bring you the latest. Only fancy! the celebrated harpist, Chamberlin, has arrived from Paris, and is going to give some concerts."

"I never knew you to be so devoted to the harp."

"Oh, I rave about it."

"And I can't abide it," put in Sujukin, in full agreement with the father.

Jevgen continued:

"His Majesty the Czar, to do honor to the harpist, has commanded a state concert to-night at the Winter Palace."

"Oh, I delight in the harp!" hastily threw in Sujukin, in order to amend his former speech.   ·

"The invitations are already issued. It will be a particularly brilliant assemblage. I just saw your invitation delivered to, your groom of the chambers. I have already received mine."

"Oh, then, of course it will be a brilliant affair!"

"I suppose you know that we must appear *en grande tenue?* Men with the *grand cordon* and all their orders."

"Upon my soul! Doing high honor to the musician."

"Besides which the Zeneida will sing something of Cimarosa."

"Is that all you have to tell me?"

"Beyond that nothing," returned the young man, rising with a yawn as he looked at the clock. "Now I must be off and change. By-the-way, shall you be at the state concert to-night?"

"What else should I do, as the Czar honors me with an invitation?"

"I thought, perhaps, your rheumatism was plaguing you too much."

"Do not forget that there is no rheumatism when the Czar commands."

"And yet it were a pity to risk your health, sir, for sake of a scoundrelly musician. You will be awfully bored. There is nothing in the world so ghastly dull as the harp."

"You just told me you raved about it."

"Oh, of course, if it is a lady harpist. But to see a man sprawling over the strings! *pas si bête!* It is for all the world like listening to some street player. I could make your excuses to the Czar for you in form if you preferred to stay at home."

" Now what the devil does it matter to you whether I go or not? What has made you such an affectionate son, so solicitous for your father's health? Have you entered upon the climacteric years which alter a man's nature ?"

Jevgen broke into a laugh.

"Not exactly, father. Your son is the same as before. But I want you to stay at home to-night, because then you could lend me your diamond Vladimir order. I can't find mine anywhere."

"Because you have not searched at the pawnbroker's for it."

"With clear conscience I can say it is not at the pawnbroker's. If it were I could have easily redeemed it with the cash in my pocket, and need not have come to you. I have searched everywhere, and cannot set eyes upon it."

"Just think, my boy; you'll remember what you've done with it."

"Well, then, I will confess. It is no disgrace; a thing that happens to many of us officers. After playing I came across a demoniacal little girl."

"Ah, you found time for that, too, during inspection?"

"What matter! When I released the said little fury I perceived that my Vladimir order had disappeared with her."

"Upon my word! It is a pretty story!" cried Araktseieff, springing up from his chair. "You have done for yourself. Did I not say that some nice mess had brought you here? Lose your order! Let it be stolen from you by a street wench! Do you know the girl ?"

"Yes; she is a street dancer — Diabolka, the gypsy girl."

"A gypsy, eh?" broke in Sujukin at that moment. "That's it! Just what might have been expected from Pushkin's verses. Ah! I can generally see through things!"

"Did you put the police at once upon her track?" asked Araktseieff.

"As though the police were to be found at once, or, to put it the other way, as though our police were likely to find any one at once! Oh, it is not lost! The gypsy or the Vladimir order will be found fast enough in Appraxin Dwor. But that's no use to me. I want to wear the order to-night; for I dare not appear without it at the state concert."

"Well, my boy, no power but death shall separate me from mine."

"Then I see no way out of it. I have tried to obtain one from the State Treasurer; but the Czar keeps the key of the order safe himself; so nothing is to be done there. It is enough to make a fellow blow his brains out!"

"Well, well, here is an idea; but, mind, I take no responsibility for it. Are you on good terms with the Czar's groom of the chambers?"

"Oh yes, excellent! We meet constantly—under the table!"

"You are aware that when the Czar attends any civil function and not a military parade, he is pleased to show his imperial favor towards civilians by appearing in a plain black coat, and wears no orders, merely the gold medal in his button-hole, which he received from the society of 'Philanthropists' in Riga for having saved a poor peasant from drowning in the river. Thus, amid

all the brilliant assemblage, the Czar is conspicuous by
the simplicity of his attire; and his Vladimir order will
be in the custody of the groom of the chambers for the
night. Bribe your friend to lend you the Czar's order
to-night."

" By Jove ! a brilliant idea ! I see, after all, that you
love me, governor."

" Ah ! were you not my son, my boy, you'd long ago
have been swinging on the gallows."

" No, no, father. Why joke with the word 'gallows'?
You may come to it yourself one day, though you are
my respected parent."

" But I give you one piece of advice : See that you
keep as far off as possible from the Czar at the concert,
that he may not recognize his own order."

" Bah ! how is he to single out one amid the forty
that will be there ?"

" I tell you this much, that the Czar is an expert in
precious stones. So make a point of keeping in some
obscure corner."

" Well, I will be your obedient son. I am pleased
with you to-day, father. It is no light matter to have
such a sensible parent to come to. I grant you permission to give me a kiss. Adieu ! Good-day, Herr
Sujukin. Pray continue where you left off."

Meanwhile the death's-head had been chewing something between his teeth, perhaps a criticism, while the
young man was making a clean breast of it. " A good
many things to strike out with the red pencil there,"
thought he to himself. The father gazed for some time
at the half-open door ; then, turning to Sujukin :

" A fine, handsome boy, is he not? A merry fellow. His worst fault is that he knows how much I love
him."

" He only needs a little of the red pencil! But to
return to the story of that red pencil."

"You shall have satisfaction, Vasul Sergievitch! Leave
the matter to me. I will place the *corpus delicti* in the
Czar's own hands, and can assure you that the culprit
will bitterly repent his offence! As though his first
intemperate actions, which he paid for by the confisca-
tion of his property and his banishment to Odessa, were
not sufficient reminder, he requites the clemency of the
Czar, who permitted him to return home, with these
fresh excesses; but we will find a means of settling
with him. Be comforted, Vasul Sergievitch. To-morrow
morning Master Pushkin will find himself on his way to
Uralsk."

" Irkutsk is farther!" said the Censor, who could not
refrain from improving on Araktseieff's verdict.

" But Uralsk is worse! Believe me, Uralsk is an awful
garrison for an officer to be disgraced to. In ten years'
time no woman would recognize him. From a gay butterfly he will come back transformed into a hairy cater-
pillar—like our friend Jakuskin!"

The death's-head was satisfied to leave matters to him
—*Typis admittitur!*—and went back to the reception-
rooms to administer a parting shot to the Frenchman.
After the encouraging words of the President of Police
his horns had grown so fast that he felt as if they would
reach to the artist perched aloft.

" I forbid you to paint a figure of Death before his
Majesty's very feet. It will give the whole fresco an
ominous meaning."

But the artist continued undisturbed to paint in his
figure of Death; and the face was the counterpart of
that of the Censor.

CHAPTER XV

THE CZAR SMILES

ONLY as Pushkin reached home did he begin to meditate over what he had done. He did not for a moment hesitate as to the consequences of his rash act. A man only just permitted to return from exile in Bessarabia, whither his hot head had banished him, and even then but received in semi-favor at court, could not expect other from his recent scene with the sacred person of the Censor than to be deported to some fortress on the Volga, or to guard the Kirghis Pustas, where he would be forever lost to sight and mind. He therefore set to work at once addressing P.P.C. cards to his friends; on that to Zeneida he added, "pour jamais." When once he received marching orders, there would be no time for such things. The report of the assault had quickly made the round of the town; such news is sure to spread quickly. Among his many friends there was but one who found his way to him on hearing of it; that one was Jakuskin.

"Well, friend, now you, too, will make acquaintance with the Caucasus. You would do well to have your portrait taken at once, that after ten years, when you come back, like me, you may at least know what you once were like."

"I am prepared for anything," answered Pushkin, sealing the letter in which he was returning the pub-

lisher Severin the two hundred rubles he had received
for his poem, not having obtained the Censor's permission to publish. "But there is one thing I cannot understand. I have just received from the Lord Chamberlain an invitation to the state concert to-night. Now,
what the devil does that mean?"

"What does it mean, my friend? That your punishment is to be carried out with a refinement of cruelty!
Had I not a similar experience? The very night I had
challenged that scoundrel, I, too, received an invitation
to a court ball. When the circle was formed round the
Czar, the Lord Chamberlain placed me among the
guests to whom his Majesty desired to speak. I was
simple enough to feel elated at the distinction. My turn
at length came. The great man stood before me, letting me feel his colossal height. Looking full at me
with his cold, green eyes, his face as immovable as a
moonlit landscape, he asked, 'You are not satisfied
with your commanding officer?' And, taking my confusion for acquiescence, added, 'We will provide against
any such unpleasant friction in the future.' And I stammered out something like thanks, never thinking that
this was only a planned humiliation for me, that every
one standing round about me knew already whither I
was to be banished, and that the honor of this imperial interview was merely intended to further humiliate
me. Oh, if I had but known it then! If it should again
happen that I— Ah, fool that I am! Fate does not
so repeat itself. But could I pass on to you my imbittered heart, my experience, and my determination at the
moment in which you will be standing there, face to
face with 'him,' apart from all, all eyes upon you, but
every man's hand turned away from you; no one near
you but a devil! Casca's devil! But what am I talk-

ing about! You are but an Epimetheus to whom wisdom only comes when the opportunity is past. A pleasant journey to Tungusia; my respects to the marmots!
Come, let us shake hands. We are comrades now."

"Eh! fate does not repeat itself? How if the soup
be not eaten as hot as it is served?" asked Pushkin,
simulating light-heartedness. But Jakuskin's words had
left a sting in his heart. Why had he received the invitation to the palace that night?

There was no evading the command. His sledge was
one among the many formed in line before the gates of
the Winter Palace that evening; the guests numbered
more than two thousand, the whole *élite* of St. Petersburg society was there.

At that time the Winter Palace, in its magnificence,
tone of society, its mode of paying compliments, and
distinguished courtesy, threatened to rival the Tuileries;
even Parisian *bon-mots* went the round. All national
characteristics had become decidedly bad form. Ladies
no longer wore the fur-lined *dolmanka*, the clasped
girdles; the singular fashion which had formerly prevailed of wearing gold watches in the hair had been
given up; feminine taste displayed itself in following
the latest Paris fashions, in which lace and artificial
flowers were *de rigueur*. The men wore uniforms. The
Czarina was the sole exception to the prevailing fashion;
she continued to wear the out-spreading head-dress, in
form of a peacock tail, which made her tall figure seem
even taller, and lent still more majesty to her countenance. The Czar, on the other hand, was wearing plain
civilian evening dress, without ribbon or order of any
description.

Late as was Pushkin's entry among the gayly attired
throng, he could not fail to notice how greatly the tone

of society had altered towards him from the night before. People did not seem to see him. His superior officers and others to whom he had been presented did not acknowledge his salute. Intimate friends, comrades in arms, seemed suddenly engrossed in conversation with their neighbors on his approach, to avoid accosting him. Lovely women, who but yesterday had welcomed him to their opera-boxes, spread out their fans before their faces as he neared them; the heat suddenly became oppressive! One lady alone, clad in rich silks, crossing the room on Prince Ghedimin's arm, vouchsafed him her attention; she was the beautiful Princess Korynthia, Prince Ghedimin's wife; her cold gray eyes measured the young officer from head to foot—she who had so often laughed at his wit—while she deigned him no other return to his salutation than a contemptuous curl of the lip, for which he promptly revenged himself by turning and exchanging mischievous smiles with the young girl at her side, Princess Bethsaba. Just then the press before them brought Prince Ghedimin's party to a standstill, and Pushkin saw the bright flush which had suffused the young Princess's face under the fire of his eyes. Almost he felt inclined to say: "Nay, fair rosebud, do not blush at my gaze. To-morrow I shall be speeding to the land where your fathers sleep!"

The Prince and Princess were now received by Araktseieff, who conducted the ladies to the arm-chairs reserved for them near the stage on which the artistes were to appear. Ghedimin disappeared among the crowd of brilliant uniforms; there were no seats for the men.

The concert began with a sonata of Beethoven, to which the Czar listened absorbed, as he leaned over the back of the Czarina's chair, his tall figure overtopping all others, his eyes fixed on vacancy. When it came to the turn of the harpist his manner became animated. Hurrying across to the performer, he led him on the stage, settled the music-stand for him to the requisite height, and then, as his chair was too low, himself fetched a cushion, oblivious for the moment that he was the Czar of all the Russias. The harpist acquitted himself magnificently, fully bearing out his world-wide fame. At the Czar's state concerts there is no applause; but the murmurs of delight passing from mouth to mouth of a crowded audience are a higher reward to the artist than the stormiest applause.

After the harpist followed Fräulein Ilmarinen.

Every one said she had never sung the Swan's song so thrillingly and exquisitely as on that evening; the tears sparkling in her eyes were as real as the brilliants which flashed in her hair.

The Czar involuntarily was beating time to her song. Zeneida looked lovelier than ever that night; her dress was covered with spring flowers; her face was radiant. It could not be all art.

Three pair of eyes are fixed most untiringly upon her. The first are those of Princess Korynthia. Filled with hate and contempt, they strive to read into the singer's inmost soul; to detect some false look of betrayal which shall expose the artiste in the part she is playing; and the Princess inwardly rages that she does not find the clew.

The second pair of eyes are Bethsaba's. Her great dark eyes are staring wide open at the charming apparition, as though to say, "Does the devil look like that? Then, indeed, one must be on one's guard, for its counterpart is very lovely!"

The third pair of eyes belong to Pushkin. He feels

10

that the better part of his soul is merged in that of the lovely woman before him ; and that soul, at this moment, is filled with bitterness against all those who would banish him from her vicinity.   He feels that in losing Zeneida he loses all that is noblest within him, and that evil alone will remain.   Already it has gained the upper hand as he recalls Jakuskin's speech : " Oh that I could infuse into you Casca's fiendish spirit, when you stand, the mark of every eye, before ' him ' !"

He feels himself touched on the shoulder.   Looking back, he sees the Lord Chamberlain.   Speaking no word, the latter was lost in the crowd of men.

Pushkin knows what that touch on the shoulder means. It means that at the close of the concert the person thus signalled out is to take his place in the middle of the concert-room, as one of those to whom the Czar designs to speak.   Exactly as Jakuskin had prophesied !   The blood rushes wildly through his veins.   The comedy may be turned into a tragedy.

Princess Korynthia turns to Araktseieff, standing behind her chair.

" Fräulein Ilmarinen seems to be in particularly good spirits this evening."

" I have done my best to spoil them.   I have struck her heart a blow which will stop her love of intrigue for a while."

" Let me be the first to enjoy your secret."

" The lady's hero, Pushkin, is about to be despatched to Uralsk."

" Do you think the girl will desert St. Petersburg and follow him ?"

" Either that, or she will commit some greater folly. Anyway, it will compel her to unmask."

The Czar, after thanking and praising Zeneida, now

began to make the round of the gentlemen; while the ladies to whom the Czarina desired to speak were called up to her.

The Czar entered into conversation with some of the ambássadors, exchanged a few words with Miloradovics; then, passing over a number of the circle, looked about him, and, perceiving Pushkin, signed him to approach.

All deferentially drew back. From the Czar and a culprit it is well to keep one's distance. All the same, every eye was fixed on the two.

At this critical moment Pushkin felt himself singularly calm. He stood, in fact, as cold bloodedly before his imperial master as he would have done before any ordinary man.

"So I hear you are not satisfied with your Censor?" asked the Czar.

The very form of question he had addressed to Jakuskin!

But Pushkin had a guardian angel—his Muse—who did not suffer him to remain silent and abashed.

"As satisfied as one is with an illness, sire."

"Do not bear him a grudge. He is a well-meaning man, but with certain old-fashioned notions. That is not his fault. I have read your poem; it is very fine. The Censor had struck out some portions; but that you did not allow?"

"No, sire."

"And do not allow their suppression?"

"No, sire."

"You are right. They are the best passages in the whole poem. But what are we to do about it? I cannot go against the Censor; for were I to permit what he forbids, the whole institution would be overturned; and it is a necessary one. What do you think?"

"Sire, I will take back my poem and burn it."

"No, no. I think we will send it to Leipsic, have it printed there, and then import it."

"And the frontier custom-house, sire?" asked Pushkin.

The Czar smiled; nay, he laughed — he laughed aloud.

"We will have it packed in among my own personal things, which are not examined in the customs. Thus will we bring the poem into the country."

Pushkin trembled in every limb, like a schoolboy who has undergone an examination.

"Stay a moment!" exclaimed the Czar. "It will be more profitable to your poetical studies were you to prosecute them in the country. It will be better for you to pass the summer on your estate of Pleskow. You will find you can write better there."

That meant the restoration of his confiscated estate. Moved to tears, Pushkin's voice failed.

"Tell no one of what has passed between us. I do not wish it spread abroad."

"Only to one woman, sire, whose silence is as perfect as is her singing."

"She knows it already," returned the Czar, with a smile. He had smiled twice.

How instantly the brightness of that smile had changed the temperature! How immediately the ice and snow in it had thawed! As Pushkin rejoined the circle he was greeted on all sides by friendly faces beaming with congratulation. Distinguished court ladies shut up their fans; they no longer felt the heat. Pushkin could not but respond to the crowd who claimed acquaintance. He was wise enough to tell every one that the Czar had restored his Pleskow estates to him on condition

that he gave up writing poetry, which raised him at once
on a pinnacle. For be it known, not to write poetry at
all is a negative merit; to write bad poetry and give it
up is some slight merit; to write good poetry, and yet
give it up, is a positive and great merit—in high society.

Even Princess Korynthia had the hero of the hour
called up to her in order to ask him why he had not
recognized her just now. Women alone are capable
of such a piece of audacity, and men are obliged to
take it from them.

Pushkin and the Princess conversed pleasantly for
some little time, and he was introduced to Bethsaba, to
whom he said many foolish things.

One woman only, Zeneida, he had no courage to approach. With the divination of a true poet, he felt that
she was the only creditor in all the world from whom he
must keep aloof; for that which he owed to that creditor he was unable to pay.

Nor had he any news to impart. Had not the Czar
said, "She knows it already"?

The Czar had smiled. The smile had lightened all
hearts. The melancholy feeling of monotony which was
weighing over society was at once dispelled. But it was
but an autumnal ray—a ray of evening sunshine on a
rainy day.

But he to whom this turn of things brought no con-
-tent was Araktseieff. Pleskow is not the end of the
world! If Pushkin went no further than that, Fräulein
Ilmarinen's intrigues would suffer no reverse. They
could meet as often as they wished. He could not
understand how it had all come about. That the Czar
favored Fräulein Ilmarinen he well knew; and that
Zeneida had been working to save her beloved poet,

that, too, he knew.   But this was not sufficient to have put the Czar in the very opposite frame of mind from that which he, the all-powerful favorite, had striven to bring about.   Some other hand must have been at work here.

Now among those whom the unaccustomed ray of sunlight had moved to creep out of their dark corners was young Araktseieff.

Forgetting his father's advice to keep well in the shade, and not thinking that the sparkling order on his breast was a borrowed one, and that its owner was among the party there assembled, he suffered himself to be enticed to the front, and joined the set of young men who were paying court to the ladies.

Suddenly he became aware that the Czar was bearing down upon him.

He was about to make way respectfully for his Majesty, but the Czar, going directly up to him, said :

"What fine diamonds those are you are wearing, Araktseieff!"

He who was thus addressed replied, with audacious humility :

"Sire, I wear them by your Majesty's favor."

"Remarkable!" exclaimed the Czar.   "Those brilliants are the very counterpart of the ones in my Vladimir star."

Junker Jevgen began to think that cheek alone would carry him through here.

"Sire, some diamonds resemble each other wonderfully."

"And yet I am inclined to think that the star you are wearing is mine, and that in my pocket I happen to have a Vladimir order bearing your name on the ribbon."

"Mercy, sire!" implored Jevgen, with shaking knees.
"Silence! You surely would not implore mercy here
before the whole court. Go to your quarters. Keep
the order you are wearing; I wear it no more, since it
has been worn by you. Away with you!"

"A bad adviser led me on, sire." The young nobleman was ready to betray his father.

"I do not ask who advised you. Go to-morrow
morning to your father. There you will learn what is
in store for you."

After this scene the Czar abruptly left the concert-
room and withdrew to his own apartments, the former
icy expression on his face. He did not even return the
greetings of the surrounding guests.

Araktseieff, who had watched the scene from a distance, followed the Czar. He was not admitted, but commanded to await his Imperial Majesty's pleasure, and the
all-powerful favorite awaited it until two in the morning.

Then the Czar entered the audience-chamber, carrying a roll of papers in his hand.

"What say you, Alexis Maximovitch," said he to his
favorite. "Was it not a good idea of mine to institute
the *posta sofianskaja?*"

"Without doubt, sire. It has given the people opportunity to bring their needs and wishes directly, in
written form, before the Czar."

"One learns interesting things through it at times.
This morning, for example, I received a letter from a
gypsy girl containing a Vladimir order set with diamonds.
The letter graphically recounted the manner in which the
said order had fallen into the girl's hands. Here, read it."

Araktseieff was never so near to swooning as when
he had come to the end of the letter. It was a cruel,
bitter blow to his heart; he was cut to the quick in his

paternal love. He had wanted to strike a blow at that woman's heart, and it had rebounded on his own in its most vulnerable place. That this was all Zeneida's doing there was no manner of doubt. Araktseieff was to be disgraced before the Czar. She meant to bring upon him what he had intended for her.

But she should find herself mistaken.

Refolding the letter, he said, coldly and calmly: .

"The criminal must suffer."

"Will it be punishment enough if he be sent to Uralsk?"

To Uralsk! That meant never to see him more! He, the well-loved only son, the arch-rogue for whom he lived, for whom he gathered up treasure, through whom he trusted to make his name live to posterity; he to be buried in a rocky fortress of the Kirghis steppes! But if it had been good enough for Pushkin, who had resisted the extinction of his poetic fervor, why not good enough for a soldier who by nights made burglarious onslaughts on the passers-by? And yet he would so gladly save him! After all, it was no crime, only a foolhardy scrape, such as had taken place in the days of old chivalry, and even been practised by King Henry of England himself when he was yet Prince of Wales. Foolhardiness, but no crime! He suppressed the defence, however, feeling that although the Czar might perhaps pardon his son at his intercession, such pardon would mean the end of the father's influence. His enemies should find themselves mistaken if they reckoned upon that.

"He was my only son," he said, sobbing. "I loved him above all the world, but I love the Czar better than my only son. He must suffer if he has sinned." And he prepared the ukase condemning his son to banishment in Uralsk, then kissed the Czar's hand.

Araktseieff parted from his son without saying farewell to him. He must carry out the part of Brutus con-
sistently, that his enemies might recognize the ancient
Roman and tremble. But the Roman in him had a
strong admixture of the Sarmatic. Like Foscari, he
could sign with his own hand his only son's banishment; but not because he made no distinction, but out
of the genuine love of a Russian subject towards his
ruler, and, by making his powerful position still more
powerful, to be able to pay back to his enemies the
cruel vengeance they had wreaked on him.

To this he made preparation. No single one should
be exempt.

On the very day his son set out on the road from
which so few ever return, Magriczki came to him with
the intelligence that the police had arrested Diabolka.
What should be her penalty? Should he have her
knouted in the open market-place, or with slit ears and
nose be transported to Lake Baikal? There was cause
sufficient. Her vagabond life, her immoral habits, could
be brought up against her—moreover, a gypsy girl! Was
not the dark skin crime enough?

" Bring her to me," said Araktseieff. " You, none of
you yet know how to punish. This is a wild animal who
only feels the smart of the lash while it is upon her. It
were no shame to such as her to be beaten half naked
in the market - place; she is brazen enough to laugh
while the punishment is being inflicted. Of what use is
punishment to her yet? First that sense must be awak-
ened in her, latent in every human being, but slumbering
yet—the sense of self-respect. Then we can inflict the
penalty when something more than her outer skin will
feel it. Send the girl in."

And soon Diabolka was standing before Araktseieff,

both hands chained to her back, her unkempt hair about her saucy face, her eyes gleaming wildly through it. Her feet, too, were chained.

"So you are Diabolka, the street dancer?" asked the President of Police.

"Of course. Don't you hear my castanets?" answered the girl, striking her feet together, and making the chains clash.

"And do you know who I am?"

"Of course. The father of a street thief."

"You are right! My son is an offender; he has paid the penalty. I myself signed his sentence. Was it you who informed against him?"

"I might deny it if I chose, but I do not."

"Was it you who wrote the letter to the Czar?"

"Though I cannot write, yet it was I who wrote it."

"Then somebody guided your hand, and you wrote down the characters?"

"But you shall never know the name of that 'somebody.'"

"Were you aware what your hand was putting to paper?"

"I was."

"Then you must have been aware that not alone he whom you denounced was lost, but also you yourself, for having stolen a Vladimir order."

"But I have returned it."

"None the less, you are a thief, and must be sent to the pillory."

"Women of higher rank than mine have stood there already."

"Your shoulders will be branded with hot iron."

"My dark skin marks me already as a gypsy. I am bad from head to foot."

"Come, I don't believe that. This very day, through you, I have forever lost my only son. All night long until the sun rose I was tossing in an agony of sobs on my bed. In the early morning I went into the chapel, and there, before my Maker, I swore an oath that I would free the unhappy creature who had been my son's undoing, body and soul. At least, I will loose your outer chains."

"No need to trouble the jailer for that. If I choose and you allow, I can be rid of them myself."

The gypsy girl had extraordinarily little hands. Easily, as if she were drawing off a glove, she drew out her hands from the fetters; and as simply, without even sitting down, freed her feet. Lifting one foot in the air, she balanced herself on the other, and, in a second, stood unfettered. So she stood before Araktseieff, holding one end of her chain in her hand, looking capable of laying about her with the other end on the head of any one who came near her; and that person would have remembered the attention to his dying day.

The keeper was alone in the cage with the unchained leopard.

"Listen to what I will do with you!"

The leopard took an attitude as if about to spring.

And this time Araktseieff was not, as usual, prodding about with his sword-stick. He had no weapon of any description near to hand.

"I will find you a respectable situation, where you can both live quietly and honestly, and educate yourself, mind and body—where, in fact, you can improve yourself."

"But I don't want it. I want neither a cloister, nor praying nuns, nor hypocritical monks. I will not work, unless I am beaten and made to; and even if I am beaten, I won't pray."

"You shall not be forced to anything of that kind. I will send you neither to a cloister, nor to a reformatory, but into the country. I have a castle on my estate where a dear friend of mine is living."

There was a sudden sparkle in the girl's eyes. Throwing away the threatening chain, and shaking back the loose hair with sudden movement from her brow, she looked with joyful smile at the President of Police.

"Ah! you would send me to Daimona?"

"Yes; to Daimona."

Ah! stern Cato Censorius then had yet one tender chord in his heart, one far more tender even than that which had been wrung by the banishment of his son!

There was much talk about Daimona, but not in her favor; and what was said of her was but a shadow of truth — the woman whom the favorite of the Czar worshipped more than all the saints in heaven or earth! It was with her he spent every moment he could snatch from affairs of state. She was the sun of his life—at once his tyrant and his happiness. She was a woman so savage, so cruel and passionate, that none but an Araktse-ieff could have loved her. Or was it just for that that he did love her? Every one who wished to appeal to Araktseieff, or hoped to escape his vengeance, must first sue to his idol and offer his sacrifice at her feet; and costly sacrifices they must be—no make-believes. Daimona's extortions were renowned throughout the breadth of the empire.

Diabolka's pearly teeth glistened white through her coral lips.

"So you would like to go to Daimona?" asked the great official.

"Why not? She is a woman after my own heart."

" I am not sending you to her to be her servant, but
to be her friend."

" Oh, we shall soon be very friendly !"

" She feels lonely ; and you will know how to amuse
her."

" I will divine her thoughts."

" If she takes a fancy to you, you will be happy with
her. She will give you smart clothes, trinkets, and
riding-horses."

" And a whip to scourge the slaves with."

" And if you get on well, and become a *young lady*,
Daimona will find you a husband."

At these words the girl's face darkened. Shaking her
head energetically, till the dishevelled hair fell over it
again, she struck her thigh vehemently as she exclaimed,
with a stamp of her foot :

" Then I will not go !"

A malicious smile curled Araktseieff's lips. Then he
continued, in a paternal tone :

" I understand. You have a lover here among the
gypsies."

" A ' brother '!" exclaimed the girl.

" Oh, a ' brother '! Gypsies are prudish ; they only
have ' brothers.' And suppose I were to send your
brother, too, to Daimona's castle ? He might make a
good overseer of slaves."

" Would that be possible ?" cried Diabolka, joyously.

" It shall be done. I will send you together to Daimona, and you shall become her confidential people."

Diabolka fell at the feet of the dreaded President and
kissed them, while Araktseieff, with Christian mildness,
stroked the gypsy's unkempt hair. And at the moment
of this scene of foot-kissing and hair-stroking the hearts
of both were filled with thoughts of direst vengeance.

In the inexperienced girl's soul a scheme of as wide-spreading a nature was developing against Araktseieff as he was evolving to the torture of the girl, while she was as deft at lying, dissembling, and hiding her feelings as was the statesman.   It is the advantage alike of savages and diplomats.

Which would triumph ?

Diabolka and her " brother " set off that very day for Araktseieff's estates, where Daimona was already expecting them.

CHAPTER XVI

SOPHIE

ARAKTSEIEFF'S chief care now was to divert the Czar from the influence of his, Araktseieff's, enemies.   And the best means to that end was a visit to the military colonies.   This atrocious idea had originated in Araktseieff's brain; he was the creator of the military colonies. Half a million soldiers, who had gone through every European war, were to be rewarded for their services by being planted as colonists, regiment by regiment, throughout the length and breadth of the empire.   The peasants were to teach them to plough and sow seed, while they in turn were to instruct the peasants in drill and the use of firearms.   A marvellous conception—on paper !   Thus in time the state would acquire three millions of well-drilled soldiers at no cost.   The scythe would pay the piper.

But one important factor in the project had been left out of his calculations by its author.   The peasant did not take kindly to drill, nor did the soldier to the scythe.

The Czar took the military colony of Novgorod for his first inspection; Araktseieff was in his retinue. They returned unexpectedly; a fact mentioned in the newspapers, as showing with what marvellous rapidity the Czar travelled. He had actually accomplished the journey to the Ural Mountains in four weeks; it was a peculiarity of his to gallop night and day. Then they went on to describe the magnificent reception the imperial cortège had met with in every town of the colony, which had sprung up with magic quickness. They dilated on the triumphal arches, deputations, the gifts offered them by the people, by which they endeavored to express their unbounded loyalty to the Czar. The great military parades which had been held were also graphically described; and no one for a moment suspected but that all these things had duly taken place.

On his return from the inspection, Araktseieff went on an official mission to Warsaw. This, too, was duly announced by the newspapers, without comment of any kind or description.

With the month of June springtide returned to St. Petersburg. Sophie Narishkin's room was a mass of lilies-of-the-valley, her favorite flower. Every vase, every available space was filled with them. With the more favorable season her health seemed to be re-established. She could now walk across the room without support, and began to think more about food than medicines. She even began to speculate on being taken to court balls in the winter. One of her aunts was to chaperon her in society; perhaps she might even be allowed to dance a minuet. She was constantly sending for Bethsaba to hear what a court ball was like. The king's daughter had already attended one.

One day, after the Czar's return from the inspection, Bethsaba came to see Sophie.

"Oh, your room is quite full of lilies-of-the-valley! Who sent them to you?"

"Who else than father?"

Sophie had no secrets from Bethsaba. She openly called the Czar "father" to her.

"Has he been here?"

"Yes; all last evening. It was a very sad one. I begin to feel quite afraid of him."

"Did you do anything to vex him?"

"Oh no! It is his great love for me which makes me begin to feel frightened of him. When he stands so long, looking silently at me, my hands in his, I feel as if I cannot endure the silence; then I ask him, 'What is it, father? What is grieving you?' And he answers, 'My grief is that I have no one to whom I can tell my troubles.' 'Can so great a man as you have any trouble for which there is no help?' Then, pointing to his heart, he said, 'Here is the trouble!' Upon which I coaxed him, and begged him to tell me all his trouble. Who could tell — perhaps even my childish simplicity might find a way to heal or lessen his sorrows? Then he drew me again to his heart, laid my head on his shoulder, and said, 'I am ill, Sophie; and there is no physician in the wide world to whom I can tell my ailment. There is something weighing on my heart, and there is no confessor to whom I can confess it. By night my dreams make me tremble; by day, my thoughts. I dread solitude, and I dread mankind. I know that no one loves me; I know that I am condemned.' 'By whom?' 'By God and man. Every one flatters me; only that which beats within me tells me the truth and accuses me.' 'And does not this, too, that beats within me tell the

truth?' I cried; 'and does it not live, love, and worship
you? Let those two hearts of ours fight it out together!'
Then he embraced me, and whispered, ' Be it so. There
is no one on whom I have wrought such ill as you. Why
should I not confess to you? You are my martyr; if
you can give me absolution, I am indeed absolved.'
And kneeling before me, he said, oh! such sorrowful
words, 'Look! I ascended the throne over my father's
body. *I accepted the crown at the hands of his murderers*,
and placed it upon my head. I wept no tears when I
heard of his death; I felt relieved. I had no longer
to dread his wrath, for he had parted from me in anger.
On how many a battle-field have I since sought expiation!
It was not for me. It was written upon my brow that
the bullets that whizzed about me should not strike me;
it was spoken of me that my punishment should be as
my sin. As a son, my heart was cold as stone to my
father. How was I to suffer in my children? I have
borne them all to the grave. You are my last and only
one! I am ground down to the earth under the iron
hand of Fate when I think of you, when I look into
your dear face. Are you, too, to be condemned for my
great sin?' I tried to console him. ' I want for nothing,
father dear,' I said ; ' I am happy, quite happy, and mean
to grow strong, and love you ever so long.' And we both
burst into tears. ' It is not for myself I tremble,' he
whispered. ' I see the sword hanging over me. I hear,
in the watches of the night, how the knife is being sharp-
ened against the corner-stone of my palace. I am ready.
*Through blood I ascended the throne; in blood I must de-
scend it.* But it is for you that I tremble! God's sentence upon me must not strike your head too!' Then
I made him rise, and said such wise things to him that
I quite astonished myself; I am usually such a silly
11

child. I comforted him in a hundred ways, so that at
last I won a smile to his lips, and he said, 'Then give
me absolution. Say, *Christe eleison!* I was so brave
that I even began to talk politics with him—actually got
to matters of state! I said, 'Why torment yourself
with such fancies? Your people are not as bad as those
of other countries. I know something of the world! I
have seen Frenchmen, Italians, Germans. When they
drink hard on holidays, they grow noisy and quarrelsome;
but your subjects, when they drink at holiday-time, only
stagger about, and laugh and embrace each other.'"

"Did not that make him laugh?"

"He only kissed me, telling me I was a wiser states-
woman than either Talleyrand or Metternich; then grew
grave again. 'So it used to be in former times; and the
distinction your wise little head draws did then exist.
But nowadays there is something in the air which seems
to infect the most peace-loving people; so that what you
are sure of one day you cannot be the next. I will tell
you what happened to me on my recent journey. It is
not talked about, and newspapers.and parliamentary reports will be dumb about it. It was growing dusk as I
neared the military colony of Petrowsk; the setting sun
was tinting bright crimson the fleecy clouds covering the
sky. It looked like a ragged imperial mantle.' Here I,
scolding him, asked who had ever seen a ragged imperial
mantle? And he, answering me, said, 'Among others,
Julius Cæsar.' 'I remarked that it was a sky which pre-
saged storm. "A mere fancy," returned Araktseieff.

"'In the light of the crimson sky the triumphal arch
erected in the street of Petrowsk looked like a bower of
molten gold. The other triumphal arches under which
we had passed had been of fir, which, taking no reflection from the sun, looked gloomy, however brightly it

might be shining. What was this made of that it shone
so brightly? An immense throng surrounded it. As
I drew nearer I discovered of what it was composed.
Oh, I have passed through many a triumphal arch
erected in welcome of me. They have been made of
velvets and satins in my honor; I have seen the two
side pillars formed of cannon conquered from the enemy; the arch decorated with standards wrested from
them; the crown in the centre formed of the orders of
fallen heroes; the glittering aureole around of the
swords of the generals who were our prisoners. But the
triumphal arch of Petrowsk exceeded them all.

" ' That which from afar in the light of the setting sun
shone golden were strips of ragged shirts and gowns;
in place of flags were beggars' sacks; the crown was
composed of crutches stuck through an old bottomless
cooking-pot. It was a triumphal arch built up of rags
and beggars' sacks. While I stood transfixed at the
hideous phantom, there stepped one from the midst of
the crowd—a fine, tall old man with flowing beard, holding in his hand the customary wooden vessel, in which
was a crust of bread—and said:

" ' " This is the bread which your soldiers have left
us. Taste it! It is made from the bark of fir-trees.
The usual salt we cannot offer you, for we have none but
our salt tears. On this triumphal arch you will find
many a token left us by your soldiers; the ragged clothing of our wives and daughters. They themselves are
not here, because they could not appear naked before
you. The twelve chaste virgins commanded by the
Hetman we could not present to bid you welcome, because in all the neighborhood there does not exist a
single chaste virgin since you have quartered your soldiers upon us."

"'At these words Araktseieff gave the command to
the companies of Guard Cossacks in our suite to disperse the rebellious crowd. But they were no rebels,
but despairing men. As the trumpet sounded they threw
themselves down by the wayside before our horses' feet,
and, with hands and face uplifted to me, implored:

"'"Deliver us from your soldiers. Take your armed
men away from us. We are loyal peasants, and will
work. You must ride over our bodies if you wish to go
farther."

"'It was impossible to make way along the ground
so densely strewn with prostrate figures. Nor angry
threats, nor gracious words availed. Without intermis-
sion they cried, "Take your soldiers away from us!"
Seldom has a ruler been in such a dilemma. At length
came help. From the military colony appeared rank
upon rank of veterans, marching in close order, at their
head a drum-major, as venerable and gray-bearded as
was the peasants' spokesman. I recognized them as
my grenadiers. They understood how to overcome the
obstacles in their way. A blast of the trumpet, and the
sappers advancing seized the peasants by their hands
and feet, and, heaping one upon another, made sum-
mary way for the brigade to pass. The drum-major,
planting his standard on the ground, said:

"'"Sire, do not leave us in this cursed place. We
served you faithfully in the battle-field for fifteen years;
we fought for you against Frenchmen, Germans, and
Italians; and are we now to wage war against field-
mice, grasshoppers, caterpillars, and, what is worse,
peasants? In our youth we learned to fight like bears;
we don't want, in our old age, to learn to plough like
oxen. We understand how to use our guns and sabres,
but we are not handy with scythe and sickle, and must

we be mocked.at by peasants? Lead us into the enemy's
country, where behind every shrub lurks an ambush;
but, for pity's sake, sire, do not leave us here among
your peasantry. Send us into the field against idolaters,
but do not leave us here to be cursed when we ask anything; cursed when we strike them; cursed if we only
look at them. Shut us up in a beleaguered fortress,
where we have only the flesh of fallen horses to eat—
must season it with powder instead of salt; and for
drink have only the water that runs down the walls;
but do not condemn us to this forsaken spot on earth,
to labor for our bit of bread, envied by a set of thieving,
treacherous peasants. Bury us under the corpses of
our brothers on the field of battle, but do not bury us
alive in the military colony. Curses on him who first
thought of it!"

"'Araktseieff here commanded the trumpeter to put
an end to the man's speech, but now peasants and
soldiers began to make such an uproar that the trumpet
notes were deadened. Tlia' (the Czar's coachman),
'without awaiting orders, turned the horses' heads, and
we drove back the way by which we had come, but
avoiding the hideous arch. Thus ended my triumphal
progress. When I reached home I read in the papers
the glowing accounts of the ovations I had received.
The red sky had truly betokened storm.' This is what
my poor father told me."

"It is indeed sad for so mighty a Czar, when his
people *will* not be happy, whom he would fain make so.
My father's people were happier. Why does not your
father go to them? They are his subjects."

"Bethsaba! What a capital idea! Don't let me forget it. I will propose it to him as soon as ever he is in
better spirits. Just now he is so depressed. After he

had said good-bye he came back to me again. 'I forgot to ask how you were?' 'That proves,' said I, 'that
I must be looking well.' Looking anxiously at me, he
asked if my face was always as red as then; and I,
laughing, said 'Yes. But why are you so anxious?
Does not the good God know how you love me; and are
you not the anointed, the chosen one of Him to whom
you pray for my recovery to health?' 'Yes, He knows,'
he answered, gloomily, 'that I love you. But was not
King David also His anointed, chosen servant? And
did not the king sing all night through his despairing,
penitential Psalm, and yet his child was taken from
him, in punishment of his sin with Bathsheba?'"

"Who was that Bathsheba?" broke in the king's
daughter. "It can only be another form for Bethsaba.
Was there really any one who bore that name before
me? I have hitherto searched in vain to find a name-
sake in society or in the Calendar. Never have I been
able to find one. My godmother, Duchess Korynthia,
who named me so at my christening—up to my sixth
year I was a heathen—in answer to my question why I
could not find it in any Calendar, told me it was another
name for Elizabeth, and that St. Elizabeth's day was
my name-day; and they give me presents on that day.
And now the Czar has told you that there really was a
Bathsheba. Who was she?"

"I do not know any more than you. I have never
been taught anything about her, although I am curious
to know. I asked old Helena, and got from her that
Bathsheba was St. David's wife; but that was all she
knew, for only the priests are allowed to read the Bible.
On that account it is written in Bulgarian."

"But why, then, should she not be among the saints
in the Calendar?"

"Of course, because she was a Jewess!"

"But he said she had sinned. Oh, why did my god-mother give me the name of a sinful woman?" And Bethsaba was ready to cry.

"Bethsaba, dear," said Sophie, "please don't tell any-body what I have told you about the Czar's tour and the triumphal arch."

"But if my godmother asks what we have been talk-ing about?"

"Tell her something else."

"What else?"

"Make up a fib."

"A fib! How does one do that? I have never done it."

Sophie Narishkin laughed in great amusement. She had learned to lie and fib as quite a little child. In-stead of "mamma" she had had to say "madam"; and if her father brought her bonbons to tell people that "Nicolo" (*la mère Cicogne*) had brought them.

What old Helena told her she dared not repeat to "madam"; what she heard when with "madam" she must not breathe a word of to old Helena; what either said must not be repeated to the Czar; and what the Czar told her must be kept from every one. So she had been so inured to lying that she had once brought her doctor to the verge of despair when, on his trying to find out her symptoms, her prevarications made a diag-nosis next to impossible. How the poor child had re-joiced when at last she found two beings to whom she might really open her heart, her father and her friend!

"So you always tell every one all you know?" she asked Bethsaba.

"Oh no; although I do not understand the art of ly-ing, if any one thinks to pump me, or to catch me unawares, I have my own way of being even with him. I begin to ask so many questions that he or she is only glad enough to leave me in peace."

At which they both laughed. The music of fresh young laughter was rarely heard in that cage.

CHAPTER XVII

BETHSABA

PRINCESS GHEDIMIN had accorded her royal god-daughter permission to visit her friend, Sophie Narishkin, frequently. To one but partially acquainted with the Princess's secret heart, such intimacy was easily explained. As appearances forbade her personally from visiting the child, at least through Bethsaba she could obtain news of her health.

But to one in possession of the whole truth there was yet another cogent reason.

The Czar, that reserved, laconic man, who had secrets from his ministers, and did not even confess to the priests, was in the habit of telling this favorite daughter everything. When an ordinary father confides things to an idolized daughter they are matters of feeling; if that father be the Czar, what he confides are matters of state.

Every word the Czar utters to Sophie Narishkin must necessarily concern the condition of the country. Alexander I.'s words form the basis of Europe's present and future relations. The softening or hardening of his heart betokens peace or war. In that heart of his rest the mysteries of great developments or upsettings of nations.

And Sophie has no secrets from her bosom friend, Bethsaba.

"Well, dear child, how did you find your little friend to-day?" asked the Princess, on Bethsaba's return.

"She is taking her medicine more regularly; and, I think, it is doing her good; for I tasted one of her powders one day, and it was very nasty and bitter."

"Was she not talking a great deal again? Talking is bad for convalescents."

"She told me that she had had a visit from her god-father."

Bethsaba had so far learned to "fib" that she said "godfather" instead of "father."

"Did he stay long with her?"

"I do not know."

"Did he tell her anything of interest?"

"Oh yes; about King David and his wife Bathsheba. Do tell me, what was Bathsheba's fault?"

"Bathsheba's fault! What makes you ask me such a question?"

"Because *he* spoke about it; and I want to know what it was. Why is no one called after her? And if she was so wicked, I don't want to bear her name either. Give me some other."

"Quiet, silly child! She did nothing wrong."

"But Sophie's godfather told her that she had committed sin with King David."

"It was love, and no sin."

"Love! What is that?"

Maria Alexievna Korynthia laughed aloud.

"Now, am I to tell you what is love? You will know soon enough, child, when you fall in love yourself."

"How shall I do that? Is love an evil which attacks

people like an illness, or is it a good thing for which people long?"

Maria Alexievna Korynthia laughed still louder.

"Both together!"

"How does it begin?"

"When a young man looks deep into your eyes."

"Into my eyes? I could not endure that; I should die outright."

"But suppose the young man wanted to make you his wife, and became engaged to you?"

"How can all that come about? I cannot imagine it."

"The young man might begin by sending the girl some special birthday present."

"And that would mean that he was in love with her? And if the girl accepted his present, would it mean that she was in love with him? Oh, how nice, how delightful! Must the girl make him a present too?"

"Only her love."

"Nothing else? Oh, how pretty, how charming! And suppose some other young man gives us handsomer presents, do we accept them too, and love him as well?"

Korynthia clapped her hands with amusement.

"Yes, of course. But only if one can keep the second lover secret from the first."

"No, no. No secret dealings. I would rather confess that I loved another too. And why not, if love is good, and no crime? For instance, when I have a husband, may I not tell him that I love strawberries?"

"Strawberries! Oh yes. That is only eating."

"May I tell him that I love Sophie Narishkin?"

"Oh yes. That is only friendship."

"And would he behead me if he knew my love for dancing?"

"Of course not."

"Then if I may love strawberries, dancing, and my friend, why not a youth, if he be good and handsome?'

"Oh, precious innocence! Do people never talk about love in your country?"

"Never."

"Are there, then, no youths and maidens?"

"Of course there are. But in our country, when a young man wants to marry a girl he settles her price with her father and takes her home. If she is loving and faithful to him, he buys her costly clothing; if not, he turns her away and buys himself another wife."

"That is not the custom here. Here a woman may only love one husband; this is commanded by our religion!"

"That is quite different. Why did you not tell me at once that love is commanded by religion? Oh, I will faithfully follow the dictates of religion! You do, too, don't you? You love your husband? Do you look deep into his eyes? I have never noticed it."

"Ah, child, life is long; and the season of love, we call the honeymoon, all too short."

"Then the honeymoon, or month, should be portioned out into minutes, and minutes into seconds, that each day of one's life should have one such second."

"You will soon find the impossibility of that."

"Now I know that Bathsheba's sin was in not loving the man whom her religion commanded her to love. Yet what had King David to do with all that?"

Yes; Korynthia, too, would fain have known how King David got mixed up in the Czar's talk. For the chattering girl had so confused her with her endless, inconsequent questions that she never thought of the prophet's words of reproof to the king.

A Russian is reticent beyond all men. None save the Czar dared to allude to the affair of the triumphal arch. Araktseieff was silent, because he did not want the fiasco connected with his military-colony scheme to spread. The detachment of Cossack guards were despatched to Kasan, and those others who had been present knew how to observe profoundest silence as to what had taken place.

CHAPTER XVIII

KORYNTHIA

The young Circassian Princess could not have been in a better school than that of Princess Ghedimin.

Korynthia might have served as a type to that Russian naturalist who, outdoing Darwin, endeavored to prove that women are degenerate cats. In vain, be it here mentioned, was it sought to soften him so far as to modify his views into their being a race of ennobled cats. He stuck to his opinion. The beautiful Korynthia could be coquettish as an Aspasia, stonily cold as a Diana. This time, however, it was not Diana, but Aspasia, who changed her lover into Acteon.

The men whom she thus distinguished with her favors, like Chevalier Galban, never succeeded in unravelling the riddle of the lovely sphinx. Korynthia allowed him to accompany her in hunts, danced with him at balls, gave him her bouquet to hold when dancing with another man, laughed at his sallies, made fun of others with him, even kissed him at parting, the while holding him as far off as a planet its satellites—and of such satellites she had more than Saturn—each and all per-

mitted to revolve about her, none to approach her too
near.

Yet when in society she fixed a man with a stony look
of a goddess, acknowledging his bow with the contraction of the lips by which great ladies express, at once,
disdain and reproach, he was the man for whom her
heart was cherishing secret flames.

No one knew it, for he, thus signalled out, an officer
of the guards, distinguished alike for his genius and his
many gay adventures, was careful to keep to himself that
one day a perfumed note was brought him by a mysterious messenger, and on opening the delicately tinted
envelope he read : " An unknown benefactress, who is
interested in your fate, is ready to pay off all your debts
if you will stay away at nights from Fräulein Ilmarinen's
Saturnalia."

We think we are not mistaken when we take, in connection with the above, the usurer's speech, who certainly did not volunteer it without good grounds : " There
are certain young, rich, and lovely ladies in St. Petersburg who are ready to come to the aid of a young officer
whom I could name."

The young Endymion's reply to the perfumed note
was that night to enter the proscribed Eleusis on the
box-seat of Zeneida's sledge.

Korynthia's hatred of Zeneida was not on account of
her husband, but of Pushkin. Zeneida's position with
regard to Prince Ghedimin was only superficial. The
devotion of great nobles to prima donnas is merely a
matter of fashion, and of cutting two ways. " What is
allowed to you is allowed to me !" The things which
rankle most in the Princess's mind are that her rival
possesses a finer exotic garden than she does ; that she
has finer horses ; and that whenever they meet, her

toilets are unquestionably triumphant. And they are constantly meeting; for her fame as an artiste opens all doors to Zeneida. They meet at brilliant balls; their horses are pitted together on the turf; their carriages are in juxtaposition at reviews; and the Princess is convinced that all this luxury is derived from her husband's Siberian silver-mines, which enable their owner to indulge in the amusement of permitting two women to outrival each other in the art of squandering. Could she but come out conqueror in the strife, she could forgive the artist her extravagance; but never would she forget that she, a Princess, had had to give in to her even one hair's-breadth. Here was the second ground of her hatred of Zeneida.

There was still a third. The moment of weakness, which in her early youth had made her all his life long an important factor in the life of the Czar, was forgotten; had been long buried in oblivion. The Czarina was the object of universal admiration, sympathy, and worship; and she was seen to be visibly fading before people's eyes. Public opinion, indeed, became so strong in the matter that it was often a question in secret societies whether there should not be a repetition of what occurred in the reign of Peter III. and Catherine II., to make the Czar prisoner and proclaim Elisabeth reigning Czarina. And, withal, Princess Ghedimin knew herself to stand nearer to the Czar's heart than did the Czarina; a silken cord — Sophie Narishkin — held them together. No such silken cord of union existed for Elisabeth. Alexander's love for her as a husband had been buried forever in the grave of the last child she had borne to him. And here, once more, did Korynthia find her detested rival in her path.

While the Czar avoided her, he lavished the wealth
of his favor upon Zeneida. The prima donna stood
between Czar and Czarina. Both loved and petted her.
They were never together save when Zeneida made a
third. When listening to her singing, reading aloud, or
the charm of her pleasant talk, the imperial couple would
forget their mutual estrangement and draw together;
when, on the contrary, the Czarina, appearing at some
court festivity leaning on the Czar's arm, would come
face to face with the Princess, their arms would fall abruptly apart, and they would turn away from each other.
That she knew right well. And, withal, she must display her favors to those who were indifferent to her, appear haughty and disdainful to those she would fain have
encouraged, seem affectionate to the husband she hated,
be humble to the man on whom she had a claim, and
play the magnanimous protectress to the rival of whom
she was jealous. Jealousy is terrible enough when it
has one head; how much more when it has three! The
three heads of her jealousy were: passion, pride, and
remembrance.

And to her had been intrusted the bringing up of the
Circassian king's daughter! The Princess began her
task by giving her at her christening a name which the
world then, and now, can only have condoned for sake of
the psalmist king, David.

Bethsaba was fortunate in that she united to her inexperience and innocence a considerable fund of imag-
inative fancy and the characteristic cunning of her people. Moreover, she remembered many a saying of her
good mother, whom now she sees but once a year—
on New-year's day, when some forty thousand people
assemble to pay allegiance to the imperial pair in the
great Throne Room. There stands her mother on one

of the steps of the throne; but her brow, instead of wearing a crown, wears furrows. And as often as Bethsaba looks upon her does she remember that her mother, to whom she may not speak, exchanged her crown for those furrows, because she stabbed the man who dared to say to her, "I love you; give me your love in return."

Then she would begin to ponder over what that "love" could be which had made it so easy for one to slay and the other to die. At one time it would seem good and sweet, and one's duty; at another, evil, full of pain, and, above all, sinful.

CHAPTER XIX

THE MONSTER

KRIZSANOWSKI had just ended his report of the St. Petersburg conference—to which a pale lady had lent most careful attention—when the duenna, keeping guard, entered hurriedly, and whispered, "Araktseieff has come." Then as quickly retreated.

"Oh, heavens!" sighed the pale lady, pressing her hands convulsively to her bosom.

"Now be strong as a man," whispered Krizsanowski. "The decisive moment is at hand!"

"Can it be that that brings him?" she asked, tremblingly.

"Not a doubt of it. Look well to your women, for he brings an arch spy with him. Handsome and dangerous with the sex."

Just then the sound of carriage-wheels was audible in the courtyard below, amid much noise and the harsh tones of a man's voice.

" Make haste away ! The Grand Duke is coming !"
the pale lady whispered to Krizsanowski.

He, rising, took her hand in his.

Again the duenna appeared, this time rushing in,
and saying, breathlessly :

"The Grand Duke is back from the manœuvres. Just
as they drove in at the gate one of the horses stumbled,
the outrider was thrown, and the Grand Duke's pipe was
so jolted that it broke one of his front teeth. He is wild
with rage."

" Alas !" exclaimed the lady, and was hastening out.
Krizsanowski held her back.

"You would do well just now to keep out of his way."

" On the contrary, it is just now that I must hurry to
him," she answered, freeing herself from Krizsanowski's
hold. " But you hasten away from here, that no one
sees you."

"Well, then, be strong as a woman," he murmured,
and disappeared.

Yet it was so difficult to disappear. Krizsanowski
was in the palace of Belvedere, in the royal park of
Lazienka, the residence of the Polish Viceroy, outside
Warsaw. The park was surrounded by a great wall,
guarded on all sides by armed soldiers. The castle itself a fortress, with high bastions and intrenchments, a
deep moat round it, and drawbridge ; every outlet was
protected by an embrasure, there was no evading the
sentries. Within cannon-range the noble forest-trees
had been cleared away, and turf laid down adorned with
tulip-beds. It is humanly impossible to go or come un-
perceived. And yet Krizsanowski did succeed in getting away, although Grand Duke Constantine had had
the Belvedere built to his own plan, and had watched
its construction with his own eyes. It was impossible

that there should be any secret passage unknown to him—and yet, supposing one did exist? The architect had been a Pole. He was capable of constructing a secret passage by night, and so building it up again that the Grand Duke had no notion of its existence. And so it really was. Constantine might have been surprised in his bed any night were not assassination detestable to a Pole.

His wife hurried out to meet him.

The tyrant met her in the armory hall. He was exactly as his contemporaries have described. Imagination had not run riot.

The Grand Duke had reason enough to be wroth with his brothers. They had all inherited their mother's beauty and noble presence. He alone possessed his father's repulsive features and person. Czar Paul was the impersonation of ugliness, so hideous in appearance that he would allow no coin bearing his effigy to be struck throughout the whole course of his reign. And Constantine was a faithful counterpart of his father. His enormous horn-shaped nose stood out from his face as if it had no connection with his forehead; his little sea-green eyes were scarce visible under his thick, shaggy eyebrows and blinking, almost shut, eyelids. His hair, beard, eyebrows, and eyelashes were the color of hemp, his face red as Russia leather. But the most remarkable thing about him was that the one half of his face was unlike the other, as though Nature had intended to crown her master-work of ugliness by joining together two different caricatures. One corner of the mouth was turned up, the other down; the scars of small-pox, wrinkles, warts, so completed the disfigurement that the painter who would have perpetuated the face could only have attempted it in profile. In fact, the artist who would have painted him full-face would have been guilty of high-treason. So he is described by contemporary writers.

His exterior was the true picture of his inner man; his features were the slaves of his passions. To look at him was to make one shudder or deride. As was his face, so was his disposition — violent, passionate, cruel to a degree. He carried a stick always in his hand, and laid it about him freely. If it be true that his brother, the Czar, spent two thousand rubles a year in quill pens, it may be guessed what amount Constantine's yearly budget showed for smashed walking-sticks. The stick he now held in his hand was broken and split all the way up. No doubt he had been again laying it impartially about the shoulders of the several commandants of division. Their morning prayers were blows.

And there must needs come this accident. And through the confounded horse stumbling, and the postilions being thrown, the pipe, which was never out of the Grand Duke's mouth, had hurt his gum and broken him a tooth. He uttered the most horrible oaths, spitting out blood the while.

"Cursed hound! As soon as he comes to himself throw him into the water to rouse him! Bring him here. Miserable rascal! I'll break all his bones for him!" Just then he became aware of a gentleman advancing towards him. "Who is that? Chevalier Galban? No, you fools — that hound, I mean; not this gentleman! What does he want? Araktseieff has come? The devil take— Humph! It's the barber I want, and not a minister. Can't he see I've got a broken tooth? Why are you hanging about, Chevalier Galban?"

At that moment a lady, coming hurriedly up, pushed the Chevalier aside.

"For Heaven's sake, what has happened to you?" she cried, throwing herself on Constantine's breast. "My life, my dearest, are you wounded? What is it?" And she kissed his bleeding lips.

Over the monster's face dawned a sudden smile—a smile joyous as the aurora borealis, sad as the depths it was, but it transformed the Grand Duke's hideous face. It chased away his violence. The wild, rugged features became more harmonious; the brutal mouth endeavored to assume a gentle expression.

"Nothing, nothing, my love!" he replied, in the voice of a lion caressing its mate. "Now, now, do not cry. Don't be frightened!"— his voice growing lower and lower. "There is nothing the matter."

"Oh, but your lips are bleeding. Your tooth is broken."

And she tried to stanch the blood with her handkerchief.

"It is not broken clean out," growled Constantine. "Only the crown of it. And the devil take the crown!"

"Why, your Highness," put in Galban, beginning to take part in the conversation, which had assumed so much milder a tone, "do you say, 'May the devil take the crown'?"

"At present it is only the crown of my tooth that is under discussion," returned the Viceroy, emphatically, in somewhat trembling tones. "Go you to Araktseieff, Chevalier Galban, and rest awhile after the fatigues of the journey. We shall have time for our talk after dinner. Before I have eaten and drunk I am in no mood to talk over state matters. Do not spoil my appetite. *Zdravtvijtjé!* And as for you, bring that good-

for-nothing here as soon as he has come to himself. I
will try a couple of good boxes on the ear to see if his
teeth are set like mine. The scoundrel! If I had not '
been holding my pipe pretty firmly between my teeth
the mouth-piece would have pierced through my jugu-
lar—"

"Oh, don't!" stammered his wife, in superstitious
dread, laying her trembling hands over the Grand Duke's
mouth.

He, pressing a kiss upon the palm of her outstretched
hand, threw his arm round her waist, and she, nestling
up to him, they retired to their inner apartments, leaving
Chevalier Galban standing in the hall.

"So you really would grieve if I were brought to you
one day dead, run through the chest to my back?"

"Oh, do not say such things!" exclaimed she, making
the sign of the cross over the spot to which Constantine
pointed. And to smother such fearful words she shut
his mouth with a long, fervent kiss.

"Child!" murmured the monster, and, taking his wife's
head between his two hands, like a bear hugging the
head of a lamb, he looked into her eyes. "Child!
Does it not go against you to kiss my mouth? Do not
the fumes of tobacco disgust you?"

With an innocent glance, she answered :

"I suppose every man's mouth emits the same smell
of tobacco. I remember my father's did."

At these words the monster pressed her with such
force to himself as though he would stifle her in his embrace.

"Oh, wondrous child! She knows neither the lies
nor the flatteries of a court lady. She does not tell me
that my breath is ambrosian. She only knows that it
was so when her father kissed her, and therefore the

lips of every man must be the same! Wife of mine, my father was as hideous as I am, and his wife loved him as dearly as you do me. And yet he was as repulsive as I."

"You cannot tell what you are like."

"Oh yes, I know. My mother used to tell me. She loved me best of all her children; spoiled me; allowed me my own way in everything. When my brothers and sisters used to complain about it, she would say, 'Let him alone. It is because he has his father's ugliness that I love him so.' But I am a bad man too, and that my father never was. True, he was hot-headed, and a blow was as quick as a word with him; but I am savage by instinct. I am bad because I like it."

"That is not true. Who says so?"

"I say it myself. Often when I come home with an inch of cane in my hand, having broken it on the backs of all who have come in my way, I feel as if I could break the rest of it on my own head." Here, for the first time noticing that the broken cane still hung from his wrist by the strap, he flung it hastily from him.

"No, no, dear," said his wife, "it is that bad men exasperate you to wrath. You have to do with rough people who are stupid and cunning, and that irritates you. If they were good you would treat them kindly."

The monster stroked his wife's cheeks with caressing hand.

"And you really believe that I am good? Wonderful! I should have thought I had done enough to give proof to the contrary. I thought I was a very devil."

Meanwhile his wife had coaxed the monster to her dressing-room, and, sitting him down before the toilet-table, had been busily occupied by the aid of all manner of brushes and combs in bringing hair and beard into

something like order. Then she bathed his hot, dusty
face with lily water, and stuck court-plaster over the cut
on his mouth.

"Am I a pretty boy now?" said he, with the look of a
child who has just had his face washed.

"That you always are to me. But to-day you will
have strangers dining with you."

"True. And, moreover, grand gentlemen from St.
Petersburg—from our Russian Paris. Of course they
are accustomed to smart folk, so make me smart. How
do we know whether these Frenchified gentlemen will
like your Polish cookery? You make light of it, after
the manner of women-folk, and then they'll praise it."

"Do you wish me to appear at the table?"

"Of course. Why not? Even were the Czar himself
my guest! Are you not my own little wife? Come,
answer; are you not my very own little wife?"

She answered a timid "Yes."

"I would not advise any one who values sound limbs
in his body to presume to look down upon you, Excellency or no Excellency!" cried the Viceroy, wrathfully,
menacing his own face with his fists in the glass.
"True, this Araktseieff was devoted hand and foot to
my father—he followed him about like a dog. Yet, for
all that, I'd rather know him to be safe on the island which
Kotzebue named after him, in the Yellow Sea, than here."

"Why, dearest?" asked his wife, as she tied and arranged the Grand Duke's necktie.

"Oh, women have nothing to do with state secrets,"
he answered, as he strove to twirl the ends of his mustache evenly—an attempt in which all his efforts were
unavailing, for one side would not keep together. Woe
to the private if the Grand Duke's eyes lighted on an ill-
waxed mustache! "I only tell you he may esteem him-

self a lucky man if I have no cane at hand during our interview."

"Oh, don't terrify me, dearest!"

"I was only joking. May I not have my bit of fun? Well, are we ready now? I am hungry. I have been working all the morning like any corporal."

"We will go, then. Won't you choose out one of your sticks?"

In every room of the palace where the Grand Duke went, even in his wife's dressing-room, stood a couple of sticks; and it was as much as any one's life was worth to move them from where he placed them.

"A stick? For what? I am not lame."

"No; but to chastise the culprit, he who ran you into such danger. You might have been killed. He well deserves to be punished."

"Does he, really? Well, then, you choose one. What, this good, stout one? Ah, that won't break so easily. So you feel more for me than for the man who injured me? Come, that is a rare trait in your sex. Women usually expend their sympathy on the guilty. Now, then, let us be off."

Johanna took Constantine's left arm; the stick was in his right hand. In the armory hall the delinquent, with head bound up and swollen cheeks, was awaiting sentence. He trembled like a dog when he saw the Grand Duke in the doorway.

"You scoundrel!" snorted the monster, swishing his cane threateningly through the air. "You deserve a good sound hiding! Can you not look out when you are driving? So you have got badly hurt? There, take these five rubles—buy yourself doctor's stuff with them. Gallows bird! What, you limp! Then take the stick to walk with, you good-for-nothing!"

And he passed on with his wife.

A monster arm in arm with his good genius!

"Humph!" growled the Grand Duke. "It is odd. You have discovered the better self within me; and now it almost seems as if I, too, were sensible of it."

The two gentlemen were already in the dining-hall. There were no other guests. The Viceroy was not particularly hospitable; nor had he much occasion to exercise that virtue, for the people over whom he ruled came but seldom to the palace. But they must stand high in favor who were allowed to sit at his table when his wife, Johanna, was present.

Araktseieff was one of these privileged ones. The two men had seen each other shed tears—once only, and no other eye had witnessed it. The occasion was when first they met after Czar Paul's death. The faithful follower loved the dead man as fondly as did the monster. Others breathed a sigh of relief when the grave closed over him. The world was rid of a burden! The assassins were pardoned; some even attained to high positions as generals. Two men only never forgave them—Grand Duke Constantine and Araktseieff. When, at Austerlitz, the French surrounded General Bennigsen, Constantine charged them like a Berserker, at the head of a company of Dragoon Guards, and, with the daring of a wild animal, rescued him from their midst, only to call out later to him, "I have saved your life, and you were one of my father's assassins!" It was this common hatred which enabled him to "suffer" Araktseieff. He "suffered" him. And that meant a great deal with him. Moreover, Araktseieff was a minister who could be beaten—be sent away—and yet who always came back again.

"*Zdravtazjtye!*" was the Grand Duke's salutation to
his guests. "One can still talk Russian with you, eh?
You have not grown into full-fledged Frenchmen? Kiss
my wife's hand!"

Chevalier Galban carried out this injunction with all
a courtier's grace. Araktseieff, with the unction characteristic of the genuine Russian peasant, pressing the
lady's hand with both of his to his lips, amid many
long-winded compliments, finally ending up with an
amorous sigh.

"Ah! the sight of this domestic happiness, this 'sweet
home,' reminds me of my own home."

Johanna alone was unconscious of the deep affront
hidden in these words. But her very unconsciousness
incensed the Grand Duke the more; his face crimsoned
with wrath. It was well that he had but now made a
present of his cane, else it would emphatically have expressed on Araktseieff's back, "My good man, this is
not Daimona!"

"Don't talk bosh!" growled the imperial host; "but
toss off a glass of schnapps in good Russian style. I
can't stand your foreign fads and fashions — French
compliments and German maunderings. I never could
learn a foreign language. I dare say you well remember, Araktseieff, the sort of school-boy I made! My
poor tutor! When he used to try to impress on me to
work hard, I would answer him, 'What for? You are
always learning and learning, and are only an usher,
after all!'"

"Better still was the answer your Imperial Highness
gave to your professor of geography: 'I do not learn
geography; I make it!'"

"All very fine. But you see I do not make it."

"All in good time."

"Shut up. Here comes the soup; set to work, and don't talk. And keep silence, gentlemen, while my wife says grace; she does the praying for me. And now, no serious subjects during dinner. Anecdotes are allowed, drinking is a duty, swearing is not forbidden; but he who makes a coarse speech in presence of my wife must straightway make full apology to her. If you get short commons, I must beg you, in my wife's name, to excuse it; she was not prepared for guests. That our fare is strictly national—Russian and Polish—needs no excuse. I cannot abide French cookery; their names are enough to my ears, let alone the kickshaws themselves to my digestion! And as for my wife, they are positively injurious to her!"

Chevalier Galban had his word to say:

"Oh, French cooks are swells among us just now. The family 'Robert' are quite aristocrats in St. Petersburg; it confers nobility to possess one of them in one's household. His French cook is a greater personage than the Czar himself; for he makes out the Czar's daily menu, and suffers no supervision in his domain. He is a more important man than the family physician, for he rules strong and weak alike. What he refuses to serve up is unobtainable. M. Robert does what the Polish Senate alone was empowered to do when the 'niepozwolim' was yet in fashion. If his master sends word that he desires this or that dish that day at table, M. Robert meets him with his *liberum veto*, which in French implies, '*Ça n'existe pas!*' Quite recently Prince Narishkin sent for his cook, that he might repeat to him by word of mouth his written refusal to prepare a blanc-mange for the dinner-table."

"What, did he give an audience to the fellow?"

" Yes; and M. Robert repeated his refusal verbally. The Prince began giving him a piece of his mind, when the *chef,* rising on his heels, said, 'Sir, you forget to whom you are speaking !' "

" The devil !   And what was the end of the story?"

" Well, the Prince went without his blanc-mange."

" Ah, ah !   That would just suit me.   I should be for eating up the cook instead of his dishes."

Chevalier Galban was a capital talker; he took the chief burden of the conversation upon himself.

" A funny thing happened at St. Petersburg a few days ago, at Prince Popradoff's, who has a French cook, and a French tutor for the children.   The cook was but so-so ; the tutor no great pedagogue.   All of a sudden the cook was taken ill, and confusion reigned.   The tutor offered his services, saying he knew a little about cookery, and he was forthwith despatched to the kitchen, where he sent up seven excellent dinners.   Meanwhile the sick cook offered to carry on the little prince's tuition, and he made surprising progress.   To make a long story short, both confessed to have only taken their situations from necessity, and, in fact, to have changed departments."

" And the Prince had not found it out?   You must tell that story to my wife, more in detail, when you go into the drawing-room.   Let us now speak of more important things.   How was my august brother the Emperor Alexander, Araktseieff, when you left him ?"

As he named the Czar the Grand Duke had risen, in which action he was followed by the others.

·' I regret, your Highness, to be unable to give a satisfactory answer to that question."

" What is the matter, then, with his Majesty my brother ?   Eh ?   Or can you not speak out before my wife ?   All right.   You do well not to startle her.   You shall tell me when we are alone. And how is her Majesty the Czarina Elisabeth? Are there any unpleasantnesses between them? . If you have no good news to give, better say nothing before my wife. Do not trouble her."

Araktseieff, in the face of this caution, found it wiser to lick his fingers and say nothing.

" It's always the case when a man marries too young!" resumed the Grand Duke, picking his teeth with his two-pronged fork. " I found that out myself, and had cause to repent it. Well, thank Heaven, that's past! I had work enough before I could obtain a separation from my first wife. But we won't talk of that before my wife. After all, it was I who was in fault; I who was to blame. A woman who could put up with me is as rare as a comet. And how does the world wag with you, Galban; have you got caught yet? Who is the unlucky woman who calls you husband? If I were the Czar I would levy a tax upon all such bachelors as you. The old-bachelor tax! Lucky for you that I shall never come to the throne."

" Your Highness! It was an understood thing that we touched upon no serious subjects at table," observed Araktseieff, deferentially.

" Yes ; you are right. I was infringing the rule. To make amends, let us empty our glasses to my wife's health."

The men's three glasses clinked together, then touched the fourth, extended to them by a white hand, while the fiery Tokay moistened a delicate red lip. Dinner was over, dessert on the table. The Grand Duke only took hazelnuts, which he cracked with his teeth. The first three he laid on Johanna's plate.

For the first time since she sat down to dinner she spoke, and then but in a whisper.

"Oh, please be careful about your teeth. You might break away another crown !"

"That may be!" said the Grand Duke, leaning his elbows on the table, and darting a quick glance from under his bushy eyebrows at Araktseiëff, who understood it. Then Constantine kissed his wife's forehead.

"Now leave us, darling. Have coffee served on the terrace, and take the Chevalier with you. He likes to end up dinner with his coffee in French fashion. While we, like good Poles, will sit over our wine a little longer."

On this Johanna, rising, took the Chevalier's arm, and, followed by a footman carrying the silver coffee equipage, left the dining-hall.

The two men, left alone, applied themselves to the wine, filling up their glasses a fourth time with golden Tokay.

"To the health of my august brother the Czar!"

They drained their glasses and refilled them.

"In truth, the Czar stands in sore need of that fervent aspiration!" quoth Araktseieff, with a deep sigh.

"What! is he seriously ill, then ? What ails him ?"

"He is suffering from the malady hardest to cure—melancholia. All the doctors' arts are of no avail. For months together the Czar gets no sleep, save a short, unrefreshing siesta at noon. By night and day he is tortured by all kinds of fancies. He is weary of life ; and what wonder ? Wherever he looks he sees nothing but ruin and decay in all that which he so painfully built up. The dreams he cherished are dispelled. Every institution for promoting liberty of thought and action which he called into life has he been himself compelled, one by one, to annul and abolish. And he has no spirit or energy left to pull himself together and devise new schemes. He feels that he has aroused disaffection, and has not the moral strength to become a tyrant and quell that disaffection. He knows himself to be surrounded by assassins, and has not energy to take firm hold of the only weapon which remains to him. Moreover, his domestic happiness is ruined. Your Imperial Highness knows the catastrophe. The Czar's spirit is clouded by the weight of religious depression; he looks upon himself as an irremediable sinner, condemned alike by God and man. Shudderingly surveying the fatality, he is hurrying it on. A mental condition such as this must in the end undermine the strongest constitution. The slightest indisposition might prove fatal at any moment; and he takes not the slightest care of himself. He will suffer no physician about him, and keeps his ailments secret. It is my firm belief that in his heart is the seat of disease, and that the heart is wounded to death."

"My poor brother!" muttered the Grand Duke, resting his head on his hand. "That noble, powerful fellow, by whose side I was at the victory of Leipsic, when he concluded peace with Napoleon on the island in the Niemen, and in the triumphal entry into Paris; and in Vienna, at the Congress; and wherever we went I heard people whisper, 'There he is, that splendid-looking man beside the deformed one!' Light and shadow; we were their true exponents."

"We must be prepared for the worst. The feeble flame which still feeds that light needs but a breath to extinguish it, and then the whole country will be given up to most terrible anarchy. The ground is undermined by countless conspiracies; we are menaced on all sides. Who can withstand the flood when the gates of heaven are opened? The Czar has no children. Who is to succeed him?"

"He whom the Czar appoints."

"And supposing he appoints no one? It is, indeed, impossible to get him to do so. The law, he says, speaks plainly enough—it is the Czarevitch who succeeds the Czar."

The Grand Duke burst into a loud laugh. He threw himself back in his chair in his fit of laughter; he laughed till his open jaws disclosed two rows of teeth like those of a yawning lion.

"Ha, ha, ha! That's a good one—the Czarevitch! No, my friend, he is much obliged; he would rather not sit on the throne! You don't catch me wearing Ivan's diamond crown!"

"Why not, your Highness?"

"Because I prefer to see your ribbon across your back than about my throat!"

Czar Paul had been strangled by his adjutant's ribbon.

"What are you thinking of, your Highness?"

"Of my father—and of my people. I should be a pretty fellow for the St. Petersburgers! Last year, when my illustrious brother the Czar, thinking himself in a bad way, was graciously pleased to command my presence, and I repaired to the capital, Hui! there was a panic! They began to take steps to appoint me his successor. As soon as I showed my face in the streets they were cleared in a trice. People took refuge in doorways rather than salute me. Ah! how they flocked into the churches! The sacristan had never had so many kopecs in his alms - bag as while I was in St. Petersburg. The priests almost dragged the angels by the feet out from heaven in their fervent supplications for the Czar's recovery. They sketched a caricature of my profile, with my huge nose, at every street corner, with all manner of slanders beneath it! And when it pleased

Providence to restore my imperial brother so far that
he could drive out again, there were rejoicings. The
people thronged round his carriage, hardly allowing the
horses room to plant their feet, and almost buried him
under flowers. And all this to show their hatred to me.
Not that they loved him, but because they dreaded me.
You just now said that even he is surrounded on all
sides by assassins; but the difference is that they would
despatch him to heaven, me to hell. They believe they
would find in me the son of my father—a man with iron
hand for their iron necks, as was my sainted father."

" And that is what they need ! The Russian's iron
neck only bends to the hand of iron."

"Well, let them have it; but Heaven preserve me
from them, and them from me !"

" But every true man sets his hopes upon your Highness !"

" Eh ! Time enough for that. But why are we talking such folly? Why should I survive him? I am but
eighteen months his junior. Fill your glass. Long
life to my brother his Majesty, the Czar ! And what
else brings you hither? We will speak no more of
that."

" I came with a commission from his Imperial Majesty. It is his pleasure that the succession be now
settled. The Czar has no heir."

"Well, no more have I ! But one may be on the
way—as you see I have recently married."

" So I see ; but only left-handed. A morganatic
marriage."

" So far. But as soon as my wife bears me a child I
will make her my legitimate wife."

" That is not possible to your Highness."

" Why not ?"

13

"Because your Highness's first wife, Anna Feodorovna, is still living."

"But the Synod has granted me a separation, and
she has already renounced the name of Anna Feodorovna and resumed that of Juliana of Saxe - Coburg ;
moreover, my fresh marriage was entered upon with the
sanction of the Czar."

"But it was only a left-handed marriage."

"Then we will convert it into a right-handed one."

"That is impossible. In the State Archives is a
ukase of Czar Alexander to the effect that only *women
descending from reigning families may be raised to the
imperial throne*, and the descendants of those who are
not of royal birth may not inherit the throne."

"Then when I—which Heaven forbid—come to the
throne I will promulgate another ukase annulling that
one."

"But there is a further obstacle, which not even the
Czar's ukase can overcome. Your Highness is aware
that *a woman may not ascend the imperial throne unless
she be of the Orthodox faith*. Does your Highness believe that Johanna Grudzinska would abjure the Roman
Catholic faith for a crown ?"

"Not for all the crowns in Europe! The heart of
that woman is so stanch that she would scarce change
a horse grown old in her service for a young one! Still
less would she change her religion. I would not advise
any one to try it on her."

"And there is yet another still greater obstacle than
even that of religion—society. Is St. Petersburg society
to be exiled from the Czar's palace? Johanna Grudzinska may be a very angel of light, but she would
by no means make a Czarina whom the Ghedimins,
Narishkins, Trubetzuois, Muravieffs, and whatever all

their names may be, would be willing to acknowledge to
stand on a par with themselves, still less to whom they
may pay allegiance."

"Then let them keep it."

"What does your Highness mean by that?"

"A very simple meaning. Let them keep their crown.
I keep my wife!"

"Your Highness does not mean that in earnest?"

"In thorough earnest and in cold blood," said the
Grand Duke, laying his hand on Araktseieff's arm.
"All my life through I had never known what it was
to be loved. I verily believe that the nurse who nursed
me thrashed me for being such a piece of deformity.
Not even a dog have I ever been able to attach to me.
Look where I will, I see that every one shrinks back
from me. My very voice, which I try in vain to moder-
ate, is rough and grating, as if I were perpetually scolding. I have never heard an endearing epithet since I
was out of the nursery. And suddenly Fate, like a blind
hen, casts in my way a pearl of women, a tender soul
who loves me with all her being. She does not say it,
she feels it—nay, she lets me feel it. She lives in me
like the very soul and thought of me. The little good
there is in me she awakens and makes me reconciled
to myself. She alone of all the world has brought sunshine into my dark life. When I am ill she nurses me;
when I am violent she pacifies me. She is my better self!
And do you believe that I would renounce her for any
prize the earth could give? That for any throne in the
whole world I would exchange this easy-chair where she
has sat nestling up to me? Ah, what fools you must be
to think it!"

"Your Highness! I have long made the human mind
an object of study, and it is not new to find that love is

the most powerful factor we have to deal with on earth.
It is strong, but not lasting. To-day your Highness may
be feeling as you say; but the human heart is as vari-
able as the sky; and earth, the fatherland, is its antip-
odes. To-day we may feel as though we had cast away
a whole paradise of bliss in descending from heaven to
earth; to-morrow we discover that our supposed heaven
was but a cloud which glistened in the sun and disappeared, leaving 'not a wrack behind.' Earth, on the
contrary, remains firm beneath our feet; it never loses
its power of gravity. What? Could your Imperial
Highness stand by with folded arms and see the whole
monarchy, a prey to the flames, sink into ashes at your
feet, that your head might rest undisturbed on the lap
of the woman you love?"

"Well, and even then?"

"Even then? Even in that case I have my clear instructions. Your Highness is the master of your own
future. But the Russian Empire is the master of its
own fate. If the Czarevitch prizes the prosaic domestic life of a citizen higher than the maintenance of the
empire he has received from his ancestors, I have yet
one other proposition to make to him. His Majesty
the Czar will elevate the morganatic wife of the Czarevitch, Johanna Grudzinska, to the rank of a Polish
princess, with the family name of 'Lovicz'! In perpetual
lien he will make over to her the royal Lovicz domain
of Masover Voivodeship upon the Grand Duke de-
claring her to be his legitimate wife; her children to
be Princes of Lovicz and heirs to their mother's king-
dom, with the rank of Russian bojars—*in virtue of which
Grand Duke Constantine will resign the title of Czarevitch
and the right of succession to the Russian Empire, for himself and his heirs, forever, in favor of his brother.*"

Constantine struck the table emphatically with his fist. " Rather to-day than to-morrow !"

" I entreat your Highness not to reply too hastily ! The sky is ever changing; not so the earth. I am convinced of the truth of your Imperial Highness's words ; but a short delay cannot be of any vital importance. Let your Highness try absence from the lady, say, for a week or a month. Or send her for a time, as in truth her delicate health requires, to Ems or Carlsbad. Separate yourself from her, so that you are not seeing each other daily, hourly ; that she may not always be your centre, but that you may both come in contact with other people, other surroundings, other interests—"

"And do you suppose that absence, whether longer or shorter, could estrange us from one another?"

" It is an old story, yet ever new."

" That one short month could suffice to cause some new face to blot out the other from our hearts? You are a fool, man !"

" It is but giving it a trial."

" I may do it ! But I tell you beforehand that you will find yourself mistaken. Do not dream for an instant that your plan will be successful. We do not stumble, like ordinary mortals. For a woman to love me is akin to madness—it is incredible ! But once to love me is never to part from me ! And to expect me to forget that woman is an absurdity. Then, of a truth, should I be the blind fowl pecking at a grain of oats instead of the pearl before her. Is the Act of Renunciation ready? Of course you have brought it with you? Give it here. To-day, to-morrow, or as long as my life lasts, you will receive from me but the one answer—' I will sign it.' "

" Let us agree to delay the decision, your Highness. The subject in question is no child's play; nor is it the

fighting down any youthful love affair. Let your Imperial Highness weigh well what you are renouncing—the
nineteen crowns of Russia! From Ivan Alexievitch's
crown, inlaid with its nine hundred brilliants, to the
simple 'cap' of Peter the Great; the Novgorod crown
with the Deissus, crown of the Republic, worn by Ruric;
the Astrakhan cap of Michael Feodorvitch; the Siberian
hat of Fedor Alexievitch; lastly, the ancient, most sacred relic, the crown of Monomachos, who dates from
legendary times. And would my illustrious chief renounce all this splendor for the sake of a 'woman's
charms'?"

Here the conversation was interrupted by the entrance
of Chevalier Galban, who appeared in the doorway
humming a ballet air.

"Well, Galban," shouted the Grand Duke, as he appeared, "how do you like the Belvedere?"

"Grand!" returned the Chevalier, "and, moreover, an
impregnable fortress!" The two last words were directed
to Araktseieff, accompanied with a meaning look. Possibly the Grand Duke intercepted it, for with sharp into-
nation he repeated :

"An impregnable fortress? I did not know that you
concerned yourself with the storming of fortresses among
other things."

"Oh yes," retorted the Chevalier, in a tone equally
sarcastic. "I have had the good-fortune to succeed in
storming many a castle hitherto held to be impregnable."

Araktseieff here cut short the allegory by interposing,
abruptly :

"I know the castles in the taking of which you have
won your spurs—Château Lafitte and Château Margot!"
—both well-known Bordeaux wines—at which the Grand
Duke, with a laugh, rose from the table.

CHAPTER XX

THE BLIND HEN'S GENUINE PEARL

WHAT had Chevalier Galban found so admirable on the terrace of Belvedere Castle, and what did he find so impregnable there?

In truth, a lovely view! In the foreground the massed trees of Lazienka forest, clad in the tender hues of spring's young green, their colors ranging from the golden green of the maple to the reddish purple of the sumach, delighted the eye. From amidst the thick foliage arose the zinc roofs of John Sobieski's ancestral home, Lazienka Castle. Red and green roofs of luxurious villas peeped out here and there from among the trees; rows of silvery poplars overtowering the rest marked out cross-roads. In the distance the ancient capital of Poland, living heart of a dead body; the terraces of the once royal castle showing where its gardens had been; on the Gothic towers of St. John's Church the golden crosses glistening. Below the city, the winding Vistula, its islands ablaze with spring-tide glory. To the right the great Belian forest, with its ancient Camaldulen Monastery, its walls glowing in the light of the evening sun; and then, dumb witness to so many an historic event, the great Wolja plain, where formerly kings were elected. On the horizon, fast disappearing in the golden haze of evening, the outline of a castle—Mariemont, whilom residence of Marie Sobieski.

"A lovely view, is it not?" said Johanna to Chevalier Galban, as, having reached the highest terrace of Belvedere, they let their eyes wander round.

"A magnificent prison," returned the Chevalier.

Johanna looked in astonishment at him with her large brown eyes, which, neither dazzling nor enticing, were full of soul.

"A prison—for whom?" she asked, surprised.

"For a saint and martyr, who is ready to sacrifice herself for her nation."

"And who may this be, and wherein her sacrifice? I do not understand you."

"Truly, it is not martyrdom to be tortured with red-hot iron if that torture be borne in patience; but it is martyrdom to give one's heart to be tortured in a manner more cruel than human imagination has yet conceived. And to be torn in pieces by a wild beast is not so ghastly a death as to kiss and embrace such a monster. Such a sacrifice could only be conceived by a Polish woman and for the Polish nation!"

"Either I fail to understand you, or you are laboring under some mistake," returned Johanna, handing the Chevalier a cup of fragrant mocha as they seated themselves.

Chevalier Galban was a practised strategist at such storming operations. He knew at once where the fortress was weakest.

"Duchess! wherever the name of the Polish Viceroy is heard, that of Johanna Grudzinska is named with it; with adoration and affection people utter it, for she is the guardian angel of all who are oppressed and afflicted."

"I know nothing of all this. Here only criminals are punished; and *such* punishment I can do nothing to hinder."

"Perhaps not in words; perhaps only unconsciously. Yet the whole world knows that Poland's terror has changed under the magic of your influence. He has sane periods in which he treats his people with clemency. And for these Poland has to thank you!"

"Herr Galban! Do you not see that any praise must be repugnant to me which reflects upon my husband?"

"Far be it from me in any way to reflect upon the Czarevitch, my master. He is as nature and circumstances have made him. The ruling of a nation is no poetry, nor is it a matter of Scriptural teaching; it has its established laws. Diplomacy is heartless, and a thorough-going statesman must be heartless likewise. Every one knows that the Czarevitch is a tyrant to his subjects."

"But to me he is my husband, to whom I am bound by every law of love and duty."

"It is just that which makes my blood boil. I can talk openly to you. I must confess, when I undertook the mission intrusted me by Araktseieff, I had conceived a very different idea of you from what I do, now that I am face to face with you. In the different courts I have visited I have come across many ladies who have deluded themselves with the belief that the love of crowned heads is quite another thing from the love of ordinary mortals. Once their mistake found out, they have been able to console themselves; and when higher state interests have demanded the sacrifice of their affections, they have accepted the title of countess or princess, with its accompanying estate as compensation, and have survived it."

"But what analogy is there between their and my position? I was solemnly married to my husband. At the altar I first placed my hand in his. I bear his name, and I know he loves me truly."

"Ah, Princess, you have no conception at present of the heartless nature of diplomacy! What you say is perfectly true; but you certainly did not notice that in the marriage ceremony the priest placed the Grand Duke's left—not his right—hand in yours. This was no treachery, no deception; it is customary with princes of the blood, and their wives and children can hold up their heads without shame. But—and here comes in the infamy—Araktseieff is set upon proclaiming the Grand Duke as the Czar's successor to the throne, because he is his ideal. But to this end it is imperative that the Grand Duke should take back his first wife, who is still living, *and who is a member of a reigning dynasty;* for the fundamental laws of the empire allow no other woman to ascend the throne. Do you now see the fate awaiting you?"

"However hard it be, I will endure it silently."

"You will be deprived of your husband's name; and as Count Grudzinski cannot give you back his, you will be made Princess of Lovicz. Can you not now picture to yourself what your future lot will be?"

"Patience and resignation!"

"Did you not notice the cruel smile on Araktseieff's face as, when kissing your hand, he said, 'The sight of this happiness reminds me *of mine'?* By that he intended to put you on a par with the woman called Daimona, who is only his paramour and was a *vivandière.*"

"I do not feel the intended insult."

"No, no; it is impossible! When I heard the scheme, I too thought, 'After all, what will it matter? She, like other women, will receive compensation, and, like them, will—survive it.' But since I have been brought face to face with those clear, pure eyes, which so faithfully mirror the noble heart within, I ceased to consult my

reasoning powers, for they counselled me to take myself
a hundred miles away and to make myself believe that
I had been dreaming.   Since that moment I have been
pondering how—at the risk of my own life—I could
save you.   It must not be that such an angel should
fall a victim to such devilish intrigues!   It must not be
that a Polish woman be forced to see her father's name
and coat of arms tarnished without any one to protect
her—without means of revenge!"

"What do you mean?"

"What do I mean?   To tell you how you can revenge yourself!   You must anticipate those intriguers,
and, in answer to their dishonoring proposal, say, 'Keep
your princedom of Lovicz for high-born courtesans.   I,
a Polish noblewoman, will find a husband ready to give
me the protection of his honorable name and whole
heart—a true man, who loves and respects me!'"

Face, eyes, the Chevalier's dramatic action, all tended
to illustrate his words.   It was not difficult for Johanna
to divine whom he meant as the "true man."   Not the
shadow of a blush tinted her cheek as, with great composure, she replied :

" Chevalier Galban, do you see those walls surrounding Belvedere and Lazienka?   Within those walls you
are my guest, and you have the right to do exactly as
you please, even to the length of insulting me ; but only
within these walls, as my guest.   As soon, however, as
you are without them, your immunity ceases.   I will
confide to no one what you have just said to me.   A
Polish woman betrays no one, not even to her husband ;
she revenges herself!   So, once you have passed without these walls, for this unpardonable insult I will order
my people to give you a sound thrashing!   May I offer
you a little more sugar in your coffee?"

Chevalier Galban burst into a peal of laughter.

"*Ma foi!* the fate of war. Out of three assaults, one may come off conqueror twice and yet be beaten the third time. Thank you, I will take another piece of sugar."

Then he strolled out with Johanna into the park, admired her tulip-bed, and, deferentially taking leave of her, went back to his chief, as already related.

"Where did you leave my wife?" the Grand Duke asked, as he rose from table.

"I accompanied her into the park. We parted at the Hermitage."

"Come, Araktseieff, let us go and find her! You take one way; I will take the other. Whoever first finds her brings her back to Belvedere."

The Grand Duke was lucky. He was first to find Johanna. She was kneeling on the grass feeding his pet rabbits; he let himself down clumsily beside her.

"Take care!" he said; "the grass is wet with dew; you will take a chill."

"It will not hurt me—I am strong."

"That's a story," he growled, "you are very delicate. I do not know how to wait the season to send you to Ems, that you may take the baths for which you are longing."

"I do not want to go there now."

"Why not?"

"I have been thinking it over. You would be unable to leave your post to go with me; and to be weeks, months, away from you, not ever to see you, is more than I could bear. I would so much rather stay here. Indeed, I am quite well."

"What!" cried the Grand Duke, with a wild outburst of joy. "You love me so much that you cannot live without me? that you would care for nothing if you were away from me? Oh, my own true pearl of women!" And taking up his wife in his strong arms he laughed, caressed, and covered her with a shower of fiery kisses. "And they would separate me from my wife! A fine idea, eh? Shall I throw you into this pond?" And he swung her in his arms like a little child. "Are you afraid that I shall throw you in? Ha, ha, ha! and do you think I would let them make you Princess of Lovicz and be parted from you? That I would repay you for your love and faithfulness with a title, and take another to wife? Are you afraid of it? Shall I toss you into the pond? Hush!"

Johanna twined her arms round her husband's neck, kissed him, and murmured, softly:

"Were you to dishonor me and chase me from you, I would come back to you again. Were you to humiliate me from your wife into your mistress or maid-servant, I would still serve and love you. I cannot do otherwise."

"Ha, ha, ha! And from such a woman they would have torn me. Hallo! Araktseieff! This way, man. I've found her."

When Araktseieff, turning into the winding path, caught sight of the Grand Duke with Johanna in his arms, he knew what had happened.

"Tell them," shouted the Czarevitch when he was still at some distance, and in a voice hoarse with emotion—"tell them that *I do not give up a wife who loves me for a whole empire that hates me!* When are you and your Chevalier Galban going back?"

"With your Imperial Highness's permission, I will stay the night. But Chevalier Galban has left the castle already, I see from a note he left for me. He says he

was compelled to hasten his departure; the ground was
burning under his feet, for Duchess Johanna had threatened him with a horsewhipping for a speech which had
displeased her."

" A horsewhipping !" cried the Grand Duke. "What !
my Johanna order any one to be horsewhipped ? *Come
on my right hand, wife !*" And releasing Johanna from
the embrace in which he still held her, he offered her his
right arm, with face beaming with joy.

" Go back to those who sent you, my good friend, and
tell them that I am about to wed Princess Lovicz in
right-handed marriage. And as she may not accompany
me to St. Petersburg, I will go with her to Ems, with the
Czar's permission. And now get ready your trumpery
papers that I have to sign."

With these words he turned away, and what he had
further to say to Johanna was inaudible from kisses and
laughter.

That which Krizsanowski had promised in the sitting
of the Szojusz Blagadenztoiga had come about—the incredible fact that a man could voluntarily resign his succession to the throne of the mightiest empire in the
world, and in such a manner that, did he ever repent, he
might never undo his act. That incredible fact had become not a possibility, but a thing accomplished. The
solution to the riddle was, as Zeneida had divined at the
time, Johanna. For the present, however, none knew of
it save the participators and the trees of the ancient
forest about them.

Ah ! what a terrific, world-wide catastrophe was this
idyl to bring about !

CHAPTER XXI

THE MOST POWERFUL RULER OF THEM ALL

WHILE the members of "the green book" were at work on their wide-spreading plans, those of the Bear's Paw had made others to their way of thinking.   Passing over the military, and turning their backs upon the league of the aristocrats, they took up a ground of their own, calling themselves "Napoleonists!"   What induced them to choose that extraordinary name for themselves?

Well, it is easy enough to make the poor believe their lot to be a hard one; it was at that time that the Russian Volkslied was written—

> "My soul I give to God;
> My head I give the Czar;
> My body beneath my master's feet;
> The grave is all I call my own!"

Within the last four years especially the iron hand of adversity had pressed heavily on the country. The earth no longer gave back the seed sown upon it; terrific fires had reduced the large cities to ashes; and a pestilence, hitherto unknown in the land, had crept over the frontier and devastated the population. The streams and rivulets had become floods, carrying away whole towns at a moment's notice; locusts, caterpillars of a kind and species never seen before, came down in shoals, tormenting man and beast; great war-ships out at sea sank with all their men and ammunition on board.

And all this was Heaven's retribution because the Czar had not gone to the assistance of the Greeks fighting for their freedom. Against miracles, counter-miracles alone can be effectual.

And the present century had produced a miracle in the form of a man : his name, Napoleon.

It was all a lie that the English had taken him prisoner at Waterloo! All a lie that he was being kept in confinement on the island of St. Helena! He was in hiding, though the whereabouts must not at present be divulged. Where was that place? Only so much might be known, that it was somewhere in the neighborhood of Irkutsk. Thence he would come, as soon as the people's cup of bitterness was filled to the brim, to tread down the mighty, and free every people under the sun.

This rumor was extensively circulated everywhere. Among the conspirators of the Bear's Paw was a plaster-modeller (our "Canova") who, single-handed, sent out of his workshop over two hundred thousand busts of Napoleon. These busts were worshipped by the mujiks as if they were pictures of saints ; they took the place of the crucifix to them. He was the deliverer, before whom the mujik and his family bent the knee ; he would bring them relief from all their troubles.

Even at the present time these plaster casts are to be seen in many a Russian peasant's hut: the well-known form, cocked hat, arms crossed upon the breast, in overcoat or short-waisted military tunic. Forty years after his death they still awaited his coming.

Hence the words "Only wait till Napoleon comes!" were a cry which spread through the land.

The people only remembered that twelve years before,

when Napoleon really did come, their masters were terribly frightened, and so merciful to the peasants. How fast they cleared out, leaving their castles as booty behind! and money then was as plentiful as blackberries. No price was high enough for corn and oats. And such brilliant promises were scattered about in all directions. The mujik was led to expect everything under heaven and earth; but his expectations were never realized. So let Napoleon come again!

And to hasten this was the plan of the leader of the Bear's Paw party.

The 8th of November, according to the Russian calendar, is the Feast of the Archangel Michael. On that day it is the custom to have great rejoicings in Isaacsplatz and on the Neva. The whole population of St. Petersburg, from the highest to the lowest, take part in it. Now when the throng should be at its thickest, and aristocrat and plebeian well mixed up together, suddenly at the corner of every street and square there should arise the cry, "Here comes Napoleon!" And in the midst of the crowd, borne on the shoulders of the enthusiastic people, should appear the well-known figure of the Corsican hero, to be represented by Dobujoff, one of the Bear's Paw community— a man the very image of the great Napoleon, and an admirable mimic. The rest would follow of itself. At the words "Napoleon has come" all St. Petersburg would be at their mercy, and the wave, thus started, would not stop until it reached Novgorod, where the brotherhood of "Ancient Republic" would at once swell the tide, overflowing Moscow and all that ventured to oppose it. They looked upon their plan as sure of success. The people may suffer themselves to be deprived of freedom, even of bread, but no one may

14

deprive them of their amusements. With the days set
apart as holidays no power on earth may meddle. The
plan of campaign was devised cunningly enough. Every
one having anything to do with "the classes" was carefully excluded. And one other circumstance was favorable to the audacious originators. The Neva that year
had frozen over in October, a succession of hard frosts
had followed, but no snow, while ordinarily in November
house - roofs were covered a foot deep in snow, which
lasted into May. It would be, therefore, no difficult
task to set fire to the city in various quarters, a thing not
usually so possible in the winter in St. Petersburg as
in Moscow, built as it was entirely of wooden houses.
With fire breaking out in ten or twelve places simultaneously the panic would be complete.

The Feast of St. Michael was at that time still celebrated in the Isaacsplatz. In one night, in the vast,
usually empty space, a perfect town had been erected,
with entire streets of booths, the principal booth being
the People's Theatre. And what a theatre it was!
in which marionettes acted like real people and fought
in real battles! And then the troops of artists of all
kinds, whose patron is not Apollo, but Pan, who amuse
the people, and are not at the beck and call of the rich
and learned, but are to be seen at fairs and in holiday
places, and who do not think it beneath their dignity to
come down among the crowd to collect kopecs after the
performance. Then there are the people's favorites, the
Bajazzos, who are not so ambitious as to work for posterity, but are perfectly content if they can earn to-day
their yesterday's score at the inn, playing the while, so
the populace think, every whit as well as Talma or Mac-
ready. They eat tow, draw whole bundles of rags out of
their noses, swallow red-hot coals and sharp swords, and

can scratch their ears with their toes, which is more than either Sullivan or Kean, or even Dimitriefsky, more celebrated than either, can do. In one booth is shown the "real original sea-maiden with a fish's tail, who lives on live fish, and can only say 'Papa,' 'Mama.'" In another the big drum is being beaten to call attention to the elephants walking on a tight rope; next door to them are to be seen men of the woods, with four hands and tusklike teeth. The giantess is also on view, under whose arm the tallest man can stand, although she wears no high heels to her shoes, and, when desired, shows that the calves of her legs are not wadded. The showman of a panorama describes, in singing voice to an astonished public, great battles, eruptions of Vesuvius, storms at sea, and ghastly tales of murders, the faithful representation of all which is to be seen in his booth for the sum of two kopecs. Then, how endless are the amusements hidden by no jealous tent! Here a group of cornet-players, each playing a different note, and so forming a melody; there a set of gypsies dancing and singing; windmill-like swings swishing through the air with their delighted occupants; while crowds in their holiday best glide over the smooth ice in sledges or on skates. High above all these earthly delights is to be seen a rope slung across between the tower of St. Isaac's Cathedral to the balcony of the Admiralty, upon which a tight-rope dancer is to wheel his little son in a wheelbarrow.

Wild spirits reign among the crowd! The samovars are inexhaustible with their supplies of hot tea, and epicures who know how to enjoy life swallow mountains of sweet ices, and salt cucumbers immediately after. The people listen to Volkslied singers, and join in with them; while those who have brought their three-sided balalaikas with them accompany the voices—no very difficult art, as it is an instrument with only two strings.

And it is not only a day for "the masses"; the "classes" are there also in all their magnificence. True, every precaution has been taken to prevent "the masses" from encroaching upon their betters. To this end the Summer Garden is enclosed, and there the world of fashion is to be seen driving in every variety of equipage, from the barouche to the national *proledotky*, the owners exhibiting their costly furs and running Bolognese dogs..

The frozen Neva, open to all, is alive with thousands and thousands of sledges, from smart gilded ones with their English thoroughbreds to those of simple Lapland construction drawn by reindeer, crossing and recrossing each other on the polished surface of the river. The Northern Babel is in full force.

As evening comes on, the terrace of the pavilion is illuminated with Bengal lights, and huge pitch bonfires spring into flame, showing up the animated picture of the people's feast in varied coloring.

After the fireworks three salvoes of cannon from the citadel give the signal for the bells in all the churches to begin ringing in honor of St. Michael.

These three salvoes and ringing of church bells are to serve as a signal to the conspirators. At the first sound they are to rush forward, armed with knives and torches, with the cry, " Napoleon is here! Here is Napoleon!" When, under cover of the noise of the pealing bells, they have forced a way into the midst of the aristocrats and soldiers, it will be easy for them, in the universal chaos, to push on to the palace and murder him of whom the *Song of the Knife* was written.

The thing was plain, a foregone conclusion.   That

afternoon a strong southwest wind from the sea had sprung up, to the discomfort of many. True, the St. Petersburger is accustomed, if one fur coat be not sufficient, to put on two; but the poor performers suffered much damage from the wind, which blew down their booths and stopped their performances. The tight-rope dancer dared not venture upon his neck-breaking exhibition, for the storm would have carried off him and his son bodily like a couple of flies. Aristocratic ladies in the enclosure lamented that the wind tore their veils off their bonnets. Greater still were the lamentations anent the fireworks, for none but Bengal lights and wheels could succeed on such a night.

Towards evening the gale rose to a perfect hurricane. Suddenly came the roar of the cannon from the citadel, and simultaneously the peal of bells. Three hundred bells at one and the same time ! A carillon truly.

The roar of the cannon deadened the bells. It is the people's habit to count the salvoes. Three were the signal for the lighting up of the Bengal lights.

But the cannon thundered on.

When the reports had reached twenty-one, people whispered under their breath, "What! can it be the birth of a princess in the Winter Palace ?"

No. Still the cannons thundered on.

At the fiftieth report the rumor arose that a successful naval engagement was being celebrated.

But still the cannons continued their volley, amid the crash of church bells.

When the iron tongue had roared for the hundred and first time, people began to ask themselves, " Can this be the Czar's birthday ?"

No; not even that. The iron monsters thundered on—102, 103, 104. At the hundred and fifth time none asked any more what it meant; for the whole city with one voice sent up a despairing cry, deadening even the crash of the three hundred bells.

"It is coming! It is coming!"

But it was not the approach of Napoleon's army which aroused the voice of panic, but that of a far mightier lord — the Neva! which, rushing back upon the city, brings the sea with it, and with foaming, roaring, resistless waves breaks up the ice of the river, flinging it abroad on all sides.

That was the meaning of the incessant firing of cannon from the citadel.

When Czar Peter I. first began to put into form his idea of building a capital in the midst of the Finnish morass, and, to that end, had the vast forest there standing exterminated, he came upon an old fir-tree, on whose bark were cut deep lines. "What is the meaning of these lines?" he asked an old countryman. "*These lines denote the height of the Neva when it leaves its banks and floods the whole surrounding land.*" The Czar gave orders for tree and peasant to be cut down; but both had spoken truly. The Neva remained the sworn enemy of the mighty city of the Czar.

Yes. It is coming, rushing on with backward movement; it has left the river-bed and increases mightily; it is no longer the Neva, but the sea—the salt sea in all its awful immensity! And once it has gone down, the walls of palaces and houses, as far as the water has reached, will be covered with salt.

The sledgers on the ice were the first to become aware of the extent of the danger. Those of them who took refuge on the right bank of the river might esteem them-

selves lucky, for there the streets were clear; but those
seeking the left side spread mad panic among the unconscious throng of pleasure - seekers with their cry,
" The Neva is coming !"

The very words sufficed to strike dismay into the
hearts of the bravest and to paralyze the cowardly with
terror ; for in such danger there is no way of escape.
When the Neva rises it overflows the whole city, and he
who would flee the danger meets it at the next turning.

Confusion reigned supreme. The crowds of carriages
in the railed-in Summer Garden had but one way of
egress, and collision was inevitable ; those which at last
forced a passage came into the midst of a maddened
press of people, who carried them along, regardless of
the crest upon the panels and the supercilious lackey
on the box. There were for the time being no princes
and no mujiks, only a panic-stricken mob. And before
disentanglement was possible the flood was upon them.

The first huge wave washed down the booths in Isaacsplatz. The terrified owners came rushing out of the
beer-houses, and, clambering on the tops of their disman-
tled booths, shrieked for help. The giantess pushed
head and shoulders out of her tent, frightened to death.
Boys dressed like performing apes flew up their poles ;
the sea-maiden found her feet, and, discarding tail, made
for dry land. The performing elephant waddled through
the crowd, his master on his back; and the wild beasts
in the menagerie roared as if they were in their native
forests. At that instant, as though in mockery of this
scene of terror, the red and green lights on the terrace
of the Summer Garden pavilion shone forth, lighting
up the flood in all its horror. The men in charge of
the fireworks were ignorant of what was happening.
Only when the festive peals of bells had died away in

distant reverberations did they become aware of their danger; and hastily putting out their lights, left the whole city in darkness. For the slippery pavements impeded the lamp-lighters; nor, indeed, could they have lighted their lamps in the storm that was raging. Darkness added the final touch of horror to the scene of danger! Among the terrified refugees were Duchess Ghedimin and Bethsaba; their carriage, in Russian style, drawn by two horses tandem. The first horse was wellnigh unmanageable; it was a spirited English mare, which the Duchess had specially chosen that day to show that her equipage was superior to Zeneida's. Only she had not attained her aim, for Fräulein Ilmarinen had not entered an appearance.

"Drive down one of the side streets," the Duchess said, peremptorily, to her coachman.

Easy to command, but not so easy to carry out! The mob surrounded them on all sides.

"Get down," she ordered her jäger, "and force a way through the people!"

The jäger, a gigantic young fellow, a Finlander, seized the foremost horse by the bridle, and, dealing out blows roundly with his other arm on the mujiks, thought to steer the carriage in this way through the crush. All very well; that kind of thing may do with the mujik, who is accustomed to the lash; but your thoroughbred has noble blood in his veins, and does not suffer himself to be led by the bridle. Violently shaking himself loose, the horse dealt the jäger such a blow on the head that he fell senseless to the ground.

"Oh, what are we to do now?" asked the Duchess, terror-stricken, bursting into tears.

"I know a way," said Bethsaba. "Have the leader led in the saddle."

"But who would venture to mount it?" asked the Duchess, wringing her hands.

"I will!" returned Bethsaba; "I am used to riding."

"Very well, then," said the Duchess.

Selfish to the last degree, she never considered that in order to reach the farthermost horse Bethsaba would have to wade through the icy water up to her knees, and in her light carriage-wrap expose herself to the bitter cold of the stormy night, and to the maddened populace, who, in the darkness and panic, recognized neither lord nor master. Also, in her emergency, Princess Ghedimin utterly forgot that Bethsaba was, moreover, a king's daughter, who had not been committed to her care to act as postilion for her.

So she merely said, "Very well, then."

And the girl, throwing off her fur-lined cloak, jumped from the carriage into the water, ran to the foremost horse, calling it by its name as she ran; then, stroking its mane with one hand, sprang lightly upon its back, using the leading-reins for bridle.

And now they moved on once more.

With her soft voice saying to the on-pressing crowd, "Dear cousin, please make way! Heaven be with you!" she effected more than any amount of violence would have done. The people made way for her, and she succeeded in guiding the carriage into a side street, clear as yet from the flying masses.

But there was a reason which made advance impracticable. The flood was already ahead of them; and the farther they proceeded the more imminent grew their danger. The waves were already washing into the carriage; the Duchess had to take refuge on the coachman's box to keep her feet dry. There she was so far secure, but Bethsaba was soaked to the skin from the spray dashed up by the horses' feet, while the water covered her knees.

" If only we could get to Nevski Prospect," gasped the Duchess. " Hurry—hurry on ! There is our castle."

At length they reached it. But what a sight met their eyes ! It was as though they were in the very midst of the Neva, with its fields of ice. Not water alone was round them, but ice — great icebergs floating on the black expanse of water. Through the Moika Canal the flood was coming down upon them.

" Holy Archangel Michael !" screamed the coachman at the sight, " save us on this your day !"

" Don't pray now, but push on the horses," commanded the Duchess, peremptorily.

" From this only St. Michael or the devil can save us !"

" Hold your tongue !" cried the Duchess, giving him a smart blow on the head. " I trust neither in St. Michael nor the devil, but in my good horses, which will take me home in safety. Drive on !"

And the Duchess struck the coachman, the coachman the horses, and the horses' feet the raging element. All three were furious. The king's daughter alone prayed :

" My God !—oh, dear God, send some one to help us !"

She felt that she could not hold out much longer, that her limbs were growing numb with cold.

CHAPTER XXII

THE DEVIL

SUDDENLY a glow of light illumined the dark waves ; a red gleam, reflected on the street of houses, was seen advancing towards them. From a side street a boat was approaching, with a torch stuck in its bow. Two

men were pulling; a third, boat-hook in hand, was stav-
ing off the floating masses of ice; a fourth was at the
rudder. In the middle of the boat stood a woman, her
head and face entirely enveloped in a bashlik, engaged
in covering up a group of children of all ages, distribut-
ing biscuit among them, and soothing their cries for
papa and baba (little Russian children say "baba" instead of mamma). Papa and baba do not take the
children to the fair, but lock up the poor little mites in
the houses before they go out. If any sudden calamity
occurs papa and baba escape. But what becomes of
the little ones? Does a fire break out they are burned
to death; a flood, then let Providence send some good-
natured gentry-folk, such as take pleasure in rescuing
children through roof or windows. It is as good sport
as wild-duck shooting. So this boat was filled to overflowing.

The boatmen were the first to see the desperate position of the carriage and its occupants, and they rowed
towards it. The torch showered sparks in the high
wind, illuminating the face of the youth who, as he stood
in the prow of the boat gliding over the dark waters,
looked like some hero of antiquity. Masses of ice
grated under the keel. The young man, steering dex-
terously through the ice, reached the carriage. It was
but just in time, for Bethsaba could scarce maintain her
seat upon the horse. Without a second's hesitation he
had seized the half-frozen girl, who clutched with both
hands at his arm, and the next instant she was in the
boat.

Bethsaba looked into the youth's eyes, and in that moment she knew the exquisite joy of losing one's self in a
look. Once before she had met the fire of those eyes—then
they had singed her wings; now her heart was the victim.

"Wrap her in this fur cloak," said the lady standing
in the middle of the boat to the young man, and threw
her own cloak to the girl, who was shivering with cold;
then going alongside the carriage, held out her hand to
help the lady sitting in it into the boat. As she did
so the bashlik fell back, and Bethsaba recognized the
face. It was that of Zeneida Ilmarinen—the devil! The
Duchess also recognized her.

Like a fury she struck back her enemy's helping hand,
crying, in a voice hoarse with passionate excitement:

"Away, away! I will not have your help! Rather
perish in the flood than in hell with you!" And, snatching the whip from her coachman's hand, she administered some smart lashes to the horses, who, madly rearing, plunged deeper into the foaming waves, already up
to their chests. She would have none of Zeneida's
help.

Bethsaba remained in the boat, trembling, not with
cold, but at the thought that she had fallen into the
devil's clutches, who already was making off with her as
his prey. Of course he had given her his own fur wrap
in order to get more sure hold of her. How warm it
was! It must come direct from the lower regions.

"You will take cold," said the man with the boat-
hook to Zeneida.

"I will row to keep myself warm," she answered; and,
taking an oar in her firm grasp, began rowing vigorously, her chest heaving with the exertion, as does the devil
when hastening off with his prey. Of course he takes
all the little children he can get hold of to hell. The
boat flew like the wind down the dark lanes.

At length they came to a large garden, the high walls
of which kept back the seething waters. Bethsaba recognized the gilded railings that surmounted them. It

was here the stag had been shot that they were hunting last spring. The evil spirit was bringing her to his lair.

The boat pulled up to the very threshold of the castle, for the water covered the marble steps. But the castle itself was built on such high ground that it was secure from all inundation.

The hall was brilliantly lighted, and an army of liveried footmen with lighted lamps hastened out to receive the party. From one end of the long ballroom to the other were rows of beds; in the centre of the room a table spread with food and steaming samovars. A number of beds were already occupied by children; another group was in the act of being fed with tea and soup. Bethsaba recognized many well-known faces among the helpers. They were those of members of the Society of the Green Book, who had been utilizing the Feast of St. Michael to hold a sitting, for that is one of the days when the attention of the police is otherwise engaged. Scarce had the sitting begun when Pushkin had burst in among them with the alarming news that the Neva had overflowed its banks.

The common danger at once put politics, new constitutions, and conspiracy out of their heads. Their one thought was to save those imperilled.

In Zeneida's grounds was an immense fish-pond, on which her guests were wont to hold regattas in the spring. In winter boats and punts were laid up in the boat-houses. These were got out in all haste, the conspirators told off to them with oars and boat-hooks, and they were quickly rowed off in all directions to carry help to the inundated city. Their first work was to rescue the children out of endangered houses, and those women who had stayed at home with them. Zeneida placed her castle, staff of servants, and wardrobe at the disposal of the rescuing party; but the lion's share of the work fell to her, and she gave herself heart and soul to it. She herself carried the young Circassian Princess in her arms into a well-warmed apartment hung with rich tapestries. Bethsaba had not strength to resist; she suffered herself to be carried like a baby. Besides, what is the use of resistance to the Prince of Darkness?

First Zeneida cut away and removed the frozen clothing from Bethsaba's numbed body — so does the Evil One with his prey! Here the king's daughter experienced a sensation of surprise, for she was accustomed to bathe very often with Korynthia, who never failed to admire her form, and to say to her god-daughter, "How lovely are you!" But Zeneida instead, with frowning brow, as if angry with her, clothed her rapidly in a woollen garment, then commenced rubbing her limbs vigorously until the numbness yielded and a pleasant sense of warmth was infused into her frame. Then, wrapping her in well-warmed blankets, she laid Bethsaba in a delicious soft bed and covered her up. Yes, so the Evil One treats his poor victims before he takes them to the nether regions!

Then Zeneida brought a steaming drink in a delicate porcelain cup, from which Bethsaba, taking one sip, felt warmed through as though with fire. This must certainly be the devil's potion! And having once tasted it she wanted more, and did not stop until she had emptied the cup. Then her eyes closed, and, fiercely as she resisted it, sleep overpowered her. In her dreams the Prince of Darkness led her through fairy-like places which, narrow at first, widened out farther and farther until they changed into one great Paradise, where people flew about instead of walking. Once in her dreams she saw the Evil One gently attending to her wants and removing her saturated garments. And next morning, when she awoke, true enough, her coverings had been changed. If that was no dream, were the other dreams equally true?

Bethsaba, sitting up in bed, looked about her. Yes; it must be the Evil One's room. No image of a saint to be seen; only Chinese and Japanese idols of every form and shape. Most likely images of Beelzebub and Asmodeus!

But what most astonished her was to find her own clothes folded on a low chair by her bedside. How could that be? Last night the Spirit of Darkness had certainly cut and torn them to shreds; and now here they were, whole and dry. Certainly he has number-less agents who can work like magic? Timorously she put on the mysterious clothing, not failing to ejaculate a "Kyrie eleison!" at each garment, in order to dispel the power of the Evil One.

And when thus dressed she tried to find her way out of the room she was in. Two or three of the rooms she passed through were very unlike those of her god-mother, rich princess as she was. One of these was full of living birds; another of stuffed animals. Sud-denly she heard a whimpering of children. This must be the place where the Evil Spirit tortures the little ones he has stolen. Curiosity made her follow the voices, and advancing she came to a half-open door, where, looking in, she saw Zeneida occupied in washing, combing, and dressing a group of tiny children. Some, who were being washed, were whimpering; but others, already dressed, were chattering, and admiring their pretty, new frocks. Surely an odd occupation for the Evil One. They were in Zeneida's bath-room. Beth-saba boldly entered. Curiosity begets courage.

"Ah, dressed already, little Princess?" said Zeneida.

"What are you doing to the children?" asked Beth-saba, with desire for knowledge.

"As you see, washing and dressing them; one cannot tell where their mother may be, poor little mites. The flood is rising higher and higher; the whole city is under water. As long as the danger lasts we must look after these little ones. Those who dress quickly," continued she, turning to the children, "may run into the dining-hall, and the housekeeper will give them some nice soup for breakfast."

Bethsaba thought she would put the Evil One to the proof.

"But who hears them say their prayers before their breakfast?"

"Nobody, dear child; for they are more hungry than devout."

"But prayer is good," returned the king's daughter. "For what?"

"In order to avert further misfortune from the city."

"My dear little Princess!" exclaimed Zeneida, "the wind which sends the Neva over St. Petersburg is called *Auster*, and were the whole twelve hundred millions of people who inhabit the earth to blow together it would not avail to blow back the *Auster!*"

This was a speech worthy of its maker. To liken the efficacy of prayer to a blowing of breath! Bethsaba now plunged into the extreme of audacity. She would name the Deity, and surely then the devil, amid sulphur and brimstone, would strip himself of his seductive exterior and appear in his conventional form of horns and goat's feet.

"So you do not believe that God has sent this awful calamity upon mankind?"

"No, dear child. For were it God who had sent this visitation upon the earth the flood would have destroyed the houses of the wicked and not those of the honest, hard-working people."

Bethsaba thought, "You must be he, or you would never have dared to utter such blasphemy." She went further; she wanted to catch the Evil One in his own net.

"You have too much to do; may I not help you? If you would let me, I would wash and dress the children, too. I should like to do it; it is so amusing."

"Yes, indeed," said Zeneida, merrily. "Why not? It will give you something to do; and I, by-the-way, must go and see that we have enough to eat for all our multitude. I leave you in charge of the nursery."

So saying she gave up her seat to Bethsaba, and, bidding the many unwashed little folk to be good, left the bath-room with a smile. Bethsaba's first care was to make the children all kneel down. Then, kneeling in their midst, she said the Lord's Prayer with them—"Deliver us from the Evil One. Amen."

Now he must be effectually quashed!

Then she began her task of washing and dressing the little ones.

CHAPTER XXIII

THE STORY OF THE MAN WITH THE GREEN EYES

But the small mites were not as good with their new nurse as they had been with the old one. A look from Zeneida had been enough to still their moanings and whimperings; but Bethsaba was little more than

15

a child herself, they were not in the least awed by her. One child set up the cry, the others following in chorus, " Where is baba ? where is pata ?" and she might have gone on forever washing the tears from the little faces.

Well, pata and baba she could not give back to them ; but she remembered what her nurses had done when she was a little child and used to cry for her mamma. They had told her fairy tales.

" Don't cry ! Be good and sensible, and I will tell you the story of *The Man with the Green Eyes*. It's such a lovely story. Now listen !"

The children were quiet as mice ; they clustered up to Bethsaba, clinging to her dress, resting their chins on her knees, and listened.

" A long, long time ago there was a little prince, as little as you are, Struwelpeter, here at my feet. He had a good papa and a good baba, who loved him very much. But one day they had to go a long journey, and were laid in long metal boxes, and the lids were shut down upon them. Then they were carried out and placed upon two grand gold and silver coaches, each drawn by six horses, and, amid bands of music, firing of cannons, and great crowds of people, they were driven away.

" When the little prince was left alone he asked his Grand Vizier, ' To what land did my father and mother go ?'

" And the Grand Vizier answered, ' Ah, little prince, to a land far away. To another world.'

" ' And why did they go to that other world ?'

" ' Because it is much better there than in ours !' the vizier explained.

" Upon which the little king's son asked, ' If that world is so much better, why did they not take me with them ?'

" ' Because you have yet much to work, battle, and suffer in this world before you will be worthy to reach that other one whither your father and mother went.'

" This admonition did not please the little prince at all, and he thought to himself, ' We'll see. I *will* get to papa and baba in the other world, whatever he may say!'

" And, taking his little gun, he went out into the woods, as if to shoot birds. There he stayed so long that he was caught in a thunder-shower; and to avoid getting wet he looked about for a hollow tree to shelter in. He had found one, and was looking in, when he saw that some one was already there. Now, Struwelpeter, what would you have done in such a case?"

" I should have cried out loud."

" Well, now, the little king's son did not do that; but, like a man, he spoke up to the intruder: ' I say, you fellow, this wood is my wood, and this tree is my tree, and I don't allow you to live in it. But if you can tell me where that better land is to which papa and baba - have gone I will make you a present of wood and tree, and you shall live in them.'

" And the stranger in the hollow tree answered, ' Not so, little king's son! I lived here before this wood existed, and no one has power to drive me away. You want to know where the better land is? That I can only tell you when I love you and you love me. Already I love you.'

" ' But I don't love you, naughty man,' said the little prince.

" ' Why not?' asked the wood sprite.

" ' Because you've got *green eyes*.'

" The stranger's eyes, in truth, gleamed like two green beetles.

"'Then Heaven be with you!' said the stranger; by which the little prince knew he was no evil spirit, else he dared not name the holy place.

"'I'm going!' returned the little king's son; 'and I will find the better land without you. I have often heard which way to take.'

"The little prince had often heard tell that far off, among the rocks, lived a fierce, bloodthirsty tiger, who had despatched many a huntsman and goatherd to the other world. He would take him along too.

"So he went on till he came to the wild beast's den. He knew it by the many human bones strewn about on the ground. The tiger was in his den; his growling could be heard without.

"Now, you obstreperous little man, would you have dared to go into his den?"

"Not even if my ball had fallen in!"

"Well, then, the king's son was more courageous. He shouted into the den, 'Heh! you tiger, come out! I am the king's son! Bear me at once across to the better land!'

"The monster came slowly out of his lair, licking his bloody muzzle and striking his long tail against his haunches, and preparing to make one spring on the boy. (Don't cry, little snub-nose!) He did not gobble him up; for at that instant a gigantic snake darted out of a cleft in the rock, threw itself round the tiger, and, encircling neck and body, bit the monster in the throat. The tiger uttered an awful roar, and wrestled with the snake on the ground. Now began a battle for life and death between the two animals, until both together they fell down the rocky precipice. They had killed each other. The prince had to go home to his palace.

"On his way home he met a huntsman, his bow and quiver slung on his back.

"'That's an odd huntsman who hunts nowadays with bow and arrow,' thought the little prince, and looked straight into his eyes. It was *the man with the green eyes!*

"'So you can't find the way to the better land unless you love me, eh?' said he, and disappeared as if the earth had swallowed him up.

"'We'll see,' thought the little prince. 'I heard once that there is a great sea, and that many people who went on that sea in ships found the way to that land. Perhaps I may succeed in finding that big sea.'

"So he commanded his Grand Vizier to fit out a great ship on the Black Sea for him; and in this they sailed to the country of the fire-worshippers, which had been the home of the prince's mother. The voyage out was propitious; but coming back they were caught in a terrific storm. It thundered and lightened, the sky grew quite dark, and as the lightning lit it up and the rifts of cloud opened, they could clearly see in the sky beyond the radiant angel host; and as the storm-winds made clefts in the sea they could see the sea-nymphs at the bottom.

"'At last!' thought the king's son. 'Whether from above or below, I shall find the way to the better land.'

"The waves ran so high they had already broken the ship's rudder; the man at the helm had been washed overboard; the ship was fast running on to a huge mass of rocks; there was no doubt but that it must inevitably go to pieces.

"At that moment the prince saw some one by the steering-gear, a stranger, who began steering the ship with an old-fashioned helm.

" ' That's an odd sort of man who thinks to steer this great ship with that old-fashioned gear !'

" Suddenly the storm ceased ; sky and sea quieted down, the ship ran unharmed past the threatening rocky shore, and reached its homeward destination in safety.

" The little prince looked round for the stranger steersman, whom no one on board knew ; but he, with a laugh, said :

" ' You will not find the better land before you get to love me, eh ?'

" And the little king's son, looking still more closely, recognized in him *the man with the green eyes ;* but he disappeared as if the sea had swallowed him up.

" And now the little prince began to be very angry.

" ' Can there be no road for me to the better land ? Oh yes, there is. I have heard that many a hero has found it on the battle-field.'

" So he commanded his Grand Vizier, then and there, to declare war against the King of the Tartars.

" And the Grand Vizier, with his army, invaded Tartary ; but its king was very powerful. He let the little prince's army go farther and farther into the heart of his country, then surrounded them on all sides.

" The Grand Vizier was frightened.

" ' We are lost, little king's son ! The Tartar knows no mercy ; he will either kill us or make us slaves. His army is countless as an army of locusts.'

" The little king's son exulted.

" ' Give the signal for attack at once, that it may be the sooner over.'

" But the Grand Vizier was so frightened that he disguised himself as a common soldier, and hid himself, not daring to lead on his army. So the whole army, becoming demoralized, were ready to lay down their arms to the enemy, when suddenly there appeared at their head an unknown general in a uniform they had never yet seen. His sword was like a flaming fire or a serpent. He encouraged the men, and led them against the Tartars; and scarce had the trumpet sounded for the attack before the King of Tartary advanced towards the prince, sword in hand, barefoot, in a raiment of goat's hair, and humbly offered him costly presents, beseeching peace. 'For,' he said, 'I cannot fight. My soldiers are dying off by thousands; they fall as they stand, their hands and feet writhing and convulsed.'

"And once more the prince recognized *the man with the green eyes* in the unknown general. This grieved him greatly. He began to see that, without his help, never could he find that land where his father and mother were. Thus he made up his mind to seek out *the man with the green eyes* in his hiding-place, and to tell him he loved him. He went and called him out of the hollow tree. *The man with the green eyes* had a garment of tinder, a hat of tinder bound with green mildew; his face was yellow as wax, his lips blue as mulberries.

"'Well, dear child, do you love me at last?' he asked the little king's son.

"'Yes, yes; I love you. Only show me, at last, the road to the better land.'

"'Never fear! I will show it you. But first you must eat one of the plums from my basket and kiss me.'

"I must tell you he had a basket in his hand filled with plums, as waxen yellow as was his face. The little king's son took a plum and ate it.

"'Now, just one kiss!' and he kissed him.

"'Huh! how cold your lips were!' said the little prince, with a shudder.

"And by means of that one plum and that kiss the

king's son found, what he had long sought so yearningly, the way to that better land where his father and mother were awaiting him. He is still there, and sends you his greetings."

While she told her story the king's daughter had been busily combing the fair locks of a little girl, who, with eyes and mouth wide open, took in every word of the fable. When it came to an end she asked:

"And what is that other world?"

"Where good people live; where the sun ever shines and it is perpetual spring-time; where man labors and every day is the Feast of St. Michael; where all people are glad and love one another; where none are hungry or thirsty; and where the children play with the baby angels."

"Oh, I say," quoth the little fair-haired maid, "if people must not eat or drink in the better land, I am sure papa and baba won't go there!"

This set Bethsaba off laughing, as she covered the little speaker with kisses. Upon which there was a loud clapping of hands from the next room.

CHAPTER XXIV

"THEN YOU ARE NOT—?"

THE pretty story-teller had had listeners.

As the door opened she perceived three well-known faces, those of Zeneida, Pushkin, her rescuer of the night before, and Jakuskin, the man at the helm of the boat. The two men were covered with mud; it was plain to see that they had just come in again from their work of mercy.

"We were listening to you," said Zeneida. "Your audience were enchanted."

"When I was travelling in the Caucasus," said Jakuskin, "I chanced to hear that very fable. The man with the green eyes is the allegorical symbol of Caucasian fever, so rife there. The meaning of it is, that whoever has received the incubation of that fever, whether he be wounded in battle, mangled by wild beasts, or swallowed up by the sea, will meet no other death than that prepared for him by the green-eyed spectre!"

Bethsaba saw Pushkin standing before her. She gazed into those eyes in which to look out one's very soul must be so sweet, and held out her hand to him.

"I have not yet thanked you for having saved my life. You came just in time. I could not have kept my seat an instant longer."

"But how could the Duchess have allowed you to be there at all?" asked Pushkin, in tones of reproach.

"I begged her to let me do it. I was so sorry for her, for she was so terrified, and even began to cry, a thing I could not stand. Do you know whether she reached home safely?"

"She is perfectly well. I inquired. I assure you that my sole reason for going expressly to her palace to make inquiries was that I knew your first thought would be for her. There is nothing the matter with her. She went off at once last night in her boat to Peterhof, where she is in safety. She must have passed this very castle; but, of course, her only reason for not stopping to take you in was because she felt satisfied that you were in good keeping."

And Bethsaba saw no irony in the words; for, in truth, she felt quite happy in the place where she had those eyes to look into.

"And now I can give you nothing in return for having saved me, for I am so poor."

"Like me," returned Pushkin.

And Zeneida whispered in his ear:

"Oh, the boundless riches that would come from the union of your poverty!"

Bethsaba turned back to her washing apparatus.

"Please let me go back to my work.   Duty before everything!"

"Blessed be the hands that perform it!" said Pushkin.

And each word of his was music in Bethsaba's ears.

"Now I know that I love him," thought she to herself.   "I am fully convinced of that.   But does he love me?"

"We must now leave you," said Pushkin.   "I only came to bring you news from Ghedimin Castle.   We must be getting back.   The flood is still rising; the whole of St. Petersburg is under water.   There is no end of work for us to do; but we shall be coming backwards and forwards many times in the course of the day. I shall have many gifts to lay at your feet, dear Princess."

Gifts!   Did not her godmother tell her that the Russian youth brings gifts to his lady-love?   So then—

"Gifts?" she asked, with naïve joy, an innocent flush upon her pretty cheeks.   "What kind of gifts?"

"Boatfuls of muddy, ragged children for you to wash and dress."

The girl laughed and clapped her hands with glee.

"Oh, that is capital!   Do bring them—the more the better!   That is the kind of gift I love."

The two men, in their sailor's dress, all wet and muddy, hastened off.

"Pushkin," said Zeneida, accompanying him to the adjoining room, "that girl is Heaven-sent to you."

"Since when have you believed in heaven?"

"Be off with you! You are a goose! What news had you of Ghedimin?"

Pushkin shrugged his shoulders.

"He is at home quite well. I saw him through the balcony window, but could not speak to him, as he did not open it. He is a good sort; spirited enough, too, when once he is put up to a thing, but with no self-reliance. He is fond of you, and is really anxious about you; but he knows that your palace is on sufficiently high ground to be out of danger, and that you have a host of friends to protect you. He is hospitable, and is generosity itself, and is certain to subscribe hundreds of thousands for the relief of the sufferers; yet he does not offer to take a soul into his own place, for fear of spoiling his carpets and floors; nor does he send out a cup of soup to them, because he has no wife to stand by him and encourage him in it. He is even philanthropic, yet fears to go out in the damp lest he should get rheumatism. He is an incorporated 'idea,' and he knows it."

"You are a calumniator! I am convinced that he is ill."

"He is certainly not ill unto death, or the Duchess would never have left him behind and gone alone to Peterhof."

"Don't be in such a hurry! What of the Czar?"

"He is rowing about everywhere in his boat. Jakuskin, come here! You met the Czar; tell us about him."

"Oh, bosh!" returned the other, impatiently.

"Come, tell. Zeneida likes to hear these things."

"I have no secrets from her; she knows me through and through, and that I shrink from nothing. Last night in my boat I twice came upon the Czar; we were but an arm's-length one from another. The torches of his bodyguard lit up his figure. He himself was lifting the weeping, raving people out of their windows—the very attitude for a pistol-shot! I had mine loaded in my pocket. I drew it out, and, to escape temptation, held it under water to prevent its going off."

"Do you see, Jakuskin?" exclaimed Zeneida.

"Draw no conclusions from that. That I would not shoot him at the moment that he was helping his people is no proof that I have given up my plan. A deed of violence at such a time would have raised up all Christendom against the perpetrator. Let's have no sentiment. I merely let him go free from well-grounded self-interest. Now I will confess to you what I had not yet even confided to Pushkin. For the second time, and not by chance, I met the Czar at the Bear's Paw. Now, the Bear's Paw is in that quarter of the town which unites one end of Unishkoff Bridge with Jelagnaja Street, a locality of whose existence St. Petersburg high life has no idea. And Nevski Prospect, with its noble palaces, leads up into that labyrinth of squalor and misery. But it is out of the range of the carriage-drive of the magnates. There the scum of Europe mixes with the refuse of Asia. And any catastrophe brings the refuse to the top. Our worthy friends must have been rather unpleasantly surprised by the Neva's unexpected performance; they had prepared one of another sort. The rising water washed them out of their cellars into the attics. And they knew how to howl! When the Czar heard so many clamoring voices he had his boat turned in their direction. I followed him at a distance, and saw him himself draw each several man out of the attic windows, and witnessed their humble subjection to him. I had to cram my fists into my mouth to prevent my laughter. The select company of the Bear's Paw was taken off by the

Czar to the Winter Palace, and Herr Marat and Company will have received a cup of 'kvass' broth from the imperial hands and returned a teeth-chattering 'thanks.' But a very convulsion of laughter seized me when our friend Dobujoff, got up as Napoleon Bonaparte, crawled out of the shanty. The Czar exclaimed, '*Diantre! Est-ce-que vous êtes retourné de Sainte-Hélène?*' Upon which Napoleon had to confess that he understood no word of French. Now comes the catastrophe. Not by hand of man, but by means of a bit of wood. In front of the Bear's Paw a tall pine staff had been erected, on the summit of which was stuck a pitch wreath. From this hung a line which had been steeped in saltpetre, and was evidently intended to have been lighted—probably as the signal. The masses of ice washing up against it had unsettled the staff; it began to totter, and must inevitably have crushed both the Czar and his boat's company had not, fortunately, a man been near who, perceiving their danger in time, seized the line with powerful grip and swayed the staff round so that it fell beside the boat instead of upon it."

"That man was you!" exclaimed Zeneida.

"No matter! But this much I see, that a nobleman *cannot* be a common murderer. He is too fastidious about time and place. So to a more favorable opportunity!"

"One thing more," said Zeneida. "Did the Czar touch, too, at Petrovsky Garden?"

"No."

"All right. I will not detain you any longer."

The two men hastened down to their boat. Zeneida went back to Bethsaba. The Princess had by this time dressed all the mujik children.

"Now, children," said Zeneida, "go prettily, hand in

hand, to the winter garden; there you will get your breakfast, and then you may play."

Winter garden! palm grove! What sounds for poor children's ears!

Then, turning to Bethsaba, she said:

"Now, dear little Princess, you remain here. Take a good hot bath; it will do you good after your yesterday's exposure. I will be back in an hour. There is a bell; ring for all you want."

Bethsaba's head was all confused. Everything was so new and strange to her.

A pleasant sense of fatigue stole over nerves and imagination after the bath. What a pity that there was no one here to whom she could confide her thoughts and feelings! It would have been so nice! If only Sophie were here! Ah, if she were here there would be no further reason for alarm. Two young girls together are the very essence of heroism! And now she began to wonder what could have happened to Sophie in this dread time. Had any one thought to go to her assistance? had she listened to the alarm signals and thundering cannon with despair in her heart? What tears she must have shed as she looked out of her windows at the rising expanse of icy water! Bethsaba shuddered. Her excited fancy pictured her friend kneeling, with uplifted hands, before her holy images, imploring help. Would that prayer be answered? Or was it but a faint breath, lost in the rushing of the *Auster?*

Folding her hands, she prayed that help might be given to Sophie. Perhaps the combined prayer of two maidens might have greater efficacy. What a pity that there was no holy image in the room! She was forced to shut her eyes, that some Buddhist idol might not think she was addressing her prayer to him.

Thus Zeneida, on her return, found her.

"What, praying again, Princess? This is the time to be up and doing."

"But what can I do?"

"First of all, drink down this wine soup that I have brought for you. I want to see you quite well and strong again, for I want your aid."

"My aid?"

"Now sit down and take your breakfast while I unfold my plan."

Bethsaba trembled. The thought of the dragon in the fairy story struck her, who first feasts the captured children on almonds and raisins and then slays them. She could scarce get down her soup.

"I dare say you know that one-storied house standing in a garden, near the engineer's buildings, where a young girl and her old servant live?"

Bethsaba lost not a syllable.

"According to water-mark measurements that house stands four cubits lower than this; hence the water which has encroached here to the castle steps has already flooded the ground floor, and is reaching up to the windows of the first story, and the water is still rising. But one cubit more and it will be rushing through the windows in the first story. Now, if the flood lasts another two or three days, which, unfortunately, is but too certain, that poor, delicate child will be in despair. Her only protector dare not go to her help on account of his high position; those he has sent have gone away without accomplishing their errand, for the girl is obstinate and mistrustful. She will not trust herself to strangers, for she dreads meeting the same fate as did Princess Tarrakonoff. There is therefore no other means of saving her from the endangered house than for you to come with us, for she loves and trusts you. On hearing your voice she will readily let herself down from her balcony into the boat; then we will bring her here, and you can occupy the same room together while the danger lasts. You will not be alone in this anxious time, and she will feel comforted in your society; and, the time of peril happily over, we will drive her back to her home."

Bethsaba had forgotten her breakfast while Zeneida was speaking; her eyes opened wider and wider, her cheeks rounded and flushed; she laughed with tears in her eyes; and as Zeneida finished she jumped up from her chair, and, placing both hands on Zeneida's shoulders, looked trustfully into her eyes, as she joyfully said:

" Oh, then, you are not the devil!"

· Zeneida broke into a peal of laughter.

" Who told you that I was?"

" My godmother. But I see now that it was all a lie."

" It was only a manner of speaking. If one dislikes any one very much, one says that he or she is a devil."

" It was on account of the stag that my godmother was so angry with you, was it not?"

" Yes; for that."

" But she need not then have frightened me so by telling me that the devil looked just like you."

" Oh, little goose! There is no such thing as a devil. Only that people like to ascribe their own wicked imaginings to an ideal being, who, in reality, has nothing to do with the evil within them."

" But you are a real fairy, then! For you read into my very soul, and how anxious I was about Sophie, and longing to see her. It was just for that that I was praying, that my darling little Sophie might be saved and brought here. And then you come in and bring me,

like the message in the Gospel, the comforting answer :
'Go yourself and fetch her!' And do you still venture
to affirm that there is no good in prayer?"

"To those who believe it is good," replied Zeneida,
kissing the girl's forehead ; upon which the latter, throwing her two arms lovingly round Fräulein Ilmarinen's
neck, said :

" Let us say ' thou' to each other."

And they signed the compact with a kiss. Then joyously running to the table, Bethsaba drank her wine
soup almost at a breath. There was a little left in the
glass.

" That you must drink; I left it for you."

And the bond was sealed.

" I am quite ready; let us go," said Bethsaba.

" Wait just a few minutes. We will let the gentlemen
get away first. We will go out by the garden gate, and
take only one man to steer and another for the boat-
hook."

" Then we will row, won't we? I am accustomed to
it, and strong as iron."

" It would be no use. The boat can only be sculled
through the ice, especially against the current, and that
will be done with the boat-hook."

" Well, I am still convinced that you are a good fairy,
Zeneida. You will call me Betsi, won't you? And
I must tell you that I am not at all afraid of good
spirits. Oh, we have so many at home! Tamara is
queen of them. For if you were not a fairy, how could
you know that the flood was going to last two or three
days longer?"

" There is no magic in that, dear little Betsi, for the
barometer hanging over there against the wall is pointing to continued storms. Moreover, the city archives
16

tell us that the danger always lasts several days when a southwest wind causes the Neva to overflow its bank."

"Well, that certainly is simple enough. So it was no prophecy? But then you said something else—that that gentleman, Sophie's only protector, could not go to her help. Now what barometer told you that?"

"Humph!" Zeneida, pressing her lips together, reflected for a moment, then said, "Do you know who that illustrious person is?"

"Of course I do. Why, how often have I met him at Sophie's and have told him fairy tales! And Sophie has told me everything; things that no one else knows anything about. But I will tell them to you, for people who love each other must have no secrets—don't you think so?"

"Certainly! Well, then, dear child, all this time that illustrious personage has been unable to go to Sophie, because, since the flooding of the Greater Neva, it has been necessary for him to show himself wherever the danger was greatest, in order, by his presence, to stimulate others to the task of assistance and to insure success. Had he, instead of this, gone to Sophie, who lives on the Lesser Neva, there would have been fearful rioting. Do you understand this?"

"Yes, indeed, I understand too well," returned Bethsaba, sorrowfully.

"But to-day they do not allow that illustrious personage to show himself in the inundated streets."

"Who?"

"His advisers."

"Why not?"

"Because they have discovered a plot against his life."

"Oh, how sad!" sighed Bethsaba. Then her mind

flew to the last link of her chain of thought: "A plot against the life of the Czar, and known to Zeneida! From whom could she have obtained the knowledge so quickly? From those two men; but from which?"

Timidly approaching Zeneida, and leaning over her shoulder, she whispered:

"It was not the younger man of the two, was it, who told you?"

"No, no," replied Zeneida, to whom the child's whole soul was revealed. "Fear nothing for him! His hand and heart are clear from it."

"And you are in it?" asked the girl, touching Zeneida's breast with the tip of her finger.

Zeneida was startled by the direct questions. Was it childish curiosity, or had it a deeper meaning? Bethsaba remarked her surprise.

"You see, there can be no secrets where love is. I will tell you all I know, and what hitherto I have told to no one—not even to my godmother, whom I believe I fear more than I love. But you I love so very, very much, and that is why I am going to tell what I know, and how awfully they plot against him. He himself told Sophie. In Petrovsko the rebellious soldiers and peasants would not allow him to go farther; they insulted and threatened him to that degree that he had to turn back. Now these people were ragged and starving, and I can understand their being angry with him? But what complaint have you against him? You are rich, beautiful, and fêted. Why, then, are you one of the conspirators?"

An idea flashed into Zeneida's mind. This child might form the link in the chain that was still wanting.

"Come nearer; let us whisper it, that even the walls do not hear. I, too, love you, and will frankly tell you all I know. I, too, am in the conspiracy, and play an important part in it."

"What reason have you?"

"I am a 'Kalevaine.'"

"And what is a 'Kalevaine'?"

"In Soumalain language, that which you are in the Circassian language. A girl who, when she came into the world, had a home she no longer has, whose nation, then Soumalain, is now known as Finnish. Doubtless you remember as clearly as I do the people and places you were among up to your sixth year, whom you may never look on again, and yet whom you never can forget?"

"Oh, it is true."

"Is it not? Amid all the pomp and splendor the world can give, in the midst of the most brilliant court festivities, do you not feel a sudden pang at heart when the thought of your dark native woods flashes across you; of the horsemen, on their fiery steeds, coursing over the rushing mountain streams; of the blue mountains in the far distance, and your ancestral castle, in which, enthroned, your father received the homage of his vassals?"

"Oh yes, yes."

"And even now you remember the legends told you by the murmuring streams of your native land?"

"You are right; you are right."

"Well, then, you see, so it is with me. My recollections, like the mighty roll of the Imatras, are forever surging in my soul. Just as little can I forget those moss-covered rocks, the most ancient peak in the whole world, the Fata Morgana of our Finnish plains; the red-roofed houses, with low beams across the rooms, from which hung strings of loaves; the legends of Kalevala, and its people's freedom, of which my father used so often to tell me. Then I did not understand all he said; now I recall all and—understand him."

"I, too, recall; but I do not understand it yet."

"The Czar has deprived you, as me, of our father-land; he has deprived our people of their freedom! And, as through him we became orphaned, homeless, so he became a father to us in place of our own fathers. For our little kingdoms he has given us a great one; for our quiet homes, pomp and splendor. As a man, he has been a father to us; as Czar, a tyrant. For the one I cannot be ungrateful to him; for the other I cannot forgive him. So I stand hemmed in by two conflicting duties. As my adopted father, it is my duty to shield his sensitive heart, to protect him from the assassin's dagger, from pain and sickness; but at the same time I am bound to deliver my country from the iron grasp of the tyrant, to snatch from it my people and their freedom. Do you understand?"

"I see you fly before me; but I cannot follow your flight, cannot catch you up. Tell me, is 'he' too in the conspiracy?"

Zeneida knew whom she meant by "he."

"No. He dare not! I will not suffer him to take part in it."

"Oh, then permit me, too, to remain out of it. Had you told me he was in it, I must, too, have been."

"That's right! You shall keep each other out of it. But, all the same, you must stand by me in one part of the hard duty."

"Tell me what I must do! I will obey implicitly."

"Our first thought must be to bring Sophie here, and to acquaint him whose heart is heavy on her account that he need be anxious no longer."

"Will you allow me to be the first to go in to So-phie?"

"You alone; she would not trust any one else."

And Bethsaba could not have desired greater happiness than to be the one privileged to step from the boat on to the balcony of the mysterious house in Petrovsky Garden. The flood had already risen to the balcony, and she it was who might hasten in to the neglected girl and say, "You are saved!"

The poor child was already without provisions or fuel of any description, for everything in the inundated cellar and dining-room was spoiled by water. Wrapped in her furs, she sat at the window, breathing upon it to make a clear space, and gazing with dismay at the huge blocks of ice floating unimpeded over the wrecked fence. Some, with their sharp edges, cut through the great trees opposing them as with a saw; others were tossed lengthwise against their barks, those following hurled upon them, until suddenly a great silver birch would go down with a crash. Once the resistance formed by the trees swept down, the house must follow. A pencil and paper lay prepared upon her writing-table, a carrier-dove in its cage beside it. They had been brought her by the Czar, that she might let him know when danger was imminent.

She was waiting to send off her message until the extreme moment, for she knew the grave difficulties which surrounded his coming to her rescue.

Thus her joy may be imagined on seeing Bethsaba appear on the balcony.

Seizing her pencil, Sophie wrote, with trembling fingers, "I am saved and in good hands; have no further anxiety for me!" Then tying her note on to the carrier-dove's wing, she set it loose. It flew up high in the air, then disappeared in the direction of the Winter Palace.

She did not ask where they were taking her, but followed Bethsaba in good faith.

CHAPTER XXV

GOG AND MAGOG

THE Czar had not undressed at all that night; but, tired out, had thrown himself upon his couch, which had no covering but a bear-skin.

Before sunrise he was up, and, without making a change of dress, went to the window. It was frosted over; he had to open it to see out. He quickly closed it again. The sight was terrible! In feverish excitement he threw on his cloak and hurried out. In the anteroom his physician, Sir James Wylie, was waiting, who at once accosted him with—

"Your Majesty may not go out to-day!"

"I may not? Who commands me?"

"I merely *prescribe*, sire—a right which physicians may exercise towards princes."

"But there is nothing the matter with me."

"But there may be. Your health is endangered."

"That rests in the hands of God." And he passed on.

In the audience-chamber he found Araktseieff.

"Your Majesty *cannot* go out to-day."

"So you, too, order me, as well as the physician."

"Your Majesty's life is in danger."

"Not for the first time. He who protected me yesterday will not fail me to-day. Be a Christian, and do not treat me like a child who lets himself be frightened by old women's tales. Remain at your post; I go to mine."

Araktseieff knew the Czar, and that opposition only made him more obstinate; so stood deferentially aside as the Czar strode past him.

The Czar passed, alone, down the long corridor hung with pictures of the battles he had fought. At the end of it a little negro groom stood waiting with a note, which he handed in silence. It was the Czarina's page, a birthday present to her of long ago. The Czar hurriedly broke open the note and ran it over, then looked down meditatively. Without a word he went back to his apartment and took off his cloak.

The note was from the Czarina: "I am afraid to be alone in the palace. Please do not leave me now!"

The words were a command; one which even the Ruler of All the Russias had no choice but to obey. His wife was afraid!

Now he is condemned to remain within the palace, like any imprisoned criminal.

For the first time for fourteen years his wife had made a request to him. How could he refuse it? Not only his sense of duty as emperor impelled him to repair to scenes of distress and danger, but also he was urged by that mysterious impulse from within, which ever drove him from one end of his empire to the other, leaving him no rest by night, until he would rise, get into his carriage, and drive from street to street. To stay in one place was torture to him. He had but returned this very week from a journey which led him as far as to the Kirghiz steppes. And now was he to sit idly at home? His wife had asked it. It is not much she asks. She does not beg him to come to her

in her apartments, to stay with her, to cheer and comfort her; she only asks him to remain under the same
roof.

Now he has leisure to pace from one end to the other
of his room, to hearken to the pealing of bells, the roar
of the wind, and the splash of the waves, whose surf
dashes up to his windows. Suddenly he utters a cry
—" Where are you, Sophie?" It is well that no one
hears him, that he is alone. In spirit, he is in that solitary house, surrounded by the waves. His eyes search
round the empty rooms where wind and weather sport
unchecked, and, not finding her, he cries, "Sophie!
where are you?" The vision he had called up was
even more terrible than the awful reality of raging
nature without. He could better bear to look upon
that. Rushing to the balcony of the palace, he tore
open the glass doors, and gazed down upon the ghastly
devastation. The sight was awful indeed!

Wide as an ocean bay, the giant river was rolling
back its waves upon Lake Ladoga. Ever and anon
from out the misty distance loomed visions reflected in
the surface of the madly rushing waters.

When Napoleon, watching the fire of Moscow from
the Kremlin, saw how the storm was rolling the sea of
flame upon the city, he cried in despair, "But what
wind is this?" So now Alexander, as he watched the
waves, lashed by the furious storm, dash up against his
palace, asked, "But what wind is this?"

Houses roofless and in ruins; half - naked creatures
clinging to their framework; here, a tiny hand raised
in piteous appeal from its mother's arms; there, a man
rowing with a plank, who finds no place to land on.
Every gust of wind, every wave, brings some fresh sight
to view. Now comes the remnant of a menagerie; its

cages, chained together, are being whirled about in eddying circles. A Bengal tiger, who has burst his bonds, dashes wildly from one cage to another. Some men, clinging to the bars, dare not climb on to the top for fear of the infuriated animal. All must perish. Men and beasts shriek and roar in chorus. The waves dash them pitilessly on. Then comes the fragment of a wooden bridge wedged in between two icebergs. Upon it there still stands a carriage, shafts in air, from the interior of which projects a pink dress. Bridge and carriage float past, a flock of croaking ravens flying about them.

Who is sufficient for all these horrors?

The current swept on, swift as an arrow, the waves playing with their icy barriers ; now building them into pyramids, now tearing them down, leaving a circling eddy to mark the spot.

Close by the Winter Palace stands the Admiralty, with its copper roof. The furious storm, tearing off a portion of this, rolls it up, with thunderous din, like a sheet of paper, flattens it out again, tosses it into the air, showering down fragments of it like a pack of cards; then, finally, rips off the whole remainder of the roof, hurling it into the principal square. Then follows many thousand casks of flour, sugar, and spices from the flooded warehouses of the Exchange—the whole winter store of a great capital a prey to the waves!

Again another picture. Arrayed in order of battle like a flotilla come a series of black boats, not originally designed to carry their inmates over the water, but under the earth. Coffins ! The flood had burst the walls of the military cemetery of Smolenskaja, washed up thousands of graves, and was now bringing back their occupants to the city, of which they had long ago taken farewell. The buried warriors were coming to march

past the Czar once more—the hurricane their deafening
trumpets, the waves their kettle - drums! They even
bring their memorial chapel with them, and their marble crosses, which tower in ghostly fashion from out the
icebergs!

Nor is the fearful cyclorama over yet. The horrors
of it are ever increasing. In the distance looms a three-
master, bearing down upon the city — or, rather, in the
cold gray mist it looks the ghost of a man-of-war. It
had broken its moorings at Cronstadt in the gale, and
now, driven before the wind, was coming down upon the
city at full speed!

At that moment the Czar, forgetful of his dignity, hid
his face and wept, never thinking whether any eyes were
upon him. And many eyes were on him.

All those whom in the course of the previous night
the Czar had rescued from the tottering houses in the
suburbs — all those who, taken unawares in the tumult
of the fair, did not know where to turn, the Czar had
lodged in the western division of the Winter Palace,
giving up that brilliant suite of rooms to the use of the
poor and destitute. Such guests as these the Winter
Palace had never harbored before! True, at New-year
it was the custom for some forty thousand guests to assemble in the Winter Palace; but they swept the floors
with silk, and illuminated the marble halls with their
diamonds. Now, however, it was the show-place for rags
and tatters. An exhibition of misery and destitution!
There were collected together all those who form the
shady side of a capital, and of whom the fashionable
world have no conception — an aggregate of bitter
want and of shameless depravity. They who did not
dare to creep forth by day from their dark cellars have
given each other rendezvous in the Imperial Palace.

The Czar sent them food and drink, and they spent the night singing the *Knife Song*, taught them by the frequenters of the Bear's Paw.

Czar Alexander heard it, and doubtless rejoiced to know his guests were in such good-humor. They opened their windows, and those in front put their heads out, and called to the others to tell them what they saw.

The façade of the Winter Palace had two projecting wings. The refugees were housed in the west wing. Between that and the east, like the middle stroke of the capital letter E, stretched the covered balcony from which the Czar had watched the panorama of destruction.

On seeing him his guests became mute.

He was an imposing figure, with expansive forehead bared to the fury of the storm. As long as he remained impassive his self-control communicated itself to the spectators. But when they saw him break down and shed tears, when they saw that the Czar was but a man after all, they grew furious. Weakness arouses indignation.

A man, brother to the French republican Marat, seizing his opportunity, sprang upon the window-sill and shouted to the Czar:

"Yes, you may cry! Cry for the loss of your fine city! The God of vengeance has sent this destruction upon us as a penalty for your sins! Plague, drought, starvation—all have come upon us through you! For you are deaf to the cry of our glorious brothers the Greeks! Their innocent blood that has been shed cries out to Heaven for vengeance! You are the cause of this devastation! Heaven is punishing us for what you have done!"

The noisy voices of the people within drowned the

concluding words; their yells outvied the storm. The mutinous speech had stirred up the already excited people to fury. The refrain of the *Song of the Knife* resounded to an accompaniment of infuriated noise and confusion. They tried to burst open the strong doors communicating with the corridor leading to the Czar's apartments.

He, standing on the balcony, was rooted to the spot by a double terror—behind him the yelling populace clamoring for his blood; before him the approaching ship. It was one of the largest men-of-war in the navy. When frozen up in the winter the crew is paid off, and the few men left in charge had evidently escaped, so that it came along without guidance of any kind, and was apparently making direct for the Winter Palace.

At the sound of raised and fierce voices every window in the central portion of the palace opened suddenly, displaying a treble row of bayonets. At one of the windows stood Araktseieff, who shouted in his cruel, harsh voice to the rebels:

"Silence, instantly, you cubs of Gog and Magog, or I will have you cast back into the flood from which your sovereign lord saved you! Ungrateful savages that ye are!"

This was adding oil to the flames.

"Oh, oh, Araktseieff!" roared a thousand throats. "There's the evil genius!"

"Come on!" screamed Marat. "Let's just see if your thousand bayonets can conquer our ten thousand knives! Make a beginning, or we will!"

The ship came nearer and nearer.

As it reached within half a cable's length of the Winter Palace, the Czar perceived a man in the wheel-house turning the wheel.

"What are you about, man?" he shouted down angrily to him.

The man knew perfectly what he was about. It was Borbotuseff, a naval officer and a deserter. How came he on board? No one knew. He steered straight for the palace, with the one hope of crashing into it, in order that all within, and he himself, might be buried under it. A red flag was flying from the mast.

The struggling crowd and the guards saw nothing of all this; the balcony gallery cut off their view.

Now the moment had come to prove which was the stronger, the house of wood or the house of stone.

But the current was stronger than either, and instead of the bow of the ship striking the palace, it came broadside on. It drew so much water that its keel crashed on to the granite coping of the moat, throwing the vessel on its side; while, like a knight in a tournament with outstretched lance, it struck with its masts upon its stony adversary. A terrific crashing and grinding—two of the masts broke to pieces against the pillars; the third crashed through one of the windows, shaking the whole massive structure from foundation to gable, yet the stone remained conqueror. The ponderous vessel broke in two; the bow half of the wreck was hurled on to Alexanderplatz; the afterpart, with the helmsman, fell back into the vortex, and was carried away with the current.

The concussion was like an earthquake. Of a sudden there was silence. People, soldiers, even Araktseieff, fell upon their knees. The man upon the balcony alone remained standing. He had seen something in the air. It was a dove.

The dove flew direct to him, hovered for a moment, and then alighted on his shoulder.

It was Sophie's carrier-dove.

Alexander found the letter under its wing, telling him that Sophie was in good keeping. Then, folding his hands in a prayer of thanksgiving, he raised them to Heaven.

But the dove is the sacred and wonder-working bird of Russia.

As it descended upon the shoulder of the Czar the fury of the people changed to superstitious worship. In it they saw the embodiment of the Holy Ghost. He who would not be lost must be converted. It was a miracle from Heaven.

Bozse czarja chrani! An old mujik suddenly started the hymn of praise, and all present joined in it. Araktseieff's bayonets had become unnecessary. Marat's brother, leaving the rostrum, disappeared among the multitude. Who could have found him among the ten thousand there gathered? And even if they had he would have denied his identity.

The flood lasted two days longer, leaving behind it three thousand houses totally wrecked and a countless list of dead.

The people firmly believed that Heaven's judgment had been wrought because the Czar had not come to the assistance of the Greeks in their War of Independence.

CHAPTER XXVI

UNDER THE PALMS

WITHOUT, ten degrees of cold, raging storm, flood, devastation, misery, revolution, scenes of horror. The palms knew nothing of all this. Upon the great, high elevation, under its glazed roof, reigned perpetual spring,

where huge lamps with ground-glass globes replaced
sunshine. And the tropical world suffered itself to be
deceived. King-ferns, brought hither from the East,
forgot that they were not growing in their native soil,
and that they were putting forward leaves, never blossoms. The soil beneath them was heated with hot-air
pipes and enriched by artificial aid.

And in this artificial garden of the tropics children
were playing who had forgotten that their fathers and
mothers were far away, perhaps not even caring. Here
they neither got blows nor were hungry; but danced
round the "mulberry-bush" and sang. Two beautiful
young ladies — wards of the Queen of the Fairies—
looked after them, just as in fairy tales.

Bethsaba had now a real true fairy tale to tell of her
miraculous rescue from the terrible dangers; the sudden
appearance of the handsome knight in her extremity,
how his beautiful eyes, his look of daring, his heroic
stature—

Sophie grew quite anxious to see him.

"You will soon see him, he is sure to come, he promised me he would. Still it does seem to be a long time
before he keeps his word!"

"He is not, on any account, to know who I am," said
Sophie. "It is to be kept secret here. Our hostess
wishes it."

"Then we will only call you Sophie."

"It is singular that we three have only one Christian name; neither you, nor I, nor Zeneida bear our
mother's names in addition, as is usual among us. I
cannot understand it."

"Nor I."

"Here he comes!"

"How do you know?"

" I know his footstep."

And, in truth, he came. Zeneida brought him in, more wet and muddy than the time before. His hair dishevelled; his face reddened by the cold wind. Withal, so handsome!

Bethsaba had told Sophie that here, too, a conspiracy was on foot; but that "he" was not in it. Who else, then? Sophie only believes what she sees.

"Come, come, Pushkin!" exclaimed Zeneida, with strangely radiant look. Relate again, fully, what you have already told me."

And Pushkin recounted all that had happened at the Winter Palace, of which he had been an eye-witness, with the enthusiasm of a poet inspired by the catastrophe.

The second girl was a stranger to him. Had he known who she was he would not have described with such poetic warmth the stirring scene when the Czar stood bareheaded, the storm raging round him, menaced alike by the fury of people and the fast-approaching vessel.

She listened tremblingly to his recital, drinking in his every word with feverish anxiety, the varying expression of his face reflected in hers; her lips seeming mutely to repeat what he was saying. Shudderingly she hid her face when the ship collided with the palace! She felt the force of the shock, and staggered under it.

When Pushkin went on to tell about the dove—her dove—how it descended on to the shoulders of her father, the Czar, with what joy the august ruler had raised his hands to heaven, and how with one voice the hymn of praise had burst forth from the lips of the rebellious people, the poor, overwrought girl's nerves could endure no more; with a cry of joy she threw herself into Bethsaba's arms, laughing and crying hysterically.

17

Pushkin, attributing her excitement to the power of his poetic delineation, was not a little proud of his success.

"But is all danger over now?" faltered Sophie, venturing to raise her tearful eyes to the young man's face.

He, not understanding the question, answered :

"The danger is not over yet, although the storm is certainly lessening, and, once lulled, the Neva will return to its bed ; but until then much damage may yet ensue."

"It was not that I meant ; but if he is still in any danger—he, the Czar !"

Pushkin was amazed. What interest could this girl, Bethsaba's friend, feel in the Czar?

"Danger at the hand of man cannot assail him, for Araktseieff has taken the most stringent measures for his protection. All those who were given shelter in the Winter Palace are being transferred to the Admiralty. Nay ; at such a time his very foes, even had he any, would be the first to protect him."

"How can that be ?" she asked, and waited for Pushkin's answer with the devout attention with which, in former times, the answers of the Oracle were received.

A secret instinct told Pushkin that he must answer in all sincerity.

"Because the feeling of ' humanity ' is stronger than that of 'love of freedom.' It protects alike the serf when persecuted by the Czar, and the Czar when persecuted by the serf !"

The two girls heaved a deep sigh of relief into the air, weighted with these significant words.

"You are laying cruel waste in these two hearts," whispered Zeneida in Pushkin's ear. "You had better go back to your work."

"And you have not brought me the presents you promised ?" asked Bethsaba, sorrowfully.

"I had not forgotten them; but from early morning we were busy trying to make fast the wreck; there must have been some one on board cutting through our ropes as fast as we threw them. And so I had no time to think of saving little children."

"When next you make a promise do not forget it," returned she, in tone of aggrieved reproach.

Pushkin could not understand her. Why that tone? How should he understand it? He promised to come again that evening to bring her good news, and something besides.

Neither she nor Zeneida had told him who the other girl was. Zeneida now took both girls into her boudoir. The time was approaching when she would be receiving many visitors whom it was not expedient for them to see.

The catastrophe offered favorable opportunity to the "Szojusz Blagadenztoiga" to hold uninterrupted sittings. There was to be a meeting of "the green book" to-day.

The two girls managed to find a "green book" for themselves. They searched about in Zeneida's boudoir until they found Pushkin's poem, *The Gypsy Girl*. This, of course, they had not read before; for, according to the dictum of "good" society in Russia, a well-bred girl up to her fifteenth year may indeed *see*, but not read, romances. Moreover, that poem was not to be had in print, only manuscript. Alexander Pushkin had created quite a distinct calling which had never existed before, that of transcriber. In every town were men who made a livelihood by copying out Pushkin's verses, sold, despite the Censor, by the booksellers. (There are still many houses in which only written copies of the works of the Russian poet Petösy are to be found.)

The two girls now eagerly snatched at the forbidden

fruit. First Bethsaba read it to Sophie; then Sophie
to Bethsaba. The third time they read it together as a
duet.

Then they conferred the name of its hero, "Aleko,"
upon the author. And when they wanted to speak of
him called him only "Aleko." And it fitted — only
the other way about. Aleko had wandered among the
gypsies (gypsy, poet, or bohemian being synonymous);
this gypsy or poet had wandered among princesses.
That evening Herr Aleko came, bringing cheering news.
The storm had subsided, and the water had fallen a
span; although it must be some time before it resumed
its proper level, for it stretched away eight versts on
either bank.

("Oh that it may last ever so long!" beat the heart
of each maiden, secretly.)

He had, moreover, brought something for Bethsaba
—a little doll, such as he had promised her, but not a
little muddy doll in rags, but a lovely, gayly dressed,
sweet little doll, made of sugar. There were no others
to be had; all the others had melted. Pushkin expected the girl to laugh at his offering; but she took the
matter seriously, accepted it with greatest solemnity,
placed it in her bosom, and it was evident that she was
not sorry to see Sophie just a tiny bit jealous of her.
Pushkin was not slow to see that he must be careful,
so he sought in his pockets until he found something
worth offering.

"See, fair Sophie"—he did not know her other name'
—"I have something for you, too. You showed a special
interest in the Czar this morning. Here is a piece of
copper from the vessel that ran into the Winter Palace."

Thankfully it was received. The platinum mines of
the Ural had never produced so precious a piece of ore.

"He can be no conspirator," whispered Sophie to Bethsaba.

"Decidedly not," whispered Bethsaba back.

"The storm has quite gone down," said Zeneida. "The bells have left off ringing. This will be a quieter night than those we have been having of late. Goodnight, Pushkin. If you do not hurry you will find your boat running aground."

The girls would not have minded if the water had not gone down so fast.

Zeneida despatched Pushkin home, and the girls to their beds. She was responsible for their good health.

But it was long before they could settle to sleep. They had so much to say about Aleko. They had made up quite a different ending to the poem than the real one: the gypsy girl was not to have been faithless, but if she were, Aleko should have despised her and have found a more faithful love. The gypsy girl should have implored his pardon on her knees, and he should have forgiven her, but not have driven her away from him. In a word, they made Aleko what they fain would have had him to be.

Zeneida, who slept in the next room, several times admonished them to go to sleep. Then they would be quiet as mice, the next moment to begin whispering again. At last her regular breathing proved Sophie, at least, to have fallen asleep. Bethsaba could not sleep; her heart beat so violently that, despite the prayers she said, midnight found her still awake. Suddenly it seemed to her as if the occupant of the next room had risen, and with light footsteps had gone out into the room beyond. The night was still. Neither sound of carriage-wheels nor patrol disturbed the quiet of the inundated streets. From a distant apartment rose a psalm, sung in a woman's voice, low and sorrowful :

"In every hour of grief and pain,
　To Thee for help I crave ;
O Thou to whom none cry in vain,
　Be present now to save."

Who was singing at that late hour? What grief could oppress her in this house? Bethsaba drew the bed-clothes over her head to quiet her trembling.

Three days longer the two girls spent under Zeneida's protecting care -- that is, it was not until then that Princess Ghedimin ventured to return from Peterhof, or that the slime-covered ground-floor and cellars of the little dwelling in Petrovsky Garden could be cleansed and thoroughly aired by old Helenka. The girls mean-while were living Elysian days. When Zeneida told them that they could now go to their homes, Bethsaba sighed :

"When I came here I thought I was coming to the infernal regions ; now I feel as if I were being turned out of Paradise !"

They saw Pushkin daily, had talks with him, and de-lighted in the great, noble soul which lay like an open book before them. Even earthly joys have their reve-lations, awaking super-earthly joy when they cease to be felt in secret. When the girls were alone Aleko was the sole subject of their talk. Bethsaba thought she must love Sophie the more for holding Aleko in such high esteem ; yet she had not, even yet, breathed a word to her friend of her love for him. At first, she had thought, it would be an easy thing to tell. But· the secret of a first love is refractory ; it will not come forth from its concealment. She delayed her confession; guarding her secret like some hidden treasure; dissembled her love for him, or, at least, learned to belie her feelings that she might not betray the happiness that took possession of her at sight of him. Her blushes she ascribed to headache, though, in reality, her head was innocent of any such discomfort.

But at the moment of parting the confession must be made. She would whisper it to her friend in few words, then run away.

When their sedan-chairs actually arrived—no carriages could yet be used—the two friends could scarce make up their minds to part. They had ever fresh confidences to whisper to each other; they wept and laughed, and quarrelled for the sake of making it up again. They talked together in a language which they two only understood; they promised to meet again very soon; they gave each other the parting kiss, then began to chatter again. Zeneida watched them attentively.

At length the declaration must come. With the last, very last, kiss the bomb must burst.

"I love Aleko—until death."

This Sophie whispered into Bethsaba's ear, then ran away.

Zeneida saw the rosy glow suffusing the cheeks of the departing girl and the deathly pallor overspreading those of her who remained, as though the one had stolen the life-glow from the other. Bethsaba stood where she had left her, white, motionless, with sunken head, and arms hanging lifeless at her side.

Zeneida at once divined the secret. She went up to her, but hardly had she taken the girl's hands in hers when, falling before her, bitterly weeping, the poor child hid her face in Zeneida's dress.

"Oh, why did you bring me here?"

Zeneida raised her.

"Stand up. Do not cry. He will be yours."

"What! I take him from her?"

"Humph! Were it only 'her' you had to take him from— But do not be troubled. Love him; you alone deserve his love."

The poor child shook her head sorrowfully. Now she understood the meaning of "love," and with it what "jealousy" and "resignation" meant.

CHAPTER XXVII

PANACEA

GREAT natural calamities often have a softening effect upon excited masses.

The "great power," the people, and the "little master," the Emperor, made friends again in the general distress.

The storm of November, 1824, had been a universal calamity. History knows no other so wide-spreading in its devastating effects. Not only did it lay St. Petersburg in ruins, but it raged throughout Asia and inundated the shores of California. Sailors saw the clear sea in mid-ocean thick with mud and slime; from India to Syria flourishing towns were laid in the dust by earthquakes; volcanoes burst forth in the Greek Archipelago; in Germany many springs were dried up. The whole world was in a state of upheaval. It was no time to think of revolutions.

Political secret societies changed themselves into philanthropic unions. Party spirit died out. The poor

went unhesitatingly to claim relief from the rich, and
the doors of the rich were ungrudgingly opened to them.
The incitements of the "Irreconcilables" found no
fruitful ground. Prince Ghedimin and Araktsejeff vied
with each other in their efforts to relieve the distress
of the people. Each impartially scattered his hundred
thousand of rubles abroad : the one forgetting that his
aim had been to free, the other to oppress, the people.
The people now were in need of neither sword nor
chains—only of bread.

Nor were the ladies of St. Petersburg backward in re-
lieving the distress caused by the inundations. Princess
Ghedimin presented her diamonds to the committee, the
sale of which brought them in thirty thousand rubles,
while Zeneida gave a concert at the Exchange for the
sufferers, the tickets for which sold for enormous prices,
and which realized forty thousand rubles. Prince Ghedimin presented his wife with diamonds double the value
of those she had given away. Zeneida received a wreath
of laurel from the *jeunesse dorée* of St. Petersburg and
an ode from Pushkin. Thus once more had Korynthia
lost the game, and her adversary had triumphed.

Those days of tribulation had made the Czar more
reserved than ever. His melancholy had dated from
the day on which he had witnessed the burning of Moscow, his capital ; and now it had been his fate to witness the ruin of his second capital. One had been
destroyed by fire, the other by water. Waking and
sleeping, the dread visions were before him.

But the saddest sight to him of all was that pale
child's face, to which nothing brought animation. One
day he said to Sir James Wylie :

" It is vain to try and cure me ; my sickness lies within, not without. Cure Sophie, and I shall be cured."

.The physician was silent.

"Tell me frankly.   Have you no hope ?"

" None."

" Has your medical skill absolutely no panacea, no
remedy to preserve a precious life to us — no remedy
which day by day might arrest Death hovering on the
threshold, and so prolong that dear life from spring to
autumn ?"

" Yes, there is such a remedy, sire !   But it does not
grow among health-giving herbs of India.   In illnesses
such as these the spirits of the patient are the most important factor.   Sorrow, grief, and care hasten the catastrophe, while cheerfulness, an equable temperament, joy,
and hope delay it.   The love of life renews life."

" Humph !   How am I to give her joy, hope, and love
of life when I have not got them myself?"

A day came which brought joy to the Czar.

His Governor in the Urals announced to him the discovery of new deposits of gold and platinum, with promise of abundant mining.   He sent a specimen of the platinum that had been found.   A truly valuable discovery!

At the same time arrived a report from the Governor
of Jekaterinograd, notifying the discovery in the great
desert of a species of beetle which fed on the exuber-
ant knot-grass (*poligonum*) of those parts, a useless plant
and one impossible to extirpate.   The beetle in question, known in the learned tongue as *Coccus polonorum*,
is identical with the cochineal, and affords the most
beautiful purple and pink dye.   He sent the Czar, as a
sample, a piece of rose-colored silk dyed with the purple
of the native beetle.

This was a greater treasure even than gold and platinum ; it grows like a weed, gives no trouble, and will
support the inhabitants of those inhospitable steppes.

But the third consignment was the most interesting. The Governor of the Amurs sent from Siberia a cask of wine grown in the Amur country. This is a still greater treasure than gold or bread, for it implies a triumph—a triumph in the face of the whole world, which proclaims Siberia to be a frozen hell! See! this wine contradicts it! It is more sparkling than champagne, sweeter than Tokay—at least, one must pretend that it is. Siberia can grow wine! Henceforth every Russian must drink it. Siberian wine must supplant foreign wines for the tables of the great; it must compete with Burgundy, the Rhine, and the Hegyalji. To be exiled to Siberia will no longer count as a punishment; those in search of fruitful soil will settle there of their own free-will. Siberia can grow wine! If any one doubts the future of that country, who would argue with him now? One gives him a glass and fills it. " Try this; this is Siberian wine!"

The Czar was as happy as a child! He still had one joy left.

And he hurried off, on the strength of it, to the Petrowsky Garden house. He had the platinum, the silk, and the cask of wine brought after him, thinking that what gladdened him must also gladden Sophie. The poor child was looking very pale ; she was not allowed to go out at all in the winter; the cold air out-of-doors was rapid poison to her; the heated air within-doors slow poison. A strange country, where the invalid cannot even love his home! He hates the sky which kills him and the earth which keeps him bound. It is the survival of the fittest; if a man be strong enough to enjoy a winter in Russia he thrives ; if not, he dies.

In every Russian lady's drawing-room is a special corner fitted up called the " Altana."

It is a space surrounded by a little railing grown with ivy and containing a bower of Southern plants and flowers which, during the long nine months of winter, thrive and blossom in the artificial light and warmth of lamps and stove, and make one forget the rigorous weather outside.

Alexander had had such a fragrant orange grove fitted up for Sophie when the house had been put in order for her after the inundation.   He had not been to see her since the court gardener had carried out his instructions; perhaps it had given her pleasure.

Alas! nothing gave her pleasure.

The Czar asked, "What is amiss with you, my darling?"

"An unspeakable sorrow."

To cheer her, he showed her the treasures he had brought with him—the ore, silk, and wine.   But her face did not brighten, she did not smile.   To his good news she had but "How nice! how fortunate!   Oh, thank you!" to say.

"Come, tell me, what is amiss with you?   There is something more than bodily illness; it is mental trouble. Tell me, what is grieving you?   To whom should you tell it if not to me?   Who shall place confidence in me if you do not feel it?"

Then, throwing her arms round her father's neck, and drawing his head down to her, Sophie whispered, very low:

"It is love!"   .

Then, drawing back with abrupt movement, she buried her face in her hands.

Astonished, the Czar asked, "But where can you have met any one to fall in love with?"

"The flood brought us together."

"And who is the man?"

"If you speak so angrily I shall not dare to tell you."

"It is not anger but excitement that made me speak so sharply. He whom you love is forgiven everything."

"Really? You do not forbid me to love somebody?"

"If only he is worthy of you. What is his rank?"

"An officer of the Body Guard."

"I will give him a regiment and make him a prince, so that he may ask you in marriage."

"Let me kiss you for that! But do not give him anything, father. Let him remain as he is; I love him for what he is now, and want him always to remain the same. He is more than a prince, more than a general! Higher far than they—"

"Who is it, then?"

"Well, Aleko."

"What Aleko?"

"Oh! do you not know his name? Then stoop down and I will whisper it in your ear."

The Czar drew her to him.

"Would you like to be his wife?"

For all answer the girl looked at him with eyes opened wide and radiant expression.

"Would you like to be his wife?"

"What else could I desire? Poor little foundling as I am, I should be happy indeed to have such a prospect. And we would be so happy together. Aleko would not murder me for my faithlessness. But how can we let him know? So far, he has not had permission to come here."

"From this time forth he shall."

"But who can tell him?"

"I, myself. I will bring him to you."

"You are as good a father as in one of Bethsaba's fairy tales."

"I will see myself to all the preparations, will arrange your dowry, settle the day, and command the Patriarch of Solowetshk here to celebrate the marriage."

"Oh yes, in summer, when the roses are out. My bridal wreath shall be of real roses."

"I will have your wedding ornaments made from this nugget of platinum. And now you really are as happy as I am, are you not?"

"Oh, happier!"

"And will you have this pink silk for your wedding-dress?"

"You have just guessed my wish—that my wedding-dress should be pink. White makes one look pale, and I am pale enough without that."

"This wine from the Amur we will drink at your wedding-breakfast."

"And I too will taste it. We will drink to each other. ' As many drops in this goblet, so many years our love shall last!' Is not that the saying?"

"Then you shall take up your residence on his estate. How strange that I should have just given him back his confiscated property! He shall have his ancestral castle put in order for you to live in, and I will come and visit you constantly."

Sophie clapped her hands with delight, her pale cheeks aglow. Then suddenly the light in her eyes died away.

"But is all this only joking?"

"Joking? Do I ever joke with you?"

"That Aleko should pay court to me, that you should give me to him for wife, that the Patriarch should marry us on a lovely day in the lovely month of roses. Is it not all a dream?"

Alexander, instead of answering, took her in his arms and closed her mouth with kisses.

Yes, poor child, it is real. The only unreal part of
it is that before those roses shall have blossomed you
will be—

Alexander commanded Pushkin to his presence that
day, and made short work of the matter.

"You have caused a young girl to fall in love with
you. You must marry her. Her name is Sophie Narishkin. Wait upon me to - morrow evening at six
o'clock. I will take you to her, that you may formally
ask her hand. You will then visit her daily, and see
that you endeavor to cause her no sorrow. Her life
hangs on the slightest thread; that thread is in your
hands. Beware that you are not the cause of her death."

Pushkin was in a very awkward situation.

The hand of the Czar's favorite daughter was offered
him—to him, the conspirator, the Constitutionalist, the
sworn enemy of the tyrannical Czar. He was to ask a
girl in marriage who was in love with him, whom he
pitied and admired but did not love. That girl's life
hung on the hope of becoming his wife; with the extinction of that hope the feeble spark of life within her
would be extinguished. Merely to breathe "I do not
love you" would suffice to kill her. And what made
his position the more difficult was the circumstance
that at Sophie's he would be constantly meeting that
other girl whom he looked upon as his betrothed, Sophie's only friend, Bethsaba, to whom he had given
his whole soul. Two hearts to be thus stricken and
betrayed!

What bitter punishment for past frivolity brought back
upon his own head! But there was no turning back.
We are in Russia, and when the Czar commands there
is no option but to obey.

The next day Alexander himself took Pushkin to

Sophie. The betrothal took place in his presence. Pushkin was able to convince himself that the heart intrusted to him was a treasure far above the merits of any sublunary being. He learned that there can be an ideal bliss infinitely more sublime than any earthly enjoyment utterly without sensual passion—a magic of sympathy which is not dependent upon the power of possession; that spiritual attraction is stronger even than love. It was to him as though one of those angelic souls already floating heavenward were drawing him thither in its train.

A few weeks later Sir James Wylie said to the Czar: "Princess Sophie's health is improving visibly."
"I have found the panacea!" was the reply.

CHAPTER XXVIII

THE WEDDING PRESENT

As Alexander had said, so it was. His health was in close sympathy with that of his daughter. With the return of color to her cheeks his spirits revived. Once more he busied himself with affairs of state. In his study were whole piles of unsigned papers from various departments and of letters through the "St. Sophie" post-box. He set to work upon them, and the mountain of papers was soon hugely diminished. The Sophien-post was a singular institution of Alexander's. In Czarskoje Zelo was an office where any one might give in letters to be delivered direct to the Czar. The official demanded ten rubles a letter, but asked no questions either as to the writer or its contents, whether of complaint, petition, accusation, calumniation of those in office, or favorable mention, or schemes for a new constitution of the empire. One hour later it was in the Czar's hands were he in St. Petersburg, or was sent after him if he were travelling.

The surest sign of his improvement in health and spirits was that he ceased to tear through the streets at night, and supped on the first holiday evening with the Czarina, having decided to communicate the happy tidings to her. Elisabeth was the first to hear it. The Patriarch himself had only been informed that on the 21st of June he was to be at the late Czar Peter's residence on Petrowsky Island, where he would find a young couple waiting to be married.

Meanwhile, every petition addressed to the Czar's clemency was being granted. Exiles were allowed to come home, political prisoners released from prison.

It was not in vain that Pushkin had sacrificed his love. His tenderness charmed back to Sophie's lips the smile of happiness which is so delusively like that of health. And that smile charmed a bright, cloudless sky over the whole empire. When he came, punctual to the minute, with his bouquets of flowers, and, with some pretty compliment about the improved looks of the girl hurrying to meet him, would sit down beside her and begin telling her the news, Pushkin was making the happiness of an empire. Or did he ask about her last night's dreams and tell their meaning; or play cards with her, letting her win and himself be laughed at; or read poems and romances to her; bring her the first hothouse fruit or delicate bonbons; watch her somewhat inartistic attempts at drawing and painting, oft stealing a kiss the while, and getting his hair pulled for it—then a whole empire was in sunshine!

18

This even the unfortunates on the far-off Baikal Lake, who break stones in Bleiberg mines, experienced; for every kiss pressed on Sophie's brow the fetters on a pair of hands were loosed.

The Czar, who purposely came to her late, after Pushkin had gone, always found her luxuriating in bliss. Her talk would be all of Pushkin, and of all he had told her.

Sometimes they talked about politics. Sophie induced Pushkin to confess what was the exact object of the secret society she had heard about. And, like an engaged man should, Pushkin candidly told her that what they wanted was a parliamentary constitution; that among them there was many a man who could speak as well as the members of the English House of Commons, and who ought to have the right to be heard. The government would then find a majority composed of Tartars, Kirghis, Kalmucks, Jakutes, Bashkir, and Finnish deputies, who would outvote the Russian revolutionists, and the country would be tranquillized. That parliament should have the control of the exchequer, so that in the case of a minister peculating he might be sent about his business, and, at least, give others the chance to do the same. Freedom of the press was also necessary, so that they might go to loggerheads among themselves instead of growling in an undertone. That was what they hoped to arrive at. The Czar was infinitely amused when he heard of it all, taking it very differently from what he did when Araktseieff told him the same things.

People began to think that the good· times were coming back. Some ten years ago they had ventured to talk of constitutional liberty in presence of the Czar, and the meetings of free masonic lodges were openly announced in the daily papers.

The improvement in Sophie's health deceived even the doctors; the bad symptoms had entirely disappeared. Miracles do happen sometimes! The power of nature is inexhaustible! Preparations for the wedding began in earnest. The Czar had the bride's trousseau, including the pink-silk gown and platinum diadem, sent from Paris, and had the satisfaction of revelling in Sophie's radiant face on seeing all the lovely things.

One day the Czar said to Pushkin:

"My son, if God permits us to live to that happy day, which will also be a turning-point in my life, what shall I give you for a wedding present?"

And Pushkin, falling on his knees, said:

"Father, on that day give your subjects a constitution."

The Czar was silent. This gave Pushkin courage to continue.

"Your Majesty, the whole world is in a state of ferment, and preparing for eruption, like Vesuvius. The volcanic eruption can be avoided by a roll of paper inscribed with the single word 'Charta'! Not I alone, but your whole country, every honest man, every patriot, every one about the throne, thinks and says the same. Do not grant us immediate freedom, do not remodel our country on foreign lines; but lead your people gradually, step by step, towards freedom; suffer the constitution to be shaped according to the habits and needs of your people. But do away with serfdom! Banish Araktsejeff, who stands like an evil genius between you and the people. Take the education of the masses out of the hands of the Sacred Synod, and restore it to Galitzin. Call the notables of the land to your throne-room, and command them to speak out candidly to you. Do away with the censorship, and grant permission to every man to publish his thoughts to the light of day; dismiss the dishonest stewards, who are robbing you and the country. Annul the military colonies, which are a very pest of oppression in the land; summon the old regiments, give them back their standards, unite them in a camp, put us at their head, and send us to the rescue of our Greek brothers in arms, who are drowning in a sea of their own blood. You will see what a nation is capable of when, in possession of freedom herself, she is fighting for the independence of other nations—how she would rise above all others! Oh, give us freedom, and we will give you glory!"

The Czar listened to the end, then said:

"Rise! I forgive you your audacious words!"

Some day later Araktseieff set off, very quietly, for his country estate, Grusino. It was whispered that, at his own request, he had been granted a long leave of absence. His departure was emphasized the more by Prince Ghedimin being chosen as his successor. He was now among the confidential *entourage* of the Czar, who might approach him, at any hour, without being announced.

More still took place. Magriczki, the most detested member of the Council of Enlightenment, was dismissed, and younger censors were appointed instead of the old ones. It was also known that the Russian Ambassador at the Porte had received instructions to energetically promote a more humane system of warfare against the Greeks in their War of Independence. It was also decided to form a camp instantly in the vicinity of Bender.

Finally—clear sign of a new epoch—all the regiments of the guards were recalled from the military colonies and concentrated in St. Petersburg.

These events filled the apostles of freedom with new hopes. The Secret Society of the North decided, on these lines, to support the Czar by all the means in their power, although the leaders of that society were not misled. Pestel sent word to Ghedimin: "It is all a comedy! They want to make fools of us ; the whole business will only last three months. I shall stick to my plan !" But the Bear's Paw by degrees lost all its associates, and the sole use Jakuskin found for his knife at that time was to pick his teeth with.

Pushkin, meanwhile, devoted himself completely to his duties as bridegroom and to versifying. He wrote a charming poem under the title of *The Spring of Bak-tshisseraj*, which he read aloud first to Sophie. And the milder censorship made its publication easy.

When the Czar was informed that the poem had been submitted to the Censor—of course such an event had to be notified to the Czar—he said to Pushkin :

"I advise you to dedicate your poem to a certain lady."

"To my betrothed ?"

"No. To the Princess Ghedimin."

Pushkin understood the hint. It was desirable in some manner to pay court to Sophie's mother. This was the most natural way.

The Czar added:

"When you take her your poem, tell her that on the 21st of June you will celebrate your marriage with So-phie Narishkin."

That, too, was quite *en règle*. Pushkin needed no ex-planation. The bridegroom-elect must himself take Korynthia the tidings of Sophie Narishkin's approach-ing marriage, and receive from her the kiss of consent. The wooing and consent would be expressed in the form of the dedication of the poem and its acceptance. The form was delicate, yet expressive. Both think differently and speak differently; it was a wooing under poetical guise.

Pushkin was quite up to the proprieties in first seeking out Prince Ghedimin.

"Ivan Maximovitch, I have written a new poem, which I should greatly like to dedicate to the Princess Maria Alexievna Korynthia. May I beg you to read it, and if you deem it worthy of the honor of bearing the Princess's name to be my advocate with her?"

"I will read your verses with pleasure, and may venture to tell you beforehand that the Princess will esteem your dedication as a great distinction, and will be proud to read her name in print on any work of yours."

And Pushkin, that same day, received a note from the Prince telling him that the Princess would receive him the next day at seven o'clock in her summer palace on Neva Island.

The great heat prevented people going out earlier. The St. Petersburg world of fashion had already repaired to their villas. Even the rich burgher lived in Neva Island on his "dotcha." The Czar had accompanied Elisabeth and her court to her favorite castle "Monplaisir," in the vicinity of which was Sophie's dwelling.

The Czar could now visit her very seldom, for in June the nights are not dark in St. Petersburg. But she had her lover to keep watch over her.

But one short week separated them from the wedding.

CHAPTER XXIX

MADAME POTIPHAR

AT the appointed hour Pushkin presented himself at Villa Ghedimin, and was passed on from one footman to another, until he finally arrived at Korynthia's boudoir.

The Princess was a handsome woman ; but to-day she wanted to surpass herself. The feminine fashions of that day were very becoming. The pale-golden silk, fine as any from the loom, thrown lightly about her head, enhanced the gold of her waving hair, arranged in a classic coil, and threw up her complexion ; as did the soft Brussels lace the whiteness of her neck and arms. Her shoulder-straps even were set with yellow diamonds, and, coquettishly placed between the lace, a pale yellow tea-rose diffused its delicate perfume. Her whole being betrayed an agitation unusual to her. She blushed and smiled as Pushkin entered. And both blushes and smiles repeated themselves during the greeting and exchange of customary courtesies. Then she signed him to a chair, while she seated herself upon a silken divan opposite to him, and opened the conversation.

" I have shed as many tears over your lovely poem as though I had been myself to the Baktshisseraj Well of Tears."

" I am rejoiced that the heroine of my lay should have

won your sympathy, Princess. For in her I imperson-
ated my betrothed, Sophie Narishkin."

Oh, what a change passed over her face !

Her cheeks aflame with anger, her eyebrows arched
like bows, her eyes shooting out arrows of fire.

"You desire to marry Sophie Narishkin?" she cried,
passionately. "Impossible !"

"I think it, on the contrary, very possible, seeing
that our wedding is already fixed for the 21st of June."

"In a week ? Has the betrothal been already announced, then ?"

"No ! A dispensation has been granted for our
marriage."

Springing from her divan, the Princess gasped : ·
"Impossible! Impossible !"

Pushkin retained his seat. He was not easily frightened by any man—or woman either. So he answered,
calmly :

"But, my dear Princess, what objection can you have
to it ?"

Korynthia saw that she had suffered her impetuosity
to carry her too far. So, commanding herself, she resumed her seat and made as if fanning herself from the
heat.

"He who advised you to this was no friend of yours !"
she hissed out.

"It was the Czar !"

Korynthia, shutting her fan, put it to her lips. After
a short silence she said :

"You know, then, that the Czar is Sophie's father?"

"I have divined it."

"And have you also divined the future which awaits
you in marrying a daughter of the Czar ? You will be
banished from the society in which you have hitherto

lived ; the circles into which you will try to force yourself will hold you in contempt. As long as the Czar
lives you will be a prisoner in the glittering cage of the
court, deprived of free - will ; an unhappy man, born to
enlighten others, condemned to be the shadow of a man!
At the death of the Czar you may be appointed to a
governorship in the Caucasus or on the Amur."

" Princess ! I shall neither become a prisoner at
court nor governor of Kamchatka. My wife will accompany me to my little estate of Pleskow, where I mean
to be sometime farmer, sometime poet."

" You do not love the girl. Vanity alone has led you
to this step."

Pushkin never took a blow unrequited—even from a
woman.

" Princess, did you know her you would know that it
were impossible not to love her !"

The Princess bit her lips until they bled. It was a
cruel thrust. Quickly upon it followed a second.

" Sophie has only inherited her father's sweetness of
disposition ; nothing of her mother."

The Princess rose. She could bear it no longer.
Her face was deathly pale, her eyes gleaming with a
dangerous light. Going up to Pushkin, she seized his
hand as she whispered :

" Has the Czar also confided to you the name of Sophie's mother ?"

"Never !"

" Have you heard it from any one else ?"

" From no one who had a right to know it."

"Come, then, sit down by me," gasped the Princess,
convulsively clutching Pushkin's arm, and drawing him
on to the divan beside her. " Listen to me ! I will
make a confession to you. What I have hitherto told

to none but the Patriarch I will confess to you." Sobs
choked her voice; then violently tearing the lace handkerchief with which she had dried her tears, she continued, "Even to my husband I have never dared to
say what I now tell to you: *I am Sophie Narishkin's
mother !*"

Pushkin, of course, appeared to be intensely surprised
at this discovery.

"You be my judge," continued the Princess, as she
threw back the gossamer covering from her shoulders.
She drew a long breath. "I was but a child, scarce
sixteen ; my parents dead. I met a man whom all con-
spired to worship. The aunt who brought me up was a
vain, ambitious woman, and had made me equally so.
Every one about me counselled me to return his love,
telling me that he was unhappy for cause of me. They
sought out old records of how Czars who had not loved
their wives had sent them into convents, and had raised
others, more beloved, to share the imperial throne. Flattery, ambition, inexperience, youthful fancy, turned my
head, and I—fell. Ah, how low I fell! So low that
my whole life since has been one expiation ! Still, I
never relinquished hope; I ever believed that the man
who had wronged me would come one day to raise me
from shame to splendor. I implored him ; I knelt in
the dust at his feet. Then he published the ukase
that only the daughters of reigning families might be
raised to the throne of Russia—that was the answer to
my dreams! In the depths of my despair a man in
my own rank of life came and asked my hand. True,
he had no love to give me, but he gave me his name ;
I, too, had no love to give him, but I have borne his
name honorably and spotlessly before the world. And
now there suddenly breaks upon me the dreaded catas-

trophe which for sixteen long years has been my nightly terror: Sophie Narishkin will marry, and people will be asking, 'But who is this Sophie Narishkin? Who is her father—who is her mother?"

"You may make yourself at ease on that score, Princess. The wedding will be conducted in all privacy by the Patriarch of Solowetshk in the Chapel of Peter the Great on Petrovsky Island. After the wedding not a soul will see the young couple in St. Petersburg, or speak about them."

This consolation was poison to the heart of the Princess. Would she see Pushkin no more, then?

" But why this feverish haste? The girl is but a child, scarce sixteen years old!"

"Princess," returned Pushkin, mournfully, " we do not reckon time by years, but by the griefs we endure; and by that computation Sophie has already lived a long life. Sixteen years of confinement, banishment, unrecognized by any one—sixteen years without knowing a loving word or ray of brightness should count for age enough! It is just this dream of happiness that is keeping the poor child in life. Sophie is a somnambulist on this earth. To awaken would be to kill her!"

"So it is a spirit of magnanimous self-sacrifice which binds you to her—you are not in love with her?"

" I worship her; am hers forever."

" I see. Permit me to meditate over the subject. This news has taken me so by surprise that I can give you no answer at present. Can this marriage not be delayed?"

" No."

"Why not?"

"The Czar is going on a journey—it may be a long— very long journey. He will shortly hold a great review

of the guards, and then start. But of this Prince
Ghedimin can inform you better than I. At any rate,
it is the Czar's pleasure that our marriage takes place
before he leaves."

"Then at least allow me to defer my answer to the
last moment. I have so much to say to you; do give
me as long a time as you can. Come again on the
twentieth, and even then not until dusk, so that your
coming may not attract attention. In order to enter un-
perceived—you will readily understand why I should not
wish a visit from Sophie's bridegroom, on the very eve
of his wedding-day, to be publicly known — take this
key. It belongs to the door of the veranda which
opens on to the park. Thence, by a spiral staircase,
you ascend direct to my apartments. We can then talk
over various matters undisturbed, which you ought to
know."

Pushkin put the key intrusted to him in his pocket,
and, kissing the Princess's hand, took leave, Korynthia
giving him the farewell kiss on his lips and accompanying him to the door of her room.

From this we glean that the Russian scientist was
right in his remarks upon "degenerated cats"—at least,
as far as this woman is concerned.

CHAPTER XXX

A MOTHER'S BLESSING

IN the villa shaded by aromatic pines the bride elect
awaited the happy day. No longer a prisoner, condemned to lifelong imprisonment. For the hardest imprisonment of all is sickness; one is made to hear at

every step, "Oh, don't run! Don't sing! You must not
drink water! Keep your shawl about your throat! Do
not eat this! Mind you don't take cold! Don't get
overheated!"

Even the doctor stays away. The panacea has done
wonders.

The lovely month of roses had come. The bridegroom had had the path along which Sophie was to
walk planted with roses, and the happy girl collected
the blossoms, morning and evening, that not a single
leaf might fall to the ground. Why did she do this?
When the leaves were dry she meant to fill a silken
cushion with them. Sleep would be so sweet on such
a cushion.

She was even now spreading out her leaves on the
sunny side of the veranda, singing to herself as she did
so. No one forbade her to sing now; it was allowed;
only old Helenka grumbled out the adage, "Sing on
Friday, cry on Sunday." But Sophie is accustomed to
laugh at such wise saws from her old nurse. Who believes in such superstitious omens nowadays? When all
of a sudden good old Helenka sighed out, anxiously:

"Holy Maria! St. Anna! What brings her here?"

And without another word she ran off, to avoid the
new-comer.

Sophie, looking up wonderingly, saw a lady of striking
beauty coming down the garden path. She wore a dress
of gay-colored embroidery, a bird of paradise in her bonnet, and upon her shoulders was a costly cashmere shawl.
At sight of the stranger's seductive beauty Sophie felt a
mysterious shudder pass through her frame; her heart
seemed to stop beating. She began to believe again in
omens.

The stranger came alone, and at an hour too early for

ladies, as a rule, to be out. Without hesitation she ascended the veranda steps, like one who knew the house well.

As she reached Sophie she raised her hand with the gesture of one expecting to have it kissed, saying, in a low voice, as she did so :

" I am Princess Ghedimin !"

The girl's heart beat audibly ; but she had no alternative, she must kiss the gloved hand.

" You have never seen me before ?" the lady asked.

Sophie shook her head in silent negation.

" Let us go together into your sitting-room, then. Is there any one with you ?"

" No one."

The lady went on first, and, having reached the room, took off her bonnet. Her abundant fair hair was dressed high, *à la giraffe.*

" Now kiss me, child. I am your mother !"

Sophie did as she was bid.

The Princess looked about her. Embroideries, pretty dresses, the whole trousseau, lay scattered about in charming disorder.

" Ah ! Your trousseau. So you are going to be married, little one ? Did it never strike you that so serious a step demanded a mother's blessing upon it ?"

The girl ventured to reply, " I had been told that I was neither to visit nor to write to my mother."

" But you might have let me know through your little friend Bethsaba, who has been seeing you daily."

" I thought she would have told you." ·

" No ; not a word. Oh, girls nowadays can keep their own counsel ! Not once did she mention 'his' name to me ; it was by mere chance that I heard it. Herr Pushkin came to me yesterday to ask my permission to dedicate his new poem, *The Spring of Baktshisseraj*, to me."

" To you ?"

" Have you any objection to his doing so ?"

"On the contrary, I am glad."

" And he happened casually to mention that in a week he was about to lead Sophie Narishkin to the altar. I was astonished. I fancied you still playing with your dolls. Who brought this big doll to you ?"

" My father."

" And do you think yourself sensible enough to marry yet ?"

" I do not know if I am sensible ; I only know that I love him !"

" A categorical answer ! How positive you are that he will marry you ! And where did you get to know Pushkin ?"

" During the flood. Oh, I was in such terrible danger ! Had they not come to save me I should have been washed away."

" Who came to save you then ?"

Sophie was surprised at the question.

" Do you not know ? Did not Bethsaba tell you ?"

" Bethsaba ? No ; she has not spoken to me a word of you or Pushkin. Sly girl—she shall pay for this. So the same fairy sheltered you who carried off Bethsaba from my carriage ? That devil in woman's form ! And Bethsaba has thought well to keep it from me ! And for whole days and nights you were in that den of iniquity ! Now I understand it all ! It is this fiend who has brought it all about !"

" Mother, do not curse her ! ·I owe all my happiness to her."

" Do you know, then, what is ' happiness ' ?"

"To be loved."

"And do you know what is its opposite?"

"That I do not know yet."

"To be betrayed."

"Who would betray me?"

"Who but he whom you believe loves you?"

"My Aleko?"

"Yes, your Aleko, who is the property of so many besides you. A more fickle man, a greater deceiver, more cruel, dishonorable, you could not have met with on earth."

"What reason could he have to deceive me?"

"Because he hopes, through you, to rise to higher rank."

"Oh no! He has refused all titles, rank, and possessions. He is taking me as I am. My trousseau and this piece of copper—a piece of the ship which ran into the Winter Palace, and which he gave me on the day of the catastrophe—are my whole wealth. He means to remain a poor man, and to make himself a name which no dukedom could rival."

"How he can deceive you! His schemes stop only at the throne. He is marrying you that in the next revolution he may figure as the Russian 'Prince Égalité.' Nay, Égalité!—as another Pugatseff! Why, do you not know that he is one of the conspirators whose aim is to oust the Czar from the throne?"

"But it was my father who brought him here."

"Because he has a honeyed tongue with which he can deceive the Czar—and lull the daughter to sleep."

"Oh, mother, you hate him sorely!"

"And with reason! Does not this marriage threaten to ruin my whole life? Will it not bring the secret of your birth to light—that birth the bane of my early life?"

"Mother! Do you curse the day of my birth?"

"Not now only, but twice daily—when I wake and when I lie down. You were as a death-sentence to me, the hour of which was unfixed. I have thought with shuddering of you. You have been my accomplice, a living witness to my wrecked honor; and now my fate is to be accomplished through you. You announce to the whole world that you exist—look! here am I!"

"No, mother; I will hide myself. No one shall see me. No one shall know of me."

Korynthia here pretended that pity and maternal love had gained the mastery. In sorrowing tones, she exclaimed:

"But, my poor child, do you not know that you are condemning yourself to a living grave—that you are choosing a life worse than hell? You will be the wife of an adventurer, who is sunk so low in sin, so fettered by vicious associates, that, even if he desired it, he is powerless to avoid the consequences. Do you want to follow him to Siberia?"

"If misfortune assails him I will share it with him."

"And suppose the mad scheme in which he is the foremost actor succeeds, and his hands are stained with your father's blood?"

"'Then I will find a path in which to implore Heaven's pardon for him."

"Blinded creature! Your self-created ideal prevents your seeing the man as he is. Do you believe it possible to confine a heart in a cage that is accustomed to take free flight, and which, moreover, you have by no means made captive? For Pushkin loves you not! I tell you, he loves you not! Be convinced; he loves you not!"

Sophie looked in bewilderment at Korynthia. The

19

instinct of her woman's heart, added to a nervous fore-
boding, told her the horrible truth. Seizing Korynthia's
hand, she exclaimed :

"*You love him !*"

"You are right !" hissed Korynthia, with wild vehemence.

Sophie, pressing her hands to her heart, turned white
as death; her eyes closed, her breathing stopped, and
she fell lifeless to the ground.

The Princess went in search of Helenka.

"Go in to your mistress ; she is not well."

And, drawing her cashmere close about her (the morn-
ings are misty by the river) and replacing her bonnet,
she left the villa.

Knowing that her farewell kiss would be of no benefit to the poor swooning girl, she let it alone.

CHAPTER XXXI

THE WILL

THAT day Pushkin felt as heavy-hearted as if he had
not only all the sins of the world, but the national debts
of all Europe, upon his shoulders. Was it one of those
presentiments to which the race of poets, whose stock-
in-trade is nerves, are so sensitive ? Nothing gave him
any pleasure. He went to Zeneida, to formally announce
his approaching marriage to her. She had long been
informed of it, for she possessed a splendid service of
secret police.

Zeneida replied, with cold, stoical irony :

"I still do not believe that the Czar's daughter *will
marry you.*"

" Probably not ; for *I* intend to marry the Czar's daughter !"

" Is Princess Ghedimin informed of it ?"

" I have announced it to her."

"Then nothing will come of it."

" It has nothing in the world to do with her."

" I prophesy it. Else why am I the pythoness ? Does Prince Ghedimin know of it ?"

" Prince Ghedimin ! *Mille tonnerres !* Am I to go to the Prince, too, to ask for Sophie's hand ? He, at any rate, is out of it."

" Not on account of your wooing, my friend, but that the Prince may erase your name from 'the green book.' You will doubtless see that the name of the son-in-law of the Czar can´ hardly adorn—I will not say blacken— its pages."

" By Jove ! you are right. I had not thought of that."

With heavier heart than he had come, Pushkin left her.

Zeneida's villa was on the Kreskowsky Island, thus some distance from Sophie's home, which lay embowered in orange groves. From afar the light-green roof was visible, standing out from amidst the pines. Every evening a white flag was to be seen floating from the flag-staff, hoisted by Sophie herself, as a signal that she was expecting him. Sometimes she would come down to the shore to meet him, her white-clad figure greeting him when he was yet a long way off.

Now neither white flag nor white-clad maiden was visible. He hastened on impatiently. Usually, as his boat approached the landing-stage, another, in which sat Bethsaba, would row away. The Circassian Princess never awaited Pushkin ; they only exchanged greetings from a distance. Now he perceived a gondola, painted

in the Ghedimin family colors, still chained to the landing-stage, the boatmen stretched on benches fast asleep.
Without waiting for his boat to reach the land, Pushkin sprang ashore and ran towards the house.

On either side of the path Sophie's beloved roses
were blooming; the ground was covered with their fallen
leaves.

"What can have happened," thought Pushkin, "that
your guardian angel has not been gathering up your
leaves this evening?"

"Go in-doors; you will soon know the reason," answered the roses.

He found no one upon the veranda. He opened the
familiar tapestried door leading into Sophie's private
apartments. There he learned why the rose leaves had
not been gathered in that day.

Sophie lay upon her bed, white as death. Yesterday's
soft bloom had all fled from her cheeks; they were almost transparent. The anguish she had undergone had
left a transfigured expression upon her face. She was
clasping Bethsaba's hand, who sat by her bedside, their
fingers interlaced, in prayer.

Pushkin advanced cautiously, concealing his alarm.
It is not well to let invalids see that their appearance
inspires anxiety.

"What is this? Are you not well?"

"No, Aleko; I am dying. Do not be startled; it is
past now. I have wrestled through it. You, too, will
live through it."

"Oh, do not speak so, my love!" stammered Pushkin, kneeling by the bed, and covering the girl's white
face with kisses. "It is but some slight feeling of illness that will pass off, as so often before. I will go and
fetch the doctor."

"You will go nowhere! You will stay, when I tell
you to. Do not oblige me to talk loudly, but obey.
Think, were you to go and alarm Wylie with the news
that I am on my death-bed, he would at once inform the
Czar. The Czar just now is engaged upon a great work
for the good of the country; he is arming for war. Millions depend upon his decisions for freedom, and a happier future in store. For this he needs all his powers.
My father loves me so dearly, and depends so entirely
upon me, that the news of this illness will completely
unman him, and render him unable to carry on the work
he has in hand; the thought of his dying daughter
would deprive him of all energy and power. Is it not
strange? In my lifetime scarce a dozen people have
known of my existence; in my death shall millions upon
millions curse the day of my birth and my death! So,
I implore you, do not disquiet the Czar with the news of
my extremity."

With passionate vehemence Pushkin answered:

"What matter to me Hellas and the Russian Constitution, now that you are ill? I must save you!"

The reason which led Pushkin to this imbittered exclamation was characteristic of the times. Elsewhere,
and at any other era, a lover, under similar circumstances,
would have said, "Very well; I will not go to the Czar's
physician, but to the first skilful doctor whom we can
trust not to publish your illness, and he shall cure you."
But at that period no one thought of going to a Russian
doctor who did not want to hasten his death. Rather
would they go to a quack, or trust to household remedies,
than confide themselves to a St. Petersburg doctor. It
was the surest way to court death. People only sent to
apothecaries for rat-powder; indeed, under Czar Alexander, Russian subjects were forbidden to be apothe-

caries; Germans only were allowed. A Russian mis-
trusted his countryman; he held him capable of giving
a sick man — in the interest of his enemies — poison instead of remedies. The aristocracy would only be attended by the Czar's and Czarina's physicians. In their
absence, it was no use for any one to be ill.

" I have begged you not to excite me ! In vain would
you bring me all the Galens in the world, with their po-
tions; I would take none of them. I will drink no
more of that odious physic that tastes of bitter almonds.
I must die ! Do you understand ? I *must.* My death
is necessary, irremediable. Not because I am ill, but
because I am condemned to die. And it is right that
it should be so !"

Pushkin, unable to solve this riddle, looked inquir-
ingly at Bethsaba, who, at this, made a movement to
go. But Sophie held her back.

" Stay ! I want you both. Pushkin, be a man — a
brave, strong man ! Are you a child, that you are
trembling so ? Grant me what I ask. I am going to
make my will. Draw the writing-table up to my bed,
light two candles, and place the crucifix between them ;
but first close the shutters and make it night ! Oh, these
terrible summer nights in St. Petersburg, with their endless gathering dusk—it seems as if night would never
come and day would never cease ! It is such an oppression ! Ah, I feel calmer now that it is dark. Now
come and sit down by me and write; or would you
rather lay the portfolio on my bed and write kneeling ?
So you shall, then. And you, Bethsaba, kneel beside
him. Attend to what I say, and write : ' Surrendering
my soul to God, my ashes to earth, I, Sophie Narishkin, bequeath, on my death, all my worldly goods to my
only friend the Circassian Princess, Bethsaba Dilari-

anoff. The only two things I desire to have buried with me are the little piece of lead which I have ever worn upon my heart, and, under my head, the little green silk cushion filled with rose-leaves, on which I shall rest peacefully.' What! cannot you see the letters that you are writing all across the paper? Pushkin, what a baby you are! Write further: 'To my one and only friend I bequeath the greatest treasure I have in the world— my Aleko Pushkin!'"

At these words Bethsaba would have started up, but Sophie would not allow it. Twining one arm round her neck, the other round Pushkin's, she pressed their cheeks together.

"Am I not to be allowed to dispose of my treasure as I like in my will? Do you think, then, that I do not know how dearly you love him? Before I confessed to you my love for him, his praises were forever in your mouth; since then you have never once mentioned his name. Do you think I did not know why you always hurried away when he came? Your cheeks used to be so rosy, and you so merry and full of fun. Now they are white, and you are so sad and lifeless. Do you think I have not divined your grief? You love him, as I do. Do not conceal it any longer. Tell the truth. Do not have any secrets longer from a dying girl, who to-morrow will be a spirit, knowing all that is in your spirit. Do not wait for my disembodied soul to come nightly to disquiet you, asking, as a spectre, the answer to the question you refused me in life. Confess that you love Aleko!"

As she heard these words Bethsaba's heart felt nigh to bursting, and with open lips and upturned eyes she fell unconscious to the ground.

"Lift her up and lay her by me on the bed," said

Sophie, tranquilly. "Now you have two dead brides to choose between. Only one will wake to life again, for she has not been killed. You can have no doubt now but that she loves you. Leave her unconscious. It is better that she does not hear what I have to say to you. But you keep every word in your heart of hearts and do as I bid you, for you know that girls who die during their betrothal change into spirits whom it is not good to anger. So listen. You are not to leave Bethsaba's side again. I know why I say this. If you let her go home, she will never look on God's free heaven again; she will be confined for life in St. Katherine's Convent."

Now Pushkin began to divine what had happened.

At the mention of St. Katherine's Convent, in Moscow, there flashed across him all the scandalous adventures he had heard the officers of the guards boast of at their mess dinners, outdoing even the scandals of Paris life. The convent had a reputation only equalled by the very worst convents of Montmartre. Young lieutenants wore the rosaries of the nuns of St. Katherine's as bracelets, and only that year a terrible case had happened which had been hushed up by the authorities. The last descendant of a noble family had disappeared suddenly from society in Moscow, and after a month of vain searching his body was discovered cut to pieces in one of the wells at St. Katherine's. And thither her godmother intends to send Bethsaba, where not only her happiness for this world, but for the next, is to be lost forever. And Princess Ghedimin was thoroughly capable of it.

"So, no indecision, no sentiment," continued Sophie. "On the day of my death you must marry Bethsaba; if not, she is lost. True, the world will say, 'The scoundrel! the very day he closed the coffin on his betrothed he could open his heart to another.' But you will be in possession of my will, dictated to you by me, and signed with my shaking hand; lay it upon your heart, and it will give you peace. And if your conscience acquits you, what.matters the judgment of the world? Be daring! The Patriarch of Solowetshk will be waiting in the Czar Peter's castle on Petrovsky Island. He is charged to marry a young girl to an officer in the guards without previous publication of banns. He does not know them or their names. Two witnesses will be necessary; I have provided for that. Zeneida can be one, Helenka's husband, old Ihnasco, the other; both are trusty friends. And while the one gondola, to the voices of the chanting choristers, glides gently along with my flower-bedecked coffin to the lovely willow-shaded vault on this bank of the Neva, you in the other gondola will be rowing across to the other bank of the Neva to catch your troika, which will be in waiting. And now, God be with you !"

Pushkin paced the room in wildest excitement, tearing his dishevelled hair.

Sophie, meanwhile, set about restoring her friend to consciousness, and, unfastening her bodice, sprinkled her face with water. Dying, she still thought of others.

At length Bethsaba began to revive; but as she opened her eyes she buried her face in the cushions.

"I have arranged everything with Aleko," said the dying girl, in a low, contented voice. "You have only to do exactly what he tells you. I leave you my pink dress and the platinum diadem. You will soon know when you are to wear them. Why, Pushkin, how can you be so useless? Why have you not written it all down in my will? Now, do not forget the pink wedding-dress and platinum diadem. Old Helenka, too, I bequeath to you; she has always been a good, faithful nurse to me. You may trust her through thick and thin. Now, Aleko, give Bethsaba pen and paper. She must write to tell the Princess not to expect her, as she is not coming back at present. Now write, dear one: 'Your Highness, my honored godmother,—Sophie is ill and in sore need of my care. I must stay here until the Lord take pity upon her. Your godchild, Bethsaba.' Now, dear Aleko, send off this note to the Princess, that she may not be uneasy. And as soon as you are ready give me my will, that I may sign it."

Sophie read it through.

"How many blots there are!" she whispered, and a smile lit up her death-like face. Those blots were Pushkin's tears. Sophie made merry over them, and wanted Aleko and Bethsaba to join in her merriment. She wrote her name in large, clear handwriting, and gave back the pen to Pushkin. Then she put both her arms round his neck and drew him down to her.

"To-day you still belong to me! Let me look once more into those eyes which have been so long a sweet home to me! Oh, it was a Paradise on earth! I thank you that you let me know such exquisite happiness! I thank you for the truth and tender love with which you blessed me!"

And she kissed him countless times. Then, letting her arms sink, she motioned him away. It was the last caress.

"Aleko! Bethsaba! I want to see you embrace each other—now at once, while I am still alive and can see it! If you love me, if you would have me know you to be sincere, if you place any value on my blessing, embrace each other."

And so across the dying girl's bed they laid their arms on each other's shoulders.

"Ah, that is right! And now, kiss each other—on the lips. Not like that; you have hardly touched each other; it was such a cold kiss. Give her a real one !"

And, laying her hands on the bowed heads, she drew them together, until their lips united in a kiss, her hands resting the while as if in the act of blessing. Then, raising her transfigured face to heaven, and, folding her hands, she breathed, scarce audibly :

"Mother, I have saved you from sin !" .

CHAPTER XXXII

NOT ONLY A BULLET STRIKES HOME

THE Czar was holding an extraordinary review.

The usual parades took place on the 21st of May, the day of the patron saint, Nicholas, and on the 20th of September ; but this time it was a special review of the household troops alone. They are distinct from the rest of the army ; each regiment has a different uniform. The Life Guards wear white uniforms, with shining gilt breastplates ; the Cuirassiers, light-blue tunics, with white, plated cuirass; the uniform of the Jerusalem Regiment is crimson-red, with gilt breastplate. The ranks, from officer down to corporal, are all knights of the Order of St. John, and even the common soldiers are all of the nobility.

And every regiment boasts its past, its history, which passes on to the successors as a tradition, and keeps up the glory of its name.

The regiment of St. John of Jerusalem was so cut to

pieces in two battles that in one battalion only eighteen men were left.

The Preobrazsenski Regiment has the proud distinction of having deposed Czar Ivan and set Elisabeth in his place.   Every man in the regiment received his patent of nobility.

The Ismailoffski Regiment bears on its colors the trophies of seven conclusive battles.   At Borodino half the troops remained on the battle-field, and not a single man came home without a wound.   These regiments compose the aristocracy of the Life Guards.   The rest of the household troops, too, are characterized by a brilliant variety of dress.   Hussars in uniforms of the most varied colors, cuirassiers, mounted grenadiers, pontoniers, Cossacks, Asiatic hordes with their fantastic arms, Kirgisians, Kalmucks with their slender spears, their arrow-laden quivers on their backs ; Circassians in their scale-armor, with their pointed helmets; and then the long row of cannon, the ammunition wagons (painted green), the pontoons, the flotilla on wheels—and the whole mass drawn up on a boundless plain in squares, in geometrical lines, and advancing, charging, halting motionless as a wall, at the word of command, like a machine.

May he not rightly deem himself a god who with a gesture can set all this in motion or make it stand? And they only need a second gesture to charge and dye the ground beneath them with their blood.

When the household troops advance from St. Petersburg it means that the army is on a war footing and is taking the field.   Then let every man concerned summon all his strength.

In the centre of the Field of Mars are pitched the sumptuous tents of the Czar, the foreign ambassadors, and the members of the government ; but the Czar himself rides at the head of his suite, and passes the assembled troops in review. As he thus rides past the separate regiments they salute him with welcoming stanzas, in time like the chorus of a giant theatre, with rifle, sword, and lance held rigid at present arms. The Czar's face beams like a day in summer; every one sees again in him the hero of Leipsic. The inspiration of the army has communicated itself to him too.

And in the ranks of these men presenting at the word of command are all those who have been conspiring against him. In the sabretache of the officers is to be found the *Catechism of the Free Man.*

But the single word " Forward !" suffices to change the whole temper of these men ; the conspiring regiments will charge down on the foe with shouts of " Long live the Czar !" When he shows them the battle-field they forget all their complaints and grievances—forget that they are seeking to kill him—and rush into the fight to give up their lives for him.

So it is with the Russian people. Their striving after freedom is silenced when there is hope of war. The private, freely shedding his blood on foreign soil, believes that therewith he will fertilize his native meadows. The priests have indoctrinated him with the belief that he who falls in a strange land to the enemy's bayonet will live again in his own country, where he will find parents, wife, and children once more; and, if he was a serf before, will rise again a free man.

After the review of the troops the Czar himself takes the command, and a series of brilliant manœuvres begins, thought out by himself. According to the then science of war, they were intended to be a masterpiece of the system of attack in close order. His aides-de-camp are dashing from battalion to battalion with orders, their spirited horses flying off in all directions. The orders are given by the Czar himself, who watches their fulfilment through a field-glass. Suddenly an adjutant dashes up to him.

"Sire !"

"What is it ?   Make short work of it !"

The enemy's cannon are already thundering upon the attacking column.

"Sire," says the officer, "Duchess Sophie Narishkin has just delivered up her noble soul to Eternity."

The Czar instinctively put his hand to his heart. It was there that he was struck !   And yet the cannon were only firing blank ammunition.

The sword he was wielding sank in one hand—the Czar covered his face with the other.

"*It is the punishment for my faults !*" he uttered, in a faltering voice.

What a change had come over the brilliant hero—the semi-god !   In his place sat a bowed figure ; a man bowed down to the earth by fate.

However deafening the hurrahs—however much the earth may vibrate under the tramp of warlike horses and horsemen—their leader's soul is fettered by the words "Sophie is dead."

Miloradovics, the general in command, sent to ask instructions from the Imperial Commander-in-Chief for the next movement.

"Call them back !" was the answer. "Send the troops back to barracks.   The review is over."

And, turning his horse, the Czar rode back to his tent with bowed head.   They who saw him return hardly recognized his white face.   The generals of division had great work to disentangle their troops and get them into position again. A murmuring arose among the men, as though a battle had been lost.

The Czar, not even awaiting the march past of the regiments, who were wont to defile past him with pipe and drum, left the whole command to the Grand Duke, and, throwing himself into his troika, drove back to the Winter Palace.

There he hastened to his study. On it were spread important, weighty documents, containing epoch-making decisions for people and nations, only awaiting his signature. The Czar's eyes rested sadly upon them, reading in them, not what was written upon them in ordinary characters, but the *Palimpsest* with which fate ever crosses the carefully thought-out plans of mankind.

Then, seizing all the documents—painstaking labors of many a night—he made them into a roll, and, throwing them on to the fire, watched them, a prey to the flames. They were all to have been Sophie Narishkin's dowry.

Soon they were a heap of ashes.

Then, sitting down, he wrote a letter. It contained but two words—"Come back."

The envelope was addressed to Araktseieff.

CHAPTER XXXIII

THE RENDEZVOUS

THERE is something marvellous in the summer nights of the extreme North. Foreigners find it harder to accustom themselves to them than they do to the long winter nights with their cruel severity. The evening glow lasts till midnight, and then begins the dawn. It seems endless until the first stars appear in the still, clear sky, and under them the brilliant planets Venus and Jupiter, burning in the firmament like diamonds on the surface of a golden lake. The pale moon describes its short orbit, a superfluous luminary; and on the Feast of Masinka the half-hour of actual night is impatiently awaited, in order to let off fireworks on the forty islands of the Neva. (For by daylight it is no use to send up rockets!) Street lamps are not lit in St. Petersburg at all during this month. Nor in the apartments of Korynthia's villa are lights needed on the evening of this 20th of June. The sky diffuses light enough until 11 P.M., and a little twilight will not seriously disturb those of whom we are about to speak.

Korynthia, in some agitation, has strayed—who can tell how often in the course of that evening?—on to her veranda, and let her eyes rove over the surface of the mighty river below. It, too, is golden in the evening light, and, like the Russian pictures of saints, on a golden ground is reflected in its sheen the capital, with its rows of palaces, the dome and columns of St. Isaac's, the florid architecture of the Exchange, the bridge of Holy Trinity, the scattered islands from amid whose wooded heights the varied forms and shapes of country-houses peep, with roofs red, blue, green, gilded, and pagoda - like. And among the islands are darting boats, gondolas, canoes, of every kind and description. Some rowed by twelve boatmen, others by a solitary dreamer; the one flashing along at lightning speed, the other letting himself drift on with the stream. The song of the boatmen is in the air.

In the uncertain light their figures stand out like black silhouettes. Korynthia asks herself which of the gondolas is bringing to her him she is expecting—which is the silhouette of his figure?

To the watcher the last half-hour seems longest. Korynthia turns from the balcony to the interior of her room,
and gazes once more at herself in her mirror. You are
beautiful, very beautiful, says her mirror; that white costume lends you quite a youthful appearance, leaving, as
it does, the rounded marble of the arms bare to the shoulder. Your wealth of fair hair is not stiffly arranged, but
floats in two thick tresses. No ornament of any kind,
bracelet or earring, enhances your charms. The confi-
dent champion enters the battle-field without helmet or
shield. Even the wedding-ring is absent. You are beautiful indeed—says her mirror.

And beside the mirror hangs a picture, set in a thick
gold frame. It is the picture of a young girl in the
garb of a mythical shepherdess—tender and delicate as
a dream. Korynthia had received it some years ago, a
present from the Czar. She may possibly have divined
even then that it was no fancy picture, but a portrait;
she may even have guessed whom it represented. Within the last few days she knows for certain. She has
met the original. It was the portrait of Sophie Narishkin.

Certainly she might long since have known it from
Bethsaba—have seen portrait and original often enough,
had she asked her. But although lying was foreign to
the nature of the Circassian king's daughter, she knew
how to be silent, and had that much Armenian blood
in her veins not to answer when not directly questioned.

So the reflection in the mirror and the portrait in the
frame were in close proximity. And comparison left
the living reflection victor.

You pale child with your dreamy eyes, your lips seeming to open in lament; your tender, shadowy frame,
how can you think to rival the divine presence of a

20

woman ? What power can you have, melancholy dream-
picture of another world, against this earthly woman
whose beauty arouses and quenches passion, kills and
inspires life? Do you possess an Aleko, he chooses
himself a gypsy maid; and that is not you. Is he not
himself a true gypsy, leading a vagabond, adventurous
life? In a word, is he not a poet?

Time went on slowly. Korynthia opened the windows looking on to the park. A concert of nightingales
came from the bushes. A butterfly — the night peacock's eye—flew in at the open window; taking her for
a flower, it flew about her, not about the portrait. Then
flew in another night moth, differing from others in that
it emits a sound—an unpleasant, shrill, yet melancholy
hum. Its name is *Sphinx Atropos*. Why has it been
called by the name of that one of the Parcæ which sev-
ers the thread of life? Because its back and head are
the exact counterpart of a death's-head. Ss—h ! The
lady brushes away the weird moth; but it had found a
refuge; it had flown across to the picture and had settled in a corner of the frame.

At length the twilight deepens. A few impatient
employés let off the first rockets from the pleasure gardens in the islands. Bengal lights are beginning to
show on Kreskowsky Island.

Ah, of course ! It is Zeneida's birthday. The court
calendar has found a place for her among the saints;
there are great doings to-night in her palace. And
something more, perhaps—a sitting of the Szojusz Blagadenztoiga. Under every possible guise and excuse, it
holds its meetings at the singer's house.

When Prince Ghedimin left home that evening he had
told his wife that he was commanded to the Czar, and
would be away all night discussing important matters of

state. It is therefore certain that he will be spending
the night at Zeneida's, and Korynthia need not fear to
be disturbed; it is a case of tit for tat. Any moment
may now bring him—the one so impatiently expected.

For as soon as the fireworks on the islands begin
they attract all the servants and watchmen yet awake.
There is no one to keep guard on the winding paths of
the park. The great clock strikes eleven; every quarter
of an hour four bells ring a carillon. At the last stroke
of the clock she seems to hear the sound of approaching footsteps on the gravel. Who else can it be? An
aristocrat's step is so different from that of a mujik.
She is right.

The new-comer, stopping at the door of the garden
veranda, opens it with a key. His footsteps now announce his coming, as they hurriedly ascend the spiral
staircase. Korynthia has studied the pose in which she
will be surprised. Leaning over the window-sill, her
face resting on her hand—a dreamy figure so absorbed
in the song of the nightingales that she does not perceive some one approach her, bend over her, and breathe
a soft kiss upon her lovely shoulder.

The Princess seems to rouse from her reverie with a
start, as, with an air of smiling reproach, she turns to
the stealer of the kiss, "Ah, how late you are!" But as
she sees him, she starts in reality. The kiss has been
no theft. The perpetrator had but taken what was his
own. It was her husband, Prince Ghedimin. Korynthia stammered out, "How early you have come home!"

"You just said how late I was."

"I was dreaming. I did not know what I was saying.
How did you get in?"

"By the garden veranda. You know that I have the
key."

And now it occurs to Korynthia that that other, to whom she had given the duplicate, may even now be coming.

" Did you fasten the door ?"

" No, for in five minutes I must be off again."

"But I beg you to fasten the door, and leave your key on the inside. You know how terrified I am of thieves."

" All right. I'll go back and close it."

During his brief absence Korynthia wrapped herself in a thick shawl. She did not need the pretext of cold ; she was shivering with agitation.

The Prince returned.

" I must briefly tell you that I come from the Czar."

" Indeed ! And not from Fräulein Zeneida's soirée ?"

" No, my love. I come from the Czar and Czarina."

"Of course, if you say so."

" You will not doubt it when I tell you what I have witnessed."

" Pray begin."

Korynthia remains by the window to announce by the sound of voices to that other that she is not alone.

"His Majesty has for the past two days repeatedly commanded me to his presence to deliberate certain matters of state; yet each time he has either been shut up in his room, and I have not been admitted, or if he has appointed me to go to him to Czarskoje Zelo, he has gone to the Hermitage. This evening I was commanded to Monplaisir. I traversed every room, right and left, until at length I found him on the upper veranda with the Czarina. Three times, four times, I saluted the Czar, but he took no notice of me. The Czarina signed to me to remain where I was. The Czar stood leaning against the marble parapet, motionless as a statue, his eyes fixed upon the Neva, the Czarina as fixedly, almost in fear, watching his eyes. Hundreds of boats were gliding over the smooth surface, crossing each other, shooting hither and thither. Suddenly a large barge came in sight, going down-stream, rowed in slow, rhythmic measure by eight boatmen. The barge was lighted by lamps fastened to poles; in the centre was a coffin, draped with a light-blue satin pall. In the open coffin lay a young girl in white funereal dress, a wreath of myrtle on her head. Round it stood choristers singing a funereal chant, which ascended to where the Czar stood:

> "'Ah, the day of tears and mourning,
> From the dust of earth returning,
> Man for judgment must prepare him.'

There were none to follow the funereal barge. As it passed Monplaisir one could read conspicuously on the lid, placed beside the coffin, the name studded in gold nails — *Sophie Narishkin*. Yes, you may well draw your shawl about you, madame! It is cold, is it not?"

The Prince had no idea of the effect of his words; he was still seeing what his memory had impressed upon him, not what was before him. He continued:

"Human language has no words to express the anguish at that moment imprinted on the Czar's countenance. With glowing eyes, convulsed lips, and gathered brows, he stood there clinching his hands; and, while with his eyes he followed the barge, a gigantic struggle seemed working within him. I have witnessed much sorrow in my life; never did I feel such sympathy for a man as for this one! He dared not betray his feelings, for the Czarina was standing by his side.

She, too, studied his face with great attention. Suddenly she bent towards him, and, taking his hand in
hers, cried, 'Why do you not weep? Why keep back
your tears? It is your own dear child who is being
borne to her last resting - place!' And, as if to open
the font of his grief, she threw · herself upon the
Czar's breast and burst into weeping. And then the
mighty ruler, before whom millions of men tremble,
knelt before his neglected, forsaken wife, embraced her
knees, and, sobbing, kissed the hem of her dress, she
joining her tears to his. It was a scene I shall never
forget. The separated husband and wife were reunited
in the hour of their bitter sorrow; they had come together again, the past forgotten. They leaned over
the balcony, saluting the disappearing barge with a
last farewell! My eyes fill with tears as I think
of it."

The Prince did well to weep. It was meet that
one or' other of them should shed tears at what had
passed.

"Then, pressing his hand to his heart, the Czar
gasped, 'And there was not a soul to follow her to the
grave!' It was indeed a bitter thought. Even a beggar has some poor wretch to follow and mourn for him.
And she had no one! Then a thought struck me,
and I rushed to my gondola and came to you. I am
the Czar's Prime - Minister; you a Princess Narishkin.
How would it be were we to catch up the funeral barge
in a light, fast-rowing gondola, and act as Sophie Narishkin's mourners? What do you think?"

But the woman beside him had not depth of feeling
enough to take her noble - hearted husband's hand in
hers, and giving her tears free course, to say, "Yes, let
us go; Sophie Narishkin is mine to mourn over!" No;

that woman had more power of self-control than had the Czar. Her woman's pride, conquering the animal instinct—sometimes called maternal—within her, she could answer coldly and calmly:

"What are you thinking of? How should we account to the world for our uncalled-for escort? And, then, it is too late; before I could put on a mourning-dress the barge would have got beyond all possibility of our reaching it. Besides, what do I care for Sophie Narishkin?"

She could even speak thus at that supreme moment. How true was the Muscovite scientist's classification—a degenerate cat. Even a normal cat mourns its young.

"What is Sophie Narishkin to me?"

Prince Ghedimin shrugged his shoulders, and, taking out his handkerchief, carefully brushed away traces of tears. It is certainly not worth while to run the risk of making one's own nose red for the troubles of other people.

"All right. As it does not affect you, let us turn to something else. One other reason brought me here, which may perhaps interest you more. As I got into my gondola my steersman handed me a letter bearing on it 'Pressing.' The letter was from *Alexander Sergievitch Pushkin*."

"Pushkin?" repeated Korynthia, in great agitation.

"Yes; from Pushkin. And the purport of the letter being so extraordinary that my understanding could not grasp it at all, I hastened to you to beg you to solve the riddle."

Korynthia felt the ground give way beneath her feet.

"Pushkin!" she stammered. "What should I know of Pushkin's riddles?"

"Listen. I will read the letter to you."

And, in order to see better, the Prince now approached the open window, while Korynthia, retreating to the farther side of the room, sought to conceal her agitation. The Prince read:

"'DEAR IVAN MAXIMOVITCH,—I find myself compelled with penitent heart to make you a confession. I have misused the high-minded confidence with which you laid open to me the sacred privacy of your home. Not as my excuse, but as a reason, I refer to my passion, which was stronger than the respect I owed to you. *I have stolen the dearest, most carefully guarded treasure of your house!*'"

"Is the man mad?" thought Korynthia.

"'If you desire to demand reparation for the affront, I shall be prepared to give you every satisfaction. You will find me in my country-seat at Pleskow.

"'Yours most sincerely,

"'PUSHKIN.'"

The Princess was amazed. The extent of the treachery never even dawned upon her.

"Well?" The Prince awaited an explanation. The best shield is cold-bloodedness, the best weapon a lie.

With a shake of the head, Korynthia made answer:

"But how does Herr Pushkin concern me? What have I to do with his mysteries?"

"Naturally, our friend Alexander Pushkin's proceedings have no special interest for you, nor should I desire it. But in this letter another was enclosed, having on the outside, in what seems to be a lady's handwriting, 'Princess Korynthia Alexievna Maria Ghedimin.' Probably in this we shall find the solution of the mystery. On that account I must beg you to break the seal and communicate its contents to me—if you do not feel it desirable to keep them secret.

It was now the Princess's turn to advance to the window, in order to read. No sooner had she the letter in her hand than she exclaimed, in surprise :

"It is Bethsaba's handwriting!"

"You know her handwriting? I have never seen it."

Korynthia tore open the letter, and as she read her cheeks flamed. Then, crushing it in her hand, she cried, with hysterical laughter :

"Ha, ha, ha! He has run off with Bethsaba and married her!"

Ivan Maximovitch took the matter as a joke. He had expected worse. Indeed, he could rejoice in that Bethsaba had been carried off, destined as she had been to St. Katherine's Convent. His wife's laughter still further misled him, and he thought well to join in it. Now, if his tears had met with but mediocre success, his laughter obtained him an open attack. The Princess first flung the crushed-up letter at his head, then, rushing at him like a fury, hissed out through her clinched teeth :

"This was your work, wretch! This was connived between you!"

"Who?" asked the Prince, in amazement.

"You—and your sweetheart—that Witch of Endor! You spun the web in which that girl was caught for Pushkin. You prepared the poison in which this dagger is steeped."

"Madame, I am at a loss to understand why the fact of Pushkin's marrying Bethsaba Dilarianoff should excite you to such fury!"

Korynthia saw that by her vehemence she had almost been led into self-betrayal ; so said, calmly :

"You do not understand! This is no question of love, but of high-treason! What would it matter to me

if a Circassian Princess chose to fall in love with my
lowest groom? He would probably be too good for her!
But do you know why Pushkin has married this girl?
In order to discover. the Czar's secrets, which he confided to his daughter, and which were repeated to her
friend Bethsaba. Now these secrets, through Pushkin,
will become the common property of the Czar's enemies! Thus, you ruin yourself if you are on the side of
the Czar; or the Czar, if you conspire against him. And
this is what you two have done!"

Prince Ghedimin stood as if turned to stone. His
wife had triumphed. Her words bore so clearly the
stamp of truth that defence was not to be thought of.

"Yes. It was a plot among you all!" continued his
wife, furiously. "You availed yourselves of the illness
of the one to entice the other from me. In order to detain me at home, and to prevent my watching over the
child intrusted to my care, you sent Pushkin to me with
a poem, and, instead of coming to receive his answer,
the cowardly fellow steals away with a foolish, inexperienced girl from the very death-chamber of her
friend. Out with such people! Such treachery, deceit,
betrayal! You are worthy one of another. A pack of
actors and actresses! Out of my room! Away with
you!"

When women take to abuse, men are nowhere. Their
reasoning powers are gone. Prince Ghedimin was a
wise and good man, and innocent as a child of this
crime; which, after all, was no crime at all. Yet after
this torrent of abuse he felt a very criminal who had
brought about an act of the greatest, most irreparable
evil with the coldest calculation, and, in this frame of
mind, was glad to be permitted to leave his home and
seek his gondola.

We who are in the secret can aver that he did not even now know who Sophie Narishkin's mother was. . But this Korynthia did not believe. She looked upon the whole scene as expressly got up to torture her—from the appearance of her husband at the very hour of the rendezvous, when he shed upon her love-lorn heart first the ice-drops of the funeral scene, then poured in the poison of the faithlessness of the man she adored.

It was a deadly poison, killing inwardly and outwardly. When Ghedimin left her, Korynthia, clasping her two hands above her head, threw herself on the ground, sobbing bitterly. Then, as there was no one to raise her, she assumed a kneeling posture, her long plaits hanging like serpents over her bosom; and, lifting three fingers to heaven, she gasped out, with hideous vengeance:

"Oh that I may repay you this some day!"

Her lips parted; the gnashing of her clinched teeth was audible. She was meditating something; her eyes flashed fire; she rose, and bared her white, exquisitely formed arm to the shoulder. Then she pressed the rounded muscle of the upper part of her arm between her teeth, and bit into it until the blood flowed from it, and sucked the blood she had drawn. It is the Russian superstition that whoever would insure the fulfilment of his curse must, after uttering it, drink of his own blood.

The melancholy hum of the death's-head moth in the corner of the picture-frame sounded like the murmur of a lost soul.

CHAPTER XXXIV

A DIVIDED HEART

ZENEIDA was celebrating three days of mourning in one. The first, Sophie's funeral; the second, Pushkin's marriage; the third, her own name-day.

It had been Sophie's last wish that the wedding should precede her funeral.

Her soul in its ascent to heaven would see and hear the bliss of the two she had loved so dearly on earth.

According to Russian custom the lid was only screwed down on to the coffin just before it was lowered into the grave; with face uncovered the wanderer to the Hereafter is borne to his last resting-place.

"Make the ceremony a short one!" Zeneida had said to the officiating priest.

The Patriarch of Solowetshk, whose feet had sufficient Russian understanding to suffer from a severe attack of gout that day, had sent a priest in his stead. Let his inferior have his beard shaved off if things go amiss, and not him. For if a priest rashly marry a runaway couple the marriage is legal, but *the priest's beard is shaved off*, and he is forced to become a soldier. During the wedding ceremony, according to custom, two doves were set flying over the heads of the bridal pair. They fluttered for a time round the veranda, then let themselves down on to the catafalque, at the head of the dead girl, where the crucifix stood; there, the one on the right hand, the other on the left, above the head of the "martyr to love," they billed and cooed through the whole ceremony.

The dead girl might well be content. All had been done as she had directed; Bethsaba wore the pink silk wedding-dress; the platinum diadem adorned her brow.

"That is over," said Zeneida. "Now follows the other—quick, quick!"

Bethsaba must now change the pink wedding-dress for a black one for the consecration of the dead. Zeneida helped her to dress; Pushkin waited without.

Bethsaba wept on and on, whether clad in pink or black.

Zeneida betrayed no tendency that day to sentimentality. Her utter callousness bordered on cynicism.

"But we shall see Sophie again in the next world, shall we not?" sobbed Bethsaba.

"Yes, yes," muttered Zeneida. "And to which of you will Pushkin belong then?"

That was the question.

Bethsaba was startled. Her large eyes remained fixed on Zeneida.

"And suppose he should belong to neither of you?" continued Zeneida, drawing her strongly marked eyebrows together. "Or do you imagine that in the hereafter there will still be a greater Russia crushing a lesser Finland beneath its heel, so that even then a fool will be found to open the gate of Paradise for some one else, while she herself goes into perdition!"

This outburst revealed Zeneida's secret to Bethsaba. Rigid with dismay, she stammered out:

"You, too, loved him?"

"Do not ask. Rejoice that he is yours, and do not wish yourself in the next world with him, but do your utmost to keep him to you in this."

"And you, too, loved him?" repeated Bethsaba, sorrowfully.

"As you have discovered it, make your discovery of some use," said Zeneida, with seeming affectation. "Now, at least, you know from whom you have to guard him. Take care to keep him away from me. Now you know the sort of person I am. I take pleasure in enticing away the husbands and causing the wives bitter tears. Your godmother was right. *I am a very devil.* Do not bring your Aleko back to St. Petersburg."

Bethsaba, throwing herself on Zeneida's bosom, embraced her.

"It is not true—not true—not true! You cannot deceive me. Tell me why you gave me Pushkin's heart, when you might so easily have kept it for yourself? There must be some weighty reason that induced you to do it. Tell it me; he is my husband now. I must know all about him. Even if it be—that he loves me not."

Zeneida, now looking down with gentle smile on the young bride in her mourning-dress, took her in her arms, and in fond embrace drew her to her heart.

"So you do not think me so bad that you will need to guard your husband from me? Well, then, I will tell you from whom you must guard him. There is a lovely woman, more captivating than any you have ever seen— more seductive, intoxicating, more insatiable. Her name is 'Eleutheria.' She can entice the bridegroom from his bride at the very altar rails, and the father of a family from his dear ones; and whom she once captivates she keeps fast hold of till his last heart's blood is spent. His every thought is hers. It is this dread woman who is your rival. Guard your husband from all remembrance of her, for he is in love with her."

"'Eleutheria!' that means Freedom."

"She bathes in men's blood. It is that which makes her so beautiful. The only presents she will accept are hecatombs; and of hearts and men she only chooses such as are worth the price of gold and diamonds. The woman who has such a diamond to call her own should guard him well. No pleasure-seeker, no drunkard, no gambler follows his besetting sin so readily as he whom Eleutheria has once enslaved. She has but to proclaim, 'My service demands the lives of men,' and thousands upon thousands of her worshippers answer, 'Here is mine; take it.' Beware that Pushkin be not among them!"

Bethsaba let the arms encircling Zeneida's waist sink until they embraced her knees.

"Oh, unapproachable saint! You who rejected his heart that you might save his head. Speak, counsel me, how shall I set about doing that which you have charged me to do. It is so difficult. How shall I carry it out, that my work be successful?"

And Zeneida, raising the young bride, began to whisper the sensible advice to her that experienced women are wont to give their inexperienced younger sisters.

"Give up to him in everything. Do not contradict him. If he change his mind seven times in a day, change yours with him. Divine his thoughts and forestall his wishes. If you know one thought of his, you can guess the others. If he be out of temper, do not irritate him with questions as to the reason. In such a mood the dearest face is unwelcome. Requite his love with your whole soul, and do not hide your joy from him. But do not flatter him, for that would turn him from you. Do your utmost to make his home pleasant to him. Let your house and his surroundings be pure and peaceful, yourself be ever cheerful and loving; never let him hear

your voice raised harshly to your servants. If he desire
to show hospitality, see that you make a good hostess.
Do not keep him back from his manly pursuits. Never
ask where he is going, whence he comes. Above all,
never betray jealousy. What woman is there who can
sufficiently stifle jealousy as not to feel it? Therefore
must her heart, his advocate, keep watch that it clear
him, even if eyes and ears accuse him. Never meet
him with tearful eyes, but keep a strict watch over your
own actions. It is not necessary to play the prude
with strangers and to be always flying to your husband
for protection; that would only render him ridiculous,
and lead to many disagreeables. But never, whether
from high spirits or feminine vanity, allow other men to
pay you attentions which might arouse your husband's
jealousy. If anything annoy you, tell it him gently and
at once. Do not brood over it until it grows and he
reads the trouble in your face. Be easily pacified.
Throughout, be yourself, equable, ever the same; for, in
an evil hour, some fatal moment may suffice to recall his
forsaken love, Eleutheria, to his mind, and to throw him
again into her arms."

The little bride listened to her words as though they
were the words of Holy Scripture.

"I will help you to keep him at home and from returning to St. Petersburg. I will write you letters saying that the Czar is furious that he whom he had chosen
as his daughter's husband should have been capable of
marrying another on the very day of her funeral. It will
not be true, for I shall show the Czar Sophie's will, and
it will disarm him; but Pushkin must be made to believe
that he is in disgrace, and dare not return to St. Petersburg without special permission. And we will expunge
his name from 'the green book,' that he receive no more

invitations to meetings. Let him be hidden in your arms until better times dawn or—what I far rather believe in—until the day of our extinction. When all is over, then you may come back to the world. Until then we must keep him in the belief that for him, exiled by his Czar, vilified by his peers, there is no other world than his love and his Olympus. And are they not, in themselves, two worlds—two heavens?"

Pushkin entered.

" Not ready yet?"

"Leave us alone! I am just about to spoil your wife. I am advising her how to keep you under her thumb. You are not to listen."

"All very fine. The first hour we are together she will tell me all about it."

The choristers in the chamber of death now began their solemn chant. It was a long ceremony, but it, too, came to an end. The priest, taking the two candlesticks, held them over the cross while he spake the blessing, walked three times round the coffin waving incense, then placed the parchment containing the list of sins, at the end of which was inscribed the absolution, into the dead child's hands as her passport into eternity; after which the candles on the catafalque were extinguished. The two doves upon the crucifix continued their billing and cooing.

They carried out the coffin to the barge draped with funereal hangings. Many blossoms from the garden accompanied it; it was covered with wreaths. The blue, green, and red lights glared in the twilight. The choristers continued their chant, the gentle plash of the oars marking time to it. Long those left behind gazed after the departing boat, until the next wooded island hid it from their view.

21

"She has gone on her journey!" said Zeneida; there were no tears in her eyes. "Now it is your turn. Quick! No leave-takings; they are so wearisome. Be off with you! I have my guests to see to, a right merry company. I must hurry back. One kiss is enough, Bethsaba; you may give the others to your Aleko. Take quickly with you what is yours."

"Alas! that is impossible," sighed Pushkin, who had the bad habit of being unable to keep back what was in his mind. "One part she who is gliding away in that gondola has taken with her; a second part you take; to this poor child belongs only the remainder."

"That is not true," returned Zeneida, with proud, radiant face. "She who has gone back to heaven has bequeathed her part in you to your wife; she who is here has, even now, given up to her that which she might have possessed. Bethsaba knows all about it. You are hers, wholly, entirely. And now, God be with you!"

And she held out her hand to him. The allies of the new epoch did not kiss in greeting.

And as Pushkin pressed the hand she held out to him, a ray of joy passed over Zeneida's countenance. Freemasons have a sign by which they recognize each other in hand pressure. *Pushkin had not given the sign this time.*

Already he had forgotten his former love. To the new one, to whom he had plighted his marital troth, he belonged wholly, entirely.

It was as "she" had desired; and smilingly Zeneida waved her white handkerchief to the vanishing gondola, which a troika awaited on the opposite bank. Only when she could see it no longer did she hide her face in the said white handkerchief, and whether it was bedewed with tears or not that handkerchief alone can tell. She did not remove it from her eyes until her gondolier addressed her.

"If you please, madame, the rockets on Kreskowsky Island have begun."

"Ah yes. You are right. The third funeral awaits me!"

With that she hastened into her gondola, and within its closed curtains sang, in a low voice:

" By the waters of Babylon we sat down and wept;
For they that led us away captive required of us a song,
Saying, Sing us one of the songs of Zion.
If I forget thee, O Jerusalem, let my right hand forget her cunning."

CHAPTER XXXV

SPARKS AND ASHES

ZENEIDA'S gondola glided quickly past the funeral barge back to Kreskowsky Island. Her guests were entertaining themselves without her. They were used to do so.

The conspirators were largely represented; even Pestel, from far-off Nikolajevsk, was there. To-night the conflicting parties were to measure themselves; the decision was to be made which plan should be the accepted one: the one which should give freedom by means of the Czar; or that which, regardless of him, living or dead, should carry the work to its completion.

As the fireworks commenced, the Bojars withdrew from the gay scene to the roulette chamber.

There were three-and-twenty men and Zeneida. Prince Ghedimin alone was still expected; he was to come direct from the Czar.

He came.

He had a long envelope, sealed with five seals, in his hand.

In extreme agitation all awaited the opening of the document. The Prince cut the seals with a pair of scissors, opened the envelope, and there fell from it the ashes of some burned sheets of paper, as they had been reclaimed from the fire. It was the anxiously awaited *charta*—reduced to ashes.

"I said so!" exclaimed Pestel, with triumphant countenance. "The whole thing was a comedy. Scarce three months has it lasted. There's an end of fine words. Now to dark deeds!"

Nothing was left but to decide if *the deed* should be consummated.

They voted openly and by name.

There were twelve ayes and twelve noes.

"There is still one to give the casting vote," said Pestel. "Here is the 'Votum Minervæ.' Here is Zeneida. Her vote shall decide it."

Zeneida saw the deadly pallor which had overspread Ghedimin's face.

With calm voice she said, "Aye."

Thirteen to twelve the majority for the deed. But when? That was the next question.

Pestel said, "At once."

Ryleieff moved that in September would be their best opportunity, at the concentration of the army.

"To-day," growled Jakuskin. "Not to-morrow!"

Fresh votes had to be taken.

"At once, or in September?"

Once more the votes were twelve to twelve. Once more Zeneida was called upon to give the casting vote.

Upon her breath hung the decision whether the world at that very hour should be shattered to its foundations.

"In September," she said; and Ghedimin gave a deep breath of relief.

Pestel shrugged his shoulders wrathfully.

"Then it were better to put it off until May, to try the success of the concentration of the army in Kiew. There in the South we are the masters."

"Shame upon us!" growled Jakuskin. "We are twelve to their twelve, and dare not do the deed. Every one of us a Brutus! More than an Armada! Were I alone I would do it myself."

The concluding set piece of the fireworks was greeted by the crowd without with clapping of hands. The golden rain fell like a shower of stars from the sky.

"Very well. The 20th of September," whispered the conspirators, as they shook hands with each other. Loud peals of laughter were heard among the gay company; the health of the lady of the house was drunk with acclaim.

Upon the smooth surface of the Neva, under the shower of golden rain, gently glided the funeral barge to its destination; the dead lay with face serene; and amid the applause and hand-clapping of the spectators arose the dirge:

> "Ah, the day of tears and mourning,
> From the dust of earth returning,
> Man for judgment must prepare him."

The psalm and noisy crowd were silenced. The golden sparks died out, the ashes were extinguished.

Morning began to dawn. Not a soul was to be seen on the Neva. Every one had gone home to sleep through the gray morning hours; the forenoon in St. Petersburg is good for nothing else.

Even morning here has its special characteristics. The sky is white, and as it is reflected on the calm surface of the Neva it seems like one plate of burnished silver, upon which the long streaks of cloud and the heavy foliage of the trees stand out black as night. Pomp of death in sky and earth!

CHAPTER XXXVI

DAIMONA

THE mistress of Grusino, who ruled Araktseieff as completely as he ruled the empire, was neither young nor beautiful. She could not have laid claim to beauty even in youth, and her stature was of manly proportions.

There are plain women who can make themselves pleasant; who, aware that they have not the advantages of good looks, lay themselves out to charm by their manner. But Daimona wanted to be beautiful. Her complexion was dark—she painted herself very red and very white; but as her beautifying only extended to her face, leaving her neck its natural hue, it gave her the appearance of wearing a mask. Having no eyebrows, but desiring to obtain them by artificial aid—being, moreover, extremely short-sighted—she usually contrived to paint first one, then the other, higher or lower than its fellow. Her teeth were blackened from much smoking and indulgence in sweets. In addition, she

selected the most ridiculous and garish of costumes
and colors, always overloaded with ribbons and jewels.
When she spoke it was in a man's barytone, which,
when agitated, broke into a sobbing squeak.

And this voice of hers, heard all day long without
cessation, inspired fear in all around her, for she only
opened her mouth to scold and abuse. In her com-
munications to her household she made use of the
most singular punctuation; the cane formed a comma,
a box on both ears a colon, and the knout a full
stop.

And this woman was the delight, the goddess, the
idol, of the all-powerful court favorite. The whole
land knew the infatuation of the great statesman for
her; whoever aimed at accomplishing any end in St.
Petersburg must first make his way to Grusino; for a
good word from Daimona outbalanced a whole wagon-
load of letters of introduction and whole sackfuls of
merit.

And that good word was never given for nothing.
Daimona understood her business; she had a carefully
made-out tariff for favors desired: So much for an
official post; so much for a concession; so much for an
order; so much to be let off from an undesired expedition to Siberia, with or without accompaniment of the
knout on the way, on foot, or by sledge. She could tell
it all off by heart.

The most aristocratic men and women did not esteem
it beneath their dignity, whenever they deemed it advisable, to present themselves with friendly or deferential
mien to the mistress of Grusino, who, wedded neither
in right nor left handed marriage to the favorite, was
originally the cast-off wife of a sailor condemned to
Siberia, and afterwards had served her time as a *vi-*

vandière to the Ismailowsk Regiment, who had given her
the sobriquet of the "squinting Diana."

And, withal, she had completely captivated the clever
man before whom a vast empire trembled. Araktseieff
was only at his ease when, throwing off the "iron mask,"
he could be himself again in the arms of the chatelaine
of Grusino.

At court, in order to retain his influence, he had
humbly, in cold blood, to receive every affront and
humiliation, to flatter, to be more courtly and diplomatic in manner than any diplomat; the while raging
internally, filled with uncontrollable pride and savage
revolt at everything that opposed him. It was of itself
a penance to him to have always to converse in French,
for it was the only language of the court, and he who
spoke Russian ran the risk of being looked upon as a
conspirator, or, worse, "member of a learned society."
And he hated the French with a deadly hatred! Their
language, dress, manners, music, drinks, diplomats, their
drama and their philosophy! Then, too, he had carefully to keep watch over every word he uttered and
every glass he put to his lips. Not only lest the contents of the glass should be poisoned, but for fear of
drinking too much! For he knew that the true man
spake in him when he was in liquor. Even worse, he
had to ape the ascetic; for women's charms were an
arch snare, in which his enemies would fain have trapped
him. Thus he lived like a recluse, with the appetites
of a Sardanapalus. And when, flying court atmosphere
for a brief respite, he could seek refuge at home in his
Eleusinian den, and, throwing off the affectations of the
French language, dress, and mask, he was free to resume the despised native Russian costume, and talk the
good old true Novgorod dialect, in which the republican

peasant of those days abused Czar and yeoman alike, he felt himself happy. Then he could vie with his well-mated companion in good round oaths, beat her in the morning, kiss and make friends in the afternoon over the flogging of the peasants, men-servants, and stewards who came in their way, and get drunk together at night. Daimona was a match for him in every form of excess. If he were violent, she incited him to increased violence; if he would vent his wrath on some one, she found him a human object on which to vent it, seconding him with all a woman's refinement of cruelty.

When the master showed his face at Grusino there was a hurrying and scurrying hither and thither, lamentations, groans, and blows; eating and drinking to excess; music and dancing through the streets; battues, dog-fights, mad revels of every description, and at least one *swacha* (girl market). For the Sultana provided her Padishah with his Feast of Bairam.

In fine, Prince Alexis Andreovitch found in the hideous Daimona his other self; and this made her more precious to him than all the beauties under the sun.

One day that fine fellow Zsabakoff presented himself, with countless bowings and cringings, before the mighty Daimona. Not this time in the torn garments in which he slipped into Pushkin's quarters, but attired as a man of position. He possessed different costumes for the different parts he had to play.

Herr Zsabakoff came to Daimona because he had learned that the Czar was sending an army against the Turks. The fact was known to none, not even to Araktseieff; only one man knew of it, and that was the Czar's groom of the chambers, the same worthy individual who one evening had lent young Araktseieff the Czar's Vladimir star. This worthy groom of the chambers often did his friends a good turn. Thus, for instance, it was solely to do Herr Zsabakoff a kindness that he gave a glance at the Czar's papers while arranging them on his writing-table. What he there saw, no one, not even the ministers, knew; nor did he proclaim it with beating of drums, but he sold the information without more ado. There is no reason for surprise at this. Other times, other manners. At that time it had happened that university professors had been known to distribute to students on one day answers to the questions to be put to them on the next. But in this affair Herr Zsabakoff was not interested to speculate as to whether the Hellenic champions of freedom would be able to hold Missolonghi until the Russian army had advanced to their aid, but merely whether the Czar's plan that every soldier, besides his customary kit, should carry a flask as a necessary equipment in campaign—consequently three hundred thousand metal flasks would be required. The contractor would make his fortune.

But the honest groom of the chambers had not only communicated this secret intelligence to friend Zsabakoff, but also to many other similar friends, who probably were hurrying on the production of flasks by day and night, for in the course of a fortnight they must be ready. Naturally it would not be the lowest contract which would obtain the order, but he who best greased the wheels of the Intendant-General's carriage. Herr Zsabakoff now came to the influential lady to entreat her to use her powers with the potent Intendant-General to persuade the Czar to have *wooden* flasks made instead of the unwholesome metal ones. Thus, at one fell swoop, would disappear all his metal-flask rivals; Zsabakoff would remain in possession of the field, and could demand his own price. In order to lend emphasis to his request he had brought a little present with him which would exactly become its charming wearer— an antique brilliant *ferronnière*, in the centre of which was an exquisite solitaire of unusual fire.

"Of course that is merely earnest-money," said the mistress of the house. "You are aware that in the case of such a large transaction I go shares in the profit."

"Your Excellency has taken the very words out of my mouth. Depend and rely on it, I am straightforward with you—I always speak the truth. I always do the honest thing. Why, then, should I deny it? According to the price of my contract I gain half a griva on every flask; of that I will make over two copecks to your Excellency."

"I tell you what, you make your contract so that it brings you in a whole griva apiece, and give me four copecks on each."

Herr Zsabakoff agreed to this proposition. But Daimona was none too delicate of her guests' feelings. One of her slaves was a jeweller, and expert in precious stones. Him she sent for, and, in Zsabakoff's presence, had the ornament valued. This was her custom. She kept the slave specially for that office. The expert valued it at one thousand five hundred rubles; but had the centre stone been pure water instead of yellow it would have been worth two thousand.

"You don't understand anything about it!" screamed Zsabakoff. "Yellow diamonds are unique; they are called 'fantaisie.' Besides, it is an antique, and great people like antiques best."

"Quite true. All the same, a pure-water solitaire would be worth five hundred rubles more."

"Do you hear?" quoth Daimona. "Don't forget next time to exchange it for a handsomer and costlier one. And then I prefer it set in gold to this silver setting."

Zsabakoff promised to obey her behests, and took his leave with as much kissing of hands and feet as though he had received instead of given.

Some weeks later Zsabakoff came back more amiable and deferential than the first time.

"My word is as good as my bond," said he. "Instead of that worn-out old *ferronnière* I bring you a brand-new one. Look at this stone, your Excellency. What a fire! how pure! a perfect Golconda brilliant! It dazzles the eyes like sunlight."

And he went on crying up the new ornament until Daimona gave him back the old one for it.

"You may have this examined. I am positive your goldsmith will value it at three thousand rubles. And, in fact, it cost every penny as much. But I don't grudge it you. All I ask is that you write his Excellency by your special courier, post-haste, that the matter must be at once decided. It is in your own interest. For every field-flask you make four copecks. I am off; I have not a moment to lose."

And once more recommending the flasks to her Excellency's immediate attention, Herr Zsabakoff, rushing out, jumped into his carriage, drawn by three horses, and drove off as if possessed. This time he did not wait for Daimona to summon the jeweller.

Daimona was in haste to write to Araktseieff anent the flasks. But writing with her was a slow process; the pen did not readily obey her untutored fingers. Only when the letter was finished did she submit the jewels to her goldsmith. He, suspiciously examining the *fer-ronnière*, begged permission to test it in his laboratory; then told her that, to a jeweller, it would be worth about three rubles. The brilliants were only Strasburg paste; the setting plated, not gold.

Daimona, at first, was merely surprised; she could not believe the man mad enough to deceive her in a matter concerning three hundred thousand flasks. It was such a clumsy trick, such an unheard-of affront. A trinket worth three rubles was only the kind of present that would be given to a *vivandière*.

" Hi, Schinko!" screeched Daimona. Whereupon her factotum appeared, a handsome, muscular fellow of the unmistakable gypsy type. " Take a horse at once, take three mounted men with you, and follow the man who just drove off with three horses abreast! Seize, bind, bring him back. See you do not come back without him !"

The next instant the gypsy was on a horse, without saddle, galloping for his life. His three followers could scarce keep up with him. Daimona was satisfied that Schinko would soon come up with Zsabakoff.

But within scarce half an hour the three horsemen, with Schinko at their head, came back the way they had gone, and behind them a troika in which sat a man alone. But not as a prisoner did they bring him; it was the other way about, he drove them before him. From time to time he kept putting his head out of the carriage, threatening the galloping horsemen so ominously with his stick that, as fast as their horses would go they tore homeward, looking back now and again with scared faces.

" What's the meaning of this?" shrieked Daimona, furiously pacing the hall. " Schinko ! You hounds ! What, run away—you let yourselves be driven back by one man ?"

Yes, when it is that "one" man! Arrived at the castle, and flinging back the leathern apron of the troika, he sprang up from his seat, roaring with all the power of his lungs after the runaways.

"You fellows! Just you wait! I'll teach you to molest travellers in broad daylight on the emperor's highway. A hundred lashes of the knout for each of you! I'll have you all fastened to the handle of the pump. Bojiriks, Bontshiks, thieves that ye are!"

It was "he" the master—Araktseieff himself. Daimona was more furious than ever. Rushing down the entrance steps into the courtyard beneath, she stood, gasping for breath, before the new-comer.

"Why did you hound back my people? They were pursuing a thief who had robbed me! He brought me false stones and stole the real ones. I will have him brought back—the thief."

But the master of the house paid no attention to her. When he was abusing some one, whoever it might be, he had no thought for anything else. His face was crimson as he alighted from his carriage, holding in one hand a stout knotted stick, in the other a flask by its strap.

Daimona thought him informed of the whole affair, so, seizing him by the collar of his cloak, she continued:

"It was Zsabakoff—do you hear?—Zsabakoff! You surely have not given him the flasks yet?"

"Flasks?" retorted Araktseieff, amazed. "I've only got this one; and I can't offer you anything from it, for it's empty."

"Oh, the devil take you! The three hundred thousand flasks, I mean, that the army are to have in the Turkish War."

And now he was more astonished than ever.

"Three hundred thousand flasks? War? Give yourself time to breathe. What have you been drinking to-day?"

The woman cursed and raved. In a medley of words she mixed up weeks and months, copecks and flasks, diamonds worth two thousand rubles, Misso-longhi and Omer Brione Pasha, and stormed on so long that at length her lord and master, in a fury, flinging his empty flask at her, pushed her aside; whereupon Daimona, to recover her wounded feelings, fell upon the jeweller, and struck his head with the *corpus delicti*, the paste tiara. Why had he said that a yellow diamond was not as good as a white one? It was all his fault that the thief had stolen the real one and made off with it.

And this was the affectionate reception of the weary statesman to his home. Perhaps others have shared his experiences—who shall say?

However, at supper they made it up again; and Daimona recounted to him the history of the field-flasks.

"Well, my dear hen,"—this was his pet name for Dai-mona—"you know more about it than I do, whose prov-ince it is, as Intendant-General, to see to the fitting out of the army. I am on leave from court—ostensibly on account of my health. This that scoundrel Zsabakoff knew, hence he got back his present to you. He knew that I am 'very' ill just now."

"But what's the matter with you?"

"The matter is, that I am a follower of the Czar."

"Try to get cured of that ailment."

"I know that I shall soon be recalled, and very soon fall back into my old ailment."

"Bungler! If only you had kept the Czar's favor until the field-flask contract had been delivered!"

"Bah! Say no more about it. Sing me something nice. It's so long since I heard a woman's voice."

Alexis Andreovitch really meant it when he said he wanted to hear Daimona sing. Now, the screech of a peacock was a swan's song compared with Daimona's croak. Her voice was out of tune, throaty, and harsh; but if it pleased her lord, what matter? And then the words of her song, with its refrain, "Give him a taste of the knife!" In truth, an extraordinary ditty to choose; and that it should just have come into Daimona's head! Yet what so extraordinary in it, after all, for the fallen favorite's *chère amie* to choose a revolutionary song, when he had been dismissed from court by his imperial master, and when the matter of the flasks was not settled? Surely reason enough that he who yesterday kissed the dust from off the tyrant's feet to-day should throw it back in his face!

And the fallen favorite did not interrupt her. He listened to every verse, enjoying the last so much that he chuckled with delight.

"Where did you hear that ridiculous thing?"

"You thick-head! Can't you guess? Didn't you yourself send the gypsy girl to me to be educated? We have made a thorough success of it."

"Right. Among the many pleasures that await me here is carrying on that joke to the bitter end. She drove my son to Archangel! Not a word have I heard from him yet. What have you been doing to the wench?"

Just what you directed. If you want some fun we'll have her in."

"Nothing better just now."

Daimona sent a man in search of Diabolka. Meanwhile she whispered something to Alexis Andreovitch, her painted eyebrows dancing with fiendish glee as she did so.

Araktseieff seemed to enter fully into the joke ; he laughed so loud that he made himself quite hoarse, and, striking his fist on the table, shouted :

"Good! Excellent! By Jove! That'll be worth seeing!"

Both were looking grave when the girl came in. She was hardly recognizable. A young lady in a long dress, wearing mittens, on her head the snood of a Russian maiden. She held both hands, in national style, hidden in the long sleeves of her dress, only withdrawing them to kiss the hand of her master and mistress. Her eyes she kept modestly fixed on the ground.

"Well, dear child, and how do you like being under your mistress's protection ?"

In a low whisper the girl answered :

"Thanks be to my gracious master for having sent me where I am so happy."

Araktseieff could scarce repress his laughter.

"You speak like a book."

"That is not my merit, but that of the reverend Herr Prokop, who has spared no pains to give me the benefit of his instruction."

"Ei, ei! You are quite a fine young lady, I see. You must sit down and have supper with us. Come, don't be shy! Here, you long-legged fellow, set a cover for the young lady! Here, you lout! Opposite me."

"It will be a great honor to your unworthy maid-servant to be permitted to sit at table with you; but I must ask forgiveness if I eat nothing. Good Father Prokop has inflicted the penance on me of eating no supper for a whole year."

"For what sin ?"

22

The girl heaved a deep sigh.

"Your Excellency! you know the great sin I have committed, and for which I never can atone." And she sank her head remorsefully.

Was she really penitent, or was it only hypocrisy?

"And what do you do while others are having their meal?"

"I read the Psalms to them."

"What! you can read already? and the Psalms into the bargain! I should like to hear that. Bring her a Psalm-book. Now sit here and read. Which one is it?"

The girl, sitting down as she was bid, rested the finger-tip of one hand daintily on the table, while with the forefinger of the other she marked the syllables as she read, "Lord, the hea-then are come in-to thine in-her-i-tance."

"Wonderful! But do you understand what you are reading about? Who are the 'heathen'?"

"The *Turks!*" The girl spat out the words, as beseems an orthodox Muscovite.

"Who is the 'Lord'?"

Rising, the girl answered:

"Our august master, the Czar."

"And what is his 'inheritance'?"

"Greece."

"Very good," returned her master. "How well you have learned to read! And can you write too? And so that you need no one to guide your hand, as when you wrote your first letter? Ha, ha! That was a joke!"

Then, turning to Daimona, he said, so that Diabolka should hear:

"Why, you have made quite a lady of her."

"And I mean to make a good Christian of her, too," responded Daimona.

Diabolka, seeming not to hear, went on spelling out her psalm.

"Come forward, Schinko!" Daimona commanded the man standing behind her chair. "Now, have I not selected a good-looking husband for her?"

"Ah! I sent him to you, too, my lady. Is he not a certain 'cousin' of your ward's?"

"That's why I treat him so well. A fine youth! I have no more faithful servant than he. The peasantry fear him like.the very devil. He is my right hand."

"Then I can guess how many floggings he has already administered to them."

"I will give them their wedding. Then I mean to make Schinko my house-steward and Diabolka my confidential maid."

"I will provide the wedding presents."

Diabolka continued reading her psalm without interruption. Any other girl at least would have simpered when she heard talk of her wedding in presence of her bridegroom.

"Now we'll finish up supper with a little singing and dancing," said the mistress of the house, signing to Schinko.

"Ah! Can Diabolka not only sing sacred songs, but dance too?"

"She neither sings nor dances; she has another calling. There is some one else to do that."

Hereupon twelve pretty young peasant girls entered from a side-door, each with a lute in her hand, their faces expressing more repressed fear than pleasurable expectation. Behind them slid Schinko, a long whip in one hand, the other leading a small, humpbacked dwarf on a chain, like a bear, with a bagpipe under his arm. He was hideously ugly, with a hump behind and before, his large bald head sunk between his high shoulders. His face was the caricature of a man's face, and so distorted with small-pox that it seemed as if the lineaments, being so grotesque, the fell disease had tried to wipe them out; here and there remained a tuft of beard and whisker; he had but one eye. He was revolting to look upon; but when his cheeks distended with the bagpipe he was a perfect monster. A worthier performer on the bleating goat-skin could scarcely be imagined.

"That's classical music," said the master; "but what about the dancing?"

"Wait a minute. That's the best."

Going out once more, Schinko returned with the *ballerina assoluta*, gripping her by the nape of the neck that she might not bite his hand. She was a deformity in woman's shape — a humpbacked dwarf, with long arms reaching to the ground; her stump nose hardly visible; matted-hair growing down to her eyebrows; her mouth awry with great protruding teeth — add to this an evil, bestial stamp on all her features. Such was the creature who was to perform a ballet for the amusement of the lord of Grusino. She was clad in a dress of gold paper; therefore it did not matter if she tore it. She had been taught to dance as monkeys are, and knew she had to do it.

"Blow away, Vuk! Dance, Polyka!" cried Daimona, clapping her hands; and as the bagpipe began its melody the dancer began her parody of a ballet-dancer, making such pirouettes that with her long arms, not her feet, she chased away the chorus, accompanying the bagpipe with their voices.

"Hopsa! hopsa!" cried Schinko, every now and then, and touched up the calves of the dancer's legs' with the point of his whip, if she did not spring high enough in the air, at which she made furious grimaces.

Araktseieff and Daimona sank back in their chairs with laughter. The great statesman, the pattern of astute diplomacy, drummed his spurs on the table in his mirth ; while Diabolka, without raising her eyes, ever continued spelling out her psalm, as though nothing were going on about her.

At the close of this edifying performance the female monstrosity caught hold of the male by the collar of his coat, and twirled him and his instrument round in a waltz, Schinko cracking his whip the while, as though he were in a circus.

" Well, these two will make a pretty couple, too, I declare !" laughed the master. " We will celebrate both weddings together."

Upon which Daimona gave him such a sharp pinch on his arm that he cried out.

The very next day Diabolka's wedding-dress was put in hand. All Daimona's female serfs were at work upon it. Diabolka now usually dined at the minister's table when he entertained the notables of the neighborhood, all of whom were welcome guests when they could prevail upon themselves to kiss Daimona's hand. A dear repast, in truth !

But his guests had still more to put up with. When Araktseieff had drunk too much he would grow quarrelsome and come to blows with them. All the same, they would come back again next day and meet the same fate. A still costlier price to pay !

Schinko was the chief flogger of the palace ; he had to execute all the scourging, whipping, and lashing with the knout. It was his office. He had no choice but to carry out orders. If his master ordered him to thrash corn, he must do it ; if to thrash mujiks, he must thrash them.   Lucky that it was his part to administer, not to receive, the lash.   Moreover, he was a gypsy ; and gypsies, it is known, have stronger nerves than other men.

The eve of the wedding-day Daimona commanded Diabolka to try on her gay wedding-dress, and to show herself in it to the master.

He admired it, and gave the girl a slap on the cheek.

"Do you see?   I am glad you have grown at last into a respectable young woman.   I raised you out of the mire into which you had sunk.   Is it not a good thing to have become a well-behaved girl ?"

And Diabolka, falling on her knees before him, kissed his feet.

"Nice to be a bride, eh ?   Now you love your cousin Schinko, don't you ?"

The girl hid her face in confusion.

"Well, show how you can give a kiss.   Where's Schinko ?"

But Diabolka would not be kissed.   Schinko might wait till he was married.

"A sensible girl," said her master, praising her. " Now take her to the priest, that she may tell her prayers and confess.   To-morrow morning her bridesmaids and groomsmen shall fetch her back.   You go with her, Schinko !"

After she had gone, Daimona sent for the other bridal couple.   They were worthy of each other, Vuk and Polyka.

The humpbacked bridegroom was dressed in a handsome seal-skin coat reaching down to his toes, his cap adorned with a pair of hare's ears ; while the bride, with mouth all awry, was attired as a Turkish odalisque, making her more hideous than ever.

"Upon my word, they're a handsome couple!" laughed Araktseieff. "I wonder if that great hunch will prevent her kissing him?"

"That doesn't matter," returned Daimona; "her arms are long enough to pull out his hair."

Nor did it need much encouragement for her to try it even before marriage; a word would have sufficed to give proof of their connubial tenderness.

"It will be rare fun to-morrow!" said Daimona.

"A splendid idea," chimed in her lord.

"Are you satisfied with it?"

"It's a masterwork."

"Well, if you love me, do as I do."

When was he not ready to do it? It was the reason the brutal pair loved each other so well that there was nothing so mad devised by the one that the other was not ready to join in.

Song followed the carousal. Daimona began the *Knife Song*, and Araktseieff joined in the chorus.

For the sweetest of all the forbidden fruit of the tree of knowledge is when a smooth courtier, whose wont is to flatter, to bow, and to scrape, in the privacy of his chamber can tune up a revolutionary song, and blacken his sovereign and fellow-courtiers to his heart's content.

"Let's have it over again! Where's a glass?" He always dashed his empty glasses against the wall. But instead of the glass, Schinko brought on his silver salver a letter, which a mounted messenger had just delivered.

Araktseieff at once knew the handwriting on the cover. Releasing himself from Daimona's arms, he sprang up from the divan, and, hastily wiping his mouth, pressed the letter to his lips and forehead; then said, in a hollow voice:

"Give me the scissors."

"What do you want with scissors? Break it open with your fingers."

"Give me the scissors when I ask for them!" shouted he, angrily, and snatched roughly at the pair hanging from Daimona's girdle. And as with trembling ʾhand he cut the seal, he said, feverishly, "One does not break the Czar's seal."

"The Czar's seal?" repeated Daimona, astounded.

It did not take Araktseïeff long to read his letter. Besides the signature were two words only—"Come back!"

"Bring water! Cold water!" he said, imperiously, to Schinko. And as he, not knowing the wherefore, returned with a bucket of water, his master, seizing the utensil with both hands, took a deep draught from it.

Daimona's astonishment increased more and more.

"What is the matter?"

"I must set off this very instant!" gasped Araktseïeff. "Hurry, Schinko; let them put the horses to; twelve horsemen to accompany me with torches; and one to ride on before to secure post-horses. Fly!"

"You are going away?" asked Daimona, amazed.

"Instantly! The Czar commands!"

"And you hurry back at his request?"

"As a Cossack pony answers to his master's whistle."

"And will not be taking part in to-morrow's sport?"

"I must deny myself the gratification."

"You are going to leave me?" asked she, reproachfully. "You do not love me any more?"

"The Czar has deigned to write with his own hand," returned Araktseïeff, handing her the letter.

"What do I care about his writing?" screamed Daimona; and, snatching at the letter, she cut out a piece with her scissors, which so enraged Araktseieff that he struck her violently on the hand.

"You have struck me! You are going away, and have struck me!" And, turning her face away, the woman wept bitterly.

But Araktseieff had no time to pacify her now.

"*Seisasz!* This means that the crisis is past."

Had there been an ocean before him he must have swam across it. How much more, then, a few woman's tears!

The celebration of a double wedding will come off, but he will not be there to enjoy the fun.

"Quick, quick, Schinko! Then come to my room to shave me."

While at Grusino the minister was in the habit of letting his beard and mustache grow to please Daimona; but always had it shaved off before returning to St. Petersburg.

"Take care you don't cut me with your razor," were his first words to Schinko, as he began. Schinko was the only one there to whom he intrusted his throat. "If you slash my face I'll shoot you dead."

His two travelling-pistols lay close to his hand. Schinko was cautious, and completed the operation without disfiguring his master's face. A lucky thing for Araktseieff. For the gypsy was resolved at the slightest slip of his razor to cut his master's throat, that he might not have the chance to carry out his threat. Never had Araktseieff been nearer to his grave.

As he finished, the bells on the horses' necks were heard in the courtyard below.

Thrusting the Czar's letter into his breast-pocket, Araktseieff hurried away to say good-bye to Daimona.

She had locked herself up in the room.

"I have gone to bed."

"Then good-bye, my dear!" He had no time for more.

Daimona, from her window, could see the carriage dash away, with its escort of torch-bearers.

It was pitch-dark, the rain coming down in torrents —weather in which one would not have sent out a scullion.

CHAPTER XXXVII

IT'S NOT THE KNIFE ALONE THAT STRIKES TO THE HEART

ARAKTSEIEFF, on arrival at the palace, was received by Chevalier Galban.

"What has happened here?" he asked, as he changed his travelling-dress for his uniform.

"A startling change. Since his daughter's death the Czar has become reconciled to the Czarina, and is with her constantly. Every diplomatic action has been broken off. The Greek deputation has not been received, the commanding officers of the various regiments of the guards have been despatched back to their colonies."

"And what do the women say to all this? That's the main point."

"The women are deucedly hard to get at just now. Since the reconciliation of the Czar and Czarina, domestic fidelity has become the rage in St. Petersburg. Every man is seen driving out with his wife. Even Princess Ghedimin ostentatiously parades everywhere on her husband's arm, and conducts herself so prudishly that she scarce returns my bow."

"And Zeneida?"

"Is in disgrace. The court chamberlain has inti-
mated that it would not give displeasure in high quarters
if she were to pass the coming season under a more
genial clime. Upon which she at once sent back her
credentials as court singer. She is having a sale of
her furniture, and is preparing for immediate departure."

"And the cause of disgrace?"

"Pushkin. You are aware that he was to have married Sophie Narishkin?"

"That is—it was a piece of medical jugglery. They
proposed to prolong the invalid's life and make it happier by her betrothal."

"All the same, Pushkin was her husband elect, and
the Czar was deeply hurt that the very day of Princess
Sophie's funeral Pushkin should go and get married to
the lovely Bethsaba, whom he ran away with from the
Ghedimins'!"

"Hullo! So he ran away with the little Circassian
princess!"

"The Czar was very cut up at his heartlessness.
Hence his displeasure with Fräulein Ilmarinen."

"But what had she to do with it?"

"She was witness to the marriage."

"What, she? And she who worshipped Pushkin!
That is a dangerous woman!"

"Fortunately she can't do much harm now. She
begged an audience of the Czar; but his Majesty answered that he would only receive her in your presence."

"Then it shall be a hot reception for her! Thanks
for the good news!"

And Araktseieff hastened off to the Hermitage, where
the Czar was to be found before noon.

Alexander extended his hand with emotion to the returned favorite, who had travelled night and day to obey
his behest.

" My only true friend !" he said, in a low voice.

" Not the only one, sire.   The Czarina stands first."

" You are right.   We have come together again, and
I am only beginning to learn that in her I have won back
a whole world.   I grudge the moments which this pile
of drafts causes me to spend from her."

" I am at your orders, sire !"

" That will greatly help.   Just you look through this
sheaf of papers, which I can make nothing of, and execute everything according to your own judgment."

" I will not stir from here before I have gone through
them all."

" Among them you will find a petition for a farewell
audience from Fräulein Ilmarinen.   Answer in my name
that I am willing to receive her, but solely in your presence.   Now I am off to church, where I shall meet the
Czarina.   We are holding a requiem mass for poor Sophie Narishkin."

Araktseieff made feint to be hearing this for the first
time ; and in consequence of the melancholy surprise
went through a theatrical scene of up-turned eyes and
exclamations, ending up with, as he kissed the hand of
the Czar, " I feel that my heart is torn out of my body
at this mournful news, sire !"   He was the only man
in the world who secretly exulted over the news of the
unhappy child's death.

The Czar left him alone in his study ; and the favorite found many more important matters to attend to
than Zeneida's petition.   From the multitudinous papers
it was plain to see that when the cat's away the mice
begin to play.   Everything was tending to lead the Czar

back to the paths of liberalism. Here must the first clearance be made!

A few days later Zeneida was surprised, in the midst of her packing, by a visit from Jakuskin.

" I have come to tell you how glad I am that you are leaving us."

" A singular kind of farewell."

" But comprehensible! It is well for you that you are going ; and well for us, too. The rôle you were playing is at an end, and I am glad of it!"

" So it seems." .

" Araktseieff is returned, and his iron hand is wielded over our heads. You, fair Madonna, had exiled him with your refined arts. Now it has become evident that the refinement of intrigue does not pay in our atmosphere. The old tyrant is back, and the Czar more completely in his power than ever."

" I know it. I have had intimation that a farewell audience will only be accorded me in his presence."

" And you are going ?"

" Decidedly. I must reconcile the Czar with Pushkin."

" Is that your only reason ?"

" What else keeps me here ?"

" The wish to depose friend Araktseieff."

" I have no power to do that."

" Well, then, I have."

" By violence ?"

" It is already done. To-morrow morning will no longer see him in St. Petersburg. I have struck him to the heart, and not with a dagger. His fate is already sealed. He is dead and buried already, though he has no idea of it. Read this letter."

Zeneida's face changed from ghastly white to fiery red

as she hastily perused the letter handed her by Jakuskin. Her lips parted with surprise and horror as she read.

"You are terrible men!" stammered she, as she gave it back.

"We understand what we are about, eh?"

"And he knows nothing of it?"

"There is not a man about him who dares to make it known to him. Diabolka wrote me herself. I have copied her letter and sent the whole affair to the Czar through the Sophien post. May he learn it from the lips of the Czar—or, what is still more probable, may it fall into his own hands in opening the Czar's letters. Ah, Zeneida! If only he received the letter at the very time that you were having audience! If only you could see him then! Oh, I could fain envy you the satisfaction of that moment!"

Zeneida's audience was appointed for the next day. It was the Czar's usual habit, on leaving Monplaisir at five in the afternoon, to pass a short time at the Hermitage, which stood near the Winter Palace and had been a favorite resort of Catherine II. His library here, where he transacted business, was furnished very simply. Hither were brought to him the letters which came by the Sophien post. The apartment was now reserved to Araktseieff's use, who sat there from morning to evening settling, on his own responsibility, the affairs of the vast empire in the name of the Czar. Matters of home and foreign policy, religion, education, trade, finance, all were dependent on his sole will; ministers and stadt holders alike his puppets. Alexander would take no part in anything—signing, unread, whatever Araktseieff laid before him. Those drafts laid aside by him were mere waste paper.

To-day, too, found the favorite hard at work at the Czar's own writing-table, Alexander restlessly pacing the room, for Fräulein Ilmarinen alone had been granted audience that day.

Zeneida presented herself at the appointed hour. She was dressed in deep mourning, her golden hair forming a striking contrast to her sombre attire.

The Czar advanced to meet her, but received her with marked coldness.

Araktseieff feigned not to see her; did not lift his eyes from the papers before him.

"Fräulein Ilmarinen," said Alexander, "you desired to speak with me personally. You may speak."

"Will your Majesty forgive the boldness of my request, but I have papers to place before you which the owner intrusted to me on sole condition that I delivered them personally into your own hands. These papers form the diary of the late Princess Sophie Narishkin!"

With a deep sigh the Czar exclaimed, "Poor child!" his voice trembling with agitation.

"It was her last wish, and I must fulfil it."

"You were with her, then, in her last hours?"

"And afterwards. She had sent for me."

"It was you who closed her eyes?"

Zeneida bowed her head silently.

"I thank you," said the Czar, and, taking from her the white-bound diary, he held out his hand to her—a soft, thin hand—but the action was not a cordial one.

Zeneida kissed the hand.

"Have you any wish, Fräulein Ilmarinen?"

"Only one, sire! That you should graciously please to read the last three pages of Sophie's diary *in my presence.*"

The Czar glanced back, as though to ask Araktseieff's permission. Then only did he resolve to accede to her wish, and, opening the diary, he read.

He bit his lips to conceal his emotion. But Zeneida well knew what it was he was reading; she knew the whole contents of the diary, as well as those last confused lines written by the convulsed hand of an unhappy child, looking forward with yearning and dread to the cold embrace of death. And the Czar, as he concluded the last page, looking up at Zeneida, saw that her eyes were filled with tears.

Mutely he nodded his head and sighed.

"She wanted me to read this to exonerate Pushkin, did she not? She wished it so. She had a great, noble soul!"

"Indeed she had, sire!"

"And it was at her desire; and Pushkin was only fulfilling her last wishes in acting as he did?"

"He could not have done otherwise."

"I believe it. He could not have done otherwise. And yet I cannot reconcile myself to the thought that he did it — that in the very same hour that he had covered the face of one bride with the funereal veil he could draw the bridal veil over the face of the other! He had to do it! And yet it seems incomprehensible to human understanding how there can be a whole eternity in one short hour of time; how, in one short hour, a man can fly from the arctic pole to the equator; how, in one and the same moment, a man can mourn over a dead love and marry a living one!"

"But if he had loved her previously?" asked Zeneida, softly.

"What did you say?"

"If that which he experienced for her who was gone

was but the adoration and boundless reverence for a being of another world, whose wings were already bearing her heavenward when first he knew her? If all the affection, tenderness, devotion which led him to the feet of his worshipped bride were but sacrifices offered at the shrine of a saint to keep her in life?"

Alexander struck his forehead with his hand.

"You are right! I never inquired into it. Never asked him if the dream of love were more than a sick girl's fancy? He suffered himself to be bound by that dream. That was the whole of it. In his heart he loved another, and would have sacrificed himself for her. It was all my doing, my fault—for everything I do is faulty, and everything that goes wrong is through me!"

These words were spoken by the Czar of All the Russias, not in bitterness, but with the deep melancholy of conviction. It moved the heart to pity.

Suddenly he turned to Zeneida.

"Do you wish me, then, to grant Pushkin permission to return?"

"No, sire. He is in good hands. Whoever is a true friend to him would rather desire that he should live a happy life *far from St. Petersburg!*"

This surprised Araktseieff. He threw his pen down and scrutinized Zeneida.

"And for yourself, have you no wishes?" continued the Czar.

"I am leaving St. Petersburg to-morrow, sire!"

"And do you not wish that I should send you back your credentials?"

Oh, how proudly she raised her head at the words! She, too, was a queen, and she proved it.

"Sire, where I am once shown that my presence is unwelcome I do not remain!"

23

It was an audacious ' speech, bordering on treason,
and not the manner in which to address the Czar of All
the Russias !

Springing from his chair, it was the favorite and not
the melancholy monarch who hastened to reply to the
haughty singer.

"Are you aware, young lady, that there are duties from
which a feeling of wounded pride does not exempt us?
To them belongs the respect due to the throne and
ruler, to whom you owe your fame."

Zeneida's bosom heaved ; her nostrils dilated like those
of a zebra prepared for the fight with a wolf. Her great
dark flashing eyes threatened to annihilate the favorite ;
her lips quivered as if with fever.

"Your Excellency," she gasped, "there are men who
have carried gratitude to their benefactors to the other
ends of the earth with them, and who, though they had
the misfortune to lose the favor of their august protectors, *have not gone home to sing the ' Knife Song ' !*"

This was such a smart slap in the face to Araktseieff
that he went back to his seat as though thinking it not
worth his while to reply to the insinuation. Did she
really know about it ? Had she her secret spies—perhaps Diabolka ?—the gypsy girl could write now !

Instead of his silenced favorite, the Czar now took up
the lance. It was but fair. If the squire defends his
lord, surely his lord should defend the squire.

"Your bitter remarks are in the wrong place, Fräulein
Ilmarinen. If there is one man in Greater Russia who
deserves to be looked upon as a perfect pattern of fidelity and loyalty, that is the man ! He who has been at
my side in every battle ; has shared with me every danger, yet never claiming part in my glory ; who watches,
that I may sleep ; who defies the world, to defend me ;

who forsakes me never, when all else desert me; that man is Araktseieff! What hard proofs of loyalty has he not withstood! How often have his enemies prevailed to banish him! And yet, as often as I have called, he has returned, without a word of reproach to me! I struck him a vital blow in exiling his son, yet he could kiss my hand and say I had done right, and remain loyal to me. Such is Araktseieff!"

But the favorite could not glory in this imperial recognition of his services, for, as he resumed his seat and, in order to mark his contemptuous indifference, opened the Sophien post-bag, the very letter Jakuskin had mentioned to Zeneida came to hand, and absorbed his attention to such a degree that he actually became deaf to the sound of his own praises from the lips of the Czar.

Zeneida saw how his face was working with demoniacal torture; how, convulsed by nameless horror, it had changed to the semblance of a maddened spectre; she saw his hair stand on end, his lips become blue, his eyes start from their sockets.

"Oh, woe is me!" he suddenly roared out, in a tone so brutalized that the Czar turned round in affright. Araktseieff beat his breast with the letter, as a man tries to heal his wound with the hair of the dog that bit him, or of a scorpion with its dead body; then, up from his seat, "Oh, woe! oh, woe! that I came back! Why was I not there at the time?" And he flung out of the room like a madman.

The Czar, thinking that a sudden fit of mania had seized the favorite, endeavored to hold him back.

"Alexis Andreovitch! What is the matter — where are you rushing?"

"Pardon, your Majesty; I must go back to Grusino."

"You will not leave me now? Affairs of state—the country?"

Zeneida, placing herself directly in front of Araktse-ieff, with arms crossed on her breast, gave him one look.

That look sobered him for an instant. Compelling his countenance to resume its cold exterior, while the Czar laid his hand soothingly on his arm, his official self fought the real Araktseieff for the mastery. But this time the man conquered. Striking his forehead with the crushed letter still held in his hand, he burst out:

"What do I care for Russia? What do I care for all this miserable earth — for the Czar — for all the gods, when they could let such things happen? Oh, woe is me!"

And, pushing away the Czar's hand, he rushed scream-ing from the room like one struck to death. The letter to the Czar he took with him.

"What can have come to the man?" exclaimed the Czar in amazement.

He had but now been investing him with virtues such as had never been possessed save by that one man, and here this very man suffers himself to indulge in so coarse and violent an outbreak as would not be ventured upon before a petty prince, let alone a Russian Czar.

Was there some witchcraft in Zeneida's gaze that could madden the soberest men, until, flinging down the seals of office at the feet of their sovereign, they should say:

"What is your country to me? What care I for you and your gods?"

The eyes of the Czar strove to read the secret from Zeneida's face.

The artiste would have withdrawn.

" Stay !"

" If your Majesty commands, I will stay altogether and not leave St. Petersburg."

" Do you know what ails this man ?"

" I do."

" Then speak."

CHAPTER XXXVIII

THE TRAGI-COMEDY AT GRUSINO

THE double wedding was to be celebrated. The whole of the tenantry had been commanded to attend. The courtyard of the castle had been thronged with wondering serfs from early dawn. Two couples—one handsome, the other loathsome—were to be married that day.

The preparations were on a magnificent scale. For three whole days the castle cooks had been engaged in making the national dishes. Long floral walks had been erected in the courtyard; the gateway had been converted into a triumphal arch by means of wreaths and colored transparencies. In the centre of the great courtyard was a stage erected, covered with gay-hued carpets of goat's hair. Upon it stood a table bearing an image of the Virgin Mary, the covered plate in which were the wedding-rings, a goblet, bread and salt—in fine, everything required for the ceremony preceding the marriage service. For there is much to be gone through before a bridal couple reaches the church portion of the ceremony—much to be gone through at the hands of the bystanders, the groomsmen, bridesmaids, and wedding-mother.

The wedding-mother has an important part to play. Until they arrive at the church doors she is the principal personage.

Daimona is the wedding-mother in this instance. She is marrying one of her serfs to her slave; she is mother to both. The high-backed chair upon the tribune is for her. At first sound of the bells the ceremony begins. From the priest's house the bridesmaids bring the bride in her bridal array. Diabolka's dress glistens with heavy gold embroidery; a costly girdle encircles her slender waist, on her neck hangs a fivefold necklace of gold coins; her head-dress is of precious stones. One might think she was a princess. From the opposite side resounds a horn, and the bridegroom, Schinko, is seen advancing with his supporters and groomsmen; his coal-black, curly hair, falling on to his shoulders, betraying, despite the national costume, the bridegroom's Indian descent.

The groomsmen welcome the approaching bride with song, and follow the bridal pair to the altar. From out the stables the second couple are now brought. Wild screeches and the squeak of the bagpipe accompany them in their progress. The pomp of wedding garments only serves to make them more ridiculous. They are received with mocking rhymes, which seem to please them highly. Both are very drunk; they kiss every one who comes in their way; but as they near each other they cut hideous grimaces at one another; and as they go up to the altar steps the bride gives the bridegroom a good pinch on the arm, while the bridegroom deals her out a smart kick with his foot.

This couple is also placed at the table, so that bridegrooms and brides stand one at each corner.

At the second peal of bells the wedding-mother descends with her whole retinue from the castle. The retinue is composed of twelve female slaves, clad in white, who line the steps on either side. The wedding-mother mounts the tribune alone, and takes her seat upon the throne.

She is dressed like a queen, and wears a purple mantle; her cap of marten-skin is embroidered with gold and pearls; her face painted white and red. She begins the ceremony.

"Schinko, what do you bring the bride for your wedding present?"

And Schinko details what he brings her:

"Two gay-colored beds, a cloak of Karassia cloth lined with fox, a breastplate with silver buttons, a kokosnik set with pearls, two pair of red boots, an embroidered linen shirt, twelve zinc plates, a dish, and a gold-embroidered head-dress and veil—if she behaves well!"

All these gifts were brought round by the bridegroom's supporters, and severally shown to the guests.

The bride, on her side, gives the bridegroom clothes, ornaments, household utensils, and, last, a bundle of birch rods, "with which he is to chastise me when I do not behave well."

Now it is the turn of the second couple.

"Well, Polyka, and what do you bring your bridegroom?"

But this well-assorted couple are not content that one should speak before the other; one interrupts the other, and they splutter out:

"I, a ragged cloak."

"I, a pot with a hole in it."

"I, a footless stocking in which ten cats could not catch one mouse."

"I, an empty jug that once had brandy in it."

"I, a bed sacking, with no blankets, and that lacks feathers."

The wedding guests laughed themselves ill over this dialogue of the bridal couple.

"And then twelve pair of 'dubina'!" shouted the bridegroom, with a loud laugh.

"With two ends to them," returned the bride, with a giggle.

The word "dubina," so soft-sounding in Russian, signifies in the barbaric English tongue—stick! The sack has found a mouth, the vinegar jar a stopper, and he his match, grinned the wedding guests.

"Now exchange rings," says Daimona to the couples. "They are in this covered plate. Those of the one couple are of gold and silver; the gold one is the bride's; the silver, the bridegroom's. The rings of the second couple are of copper and lead."

The wedding-mother, removing the silken cover from the plate, signed to Diabolka to set the example.

Diabolka, taking the gold and silver ring, placed the gold one on her own finger, and was handing the silver one to Schinko.

Daimona seized Diabolka's hand.

"Not so! You will give the silver ring to Vuk; and Schinko the copper one to Polyka. *For your bridegroom is Vuk, and Schinko's bride is Polyka.* That is the arrangement."

A burst of loud laughter followed upon these words. Now there would be some real fun. Diabolka and Vuk, Polyka and Schinko. The wedding-mother had the right to marry her serfs as she chose. Her serfs belonged to her, hand and foot, as did her horses and her asses. She can pair her serfs as she chooses.

The laughter of the assembled guests grew louder as the two drunken monsters, at Daimona's words, threw themselves on the handsome prey given over to them.

Their laughter was only stopped when Diabolka, before them all, gave Vuk such a blow on the chest with both hands that he went backwards off the table, and, rolling from the tribune, fell among the people.

Things were indeed going badly.

Daimona, springing towards the table like a fury, struck her fist violently upon it. At that sound the spectators' laughter suddenly ceased. The grin was still on their faces, but every sound died away on their laughing lips.

It was fun no longer.

"You will not take the husband I have chosen for you?" shrieked Daimona, in fury.

"No," returned the girl, stamping her foot, "no!"

"Dog! gypsy devil! You dare to oppose me—me, who raised you from a dung-heap!"

"Then let me go back to the dung-heap."

"So you shall! If you will not have the bridegroom I have given you, then take off the bridal dress I gave you, and be off in the gypsy rags you came in. But they want something to complete them—the addition of a thrashing for your audacity. Schinko! Here!"

He himself, her elder brother, her lover, her bridegroom!

Schinko was wearing, as bridegroom, the symbol of his office hanging from his girdle—the short-handled whip. At his mistress's command he raised the whip.

"Strike!" ordered Daimona.

The girl, white with fear, held her face between her hands.

"Brother, can you strike me?"

She had even got so far as to fear the lash. Or was it the thought that it was Schinko's hand which was to strike that made her shrink back? The gypsy's heart was not hard enough to let him strike the blow. He threw the whip away.

" Dog, pick up that whip ; or shall I have you and her tied together to the tail of a wild horse? Go on. Slash away until I say enough; fifty lashes for me, fifty for Junker Jevgen."

Schinko picked up the whip.

Despairing, the girl, flinging herself at Daimona's feet, clasped her knees, and, sobbing, implored for mercy.

"Ah, you abomination, that's the place for you !" cried Daimona through her clinched teeth ; and seizing the girl at her feet by her long plaits, she shrieked to Schinko, " Now, have at her !"

With one spring the gypsy, like a panther, was upon them, and, seizing Daimona by the throat with his left hand, with his right he whipped out his dagger. Terrified, Daimona released her hold of Diabolka and defended herself with one arm; the serf's dagger had pierced her shoulder, the blood spouted high from it.

" Heh ! varlets ! seize him ! help !" stormed the woman.

But not a person stirred among the crowd. Daimona saw that she was left to herself. She was a powerful woman who knew how to fight; so, freeing herself from the gypsy's grasp, she pushed him from her, sprang off the tribune, and rushed towards the castle steps, Schinko after her.

Nor did a hand stir to hinder the serf. The crowd, the whole body of servants, looked on, and saw Schinko dash after the mistress and wound her afresh. The woman, turning upon him, began to wrestle with her pursuer ; his dagger was plunged again and again into

her breast. Once more she succeeded in pushing back
her adversary, and, darting into the midst of her women
servants, shouted, " Help ! protect me !"   The women
put their hands to their ears that they might not hear
her cries.   They all hated her.   Then she was seen flying down the long corridor, screaming and shrieking,
her murderer close upon her heels.   Still no one went
to the rescue.

At the extreme end of the corridor was the picture of
a saint.   Thither she fled, and fell down before it in
beseeching attitude.   But the saint did not stir a hand
to protect her.   Then rushing to the parapet of the
balcony, she attempted in vain to spring from it.

The murderer slowly comes down the stone steps
into the courtyard.   A path is made for him.   He as-
cends the bridal tribune.   There, her face to the ground,
lies a girl motionless with terror, shame, and despair.
Close to her the wedding garments.   The murderer
wipes the blood off his dagger with the bridal veil, and,
taking the girl by the hand, raises her to her feet.
They look each other in the eyes.   One look, like a
couple of wild wolves.   No need for speech !   Then
they run, hand in hand, into the steppe, into the
woods—anywhere.   No one seeks to hold them back.
They were never seen again.

Who would attempt to find two wolves escaped
from captivity, in their native lair, amid the dwellers
of the endless steppes, whether in forest or jungle?
Only·once did the two call a halt, where Diabolka,
having reached her gypsy encampment, wrote the letter to Jukuskin, in which she related the tragi-come-
dy of Grusino, and of which a copy fell into the
hands of the Czar's favorite, acquainting him with
the horrors that had taken place.   The starosts of

Grusino had not had the courage to give him the tidings.

Zeneida acted wisely in having personally related the events to the Czar; for those who later informed him of what had occurred at Grusino made a point of causing it to appear that this murder was in connection with St. Petersburg secret societies. Many were set upon finding the motive for the deed in high circles, where it was a matter of interest to keep the favorite from the person of the Czar, and where it was hoped, by the banishment of the son, to have effected a rupture of the close bond uniting Czar and favorite. Schinko and Diabolka were hired by the conspirators.

Was there any truth in this? No one has ever cleared up the mystery. But if any hand had prepared the blow, it had struck home.

Araktseieff was to be seen tearing through the streets of St. Petersburg, hatless, with hair wildly streaming. Your orthodox Russian, when he mourns, goes in sun and snow with head uncovered.

On the day of his flight two great wagon-loads of state papers were despatched from the favorite's palace to the Hermitage. His orders, his sword, his keys of office, he sent by his house-porter to the Lord Chamberlain. And, at the moment of his departure, the thunder of "Holy Christopher" startled the inhabitants of St. Petersburg out of their rest. This father among cannons is only fired when a general dies. The court favorite had himself gone to the commandant of the fortress and ordered the cannon to be fired. The commandant had no choice but to obey. Araktseieff was commander-in-chief of the artillery. When the firing was over the commandant asked:

" What was the name of the deceased general ?"
" Alexis Andreovitch Araktseieff !"
Some days later the Czar had terrible news of Arak-
tseieff. His reason had entirely left him.

CHAPTER XXXIX

THE HERMIT

ONLY when Araktseieff had left the Czar did the
emperor realize how completely alone he was in the
world.

There was not a man in whom he could place confidence; in every one he saw an enemy, a conspirator;
and his true friends, if he still possessed any, he had
imbittered by Araktseieff's recall. His generals were
disaffected by his not supporting the Greeks. Secret
treaties were directed against him. Those who were already apprised of his declaration of war, and had sufficient energy to act counter to him, had left the field at
the beginning of operations.

On Araktseieff's return to Grusino he had hurried
without delay to the mausoleum, and, barring the door
behind him, had cast himself down beside Daimona's
coffin, and for two whole days nothing was heard within
but his bitter sobs. He would eat nothing, would make
no answer to words or entreaties. " Daimona " was the
only sound he uttered.

He had loved that woman as only giant beasts love
their mates; when the hunter has shot the female he
may shoot the male, for it will not leave its dead. For
two whole days Araktseieff's household in vain besieged the door of the mausoleum; Chevalier Gal-

ban's representations also that he should come out and take care of his valuable life were fruitless; he paid no heed to his faithful followers. In vain they called him their sweet, good master, "sweet friend," "Alexis Andreovitch"; he was deaf to their voices.

On the third day Photios, the Archimandrite of the Monastery of St. George, came to the mausoleum. He is the holy man, to receive whose blessing hundreds of thousands make the yearly pilgrimage to the monastery from all parts of Russia. The decree of the saint is as much esteemed as is a papal bull.

When Czar Alexander I. gave into the hands of Prince Galitzin, the freethinker, the portfolio of Public Instruction, the Archimandrite, going up to the Czar, exclaimed threateningly:

"If you take the ancient faith from your people you will shake your empire to its foundations."

Whereupon the Czar dismissed Prince Galitzin, and the education of the people was left in the hands of the Sacred Synod. Russians always have their "living saints," some of them miraculous.

Photios, standing at the door of the mausoleum, called to Araktseieff within, in language unmistakably plain.

"Abandoned criminal, come out!"

The cries within were silenced.

"Come out from there!"

Araktseieff staggered out. He was scarcely recognizable. His beard, untouched for several days, stood out in gray bristles round his face; his eyes were blood-shot with weeping; his lips swollen; his hair lay wildly matted on his forehead; his general's uniform was streaked with green mould.

" What seek you in that grave?"

" Death."

" Of course you will die, we all shall do so, as penalty for our sins. But do you desire to crown your evil deeds by dying unrepentant? Do you desire to die beside the coffin of her for the loss of whose soul you are guilty? You were the cause of her sin; will you drag her down to hell? Instead of thinking of repentance, would you follow her to condemnation? Defiantly would you burst the barriers of that fearful next world instead of entreating admission with bended head? Of course you will die, but not when it pleases you; rather when it pleases your Maker to grant you death as a reward for penance.

" Your place is in the deep catacombs," continued Photios; " not by the side of your concubine. Under the rays of the burning sun, in storm, in the roar of the tempest, under drenching rain, shall you seek repentance! Stand up! follow me!"

Araktseieff crawled towards him on his knees.

" Now eat!" commanded Photios, throwing him a couple of turnips.

Picking them up, Araktseieff obeyed.

" Now put on these!" And he threw a dilapidated monk's dress towards him, faded out of all color by sun and rain. Araktseieff, taking off his general's uniform, put it on. And as saints on this earth do not drive in carriages, he followed the saint on foot and barefooted to the gates of the Monastery of St. George.

St. George's is one of the wealthiest monasteries in all Russia. It is situated near Grusino, at the end of the long peninsula formed by the river Volkhov and Lake Ilmer. Its gilded cupolas, green from the verdigris which centuries have brought out on the copper, tend to spread its fame far and wide. But entrance within the walls of the monastery oppresses the spirits. Silver dais upon silver dais reach to the dome; the organ towers aloft, with its pipes of gold; there are pictures of saints dazzling with rubies; mosaics composed entirely of precious stones. Upon the elaborately decorated altars lie costly Bibles bound in silver, and enamelled books of the mass. Over one of the altars is a picture of St. George in beaten silver. But it is only when we come to the "treasure chamber," with its priceless store of mitres, crooks, crowns, pearl-embroidered stoles, golden monstrances, that we realize how rich is Heaven's vicegerent—the Church. While the priests who guard all these treasures wander in among them in coarse cassocks and bare feet, that the world may see how poor is man.

But the most jealously guarded of all the treasures stood before the altar. It was a granite pillar enclosed within silver rails.

On the granite was engraven: "Upon this spot knelt Czar Alexander, attended by his faithful servants, the Archimandrite Photios and Alexis Andreovitch Araktseieff, in the year 1818."

Thither Photios brought the statesman, that he might see his name perpetuated beside that of the Czar.

"So high you had raised yourself. Now come and see how low you have sunk!"

The Archimandrite led the penitent back to the cloister and showed him his, the Archimandrite's, cell. It was a space six feet broad by eight feet long. But there was one luxury in it: it had a window through which sunshine penetrated. His bed was a coffin roughly put together; his *prie-dieu* a stone hollowed out by constant kneeling; a jug and a bowl for the daily *kwas* the sole furniture of the cell. Yet all this was luxury compared with what awaited the penitent.

In the catacombs of the cloister were caves hewn out of solid rock, just large enough to contain a man kneeling or recumbent; a small hole in the heavy iron door let in air. Total darkness reigned. These caves were inhabited by the whilom great, powerful aristocrats, masters over hundreds of thousands, now no longer masters of their own souls. It is not tyranny, not the power of the sacred hierarchy which holds them bound here, but their own blind zeal. Despising, hating the world, they are self-condemned to the awful imprisonment. The catacombs of the cloisters of St. George and of Solowetshk ever harbor numbers thus self-condemned to a living death.

It pleased Araktseieff.

Lying upon his straw he passed days and weeks. His door was kept locked by day, only to be opened at sound of the vesper bell, when he went to seek for food, for food is not brought to penitents. Only at dusk may they steal into the cloister garden to seek for mangel-wurzel, samphire, potatoes, and such like produce of the earth, their sole sustenance. One day Araktseieff came across a still more remarkable penitent than himself.

He, too, had once been a distinguished bojar; but none knew what his real name was. Here he was only known as " Little Father Nahum."

Nahum did not even allow himself the luxury of a ragged cassock. His sole covering is a rush mat woven by himself, his white hair and gray beard flow wildly down over his dirt-begrimed limbs. Nahum does not allow himself lodging in a cave. In summer

24

he sleeps in pools, in winter he creeps into a dung-heap. To kneel day after day in his cave is not humiliation enough for him ; he prostrates himself across the threshold of the church door, that those who enter may walk over him, kick him, spit on him. To gather fresh roots out of the earth and eat them Little Father Nahum looks upon as sinful gluttony. He seeks his evening meal from the dust-heap; what is thrown there is his sustenance.

Araktseieff had been doing penance three weeks in the catacombs when, one evening, as he was returning with a bundle of leeks in his hand, he came upon Nahum feasting off his self-laid dinner-table, the dust-heap.

" Ah," said Little Father Nahum, accosting the new-comer, " I have found so much to eat here to-night I can share with a friend."

" What has Providence provided for you ?"

" Mouldy cheese."

" All right.　Give me some."

" Here it is.　Take it all," returned Nahum.　" He who hankers after a penitent's food should have it all given up to him."

And he handed him the mouldy cheese, with the paper in which it had been wrapped and thrown upon the dust-heap. Truly, loathsome food! But Araktseieff's attention was not so much arrested by the contents as by the paper in which the cheese was enclosed. It was a letter, and in it Araktseieff at once recognized the handwriting of the Czar. His blood surged within him. The Czar's writing a cover for stale cheese! And then the contents! It was a letter addressed to Photios.

" Call him to you. Speak to him in the name of holy

religion; strengthen him in the faith. Admonish him to preserve his life for the good of his country, which is beyond all other considerations. Thus will you preserve to the empire a servant of inestimable loyalty, and to me a faithful friend whom I sincerely honor and esteem."

And this was the paper chosen as a cover for mouldy cheese and thrown upon a dust-heap!

"Well, eat away, man," murmured Little Father Nahum, and, taking up the cheese which Araktseieff had let fall on the dust-heap, offered it him in the flat of his dirty hand.

Thrusting his fellow-penitent aside, Araktseieff hastened to Photios.

Photios was in the act of reading vespers. Araktseieff did not suffer him to come to an end.

"Was this letter from the Czar addressed to you?"

"To me."

"And you threw it on the dust-heap?"

"That you might find it there."

"I have found it. My penance is over. I return to St. Petersburg."

"Just what I wished to accomplish."

"You have accomplished it. But you do not yet know what you were doing when you brought Alexis Araktseieff forth from the grave? You constrained him back to life and the world, once more to prove the stuff that is in him. Well may you tremble before a resuscitated Araktseieff!"

"A blessing be upon all your actions!" stammered the Archimandrite, and continued his vespers.

Araktseieff left the monastery that very hour. He left it with the same wild frenzy of destruction with which he had entered it, only that then his desire was for self-destruction; now had returned the old desire for the destruction of others.

When Araktseieff, after those three weeks, was seen again in St. Petersburg, every one started back in terror at his appearance. His face was emaciated, his hair had turned quite white. It was plain to see that he had risen from the grave.

CHAPTER XL

DISCORDS

ZENEIDA was strolling alone through the shady winding paths of her park in the twilight of evening. Nightingales were singing; from a pond close by came the sound of croaking frogs; ever and anon the song of a boatman on the Neva broke the stillness, or the distant sound of a violin or clarinet in an inn, or the howl of a chained-up dog. Again would come the tones of the passing-bell, announcing a death, or from the vicinity of Monplaisir a sharp "Who goes there?" "Halt!" sometimes followed by a shot. Why that shot? Then again the song of nightingales, the croak of frogs, sounds of clarinet and passing-bell. These discords found answering echo in her heart.

Araktseieff's second return was hurrying on the crisis. No sooner had the Czar passed over the cares of government again to his favorite's shoulders than he had secluded himself completely in the solitude of Monplaisir. Just as he had formerly avoided his consort, so now did he devote himself exclusively to her. He seemed as if he could not live an hour without her, as though he were endeavoring to atone by this devotion for his fourteen years of neglect. Now first he recognized the treasure he possessed and had neglected ; now first he perceived that the wife he loved was ill, that her protracted sorrows, her secret grief, had undermined her strength. And he trembled to think he might her.

But the Czarina was happy. She blessed the sickness which had given her back her husband. The Czarina's physician, Dr. Stoffregen, had recommended a milder climate for her through the severity of winter, perhaps that of Venice; but Elisabeth had answered, "A Russian empress should not die anywhere else than on Russian soil." And it was this thought alone which absorbed the soul of the Czar.

Of the devastations wrought by Araktseieff, armed as he was with unfettered power, none told the Czar. Of all that was passing on the other side of the poplars of Monplaisir he was ignorant. He was not informed that Araktseieff's first step was to have the entire household of Grusino, who had been witnesses to the murder, consisting of ten men and twelve maid-servants, brought to St. Petersburg to the pillory and lashed until they were half-flayed, for not having gone to Daimona's rescue. He was ignorant that the severity he had previously practised as a system was now, by his thirst for vengeance, increased to gross cruelty ; that he had dismissed high officials of every kind from their posts without any other reason than simply because they did not please him ; that he was filling the dungeons on mere suspicion ; that he had even cruelly oppressed the poor Finns. Possessing nothing more that he could take from them, he punished them through that which he " gave " them, his latest edict being that their toasts at public dinners must be

given in Russian. All this had strained disaffection and
discontent to its utmost limit. Of all this Alexander
knew nothing. No. He was absorbed in devising how
to procure fresh air without draught in his beloved
patient's room ; how to keep out the gnats ; and, among
the flowers for her apartment, how to select those that
would not give her a headache.

And Zeneida well knows what is looming in the distance. Secret societies are no longer holding meetings; they are agreed what is to be done. The only
question now is—" When ?"

The outbreak must be general throughout the empire.
The threads are in Zeneida's hands. The artiste has
retired from the stage. Moreover, the opera is closed
during the summer months in St. Petersburg, and she
will not again appear as a member of the Imperial
Opera Company, but will give a concert for a charitable
purpose in the course of the autumn. The day was to
be publicly announced in official papers ten days previously. When the announcement, therefore, appeared
that " Fräulein Ilmarinen would sing for the benefit of
the Orphanage " on such and such a date the conspirators would know that this was the day fixed for the
rebellion. The government organ would itself spread
the word throughout the empire. Thus in her hand are
the shears which shall sever the fatal thread ; and the
grave foreknowledge of all that it must bring with it is
oppressing her spirit. The rebellion is unavoidable ;
no one will longer bear the heavy burden ; from ragged
mujik to titled magnate, all are yearning to burst the
yoke, and the Kalevains have more reason to weep
than their fellows. But what is to happen to the
imperial pair in the outbreak? Both have been such
kind protectors to Zeneida. The palace had been a

home to her. How will it be possible to save their lives without proving a traitor to their cause?

And then a second trouble—Pushkin. True, he had promised her he would withdraw his name from "the green book"; but, when giving the promise, he had thought he would have the daughter of the Czar to wife. That is over now, and Pushkin has no further reason to withdraw from the Northern Union. He, too, is in possession of the conspirators' plans; there is not a doubt but that as soon as he reads the announcement that Zeneida will sing for the benefit of the Orphanage he will appear that day in St. Petersburg, even he must leave Paradise itself to be there.

How is she to hinder this without casting the slur of cowardice upon Pushkin? The delights of love alone would not be strong enough to hold him back—a yet stronger motive must be found. And she paces backward and forward under the trees in the dusk; in her soul reign the same discords which disturb the brilliant night, and she seeks in vain some quieting thought.

The Czar has grown melancholy; the Czarina is sick unto death; they live but for each other, have shut themselves up from the world. Their example is contagious. Even Prince Ghedimin has become reconciled to his wife, and no longer visits Zeneida. St. Petersburg society has scattered itself among the forty islands of the Neva. Every one lives to himself; all social life is extinct. Every visitor is looked upon suspiciously by the host as one of Araktseieff's spies. There is an oppressive calm over everything. People do not even write to each other any more. They tremble at the black inquisition.

Pushkin gives no news of himself. He sits at home in his desert at Pleskow. If he keeps silent about his

happiness, he has a hundred good reasons for that silence. It is possible that Bethsaba has written more
than once to Zeneida; but letters are an uncertain medium of communication. Who knows into whose hands
they may fall?"

This great calm, this isolation, this striving to keep
up the spirits, began to be oppressive. Chevalier Galban received orders to go from villa to villa and organ-
ize some amusements among the aristocracy. Husbands
were no longer to be tied to their wives' apron-strings.

It was rumored that the lovely Princess Ghedimin
would break the ice and bring society together again
by means of a great reception on the day of the Feast
of Masinka, and, in order to make the reconciliation of
the Prince and Princess more publicly known, that Zeneida would be included among the Princess's invited guests.

The haughty Princess sending an invitation to the
equally haughty Queen of Song, whom the world cred-
ited with having been one of the Prince's flames! It is
hard to say which woman has the greater courage, the
one who sends or the one who accepts the invitation.

But Korynthia has made a still more difficult decision.
She means to send Bethsaba an invitation, accompanied by a coaxing, forgiving, affectionate letter, written
by her own hand. And in order to insure the young
wife's acceptance, the Princess intends to offer the prospect of the imperial pardon. Bethsaba shall have the
opportunity of soliciting forgiveness from the Czar for
her own bold step, and the return of imperial favor
towards her husband, banished by the Czar's displeasure to Pleskow. This bait would be irresistible.

All this had Zeneida gathered from Chevalier Galban.

What did Korynthia hope to achieve by this? What
does she aim at in getting hold of Bethsaba?

It is next to impossible that the young wife should be tempted to leave her home during her honeymoon, and alone, without her husband, who may not leave the precincts of his estate. And yet, did she do so, what would be the consequences?

Zeneida thought she had found in the person of Bethsaba the missing link in the chain. Now it is her work to fit that link in its place.

CHAPTER XLI

HOW TO ROB A MAN OF HIS WIFE

It must be a poor toy that cannot amuse children. And there can be no greater children than a newly married couple who are deeply in love with each other.

There is kite-flying in the park at Pleskow; Bethsaba is in high glee at her kite always flying straight up and remaining aloft, while Alexander's is always coming to grief. Her kite, too, is much handsomer than his. In the form of a dragon, it has two large eyes, a mouth, nose, and movable ears; while Alexander's is just a commonplace thing, made out of old scraps of manuscripts pasted together. The wide expanse affords the two grown-up children room enough to run with their kites. No eyes to see them but those of the stag on the edge of the forest.

A post-chaise rolls quickly along the highway skirting the park walls; the postilion blows his horn cheerily.

"I think that post-chaise must have stopped at our gate," observes Bethsaba.

"So it has. It means either a guest or a letter."

"Oh, I hope no guest," sighed the little wife.

Newly married folk are not hospitable, as a rule.
Still, somebody appeared to have come. The dvornik
came out towards them from the castle. They hastily
let down their kites; they must not be caught at such
childish amusements. In the hurry the dragon caught
in the withered bough of a pine-tree and lost one eye.

"What a pity!" murmured Bethsaba, in vexation.
"Now my dragon has only got one eye. Have you a
scrap of paper about you to repair the damage?"

"Where should I get it from? Haven't you already
seized upon every vestige of paper to make your dragon
with?"

"Do look! Perhaps you'll find some old bill or
other."

Meanwhile the dvornik had come up to them.

"Well, Tanaschi, what is it?"

"A letter."

"To whom?"

Bethsaba seized the letter from the dvornik.

"Oh, oh! A woman's handwriting! Take it. A
love-letter. Some former flame writing to reproach
you. Read it. Of course it is to make an appointment."

"You are right enough. It is a woman's handwriting, but addressed to you, not to me, my dear."

"To me?" cried Bethsaba, in surprise. "Who can
have written to me? Perhaps Zeneida?"

"No, it's not Zeneida. I know her handwriting."

"Perhaps too well. But who else could have written
to me?"

And they began guessing who the writer could have
been while the letter passed from one to the other. At
last Alexander proposed that the best way to see who
had written the letter would be to open it.

As they saw the signature both simultaneously cried,
"My godmother!"   "Your godmother!"

"What can she have written about?"

Presently, as if it were intended for a joke, Bethsaba
laughed heartily over the letter.

"Ha, ha, ha! She wants me to go to the Masinka
Fête! Alone! Without Alexander! 'It is to be a grand
affair; the Czar and Czarina and several foreign princes
will be there ; I shall have an opportunity to entreat the
Czar to grant Alexander permission to go back to St.
Petersburg!' Ha, ha, ha! Did you hear that, Alexander Sergievitch? My godmother sends me an invitation to a ball without you! The letter could not have
come at a more opportune moment—I just wanted it!"

And with these words she seized the precious epistle ;
it just covered the damage the dragon had sustained,
and a couple of pins fixed it in place—the black seal
just forming the pupil of the eye. (The court had gone
into mourning for six weeks after Sophie's death, and
society used black sealing-wax during the period.)

"A large case also arrived by post-chaise," said the
dvornik.

"Put it on one side. I have no time now to look at it."

What more incomprehensible than that one of the
fair sex should have no time to look at a ball-dress
sent direct from the capital? The dragon was mended,
and ready now to resume its flight in the air.

Laughing and shouting, Bethsaba ran along with the
tail of her kite dragging after her ; the second child
stood looking on, laughing, while the dragon disapprovingly waggled its foolish-looking head. While starting
a kite, the flyer has to run back with head turned up-
ward. Bethsaba, therefore, was not aware that she was
running directly against some one coming towards her

from the English garden; and was startled to find herself suddenly embraced from behind, and a long kiss
impressed upon her face. Then she gave a loud, joyous
cry, and the next instant her arms were round the intruder's neck; and, not content with hanging upon that
neck, she pulled its owner on to the grass, and, rolling
over, kissed her enthusiastically, interposing the most
endearing epithets: "You love!—you darling!—you
precious!" Pushkin was fain to go to the rescue, and
help them both up again.

It needed no extraordinary acumen to guess who the
guest, so affectionately welcomed, could be.

"Do not quite strangle me, you little goose!" exclaimed Zeneida. "Look; your dragon has meanwhile
flown away."

"Let it fly out into the wide world, and my godmother's letter with it. Do you know I have had a letter
from my godmother? Do you know she has invited
me to the Masinka Fête without Alexander? Do you
know what I did with her letter? My dragon had a
slit, and I mended the slit with it. How dear and good
of you to come and see us!"

"It is the correct thing. Six weeks after marriage it
is the wedding-mother's duty to come and look after the
young couple and see that they are happy together—
and if they really care for each other. Has your husband beaten you yet?"

"Oh, dreadfully," said Bethsaba, pretending to complain. "The last time it was here!" And she secretly
rubbed a place on her arm until she had made it red;
but a redness, Zeneida detected, which had come from
no blows.

"And you, Pushkin, have you been writing many fine
verses?"

"Not a line! You know my muse is never active in fine weather. It requires storm, rain, and snow."

"And your sky has remained sunny?"

"As you see. I have not written a word."

This was very possible. There are times in his life when a poet only feels poetry, does not write it.

"Why, we have not a sheet of paper in the house," said Bethsaba, whose woman's instinct whispers to her it is her greatest boast when a poet's wife can say that it has been through her that the poet has been faithless to his muse. "We really have not. I had to use my godmother's letter to make my dragon's eye."

"Indeed! Is that how you treat your correspondence? That is a good thing to know. I will never write to you then, but, when I have anything to tell you, will rather come myself."

"That will be nice."

"Or I will take you with me."

To this the same response, "That will be nice," did not come. Clinging to Alexander's arm she looked up to him, saying:

"You will not let me go, will you?"

Zeneida answered for him:

"To that we shall not ask Alexander Sergievitch. His business it is when his little wife wants to go visiting to order out the carriage and horses, and to take care of the house in her absence."

"But I could not go anywhere if I wished it. Do you not see how I am dressed? It is the Pleskow costume! Alexander tells me it was also the costume of the first Russian Christian, Princess Olga. And I like it so much. Admire this sarafan with its many buttons, the pearl-embroidered povojnyik on my head, my red boots and striped silk stockings!" And with childish *naïveté* she lifted up her dress to her knees. " How people would stare if I were to appear among them in this costume! I have no other dress; this is what pleases my Alexander to see me in !"

She told the truth. The ball-dresses sent her were not her own property yet; she had not accepted the present.

Alexander drew his little nestling wife closer to him.

" We have become thorough peasant farmers."

"Heaven grant that you may remain so!" thought Zeneida to herself. " I fear, however, that some day you will be leaving wife and village, and it will no longer be the pearl-embroidered cap upon your wife's head you will then consider the greatest adornment, but the Phrygian cap you will be running after !"

That which Dante omitted among the tortures of hell was that a woman should be condemned to see the man she loves, who might have been hers, revelling in the love of another woman, and she his wife. Had Zeneida's love been that of ordinary women, it would have mattered little to her that the man, round whom her fetters had been cast, should, sooner or later, be dragged by these very fetters to the grave. The joys of the present would have outweighed the tortures of the future, the dread secrets of eternity. But so dearly had she loved Pushkin that she sought for him a happiness in which she had no part. It was an unnatural situation, and one requiring a nobler courage than most possess. But is not the woman who devotes herself to play a part in politics an unnatural, abnormal creation? Upon the altar of politics the heart is the lamb of sacrifice. In the service of a Moloch sensual passion may exist, but not love. Those who become political leaders have no longer fa-

ther or mother, brother or sister, lover or friend; they
recognize no difference between honesty and roguery,
between the laws of God and the expediencies of man.
Hence the pursuit of politics is an unnatural occupation
for women, with whom love and justice are ruling prin-
ciples. The Amazon who went forth to war had first
rooted out the gentler feelings.

The possibility of women taking up such a part is
only comprehensible in countries where oppression is
so unbearable, so utter, that the thirst for freedom ex-
tends from the starved hearts of the men to those of
the women. The poet-laureate might love the court
prima donna, but not the plenipotentiary of the Szojusz
Blagodenztoga. Between those two lay " the green
book "—a far more efficient obstacle than the green
ocean.

But, all the same, the anchorites of St. George's Monastery had not carried their self-torture to greater perfection than had this woman who had forced herself to
come as a guest to the house where she would be witness to the happiness denied her, and which she had
voluntarily given to another. And now she has come
to guard that happiness against the storms of the future. •And she is not only witness to their happiness
when they are together, but even when his farm-yard
or stables tear Pushkin for a short hour from Bethsaba's
side, the young wife can talk of nothing but to boast
of her happiness. No peacock is so proud of spreading
his tail as is a fond wife of telling of her happy lot.
She has so many things to tell. Her husband is a perfect model of virtue and perfection! And to all this
Zeneida must listen with utmost composure; to see, if
the husband were absent over the expected half-hour,
how uneasy and distraught the young wife grows; to

read from her face: "Oh, you dear benefactress mine, my good fairy, my goddess, how gladly, were you not with me, would I run out to seek him!"   And this, too, must she bear with a smile on her face! Oh, this Moloch!

"Listen, child: my sole object in coming was to steal you away from Alexander Sergievitch for a time."

"Ah! If you want to steal either, take both of us. Alexander would not mind being run off with by you."

"Only, as it happens, he is neither invited, nor may he come. You must accept your godmother's invitation."

"What! The invitation to her ball!"

"There you will meet the Czar and Czarina; they will speak to you."

"I—there—without Alexander?"

"Upon you it depends that Pushkin may be free to go where you go. Your marriage with him has entirely marred his career. He does not feel it now, but in the course of a year or two he will remember that formerly every step he took was accompanied by the clank of spurs. The soul of a man is not to be confined in a cage like a tame bird, especially when he has eagle's wings. Be it your task to implore forgiveness from the Czar for your husband, that Pushkin may proceed on his interrupted career. Now the meadows are still green; in another month they will be covered with snow, and the couple condemned to fireside and indoor life will not be so light-hearted as the one flying their kites in the open meadow."

"Then it is your wish that I should intercede for Alexander's return to St. Petersburg?"

"Not for all the world! No; a thousand times rather entreat the Czar to give him a mission that shall take

you and him to your own people and country. Describe to the Czar and Czarina the land in which you
were born, as it lives in your memory, with its genial
climate, its aromatic woods, its fruit-bearing trees. Tell
them all the lovely and beautiful things of it that your
memory can recall, and entreat the Czar, as an act of
mercy to yourself, to send your husband there."

"Oh, the tempting thought!" sighed Bethsaba.

"But he will never consent that I should leave him
and go away, and stay days and weeks away from
him."

"It would only be one week."

"But that is a century! Oh no! Alexander would
never consent to it."

"You leave that to me; I will talk him over."

"Oh, if you succeed in that you will be a real fairy.
But what an odd fairy! Had you wanted to carry off
Alexander from me, I could have understood it; but me
from Alexander—that I cannot understand."

"See! here he comes through the garden. Place yourself here at the window and watch. I will go and meet
him. You listen how I am going to bewitch him!"

"That I am curious to hear."

One intrenchment was already taken. Zeneida hastened to besiege the second.

Pushkin, crossing the lawn, was astonished to see
Zeneida hurrying towards him.

"Turn back, and let's have a little talk," said she,
putting her hand on Pushkin's arm. "Are you quite
happy?"

"One can never be too happy."

"My object in coming is to ask you to spare me a
portion of your happiness. I want to run away with
your wife for a week."

25

"My little wife! What to do with her? Already she loves you ever so much better than she does me."

"Do not fear. She loves you above everything in heaven and earth, and all that lies between them. She positively must accept the invitation to Princess Ghedimin's ball."

The girl wife, watching at her window, sees how her husband vehemently draws away his arm from Zeneida's retaining hand. Zeneida does not shrink; she takes possession of his arm again.

"Hot head! She will not be staying with the Princess. but with me; I will be her chaperon. Since I gave up the stage my house has become strictly proper; I have held no more frivolous gatherings; since the Szojusz Blagadenztoiga made its final decision I have had no more conspirators coming near me; no need for masquerades or riotous meetings; I live a quiet, secluded life. The Czar has sent me the Order of the Cross as an amend for my recent dismissal; and, *noblesse oblige*, the bestarred Zeneida no longer consorts with Diabolkas. So, have you not the courage to trust your wife to me if I keep vigilant watch over her?"

"But to what purpose? If you want to beg some favor of the Czar for me—you little know me!"

The woman at the window saw Pushkin fiercely slash off the heads of the asters at his feet.

"I know you perfectly well. You have made up your mind to stay on here at Pleskow, see the grass grow, hunt hares, shoot wild duck, smoke the house out, play ombre, and discourse of dogs and horses. It will be your ambition to keep a good cellar, be known as a good dancer, to occasionally slash an officer or two in duels, and to leave your papers and periodicals uncut. You

would have just strength and energy for such a life!
But there are others interested in your wife's coming.".
    " Who ?"
    " First the Szojusz Blagadenztoiga; then the Czar."
    " At my little Bethsaba's coming ?"
    " Do not interrupt me; I must speak quickly. You are
aware that this second return of Araktseieff has made it
impossible to stave off rebellion. His violent measures
have had so imbittering an effect that no one any longer
attempts to defend the life of the Czar save I alone.
Perhaps because I am a woman; yet there have been
illustrious examples enough to show that women can be
as cruel in the matter of blood-shedding as men, and
even in a more cold and calculating fashion. Any outbreak initiated by Kubusoff's air-guns or Kakhowsky's
infernal machine, or, as Jukuskin has planned, by an
opportune ball, giving the signal for attack upon the
entire imperial family, would have no beneficial result.
It would simply bring about the overthrow of the em-.
pire, the war of the knife and the axe *versus* bayonet,
the war of rags *versus* gold lace, inaugurating a reign
of chaos which would make the country bless the return of despotism, and welcome a peace, even though
accompanied by their old fetters. Now the Czar and
Czarina must not be hurt! This reason, not sentiment,
dictates.
    " My plan is as follows : The Czarina's physician has
advised her being taken to a milder climate. But her
Majesty will not hear of leaving the Russian dominions, and the Caucasus she looks upon as a wilderness
in which it is impossible to live. She gives no heed to
the naturalists who describe the country, saying they
are mere flattering official reporters. But if a young,
unsophisticated little bride, presenting herself to the im-

perial pair, were to petition as a special favor to be allowed to go back with her husband to her beautiful native land, describing this native land with enthusiasm of early and tender recollection, it is possible that though this request may be refused, yet the Czarina herself might be attracted to the idea of going to that lovely land. The Czar worships his consort to such a degree that he would accompany and stay with her there; with this result, that those who want to inaugurate the outbreak with the violent death of the Czar would be constrained to devise some other nobler, more humane, more politic plan of action. On the Black Sea the Czar will live his life without cares; here we should have the imperious favorite only to bring to judgment. The constitution would be proclaimed in St. Petersburg without blood-shedding; the army would declare in its favor; and Czar Alexander will be free to choose either to fulfil the universal wish of his people, and come back as their beloved monarch, or, if he prefer it, to embark on board a ship in the Black Sea and sail away to seek the hospitality of—say, the Sultan of Turkey, if he wish it. Anyway, his life would be preserved."

The young wife at the window sees her husband kiss the hand of his guest. He is won over already. Zeneida has succeeded in carrying off the wife from the husband.

"Those whom you love are loved indeed, even when they are tyrants!" said Pushkin, deeply moved.

"It is the holy cause, not the Czar, I wish to save!"

"Both! Come, I will trust my wife to you! Take her with you! Let her, with her lark's song, bid the storm to cease!"

Bethsaba standing at the window sees her husband and

Zeneida come quickly back to her. "Truly you are an enchantress!" she thinks.

Pushkin comes in to his wife.

"Only think! your kite has been brought back from the far end of the town! Here is your godmother's letter, as kind as can be. You must do as she wishes. How could you refuse an invitation so worded, especially as Zeneida undertakes to be your chaperon?"

Bethsaba looked at each in amazement, and then raised a threatening finger and shook it at Zeneida.

"You are a fiend, after all, then. Well, then, come along, and let's see what kind of ball-dress my godmother has sent me."

This may be called a thorough capitulation.

The box was brought in and opened, the most exquisite of ball-dresses produced, and, with Zeneida's aid, duly tried on. In it Bethsaba showed herself to her husband.

"Shall I look lovely? Shall I turn many men's heads?"

"Every one of them!"

"Oh, take care, take care! You must not embrace me; you will crush my lace!"

This is the way in which a man is deprived of his wife in the very midst of his honeymoon.

CHAPTER XLII

THE FEAST OF MASINKA

THE Assumption of the Virgin Mary is, according to the Russian calendar, at the end of August, thus twelve days later than according to the astronomical calendar. By this we see that the Czar of Russia has power to command even the sun. As, according to the Russian calendar, every four hundredth year is short of three days, in the course of twenty thousand years it will be summer in the winter quarter, and winter in the summer quarter, in Russia. The Czar can even effect this.

However, now it is the beginning of autumn, the best time of all the year in St. Petersburg. The days are shorter and not so hot; the nights are moonlight; and, one-third of Russian women being named Mary, there is a festive tone in all houses; and at night, when fireworks begin, there are more stars to be seen on the earth than in the sky.

Korynthia, too, was a Mary; hence had every right to celebrate the day.

The summer palace of Prince Ghedimin on the island of the Neva rivalled in magnificence the Imperial Winter Palace in St. Petersburg. The ballroom was large enough to hold a thousand people.

Among those invited were the Czar and Czarina, the Grand Dukes and Grand Duchesses, their relatives then staying at the Russian court, the Czar's brother, the Grand Duke and Duchess of Weimar, the Prince and Princess of Orange. All combined to add brilliancy to Prince Ghedimin's ball. And yet Maria Alexievna Korynthia was far more anxious to know if Zeneida and Bethsaba were coming than about any other of her guests.

Fräulein Ilmarinen and Frau Pushkin had certainly written in most courteous and gushing terms the day before, stating that they would be there. Russian women, by-the-way, surpass even French women in the art of writing flowery notes—especially if they hate each other. But every one knows the value of such promises. No

one can write the day before, " I shall be having a headache to-morrow," but an hour before the ball any one
can send a note of excuse by the footman, " I am in despair at being unable to come. I have such a violent
headache." Of such excuses women possess a perfect
arsenal.

To the Princess's great content, however, instead of
the expected letter of excuse, both ladies put in an appearance; and in good time, before the dance music
had begun, it being etiquette to arrive before the imperial guests. Zeneida always knew what was the right
thing to do.

Fräulein Ilmarinen was wearing for the first time that
evening the order conferred upon her by the Czar; Bethsaba, the ball-dress sent her by her godmother. She
was strikingly lovely; even the close vicinity of Zeneida
did not detract from her charms.

Korynthia, rising, advanced to meet them; first she
greeted Bethsaba as the married woman, then she turned
to Zeneida. Zeneida forestalled her greeting.

"You forestall me!" exclaimed the Princess. "Of
course, *queens* ever give the first greeting."

" Not so, Princess; but they who desire to offer their
congratulations on their hostess's name-day."

And the two ladies shook hands. They knew that
every eye was upon them, wondering how they would
meet.

Both were well-seasoned warriors.

The ballroom was so arranged that all about were
small groves of exotics, with openings just large enough
for a couple to retreat into, and talk scandal or flirt, as
the case might be. Little tables were there placed, and
footmen went in and out handing refreshments.

Korynthia drew Zeneida into one of these floral re-

treats, and, as they sat down together, whispered laugh-
ingly into her ear :

"You understood me. I expected no less from your
clever intellect."

Zeneida, adopting her tone, replied in equally laughing voice.

"That I have brought you the dove out of her
nest ?"

"Just so — that we have thus become allies?" resumed the Princess.

"An alliance *ad hoc*, in the language of diplomacy,"
interpreted Fräulein Ilmarinen.

"For the object of discomfiting a third adversary,"
filled in Korynthia.

"And meanwhile England and Russia have signed de-
fensive and offensive alliance—"

"In order, as allied powers, to conquer Paris," laughed
Korynthia.

"The same Paris who keeps the golden apple, in
order to give it to—whom?" exclaimed Zeneida, with a
peal of silvery laughter.

"You are a demoniacal woman !"

"That I know. Your Highness has said it already."

"How you remember everything ! But, to change
the subject, three of your admirers are here to-night.
We will soon settle the third of them. See, your little
protégée is already absorbed. Her former admirer, Chevalier Galban, has caught her like a spider in his web.
Do not be uneasy about her ; she will not go back heart-
whole. We will see to that. We understand one another !"

"Perfectly, Princess."

No harm to her ! All loss is gain to her, but I do
not think it will be her last conquest. For any one
who has *begun* as has my goddaughter, it requires no

great sagacity to prophesy how she will *go on*. No need for us to grieve about her."

" Nor in such a case can we show any mercy."

" So, for the present, peace is concluded between us ! After that, war to the knife."

" I first pull down my flag."

" Oh, that is only tactics, Fräulein Ilmarinen. Women never capitulate. That we both know too well. Do you know, I have never had opportunity to see you so close, though I have been so curious to get a good view of you. Tell me, do you dye your hair with saffron to make it such a lovely gold color ?"

The golden hue of Zeneida's hair was a natural beauty ; but she whispered confidentially to the Princess :

" No ; saffron has too pungent a smell. I dye my hair with berberis roots in which purple snails have been steeped."

" And I never could understand how you get that exquisite complexion. Do you use violet roots ?"

Zeneida laughed ; the blush which heightened her complexion should have been answer enough—could she have told the truth. But she had come here to lie ; therefore answered, in laughing accents :

" Oh, Princess, the preservation of this complexion is a perfect science. I have an old book, published in the times of Poppæa, which contains the receipt."

" Oh, among other things does that receipt advise laying a slice of beef upon one's face on going to bed ?"

" Yes, that and other things. I could send you the book ; though, in truth, you do not need it. It would be the Graces clothing Anadyomene."

" Oh, you are as magnanimous an adversary as that French naval captain who shared his powder with the Englishman and let himself be shot by him. To that I

can only answer as did the Persian king to the Armenians : ' What use is it to send me your sword if therewith you do not send me your arm also ?' Of what use
the secret of the cosmetic if you do not make me an
adept in that bewitching smile which none may resist?"

" Princess, you are just like Napoleon, who had the
art of raising a fallen foe."

" This time we are not foes, but allies."

The common foe (Bethsaba) here interrupted the ami-
cable warfare by coming up to put the naïve question if
she might dance the first polonaise with Chevalier Galban? She was heartily laughed at.

" You may do whatever you like. You are a married
woman now."

What is known as a polonaise in the court balls of
St. Petersburg is a promenade round the ballroom in
short dance step, performed by the whole company according to the fancy of the first couple. We are therefore not to understand under that appellation the wild ma-
zurka of former days, when the floor groaned under the
stamp of the dancers. That was the dance of a period
when every Polish nobleman was as good as the king ;
this is the dance of a time when every Polish nobleman
is equal to—a peasant.

In former times both Czar and Czarina had headed
the dance ; and it happened to have been a polonaise in
which Alexander had wounded the feelings of Elisabeth
for the sake of the beautiful Korynthia Narishkin—an
insult the former had never forgotten.

The arrivals of the great, greater, and greatest personages put an end to conversation. Once arrived, people
formed themselves into a circle and waited for the august
couple to make the round of the ballroom, after which
the polonaise began.

Zeneida was presented to all the foreign princes, and received so much homage that in its intoxicating atmosphere she might well have lost sight of the one intrusted to her care. She was, however, a tried general in such campaigns, and knew how to keep the whole field well under supervision, even to the slightest detail. Attentively her eyes follow Bethsaba. She sees Chevalier Galban, with languishing expression, whisper in her ear; sees the young wife hasten up to her godmother with glowing cheek; sit down by her and then listen, surprised and startled, betwixt laughter and tears, to what her godmother is saying to her. She even divined what it was that was being said to her. She also saw the Czarina address Bethsaba, and enter into conversation with her with gracious condescension. And she saw, moreover, that these thousand guests here assembled to discourse sweet nothings, to jest, to trifle away the hours with orgeat, sorbet, and punch, were often the bitterest enemies, full of deadly hatred, ready at the first opportunity to give vent to their true feelings; that the men in their uniforms, stiff with gold lace, their breasts literally sown with orders, who, hat under arm, bowed low to the Czar or to each other, were thinking, "To-day or to-morrow either you or I will be giving each other a 'How d'ye do?' with our heads, instead of our hats, under our arm"; that she, the singer, had but to say, "I am singing for the benefit of the Orphanage," and in an instant every sword would be out of its scabbard, and the men now dancing *vis-à-vis* to each other would be running their swords through each other's bodies, and the crowned chairs on the dais be overturned, no one asking themselves, "Who is sitting on those chairs?" or, worse still, that same dais be turned into a scaffold. Conspirators and oppressors, murderers and executioners, all assembled in one ballroom; every one knowing who everybody is so well that when the master of ceremonies, in mistake, called out, "*Coup de main !*" instead of "*Tour de main !*" there was a shout of laughter. Only the Czar asked, "Why are the gentlemen so merry?"

All this Zeneida saw. The secret of every man there lay in her hands. Ah, she saw, too, very well, what motive the gracious lady of the house had in giving this brilliant entertainment. In order to seduce a young wife from her truth? Oh no! But in order to discover the key to a secret which he to whom it was intrusted had not divulged to any one—not even to his well-beloved wife.

With the departure of the court from the ballroom the whole assemblage, as etiquette dictated, at once broke up. No one, moreover, was inclined to stay for the sake of enjoyment on that occasion.

Zeneida, taking Bethsaba under her protecting wings, went off with her to Kreskowsky Island. In the gondola the young wife was very silent, and Zeneida purposely abstained from asking her how she had enjoyed herself. Even after the two women had divested themselves of their ball-dresses Bethsaba remained dreamy and melancholy. The chill of the river made hot tea a necessity before going to bed—in the paradise reclaimed from the marshes lurked ague. When they were alone together, wrapped in warm dressing-gowns and drinking their steaming tea, Bethsaba broke her melancholy meditations with :

"But tell me, then, is this, too, a part of religion?"

" What?"

" That a Christian wife, should another man choose

to say to her, 'I am wretched, dying for love of you, I will shoot myself if you remain cruel to me,' be bound to turn her love from her husband, and give it to that other, that he may not be unhappy—may not be forced to misery and suicide."

"And they have told you that such is a woman's duty?"

"Yes. And if religion requires that woman's love should resemble that of St. Martin, who, when he met a shivering beggar, tore off half his mantle to give it him, I will return to my heathen belief, in which I am not required to distress myself about the welfare of any one but of my husband."

"And all this was new to you?"

"I could have cried outright when I heard it. I thought my eyes would be burned out of my head; I felt contaminated at listening to such words. The mere separation from Alexander had already made my heart as heavy as if I were mourning my dead; the very touch of another man's hand in the dance had pained me as if, in taking it, I were killing a dove; when I laughed my heart accused me as if I were committing a theft; and with the laugh came the thought, 'And he has nothing now to cheer him. He is sighing for me, he is lonely, while I am merry!' And all the time an evil curiosity was urging me on to hear more, to sound to the very depths the quagmire from which I was shrinking; and so I feigned to listen willingly."

"In that you did well."

"It would not have been good manners to run away, would it?"

"You would simply have been lost. A woman should never let it be seen that a man's seductive arts terrify her; a demonstrative repulse makes her at once his prey. I was watching you—you behaved admirably. Your expression was that of a woman who does not understand what is being said to her, who takes it all as a joke; and by so doing you led him on to speak still more explicitly."

"That is just what he did. Only think, impertinent fellow! He actually had the audacity to tell me that for love of me he had bought an estate but half a day's distance from Pleskow, where he means to be spending the winter and to be visiting us constantly. I was inclined to say, 'Oh, please, do not come!'"

"You did well not to say it; rather you should have replied, 'Alexander Sergievitch will always be glad to see you.'"

"That is what I did say. But then he sighed so deeply: 'Oh, if you will only tell me one day Alexander Sergievitch is going from home to-morrow!' I should so have liked to give him a box on the ears for saying it!"

"But, instead of doing that, with naive, unconscious expression you asked, 'What good would that be? You surely would not be coming to see me when my husband was not at home? All the world would know of it.' To which he made reply, 'You are right. But you could come to my castle.'"

"How *do* you know that?"

"From what you have told me and from what I saw. It was then that you felt inclined to cry."

"He said still more. 'You would have an excellent excuse to leave home while Alexander Sergievitch is away. Your mother, the Queen of Circassia, is in St. Ann's Convent in Novgorod. You would only have to say, "I am going to my mother, who has not seen me since I was a child, to tell her of my marriage, and ask her blessing upon it." ' So even my poor mother he dragged into this infamy !"

"And upon that, leaving him, you took refuge with your godmother ?"

" Did you notice that, too ?"

" In doing so you had gone to the right place, and could tell all your troubles to sympathetic ears."

" Oh, if only you had heard what she did say !"

" I saw."

" How saw ?"

" By your face. Every word of hers was reflected on your face. Did she not say, ' Poor Galban ! If only you knew how much he has suffered on your account ! He has actually been on the point of making away with himself. Then he wanted to bury himself in the cata-combs of Solowetshk. It would but be giving a copper to a starving man out of your wealth. It should be kept secret ; no one should know. It is the way all we women act ; there is not a single exception among us. Besides, it is only paying back in the same coin. Every one of us is deceived by our husbands ; you and I, and all of us. At the moment that Galban made his confession to you, you may take it for granted that Pushkin was vowing his love to some other woman, who would not be so scrupulous as you.' "

" So he really did say ; and yet more. This man— whose name my lips can never more utter—is capable, for sake of me, of exiling himself from St. Petersburg, of renouncing his brilliant position, merely that he may live near me ! He is capable, in his despair, of killing Al-exander, me, himself, if I torture him longer. Oh, how he has terrified me ! As soon as I get home I will tell it all to Alexander, and, taking his hand in mine, will implore him to run away to the other end of the earth with me."

"By so doing you would attain just the contrary to what you desire. Just this: that Pushkin would be aroused, and, not having been conceded permission to return to St. Petersburg, would challenge Galban to go to him, and their duel would end fatally. Do not be afraid of him! Fight him yourself!"

"I? I fight him? Galban? I, a weak, foolish, cowardly little creature, who tremble at every word he utters?"

"You tremble and are fearful because you believe your heart in danger. But how if you knew that the net is not thrown out to catch your heart, but Pushkin's head — that it is his life against which every mesh has been woven? Then you would not be a coward."

"What do you say? — that it is against Alexander's life their plots are directed?"

"Silence! Question no further! When we have retired to bed, when we are quite alone, and there is no ear to overhear us, I will tell you all, and will teach you what you have to do. And now put your hair in curl-papers. The day after to-morrow we have to attend the grand farewell ball at Peterhof. There you may tremble; there show what a weak, innocent, timid little wife is capable of when her husband's life is at stake!"

"If that be so I will not be afraid; I will be bold and sly as a cat! I have not the courage of myself to pin a butterfly, but the man who threatens my Alexander I could pierce to the heart. Mashallah! *I am the daughter of my mother!*"

Zeneida then instructed Bethsaba in a part which she played to perfection to the end. At present, however, we may not divulge the plot of the play.

The link had been successfully forged into the chain.
At the brilliant farewell ball given by the Czar to his
royal guests at Peterhof, the Russian Versailles,˙ Bethsaba had the honor conferred on her of being presented to the Czarina. The Czar had long known
her as Sophie's playfellow. It was he who led the
Georgian princess to tell the Czarina of the land of her
birth. Bethsaba, the little Scheherezade, half closing
her eyes that she might not see those around her,
began to tell of the land where winter is unknown.
Who could fail to be eloquent when speaking of his
native land? Of sky clear as crystal, of air aromatic
with balsamic fragrance, of woods where the leaves
of the trees neither wither nor fall, of rivers which
never freeze, of fields always gay with flowers, of the
mighty ice-covered mountains which shut in the laughing valleys; and where vital power and buoyancy are
diffused in grass, trees, water, and air, and the dwellers in that sunny clime know neither sickness nor
decay?

That to which all the most learned doctors in the
world had been powerless to persuade the Czarina—
the change to another climate—was brought about by
the enchanted chatter of simple, childlike lips.

Taking her husband's hand, the Czarina uttered:
" I should like to see that sunny land."

Those words, " I should like," are often more powerful than any mere word of command.   •

Courtiers and conspirators, who at this dazzling entertainment had grouped themselves about the superb
fountains of the Sampson Springs, had not the slightest conception that in the course of a short ten minutes one delicate woman, with her rosy, childlike lips
would effect such a complete revolution—that one peal

26

of silvery laughter would blow to the winds their cannon, their army, their plan of campaign.   The fairy
tale of the Circassian king's daughter had this pre-
eminence over all other fairy wonders, that it extinguished the impending outbreak of a volcano by a drop
of water.

This drop of water had shone in the Czarina's eyes
when she said :

" I should so like to go there!   There I should get
well again !"

That same evening Chevalier Galban met Bethsaba
again.   She was afraid of him no longer ; she had
learned from Zeneida how it beseemed her mother's
daughter to act.

At the close of the ball the Princess and Zeneida met
in the vestibule.   They were waiting for their carriages.
From Peterhof to St. Petersburg people go by road.

The Princess accosted Zeneida with :

" It is settled.   I thank you for your co-operation."

(Bethsaba was under the escort of Chevalier Galban.)

" We are quits now."

" The little goose has confessed all.   She has gone
thoroughly astray.   She even acknowledged that you had
helped her on."

" The chatterbox !"

" I fancy that she will be making somebody very,
very unhappy."

" So do I."

" Then the fight between us can begin afresh."

" I think not.   I renounce any claim to console the
unhappy."

" Oh, you do not want to make me believe that you
are acting without personal feeling."

"Certainly not. But what will result from this evening's work will be a monster needing two mothers. The
one revenge; the other love."

"And you choose revenge?"

"I give you the second, Princess."

"I have not yet forgotten the diplomatic saying that
two only make a compact together in order that one
may deceive the other."

Meanwhile Prince Ghedimin had come up to conduct
his wife to her carriage. Seeing Zeneida, he started.

"Do just see," exclaimed the Princess, in an affected
tone, "how low-spirited he is! He has grown quite
melancholy. For days together I cannot drive him from
my side; he will not stir from me. If only he had something to talk about! But all he can do is to knit his
brows and ruminate. I do beg of you, Fräulein Ilmarinen, in consideration of our alliance, to do me a favor.
You are a perfect enchantress — just say one word to
him. I am convinced it will cheer him."

"Do you really desire it?"

The look Prince Ghedimin cast upon Zeneida expressed
both fear and uneasiness. He was "the chosen dictator."
If Zeneida uttered the words "I sing," he must forthwith
draw his sword out of its scabbard, exclaiming "I fight!"

Zeneida attempted the magician's feat of curing the
Prince's melancholy with one word.

"The summer has quite left us, Prince, has it not?
Winter is upon us."

A sufficiently commonplace remark! Imagine talking
about the weather!

Prince Ghedimin acquiesced.

"And I fear we shall have a very unpleasant winter
if we 'too' do not go to the Crimea or the Caucasus to
luxuriate in a second summer."

A very ordinary speech ! But that little word "too" had electrified the Prince. He seemed a changed man. His face brightened, his figure grew elastic; surely a miracle had happened to him !

" Come, my love," he said to the Princess, and, to her amazement, began humming an air from the overture of the *Czarenwalzers* as they went down the stairs.

That woman is surely the devil in person ! She says the most commonplace nothings, and, doing so, brings a dead man back to life.

And yet the Princess has carefully weighed every word spoken by Zeneida. Which can have been the magical one ? There was none. The little word "too" had escaped her attention.

And it was from that one word that the Prince knew that the Czarina would go to the Crimea, and with her the Czar. His breast was relieved of a heavy load.

Chevalier Galban escorted the ladies to their carriage, and Bethsaba, leaning out of the carriage-window, looked back at him.

" I have caught her !" thought Chevalier Galban to himself.

CHAPTER XLIII

UNDER THE COMETS

In the summer of the year 1825 no oil was needed for the streets of St. Petersburg, the nights were so light. The first lighting of the lamps falls on the day the court leaves Peterhof for the Winter Palace. The lighting of the lamps, on this occasion, was looked forward to by many.

A great plan was in course of operation among the

lower strata of society, which they had imparted neither to the *matadores* of the *Szojusz Blagodenztoga* nor to
the *Szojusz Spacinia.*

A succession of gloomy, rainy days came with the new
moon. When on the fourth day a keen north wind blew
away the clouds from the sky, people were astonished to
see near the silver sickle of the moon yet another wonder, like a fiery sword—a comet. So quickly had it come
that it was only perceived when in its full blaze of glory.

What is a comet?

Scientific men themselves do not know; how, then,
can poor ordinary mortals?

A comet is the herald of pest, of war, of downfall!
Let him who does not believe this show reason why he
is unbelieving. In wine-growing countries it is true
that a comet year is said to promise a good wine year.
But that does not affect the people of St. Petersburg,
where they only make brandy. And a comet has no influence upon the increase of brandy. On the contrary,
when there is any trouble brewing in the empire there is
always but little brandy consumed. It is a peculiarity
of the Russian that he does not drink when in great
trouble. When the head of the police learns that in
St. Petersburg, instead of a daily consumption of five
thousand casks of brandy, only two thousand are being
consumed, he redoubles the patrols.

The appearance of the comet only heightened the
general feeling of excitement. A comet is the prophet's
material symbol concerning which he can cry, "Look!
the fiery sword has appeared too in the heavens!"

When Czar Alexander was leaving Peterhof he gave
orders that the Lord Chamberlain should precede the
Czarina, to see that her apartments were in order on her
arrival.

It was evening when the Czar, with a small retinue, neared the capital. Arrived at Alexander Nevski Monastery, he called a halt, and, going into the church, commanded that a mass for the dead should be read the next day. As he left the church, standing on the terrace, he cast one long look at the capital, lying before him veiled in mist. The distant sounds came up to him like the roar of the sea; the traffic in the streets, the murmur of voices mingled together like the buzz of a beehive.

He stood there a long time, lost in meditation. The giant conflicts of a quarter of a century rose before his eyes out of the sea of mist, and he experienced that agony almost beyond human endurance—the consciousness of an approaching end, the mighty tasks of his life still unaccomplished. He had risen so high that he had half thought himself a god; he had fallen so low that there was not a man who would have changed places with him. Napoleon and he had been the dominating personalities of that quarter of a century.

Nor did that lonely figure on St. Helena look with other feelings on the ocean surrounding him than does Czar Alexander on the mist falling thickly over his capital. This mist is vaster than the ocean, because it is formed by the breath of man; and as many breaths, so many curses against him—against him, once so idolized.

The only difference between them is that Napoleon's people ardently yearn to have their conquered hero back, while this conquering hero has become a weariness to his country.

And that comet in the sky is like an illuminated pen with which an invisible hand is writing the fate of empires and their rulers amid the stars. Alexander's

spirit was ever inclined to mysticism. He was filled
with forebodings and terrors. He was a believer in
fate and its portents. Comet and moon had both sunk
beneath the horizon of the thick sea of mist.

The Czar had an old coachman, known to every one
by his long, gray beard, which reached down to his
girdle. This coachman always drove the Czar long dis-
tances; he was the most faithful servant he had. As,
on returning to his three-horsed troika, Alexander asked:

" Ilias, did you see the comet?"

" I saw it, your Majesty."

" Do you know that the comet is the forerunner of
misfortune and mourning? Ah, well! The Lord's will
be done!"

And he gave orders to drive to the noisy city.

People told each other that the Czar was about to
take a long journey; whither was not known. He intended taking the Czarina away from the inclement
climate of the capital to more genial skies; whither
he had as yet told no one. He was himself going first,
to secure quarters. Whenever he undertook a long
journey it was his custom to hear the *Veni Sancte* in the
Church of the Holy Virgin of Kasan. It was his own
church; he had built it, and had had it consecrated, and
from its threshold he would get into his travelling carriage. The entire body of the clergy would await him
there betimes, wearing their richest vestments; his favorite choir, too, would be in attendance, to sing the collects.
And the murmuring capital whispered to itself, when once
priests, Czar, and Grand Dukes were collected together
in the Church of the Holy Virgin of Kasan: suddenly,
at the invocation, " Come, Holy Ghost!" a determined
man would start up from the crypt below, and, presenting
a loaded pistol, would say, " Come down, then, to him!"

And straightway church, holy images, Czar, Grand
Dukes, priests, and choristers would be blown into the
sky. An awful thought !

Perhaps to be realized. Perhaps already for days
past some bold spirit—one of the Irreconcilables—has
been crouching below in the crypt, the coffins filled with
gunpowder, waiting for the signal of the bell which calls
the faithful together to carry out the awful deed which
shall overturn a mighty empire. The fatality was prevented—forbidden by the ashes of the dead.

The next day, at early morning, the Czar was not
driven to the Church of the Holy Virgin of Kasan,
where the richly clad Metropolitan awaited him, but to
the Chapel of Alexander Nevski, where an ascetic attired in black, the " Simnik," advanced to conduct him
to the mass for the dead.

An official paper has categorically described this ceremony. How the Czar knelt before the Icons ; how the
protopope Seraphim placed the New Testament upon
his head, lying prostrate in the dust ; how the Ruler of
All the Russias did penance in the poor Simnik's cell,
and how the Simnik told him of the degeneracy of the
people. The account being authentic, it, of course, does
not contain a single word that is not true.

A very different reason was it that had brought the
Czar within those walls. Here rested the ashes of his
three dead daughters, side by side—for he had had
Sophie's remains brought here secretly. And it was
these three children, deep down in the earth as they
were, who combined to save their father, calling him to
their calm, secure resting-place.

What had the father to say to his dead ? The walls
alone can make reply. Official report is silent.

As the Czar left the church, in which he had heard

the mass for the dead to the end, the sun was just rising, its reddish rays gilding the towers of the Church of SS. Peter and Paul, and the cupolas and cross of the Isaac Cathedral, through the sea of mist, the hollow tones of the early bells vibrating long in the stillness.

All sounds were hushed as Czar Alexander looked upon the capital of his vast empire for the last time. And as the troika, drawn by its fiery team, rolled rapidly away, the Czar turned to gaze, the better to impress the scene upon his memory, a scene which the rising mist was slowly, slowly shutting out from his view.

CHAPTER XLIV

THE MAN WITH THE GREEN EYES

THERE was alarm, almost panic, in the capital when the news became known that the Czar had started by the Sea of Azof and the Crimea to the Caucasus! Now people understood the meaning of the comet! It was the agent which had upset the calculations of wise men and fools alike.

Fearful curses echoed through the catacombs of the Church of the Holy Virgin of Kasan when it became known that the Czar had changed his plans and gone to Alexander Nevski Chapel! The plots, the fulfilment of which was to shake the world, had been a failure! The Czar had left St. Petersburg and betaken himself to a remote spot nineteen hundred versts away, nearer by thirteen degrees to the equator. He had betaken himself to a land where conspiracies do not flourish; he had escaped the giant trap laid for him. The plot of the " Free Slavs " had come to naught, which was to have begun the work of freedom with the immediate murder of the Czar. Now the plot formed by the " Northern Union " came to the fore, which was to carry out the constitution planned by " the green book," either by forcing the Czar to initiate it or by his exile. In either case, without violence to the crown.

The Czar started on September 13th, seven days before the date fixed for the grand review. By this means the net of the military conspiracy was also rudely torn asunder.

The members of the Szojusz Blagadenztoiga hastened to confer at Zeneida's palace, not waiting invitation. What was to be done now?

Twenty-three among the twenty-four said the whole thing must be begun afresh. The four-and-twentieth was Jakuskin, who said:

" If all of you fall away, I remain firm. Discuss as you choose; I act." And with these words he left the meeting.

Hence the chase had begun. As the hungry wolf pursues the hare through steppes, forests, marshes, so Jakuskin pursued his prey.

The Czar had a six hours' start of his enemy, who fully expected to get over the ground quickly enough to come up with him. He had a strong Caucasian mare accustomed to do its twenty hours a day and then graze on any grass at hand. The rider was worthy of his horse; he, too, could content himself with a piece of bread and bacon, and take his four hours' sleep under any shrub by the wayside.

But the pursued went fast. Every day the Czar covered one hundred and fifty kilometres — *i.e.*, a twenty hours' post—only allowing himself four hours' sleep. He was also accompanied by a large escort; but that was no impediment to Jakuskin's plan.

Once to stand face to face with him was all he needed. He knew the way in which the Czar travelled. First a picket of Cossacks, well in advance of the rest of the cortege, that the Czar might not be incommoded by the dust of their horses' feet. Then in the first carriage the Czar, easily to be recognized by his coachman, Ilias, his long beard fluttering like a couple of flags on either side the carriage. With him is his adjutant, Count Wolkonsky. The Count is a small, undersized man; the Czar a man of splendid physique—tall, athletic, with a head small in proportion to his size. Impossible not to recognize him.

If only Jakuskin could get in advance of his intended victim! But this he could not do. The pursuer's worst hinderance was the moonlight, which, turning night into day, enabled the imperial cortege to travel continuously, and thus prevented his stealing a march. Fortunately, on the seventh day, when they reached Kúrsk, the sky suddenly clouded over and stormy weather set in. The moon no longer replaced the sun, and driving by night was impossible—but not riding.

This gave hopes of overtaking the Czar. But these hopes also were doomed to be frustrated.

He was to experience that nothing is impossible to the great of the ear' . 'hen the Czar is in haste even da·' ss must yielu. Once when Jakuskin, galloping ' pitch darkness over breakneck paths, had g' ᴜ,y up with the escort, it was but to see that thᴜ Czar's way was illuminated. Men carrying lighted torches were riding on either side of the imperial carriage.

" All the better!" thought Jakuskin to himself. But when he reached the high-road, he saw that as far as the eye reached, at a distance of three hundred paces, were fagot heaps, serfs standing beside them with lighted matches; and as the Czar approached, one fagot heap after another, blazing up, lighted the way. This went on till break of day. The Czar rattled over the ground by artificial light.

Thus the wolf hangs back, gnashing his hungry teeth, when he sees fire-light. These bonfires along the highway destroyed his calculations. He must give up the pursuit; now he might allow himself time for sleep.

He did not move from the hut in which he had taken shelter for a whole week, till the second cortege came up with the Czarina. She travelled more slowly; that which had taken the Czar twelve days she accomplished in twenty-four. Jakuskin followed on her track. The journey came to an end at Taganrog.

Taganrog is a seaport on the Sea of Azof. It is a modest little town which has twice been entirely deserted by its inhabitants, having once been made over by the Russians to the Turks; the next time, at conclusion of peace, by the Sultan of Turkey to the Czar. At present it is inhabited by Greeks. It was only due to the chance throw of a . . 'e that it did not form the site of the capital of the . . . When Czar Peter conceived the idea of founding a . . . tal on . . sea he was in doubt whether to build it i. . . . marshes or the Tartar steppes. The thro . . . . knife d . . . d it. If it had fallen point down d Taganro 'd now be St. Petersburg, and the cupolas . . . . . hedral would be reflected in the Sea of Azot . . . . in the Neva.

Jakuskin knew beforehand that the Czarina would not be staying here. There was not a single garden in the whole town. No one planted a tree lest his neighbor should gather the fruit. The first cutting wind that blew would teach the Czarina's physicians that a place is not Italy because it happens to be a certain latitude. The Czar would seek some place in his vast empire for his beloved invalid to rest where the trees are green all the year round. He has two places to choose between, Georgia and the Crimea—both countries a paradise to the Russians, who for eight months in the year are accustomed to see nothing but icicles about them.

Hardly had the Empress Elisabeth installed herself in the castle at Taganrog when the Czar started upon his voyage of discovery. He set out in the direction of Novocserkask.

Jakuskin concluded that he would go on to the Caucasus. All preparations were made to that end—posthorses and escorts bespoken as far as Tiflis. Easy to choose a point where to lie in ambush.

But the Governor of the Crimea, Prince Woronzoff, came, and had so much to tell of the lovely climate and surroundings of the Crimea that the Czar, suddenly altering his itinerary, turned back, and Jakuskin only first knew of the change when he   a day's journey before the Czar.

Once more he poste   reached the marshes of the Dead Sea,   spirits of malaria await the travel'   catch up with the Czar until his arriva.   pol, reaching it at the very moment when the   ity was blazing with illuminations in honor of its illustrious guest.

But the C   d not go out again to enjoy the brilliant sight.   Tired out, he had gone to bed. Jakuskin learned that the horses were ordered early next morning; the Czar was going to visit Prince Woronzoff's farfamed palace in Jusuff.

Jakuskin caught up the carriages at Bagdar; they were empty. Leaving his carriage to pursue its way along the high-road, the Czar, on horseback, accompanied by his escort, had taken the steep mountain-path of Tsatir Dagh, a distance of some five-and-thirty versts.

The Czar's whole journey was conducted in as capricious a manner as if it had been dictated by some one knowing that he was being pursued, and as if this zig-zag progress from valley to valley by impassable paths were intended to deceive.

And how many favorable opportunities had Jakuskin missed! The Czar had felt so free from care among the simple Mohammedan populace that he had wandered for hours on foot and on horseback among the exquisite gardens and woods. As he strolled along the lovely valley of Oriander, in full bloom, he had said, meditatively, " Here I would fain spend the rest of my days!" Torturing care, melancholy's dark phantom, found no place here ; they were as effectually scared away as were the conspirators. At his physician's earnest entreaty, at length leavin~ *'   ?ast, he turned to the interior of the penin!   ' '' m capital of the Tartar Sultan, Bakca ᴗ.   .   e palace of the former Ghiraids passed th\   ,ᴧ..

All through tha   \ ɪt and the following day there sat at the gate of the palace, beneath the cypresses which have made Bakcsi Seraj so famous, a dervish. That dervish was Jakuskin.

At length he had found the Czar. Wrapping himself in his burnous, he sat and waited until the Czar should come forth. He is certain of his object. In his girdle glistens a good sharp dagger. His hand does not tremble.

And yet once more the Czar escapes him. He passed close to him; his dress brushed him by, and yet Jakuskin does not recognize him; for, dressed as a Tartar chief, the Czar had gone out of the palace quite alone, without attendant of any kind. Had he but been attended by a single person Jakuskin must have detected him; but one man alone escapes notice. The Czar had wished to visit the "Valley of Tears," about which the bridegroom of his favorite child had written. This romantic fancy had saved him from the assassin's knife. Thence he went, still in the same dress, to a Mohammedan mosque and stayed through a Moslem service. After which, not returning to the palace, he met his retinue at the Stadtholder's castle. There he found a despatch containing news of the death of King Maximilian of Bavaria, brother-in-law to the Czarina.

Alexander was alarmed. Should this news have reached his wife it might, in her delicate state of health, have seriously affected her. So, giving command to start instantly, he did not return to the palace.

The dervish sitting at the gate awaited his prey in vain. When at length he heard that the Czar had gone, the latter had already got a considerable way towards the other side of the isthmus.

And now the pursuit began once more, and with it came to his mind the saying, "For him who has been chosen by the man with the green eyes it is in vain to whet the knife." He was growing superstitious — his imagination filled with green-eyed spectres.

The Czar pursued his way by the Dnieper, thence through the Nogai Steppe, and over the silk-growing plains of Mariopolis to the shores of the Sea of Azof, where his beloved consort was awaiting him.

Jakuskin followed close upon his track. As he crossed a bridge, after passing Orekhov, his horse, stumbling, broke his leg. Jakuskin had to proceed on foot. It was not far from the post-house; thither he went. A horse he must have at any price.

The postmaster led him to the stable.

"Look, my lord, I have not a horse left. The Czar has just passed through; every horse I had has been taken for himself and retinue."

"And that one in the corner?"

"That horse is not mine. It belongs to a courier just arrived from Kiew, who went at once to bed and is fast asleep."

"A courier who can allow himself to sleep on the way cannot have any very urgent business. Perhaps I can persuade him, for some good gold pieces, to sleep on until I have reached Mariopolis on his horse, whence it shall be sent back to him."

"You can try it, my lord!" It was not such an unheard-of thing in Russia for a courier to sell his horse from under him.

"If he will not lend me his horse I'll put a bullet through him," muttered Jakuskin to himself as he entered the guest-chamber.

A young officer of a lancer regiment lay on the bed wrapped in his cloak.

"Good-day, comrade," said Jakuskin.

"Don't talk of good days," returned he, his teeth chattering. "I am shivering all over. That confounded Caucasian fever has laid hold of me on the road. It's all up with me. And I had a despatch to deliver into the hands of the Czar himself wherever I might come up with him. General Roth sent me — delay is most serious. And I cannot sit my horse! I say, my dear

fellow, do me a good turn and take charge of this despatch. Take my horse. The Czar has gone to Taganrog. Hasten after him! Give him this despatch—into
his own hands. Those were my orders! As for me,
I shall only be able to report myself to him in the next
world. Lose no time, I entreat you."

Nothing could have been more welcome to Jakuskin.
A despatch which must be delivered into the Czar's own
hands—the Czar!

"Heaven be with you, comrade! You may die with
an easy mind. I will faithfully carry out your commission; and if you have a betrothed I will write her where
you breathed your last, and will send your mother your
watch and chain. You could not have found a better
substitute."

The officer probably died and was buried in that picturesque steppe. Jakuskin, mounting his horse, placed
the despatch intrusted to him in his breast-pocket.

But the horse given over to him was a sorry jade, and
not accustomed, as his other had been, to the steppes.
He could make but few miles a day, and whenever he
came to a bridge his rider had to dismount and drag the
animal across. He would not go over a bridge.

Owing to such a bad mount he did not reach Taganrog until four days after the arrival of the Czar.

One day Jakuskin found out that the Czar intended
going from Alapka to Mordinof. Now there was but
one road to it, and that only a bridle-path—a path called
by the natives "the ladder." It well merited its cogno-
men, rising so steeply up the mountain-side that sometimes the horse has to force its way through narrow
clefts in the rock.

Jakuskin hired a Tartar guide, who was to lead him
through the forest to the summit of "the ladder."

27

Before dawn, in the dead of night, he made his start, to be there before the Czar. He was dressed in the costume of a Tartar huntsman, a double-barrelled gun slung over his shoulder. Emerging from the thick forest, he saw the steep mountain path before him. Over a spring, gushing from out the rocky wall, grew a bush some ten feet distant from the path. The path itself was intercepted here by a cleft in the rock, across which a narrow bridge had been thrown, only wide enough for one horseman to pass at a time.

The most favorable spot possible for an ambush.

"Hi, lad! How green your eyes are!"

The man laughed a hollow, low laugh, as though out of an empty cask.

"You're right; my eyes are green." He spoke, and disappeared in the thick underwood.

Bethsaba's tale came into Jakuskin's mind. He drew back behind the tree, loaded his gun, and waited.

A vulture flew over him with hoarse scream; he took the waiting man for a corpse, so motionless was he.

At length was heard the long-expected signal. The path groaned beneath the tramp of horses. The horsemen must perforce pass quite close to him. He could aim as slowly as he pleased.

Only when the horsemen came up did he see how he had been the sport of fate. They were only outriders; the company passed; the Czar was not among them.

Where could he be?

"Confound you, you fellow, with your green eyes!" said Jakuskin, with an oath. "You will be making me into a superstitious fool!"

There was no sign of the Czar. He had escaped.

It is a delicious autumn day, such as is only to be met

with in the enchantingly beautiful mountains of Tauris.
The air is so pure that the distant ranges are brought
near; silvery threads of gossamer flutter from every
branch ; the autumnal tints are an exquisite mixture of
gold and red; the turf is strewn with pink anemones.
That little spot of earth is the orchard of the world.
There is a perfect forest of fruit‑trees here, groaning
under their ripe loads.   Fallen apples and pears cover
the ground.   Blackbirds sing their praises to the owner
of the woods, who grudges of his plenty neither to the
wanderer nor to the birds of the air.   The giant trees,
which in other countries only bring forth wild pears,
are here laden with luscious fruit sweet as honey.   What
can be gathered with the hand is the passer‑by's; the
rest is the property of the owner.   ,

Czar Alexander was delighted with the wealth of fruit
in this fairy‑land.   He began to believe in Bethsaba's
fairy stories.

In one place, where the path led up through two rocky
walls, the sound of bells came wafted down below.

The Czar, accosting a Tartar who was coming down
the rocky path towards him, asked :

" Where are those bells which are ringing ?"

" In St. George's Monastery," was the answer.

" Who built a monastery in this wilderness ?"

" It is the former Temple of Diana.   Among its ruins
the black monks, who came here from Mount Athos,
have settled."

" So this is, then, the famous Temple of Diana in
Tauris?" returned the Czar, suddenly recalling to mem‑
ory the tradition of the lovely priestess of Artemis,
Iphigenia, of whom poets from Euripides down to
Goethe have sung.   "And is this temple a monastery
now ?"

The Czar never passed by a church without entering
it. And here was an attraction over and beyond his
yearning for the sacred building. It was a piece of
historical antiquity, a relic of classic times, as well as a
Christian asylum in a Mohammedan province.

"How does one get to the monastery?" he asked the
Tartar.

"By a footpath which forks off from the ascent and
leads round past the monastery to the regular path again.
The horses would have to be sent on; the way can be
only accomplished on foot. It is somewhat difficult to
find. I could guide you."

The Czar was now more than ever anxious to see it;
so, alighting from his horse, he ascended the path with
the guide to the Temple of Diana. It led through a
thick forest. On either side picturesque groups of trees
lined the way; wild vines festooned the branches, forming a green roof overhead, from which hung bunches of
little round grapes, called in Tartar language "kacsi."
Other fruit-bearing trees abounded; among them towered
two thorn-bushes bearing plums—the one rosy red, the
other waxen yellow. The yellow plum has a large stone;
the red one grows in the form of a grape, like cherry-
plums.

"What do you call this fruit?" the Czar asked his
guide.

"The yellow is called 'alirek,' the red 'isziumirek.'"

"Gather me some. I should like to taste them."

The guide, hastily breaking off some blackberry
leaves, formed them into a basket and filled it with red
and yellow plums.

The Czar was heated from the mountain ascent, and
thirsty. The ripe, juicy fruit, with its pleasant acid, was
very grateful to him. He left none. Only on returning

the empty basket to his guide was he struck by something in the man's appearance.

" Countryman, what peculiar green eyes you have !"'

" Yes, so people say. I have never seen my own eyes."

After an hour's walking the Czar and his attendant
reached the classic ruins, now the monastery. He was
wet through with perspiration from the exertion of the
long climb on a hot autumn day; still overheated, he
passed through the subterranean passages, visited the
caves at one time appropriated to youths destined for
sacrifice, and those secret hiding-places cut out of the
rock whence Orestes had formerly stolen the golden
statue of Artemis. After which he visited the chapel
and remained some time in prayer.

On leaving the monastery he sent to seek his guide,
but he was nowhere to be found. No one had noticed
when he left them. The monks themselves conducted
the Czar through the woods on the way to " the ladder,"
where his horse and horsemen awaited him.

Thus the Czar avoided passing the yew-tree where
Jakuskin lay in wait for him.

That same day the Czar was forced to confess to his
physician that he was feeling a strange languor in all
his limbs, accompanied by attacks of shivering. But
he would not be persuaded to take any remedies,
saying it would pass off of itself, and continued his
journey.

He visited the ancient Akhtia, which now bears the
high-sounding name of Sebastopol, was present at the
launch of a man-of-war, and inspected the Pontus fleet.
Despite the recurrence of fever, he was untiringly occupied throughout the day; late in the evening he again
went into the church to pray.

When Jakuskin took the despatch from the dying

messenger and placed it in his bosom the thought
flashed through his mind that it might carry infection;
but he dismissed it with :

"Bah! How ridiculous to fear a scrap of folded
paper !"

And yet Jakuskin would have done himself and his
friends better service had he taken to his bosom one of
the horned serpents which lie in wait for the traveller
by the side of ditches, or in coach-tracks, rather than
that piece of paper.

He thought to himself, "Let the despatch contain
what it may, as long as I deliver it to the man for whom
it is intended !"

The story of the despatch was this :

In the Southern Army all preparations had been
made for the proclamation of the Constitution. Pestel
—called the Russian Riego—had up to now won over
one thousand officers, including even generals, to the
conspiracy. Pestel himself had been chosen as the
future Dictator, who, with the Southern Army, was to
hasten to aid in proclaiming the Greek Republic; while
Ghedimin, as civil governor, was to construct the new
republic within the empire. It had been planned that
on January 1st, 1826, the "Viatka" regiment commanded by Pestel should march into the headquarters
of Tultsin. And that very day every officer not among
the conspirators should be slaughtered. From Tultsin
they were to rush on to Kiew, take the commandant of
the First Army Corps, General Osten-Sacken, prisoner;
proclaim the Republic; incite the Poles to rebellion, and
declare the abdication of the Czar. Entire regiments
of infantry, hussars, and artillery had been won over to
this scheme, the commandants never even dreaming
what was going on about them. Privates were won over

by being told that the "German" officers were to be massacred. To massacre the Germans is naturally always a popular idea. The generals at the head of the army, Osten-Sacken, Wittgenstein, Roth, Diebitsch, were all Germans.

The whole of this bold plot had been wrecked by the weakness of one man. One among a thousand, a certain Captain Mairoboda, could not act against his conscience, and confided to his commandant, General Roth, the whole details of the conspiracy, giving the names of the superior officers, the leaders of the whole affair.

General Roth had written fully to the Czar, sending his report by an officer to his imperial master at Taganrog.

The officer was seized by fever on the way, which quickly turned to typhus; he was unable to press on to Taganrog. Fate brought Jakuskin that way, that he might be the one to replace the broken wheel of its chariot. Such were the contents of the despatch he had undertaken to deliver. With it in his bosom he was himself converted into a witness against his fellow-conspirators.

When at last he pulled up his poor staggering horse at the gates of the imperial castle at Taganrog, his first question to the officer on guard was if the Czar were here?

The answer was that the Czar was here, and had not left his room for some days past. It was understood that the Czar was ill, but scarce four hours since an imperial messenger had been despatched to carry the joyful news to the Czar's mother that last night his illness had suddenly taken a favorable turn and he was recovering.

"Heaven be thanked!" sighed Jakuskin, while his hand sought his dagger.

Every circumstance combined to favor his awful scheme. The guard of honor of the imperial palace happened to have been taken from the "Viatka" regiment, both officers and men of whom had been won over to the conspirators. Well-known faces on all sides gave him secret looks of intelligence.

With determined tread he hastened up the staircase. The two grenadiers on guard at the door of the Czar's room, saluting, let him pass.

In the anteroom was the officer on duty, who greeted him by name as a friend.

"I seek the Czar, with an urgent despatch."

"Go through. You will find there Adjutant Diebitsch, who will announce you."

Jakuskin opened the door. At the same time the door was opened from the inside, and the man coming out and the one going in met on the threshold.

Jakuskin trembled. The face before him had *green eyes*. Or was it only his fancy? The man was wearing a Tartar costume; his expression at once so singular, awe-inspiring, defiant, arrogant! Contempt, scorn, and sorrow mingled in his look; his eyes glittered like green beetles. As he pushed by, an icy shudder passed through Jakuskin.

Jakuskin staggered.

"I say!" he exclaimed to the officer, as he pointed to the man passing through, "who is that fellow?"

"Some messenger or other."

"Did you not notice what green eyes he has?"

"'Pon my word, no. What the deuce do his green eyes concern you?"

Jakuskin passed on to the inner room. Here he found Diebitsch sitting at a table writing. He seemed in haste, for he did not raise his head.

" Am I permitted to go in to the Czar ?"

" You are."

" Is he alone ?"

" Alone."

" What is he doing ?"

" Sleeping."

" I am the bearer of an urgent despatch to him. May I wake him ?"

" Wake him."

The general did not look up from his writing—did not observe to whom he was speaking. Jakuskin resolutely approached the door of the adjoining room. It seemed remarkable that the man he had addressed had not perceived, by the wild beating of his heart, what he was meditating ! A door only separated him from his victim—and that door stood open !

The Czar was already very ill on his return to Taganrog. Still he would hear of no remedies. It is a characteristic trait of Russian czars to defy illness. They will not believe that Death (their chief agent), who has been so long in their service, who at their word of command has mown down rows of men like ears of corn, should ever—brandishing his scythe backward—cut down his lord and master. They are far too proud to concede that the pale spectre should ever see their weakness, hear their groans, limit their wills. Even Death, when he knocks at their door, they would bid to " wait."

Or, was it not so? Was it that the great colossal figure which, like a second Atlas, had so long borne the whole world on its shoulders, had grown weary of the burden? That he who had been accustomed to hear his praises echoed from the four corners of the earth now shrank from hearing the murmurs born of revenge and bitterness, and that his soul yearned for the rest of

the grave? Earth has nothing more for him to do. He
feels that he stands in the way of history. He has lost
all that his heart held dear; his last ray of sunshine,
his sick wife's smile, is but a fading light in the sky of
evening. Is it not possible that the giant, weary of
life, and becoming aware of a call to another world,
should, far from shutting out that call, open wide the
doors, saying, " Here am I—let us go "?

That day he had so far recovered that his illness
seemed entirely to have disappeared. Even his physician was deceived by the outward symptoms; and late
that evening a courier had been despatched to the
Dowager Czarina in St. Petersburg with the glad news,
" Alexander out of all danger. No further fears for him."
(None further than some hundred thousand attempts at
assassination.)

But the next morning the benevolent spirit, which
comes alike to kings and beggars to ease them of their
burdens, had appeared to him, saying, "Come home."
For three days and nights Elisabeth had not left her
sick husband's room. She was his constant nurse, her
wifely affection his one consolation.

And to the Czar of All the Russias was granted the
happiness—at the moment when every arm was turned
against him, when the altar itself at which he prayed
was undermined, when a whole vast empire was about
to crumble to pieces about him—that for the last time,
by the rays of the rising sun, with the life-giving
warmth of the day-star bathing his brow, he could yield
up his soul to Him who gave it with the words " *Ah,
le beau jour!*"—the happiness of having tender hands
to close his eyes, and to cross his arms upon his
breast.

Then the sick wife's strength broke down entirely,

and she sank swooning to the ground. The two physicians, hastening to her, lifted her, and carried her to her
apartment. The third man, who had been witness to the
dying scene, hastened back to the study to send off the
despatch to the Czarina-mother announcing the death of
the Czar, giving the messenger instructions to make all
speed in order to overtake the courier of the previous
night, and, if possible, precede him. After which his
next care was to send off a letter to the Grand Duke
Constantine, in Warsaw.

At that moment Jakuskin had entered.

Diebitsch hastened on with his writing, his mood
that of Russian cynical humor. "What is the Czar
doing?" "Sleeping." "Dare I wake him?" "Wake
him if you like!"

Or had there been something in Jakuskin's face which
betrayed his plans, and was that why the adjutant's utterances had been framed so sarcastically?

The conspirator advanced into the room. At that
moment no one else was there. The Czar was alone.
Jakuskin saw him whom he had been seeking lying before him—silent, motionless, with eyes closed, his arms
folded on his breast.

A mighty man—invulnerable—dead. Jakuskin dared
not draw nearer. Before the dead Czar he trembled.

He rushed staggering back into the adjacent room,
holding the despatch still in his hand.

"The Czar—" he stammered.

"Is dead!"

"When?"   •

"In this very hour."

"Why did I not arrive one day sooner, in order to
deliver up this despatch to him!"

The adjutant thought this exclamation somewhat odd.

"I give you a piece of advice," said he to Jakuskin. "Make this letter into a bullet, and shoot yourself through the head, and you will overtake him yet."

In truth, no bad piece of advice! Jakuskin would have done better had he followed it; instead, he dashed the despatch on the table, and flung from the room, uttering curses on his fate.

At the gate of the palace he again came across the man of the green eyes in the act of mounting his horse. Looking at him with his cat-like eyes, he laughed.

"You came too late, eh?" cried he, and, driving his spurs into his horse's sides, dashed away.

Jakuskin shivered and trembled in every limb.

Elisabeth, as soon as she had recovered from her swoon, went back to her dead, and wrote the following letter to the Czarina-mother from the chamber of death:

"BELOVED MOTHER,—Our angel is already in heaven, and I still am left on earth. Who would have thought that I, the invalid, should have outlived him? Mother, do not forsake me, who now stand alone in this world of care and suffering. Our beloved has recovered all his sweetness of expression in death; the smile upon his face shows that he is looking upon more lovely things in the next world than here on earth. My one consolation is that I shall not long survive him, and shall soon be reunited to him."

Her presentiment was a true one. Next spring brought her to that land where Czar and serf·alike are happy and there is no difference between them.

CHAPTER XLV

THE HERALD

THE science was not then discovered by which man can compel lightning to convey his messages, and by means of which any linen-draper nowadays can flash to the other half of the world the news that a son is born to him, or extend an invitation to his partner at the other end of the kingdom to attend the christening next day.

At that period it took eight days before so important a matter as the death of Czar Alexander could be transmitted, by means of the fleetest Ukraine pony and its rider, from the remote end of the Russian dominions where it had occurred to the capital. The first messenger bringing the news of the Czar's recovery, in fact, arrived before the second. He was spurred by the good tidings ; sorrow went a more leaden pace.

Upon the arrival of the good news, ten members of the imperial house of Romanoff—the eleventh, Grand Duke Michael, being then at Warsaw with the Grand Duke Constantine — assembled to early mass in the chapel of the Winter Palace, the highest ecclesiastical dignitary being the celebrant. The chapel was crowded with high officials, magnates, and officers of rank. The choir intoned the collect, "God preserve the Czar !"

As the protopope was in the act of opening the jewelled book upon the altar, and with trembling voice was about to begin intoning the prayer for the Czar's recovery, suddenly, in the devotional stillness, a harsh voice, like the sharp stroke of a bell, called out:

"He is dead already!"

The terrified congregation mechanically made a passage for the new-comer, whose light-green beshmet was streaming with the mud of many a Russian province— the black mud of the Nogai steppes, the yellow mud of Moscow, the chalky clay of Novgorod, and the greeny slime of Czarskoje Zelo. In his hand the messenger held a letter, with which he pressed forward through the throng direct to the Grand Duke Nicholas. It was the Czarina's letter to the Dowager Czarina.

The Grand Duke, taking the letter, opened it himself.

Then, hurriedly going up to the protopope, whispered something in his ear. Upon which the protopope, covering the crucifix he held in his hand with crape, advanced to the Czarina Marie, saying:

"Thy son is dead!"

And, the choir breaking off their *Te Deum*, in another minute the burial hymn mournfully resounded through the chapel:

"Lord! send him eternal peace!"

The service which had begun as a *Te Deum* had ended as a requiem.

CHAPTER XLVI

"BEATUS ILLE . . ."

WHAT, on this earth, is true happiness?

To be able to dissociate one's self from the tussle and tangle of the political arena.

There is no such happy man on this earth as your

landed proprietor, who only learns what is going on in
the political world from the columns of his daily paper.

In the morning he goes out coursing; starts three
hares, two of which are caught by his terriers; this is a
real triumph. The third they let run; this is a disgrace.
But on the way home his dogs seize and throttle a wild-
cat; that makes up for the former vexation. His horse
stumbles over a stone; that is a great misfortune. But
neither man nor horse are any the worse for it; and that
is a piece of good-luck.

Within easy distance live some men—jolly fellows—
to whom he can detail the morning's doings, and who,
in return, give their adventures.

At noon the wife awaits her husband's return to a
well-spread board, and she hospitably presses his friends
to stay. Cabbage with fried sausages is very acceptable
after such an active morning! After dinner they find
they are just enough for a game of tarok, and the husband can boast next day how he has conquered against
long odds.

The only political allusion made was when Pushkin
named the "fox" Araktseieff; but even at that the postmaster shook his head disapprovingly. Why disturb
the harmony of the evening by such reference?

Then, as the company is about to separate, the postmaster suddenly remembers that he has forgotten to
give Pushkin his newspaper, which he had brought in
his coat-pocket.

The paper was opened. Old-fashioned newspapers
used to be sent out in envelopes. What news?

"A military review."

No one reads that.

Well, then, France: The French are content. How
satisfactory! Turkey: Peace concluded with the Greeks.

Evident enough! England: The Channel Fleet returned
to Dover. And a good thing too! In Russia nothing
of interest has transpired. Heaven be praised !

After which each, lighting his lantern, repairs home.
The master of the house seeks his wife's room. The
good little woman has had time for her first sleep, and
is not angry with his friends for staying so long at cards.
Good little wife! Next day they rise late, because the
snow has fallen so deep in the night that their windows
are blocked and they cannot see out. What matter!
One is not merely a Nimrod, but a Tyrtæus as well. If
one cannot go forth to Diana, one can toy with the
muses at home ; they are good friends, too.

A man lights his pipe, paces the room, and poetizes,
pausing at every comma and full stop to give his dear
little wife a kiss; she, the while, busied in doing her
hair in becoming fashion. If a rhyme be hard to find,
he takes his wife on his knee and looks into her eyes,
and—the rhyme is soon found.

In the afternoon the friends turn up again—the postmaster, a gentleman farmer, and a landed proprietor.
They have not been deterred by the heavy snow. Two
had driven over; for the third, Bethsaba had sent the
sledge, that the party might be complete. She set out
the card-table.

"It is paradise—perfect paradise !"

But once the serpent succeeded in wriggling into
paradise.

At the end of the game, when the long score had to
be reckoned up, in order to see how many copecks had
been won, the postmaster was fain to turn out all his
pockets to scrape together enough small coin wherewith
to pay his debts. In so doing he extracted several
letters.

"No news to-day?" the gentleman farmer asks him.

The only newspaper in that part came to Pushkin, so the neighbors always came to him to hear the news.

"What are you twaddling about? Did I not bring a paper yesterday? Do you think a press correspondent can afford to lie every day? Quite enough to have to do it three times a week. Poor devil! he must bless the intermediate days. If you must have a paper, read yesterday's."

"So we have, from beginning to end."

"I bet you've not read about the review."

"Right you are. Hand it over."

And it repaid the trouble of reading. For it stated that each regiment of guards quartered in St. Petersburg had severally taken the oath of allegiance in the chapel of the Winter Palace. And why not, if they liked to do so? It would do the soldiers no harm. Ah, but it was to Czar *Constantine* that they had sworn allegiance.

"Czar *Constantine?* Who ever heard of a Czar Constantine?"   .

In the great confusion the press had *entirely forgotten* to officially announce the death of Czar Alexander.

"It's a slip of the pen," quoth the postmaster. "Perhaps the correspondent was drunk. Why should they not get drunk, poor devils, just once a year?"

So the matter dropped. The writer of the article in question had been celebrating his name-day too freely, had got mixed, and had written, instead of Alexander, Constantine.

In the next number, under *errata*, the mistake would be rectified.

But the next number brought no correction; rather the "error" was repeated twofold, threefold—all edicts

28

being published in the name of " His Majesty Czar Constantine."

The death of Czar Alexander was never officially announced.

The worthy news-reading public only saw from their
Sunday papers what was going on.   These papers gave
full details of the funeral services held in all the
churches of St. Petersburg, and the official odes to the
dead, which sang the fame of the deceased Czar in Russian, Latin, and Greek.

After that no one wondered that future edicts were
promulgated in Constantine's name ; he was the Czarevitch, and, according to Russian laws of succession,
heir to the throne.   That the people did not love him
did not affect the question.   What had the people to do
with it?   The soldiers had sworn him allegiance, and
the soldiers are the empire.

And what matters all this to those " happy folk " in
the country-house?   Their home was dear to them in
Czar Alexander's time ; that Constantine now reigns in
his stead only makes that home dearer.

The Winter Palace has got a new inmate more unwelcome than the last.   The former, as he wandered
silent and melancholy among his courtiers, was hard to
serve ; how much more the new one, who knouts, kicks,
breaks men's bones, and swears !   His cheerful moods
excite more terror than did the other's depression.

On these accounts the officer of the guards, among
whose private papers was a ukase, " by command of
the Czar " forbidding him to leave Pleskow beyond a
day's journey, might well be called a lucky fellow.

CHAPTER XLVII

THE TEMPTER

ONE stormy winter's day, on which not even his neighbors dared venture out of their houses to make their customary visit to Pushkin, a sledge, amid the tinkling of many bells, drove into the courtyard, and from out the midst of his fur wrappings and high felt boots emerged Chevalier Galban.

A host stifles all inimical feeling towards his guest, the more so when he comes in such vile weather. The road was invisible from snow-drifts; it was impossible to see where one was driving.

Pushkin welcomed Galban cordially. The pipe of peace was lighted in the warm, cosey room. Bethsaba prepared the tea.

" But, in the name of all that's wonderful, what brought you out of St. Petersburg in such weather ?"

" H'm ! My dear fellow, that your own experience can give you a good inkling of ! Your windows do not look on to Nevski Prospect either ! You, too, have your reasons for being here."

" Right you are," said Pushkin, blowing the smoke in blue rings into the air, which rings gathered together over Bethsaba's head, as an aureole over the head of a saint; and, ostentatiously drawing his wife towards him, he put his arm round her waist as he said, " This is my reason !"

Galban laughed. "Well, I certainly cannot lay claim
to such a reason! As far as I am concerned, it is *Ve-
teres migrate coloni*" (Old cottagers take to wandering).
"The world is topsy-turvy. The old set have to fly for
their lives. Even Araktseieff is smoking his pipe at
Grusino."

"That surprises me. Czar Constantine was his ideal.
And I know that there is no one Araktseieff loves better
than Czar Constantine."

"Yes; if Constantine were the Czar, I, too, should
have known what I was about; but he is not."

"Not Czar?" said Pushkin, amazed. "But the papers
give his name in all proclamations."

"But, my dear Alexander Sergievitch! You a writer
yourself, and yet are naïve enough to believe what is in
the papers?"

"The devil! But one must believe them when they
announce that the Senate has proclaimed Constantine
to be Czar, and that the household troops have sworn
the oath of allegiance to him."

"All the same, Constantine is not Czar. We live, my
friend, in an age of miracles and absurdities. Official
papers do not publish everything; still, in St. Petersburg people pretty well know what is happening. When
Constantine was proclaimed Czar, and from Grand Dukes
to guards all had duly sworn the oath of allegiance to
him, the President of the Senate, Lapukhin, produces
a sealed packet, upon which was inscribed, in the late
Czar's handwriting—'To be opened in cabinet council
after my death.' The seals were broken, and within was
found a document in which Grand Duke Constantine,
the Czarevitch, renounced his succession to the throne
in favor of his younger brother, Grand Duke Nicholas.
A second document contained in the packet was Alex-

ander's will, wherein he states that he had accepted
Constantine's renunciation of the throne, and naming
Grand Duke Nicholas as his heir."

"So, then, Constantine is not Czar, but Nicholas.
That is plain." Pushkin said this in a tone from which
it was easy to infer that it was a matter of indifference
to him.

"Not quite so plain as you think. Grand Duke
Nicholas refuses to accept the succession. He is a
follower of the old régime, which suffers no changes, and
now the war of high-mindedness runs high between St.
Petersburg and Warsaw. Grand Duke Michael, the
third brother, acting as intermediary, goes from one
brother to the other with the request that he should
accept the crown."

"Anyway, a display of great brotherly love, unexampled in the world's history. Up to now princes have
been more apt to dispute a crown!"

"And what makes the farce complete is that two accomplished facts, contradictory to each other, have to
be surmounted. It is an accomplished fact that Constantine has been proclaimed Czar and cannot relinquish the throne; and, equally so, that he has taken to
wife Johanna Grudzinska, a Pole, a Catholic, and only
of aristocratic birth, three circumstances which render
it impossible for her husband to wear the crown. And
so, on the one hand, Constantine *cannot* relinquish the
throne; on the other, he *cannot* ascend it."

"For all I care, let him stay where he is."

"You, in your Tusculum, can afford to make cheap
jokes; but what are all the poor devils about the court
to do in such an imbroglio?"

"Especially as his wife is more to the Czarevitch than
his crown!"

"No more of that! With that overdrawn conjugal love we do not throw sand into other people's eyes. I had opportunity of putting that love to the proof. I assure you that it needed no magic to have led Frau Johanna to forget her Grand Ducal lover for a *knightly* one. At that time she had not the right to call him husband. Ah! had not a more powerful feeling swayed my heart"—a suppressed sigh and secret side-glance at Bethsaba here explained his words—" truly in my hands would have lain the power to present Grand Duke Constantine the nineteen crowns of Russia—even a twentieth. It only needed me to have stayed one day longer in the gardens of the lovely Lazienka."

Pushkin was disgusted at this bragging. He knocked the ashes out of his pipe. Galban's boasting he valued at the same rate as those ashes.

" I happen to know, however, that the Czarevitch and his wife are so devotedly attached to each other that Constantine would not exchange Johanna's head-dress for Rurik's crown."

" But what if that is not due to Johanna's head-dress, but is the fault of Rurik's crown? A sensible man does not shelter from the storm under a fir-tree if he means to keep dry, and of all fir-trees the crown of a Russian fir is the most dangerous in a storm. Every one knows —even the sparrows twitter it—that the late Czar was only saved by the kind agency of Caucasian fever from the fatality which awaits every Russian czar. There are many rumors, even, about his end. People talk of poison. The *bon-mot* of Talleyrand is going the round: ' It is really time that Russian czars changed their manner of dying.' One shudders to say it, how assassination, treachery, conspiracy, await him who sits upon Rurik's throne. The very kneeling-chair, the altar, the church

wherein he prays, are undermined. Is not this explanation enough why one brother vies with another in re-
fusing the throne? The most open expression of feeling was that which caused the Czarevitch to explain
the reason of his hesitation to the Queen Dowager of
Saxony in these words: 'Russian czars need to have
very strong necks, and I am not fond of having my neck
tickled.'"

So outspoken! Only *agents provocateurs* venture to
say such audacious things.

Pushkin shoved the amber mouth-piece so far into his
mouth that he could not bring out a word. Bethsaba
saw that her husba..d was on thorns, and left the room.
She had divined his wish, and ordered three sledges to
be horsed and despatched to fetch their neighbors, hindered from coming by the snow-storm.

Galban, meanwhile, continued the conversation.

"You know very well who I was and what I am. My
whole life long I have been a courtier. I loved to serve,
to obey, to intrigue. Never did I have the least in-
clination to join a league of conspirators. I tell the
truth. But under the present circumstances a man's
ordinary loyalty is of no account whatever. The whole
country is at sixes and sevens. Even political leagues
are disrupted. By the death of the Czar the ground
has been cut from under their feet. There is no Czar.
Against whom should they conspire? They have split
up into two parties. If Constantine take the crown,
Nicholas will immediately be proclaimed Czar as well;
if Nicholas, Constantine will be set up against him.
The soldiers are ready to fire upon each other; each
party will fight for their legitimate head. Under the
counter battle-cry, 'Long live the Czar!' we shall have
a fine revolution breaking out. Nor can one tell who

will come out conqueror. If Constantine's party win the day, Nicholas's followers will be the rebels ; if Nicholas's party gain the upperhand, it will be Constantine's followers who will suffer. The position of a man like myself is simply terrible. Whichever side I take to-day, how am I to tell if, with all my loyal devotion, I shall not to-morrow be proscribed as a rebel? Under such circumstances a wise man cannot do better than to leave the chaos to take care of itself and flee to the woods to hunt wolves. And, I trust, Alexander Sergievitch, that we shall often join in that healthful pursuit together."

"I am not allowed to go a day's journey from Pleskow."

"Well, then, my estate lies within your boundary—just a short winter day's distance. Let us get all the enjoyment out of it we can as long as this chaotic world endures."

Pushkin promised to return the visit shortly.

"Then, now we are friends and companions," continued Galban, garrulously. "You may imagine the lamentations under the tsinovniks in St. Petersburg. Next March Czar Alexander was to have celebrated his five-and-twentieth year of accession. Every man about the court was congratulating himself on the prospect of ascending a step on this ladder of rank ; instead of being 'vasé blagorodié' that he would become 'vasé vomszkoblagorodié.' Numbers of them had had their uniforms made beforehand, and had prepared their answers for the forthcoming examinations. You are aware that all of us, when we get preferment, have to undergo an examination? Luckily for us the professors give out the papers in good time ; a golden key lets them out the sooner. And now all this has come to naught. I myself stood on the list, in the third rank of nobility,

as director of the St. Petersburg Theatre, and you fig-
ured in it in the rank of major. Three thousand aspirants! most of whom had paid pretty heavily for their
chances into Daimona's fair hands. Money thrown
away now."

This dangerous conversation was brought to an end
by the noisy entrance of the three neighbors. Never
had doors opened to more welcome guests. They had
not, moreover, come to quarrel over involved questions
of succession, but to play tarok; and it is an acknowledged axiom—tarok before everything!

Chevalier Galban excused himself on the plea that he
only played hazard, and that for high stakes.

"Well, then, sit down and have a game of chess with
my wife. But look to your laurels; Bethsaba plays a
good game."

Thus Chevalier Galban settled to a game that is the
greatest hazard in all the world, and is played for the
highest stakes of all.

CHAPTER XLVIII

THE MOUSE PLAYS WITH THE CAT

THE men flung their cards upon the table as though
they meant to make it suffer, and after every game set
to quarrelling. "This card should have been played,
not that, for we were winning!"

The men said things to each other which, had not the
cards been in their hands, must have led to affairs of
honor. In the opposite corner of the room things went
much more quietly. Here they only spoke in whispers,
as is customary at chess.

" Sun of my life, now you can see of what a wounded heart is capable ! Who other than a man made a very fool by his love would be paying visits at such a time?"

" Then you have not fled, in the political chaos, from the capital ?"

" I ? It is my element, in which I live as a fish does in water. It is my natural element. There has not been a change of sovereign throughout Europe at which I have not assisted. When Mars armed himself for the battle-field I was the Mercury who bore his message. It is in order to win your smile that I have rent a career in sunder, have thrust a princely crown from me."

" And if I do not smile ?"

" I should go mad."

" Oh, you are going back on your words ! The last time we met you vowed you were mad for love of me ; and now are you only beginning to take precaution against it ?"

" Every day I begin to get mad afresh."

" That proves that every day your madness is cured."

" Does not my presence here prove that I am incurable ?"

" It was only the snow-storm that brought you here."

" The storm befriended me ! It gave me the right to come."

" Oh, our house is always open to guests."

" Our house ! What torture in those two words !"

" Shall I say, ' My husband's house ' ?"

" That is preferable ! That manner of speaking in the plural only beseems kings, not even queens."

" Russian women are no queens ; they serve a praiseworthy custom of antiquity."

" But your province is to make slaves."

" I have heard tell that the Turks once conquered a

citadel which they had been permitted to enter as guests. Do you not perceive that you are misusing the rights of hospitality?"

" Show me by one look that my presence here is obnoxious to you, and neither storm nor night will exist for me. I will have my horses put to, and, despite snow-drifts, despite the howling of wolves, I will set out on my way."

" You are perfectly aware that you could find no reasonable pretext for such a step—that Pushkin would not suffer it."

" I knew how it was! Check to your king! You will soon have lost the game. Then you will jump up indignantly, complain of the smoky atmosphere, and retire to your own room. I shall sit down behind Alexander Sergievitch's chair and criticise his play. That is the way the best of friends fall out. One word leads to another. I am hot-headed, so is he. Finally, I let myself be turned out of doors. Now do you understand my game?"

" Not yet. I can still castle my king. I will not allow you to leave our house."

" If you say 'our' house again I will leave it on the spot. The very thought that the same roof covers me, my happiness, and the robber of that happiness makes even this paradise into purgatory to me. Check to your king and queen!"

" Then we shall be compelled to exchange queens. I take yours, you mine. I will not have you leave me. Who knows, after all, if the angel be as white as she is painted?" she added, with a fascinating glance at the Chevalier. Zeneida had thus taught her. "You overlooked this move. Checkmate!"

" By Jove! you have won!"

" Shall we begin another game?"

"The conqueror has the first move."

"Have you heard anything since of my poor, dear mother?"

"It is well that you have touched on the theme yourself. I assure you, had you not asked me I would not have started it. And yet it was principally that which brought me here. The queen wishes to see you."

"Really? Since I was parted from her I have only seen her twice, in the Winter Palace, on New-year's day."

"Now you will be seeing your mother face to face. I have managed to obtain permission for you to visit the queen in her convent."

"Have you got it with you?"

"Do you want to show it to Alexander Sergievitch?"

"Oh no. It must be kept secret from him."

"Then leave the permit in my keeping. It is in very good hands. Pushkin dare not accompany you himself; it were an act of misdemeanor. As soon as you have opportunity to use it, you can obtain the permit from me."

"Yes. If Pushkin were leaving home for a few days."

"You send to me and I will forward it to you at once."

"But with this sending backward and forward two whole precious days will be lost. Would it not be better if I were to come and fetch it myself?"

Clever little woman!

"Were this happiness to fall to my lot I would set fire to all four corners of my castle instantly upon your departure, that, after you, no other guest should be received there."

"Checkmate! I led you on beautifully! I merely went on chattering to take your attention off the game. It was a thorough stalemate. And now you can retire to rest, Chevalier. Good-night!"

Bethsaba left the room.   Chevalier Galban, however, rose from the chess-table with a full sense of triumph; he was convinced that he had won the game.   As a rule he was accustomed to win two out of every three games he played.   The third he usually lost.

The tarok-players had perceived nothing of what had passed.   It had been a fearful battle that had been fought at this table.   Alexander Sergievitch had lost a "solo" with Quint Major, *tous les trois.*   It was a thorough defeat.

"Two kings in my hand, and both taken—a hundred thousand devils!" swore Alexander Sergievitch.

"Yes, those kings," boasted the postmaster, proud of his achievement.   "We beat every one of those kings!"

"What!" began Chevalier Galban.   "You beat kings? Upon my word!   A thorough republican movement!"

The postmaster's interest in the game was so sensibly diminished by this speech that he proposed adjourning, and the exciting game came to an end.

Pushkin accompanied his guests to their sledges, then returned to Chevalier Galban.

"Well, how did your game go with my little one?"

"I was thoroughly thrashed.   She played with me like a cat with a mouse.   From whom did she learn to play such a capital game?"

"What, chess?   Our dear Sophie Narishkin was her teacher.   They used to play together every day."

But that was not the case.   It was not Sophie, but Zeneida, who had taught the "little one" this game. This time it had been the mouse playing with the cat to her heart's content.

CHAPTER XLIX

THE ANTIDOTE

LOVELY, sunny December days followed on the past arctic weather, with its snow-storms. Chevalier Galban returned home, having received a promise from Pushkin to make him a return visit very soon. Post traffic was resumed; that is, communication by means of sledging was once more practicable.

The official newspaper outdid itself in dulness. But at the end of the so-called news of the day was an announcement to the effect that "*on December 26th Fräulein Ilmarinen would sing in the Imperial Exchange for the benefit of the Orphanage !*"

The concert was announced eight days in advance, in order that all who desired to attend should have due notice.

Pleskow to St. Petersburg is two good days' journey. Allowing for the time for post to reach, Pushkin had six days' notice.

Bethsaba, too, read the announcement, and said :

"Oh dear! How I should like to be there, to hear my dear Zeneida sing !"

Her heart was filled with dread. She, too, knew full well—Zeneida had told her—what this concert and this singing heralded.

From that moment Pushkin was utterly changed—morose, melancholy. Bethsaba read in his face as in an open book. Had she not had the key to the hieroglyphics from Zeneida? She knew exactly what Pushkin was brooding over; she knew perfectly well that " Eleutheria" was the name of his old love. And she concentrated all her love upon him to hold him fast.

Was it such an unheard-of thing for men, renowned statesmen, to forget, in their domestic happiness, an appointment they had made with friend or enemy on the battle-field? How often it had happened that great men, when once they had learned to know "the little world of love," had been fain to think how good it was to be " little" men! What happy people Lilliputians must be!

Vain endeavor!

For two whole days Pushkin fought with himself; then told Bethsaba that he must leave home on December 24th.

Bethsaba never asked whither, nor for how long; she only said, "And you are not taking me with you?"

" No, love. It would be impossible for you to travel in this cold weather; the roads are so bad."

" But not too bad for you! Can you not put off this journey?"

" Impossible!" returned Pushkin, irritably.

The tone in which he spoke forbade further question. Bethsaba saw that the hour of the dreaded danger had come. The poison was already working in his veins. An antidote must be administered.

Going to her room, she wrote to Chevalier Galban :

" Alexander Sergievitch is making preparations for a journey very shortly. I await your answer."

This significant letter she gave to a footman, with in-

structions to convey it to its address as fast as a sledge
would take him.

After their conversation, Pushkin, seeing that his mo-
roseness betrayed him, forced himself to be in high
spirits.   His friends said they had never seen him so
merry.   Bethsaba alone was not deceived.

At last came the morning of the dreaded day.   Both
rose early, that Pushkin might not be late in starting.
Just as he was getting into his fur coat, Bethsaba, throwing herself on his breast, said, tremblingly :

" I cannot let you go without confessing a sin which
I have committed against you."

" Against me ?   What can that be ?"

" I have been jealous."

" About this journey ?"

" Yes."

" You are a little goose !   Are you always going to be
jealous when I go away for a day or two ?"

" Only this time.   I had been told that you were going
to visit your old love, and that is why you wanted to go
alone."

" Was it Galban who gave you this information ?"

" He said so when he was here.   I asked him the
lady's name.   He answered me he would tell it me *if I
asked it again.*   When I saw you making ready for departure, jealousy revived in me in all its strength.   I
lost my judgment.   Kill me !   Trample me underfoot !
I wrote to Galban, entreating him to tell me the name
of her for love of whom my husband was leaving me, and
asked him to prove to me in writing the statement he
had made by word of mouth.   Read what he answers."

And she gave him Galban's letter.

As Pushkin read the letter to the end the world
seemed to swim in blood before his eyes.

"ADORED LADY,—If you would possess the desired document, deign to visit my modest dwelling ; I cannot intrust it to strange hands.   Your ever-faithful slave,

"GALBAN."

Pushkin looked in amazement at Bethsaba.

Trembling, his wife fell on her knees.

"Oh, forgive me! I did not know what I was doing! Do not beat me; I am punished enough by the shame I have brought upon myself! I am forever disgraced!"

Pushkin gently raised his wife.

"Do not cry. You have been a foolish child, that is all. In my eyes you are purer than the angels. And I swear by Heaven that no shame shall ever attach to you for this. Kiss me, and take comfort."

"And you forgive me?"

"I have nothing to forgive. A woman has the right to demand that her husband is as true to her as she to him. Such truth I will preserve to you. Now embrace me, and take good care of your dear little self. On my return I will tell you who she was at whose invitation I am undertaking this journey."

Bethsaba knew her well—"Eleutheria."

Pushkin, taking his weapons, sprang into his sledge, giving his coachman instructions where to drive.

The jemsik shook his head. They would never reach St. Petersburg by that road.

It was evening before Pushkin arrived at Galban's castle. It was an old-fashioned building, standing in the midst of extensive pine woods—a hunting-box.

The antidote was working splendidly.

Happiness had never succeeded in causing Pushkin to overlook an appointment; but jealousy is a strong antidote. There are men enough ready to give up love,

29

happiness, means, rank, for freedom ; but the world has
not yet seen the man who would sacrifice honor for it.
Place in one scale all the workings of passion, in another
those of jealousy—the latter would weigh heavier. No
tyrant in the world is hated so intensely as is a rival.

Had Brutus been told on the Ides of March that Casca had paid court to his wife, it would have been Casca,
not Cæsar, who would have died.

Zeneida had laid the train cleverly. She knew the
whole position.

For months past the two parties had been playing
with open cards. Their plans had long been known to
one another by means of secret agencies; their very
names known. But each hesitated to begin the attack.
The members of the constitutional party were to be
found among the highest statesmen, and even generals.
That a collision would take place all were convinced,
but none knew when. But there was a key to the exact
period of the outbreak ; that key was the day of Pushkin's leaving home. The day he left Pleskow to appear against his edict of banishment in St. Petersburg
was the signal. Chevalier Galban, Princess Ghedimin,
and the followers of Araktseieff were on the watch
for it.

Knowing this, Zeneida had planned the intrigue which
would effectually keep Pushkin out of the charmed circle
on the eventful day.

Among certain nationalities her little game might
easily have ended dangerously. Jealousy has often led
to fatal results. But in Russia social opinion is different.
At that time duels were almost unknown there. We
saw from Jakuskin's experience that the challenger was
simply despatched forthwith to the Caucasus. Bethsaba
risked nothing more than that her husband should be

sent to Georgia, in the event of his challenging Galban, for Galban was certain not to fight. At the worst, it would only lead to fisticuffs, and there the strong-wristed country gentleman would be more than a match for the effeminate courtier.

In order that the noise of his approaching sledge might not attract attention, Pushkin left it in the road, and, taking his case of pistols and whip in his hand, walked to the house.

It had a deserted appearance; not even a dog barked in the courtyard. It was after some time that Pushkin at last succeeded in getting a dvornik to open the door in answer to his repeated knocking.

"Where is Chevalier Galban?"

"Ah, little master, that I can't tell. He went away yesterday."

"Tell me no lies, or you shall have a taste of my whip! Go and tell him that some one from Pushkin's is here."

"Ah, soul of mine, you have come, then, at the right time, for the Chevalier left a letter for the Pushkins. True, he said it would be a lady who came for it; but I suppose it's all the same if I give it to you?"

So saying, he drew out a letter from the leg of his boot. No matter if the scent of patchouli became slightly mixed with the smell of leather.

Pushkin, tearing open the letter, read:

"MADAME,—I ask you ten thousand pardons; but this time it was not your heart but your husband's head I was after. I hasten to meet him beside the lovely woman whose name is 'Scaffold.'
"GALBAN."

"Drive back!" growled Pushkin to his jemsik. "Drive as hard as your horses will go to St. Petersburg!"

It was too late. A day had been lost. Pushkin could not possibly arrive at the scene of action on December 26th. A woman's intrigue had succeeded admirably. If all else were lost, the poet's head was saved.

.

CHAPTER L

"DEREVASKI DALOI"

THINGS had never gone so quietly in St. Petersburg as during those three months preceding the 26th of December. Night noises, public-house gatherings, had ceased entirely. In the kabas, instead of the daily three thousand pots of drink, not more than two hundred were given out. It is a serious outlook when the Russian people do not drink.

For five-and-twenty days Russia had been without a Regent. What had occurred during those five-and-twenty days?

The vast empire had had two heads and two hearts: one at Warsaw, the other at St. Petersburg. In St. Petersburg, the Viceroy of Warsaw had been proclaimed Czar; in Warsaw, the Grand Duke Nicholas.

Their youngest brother, Michael, was on a visit to Constantine when the news of Alexander's death at Taganrog reached him—two days earlier than it was received at St. Petersburg. A grand gala was going on at the time, which was stopped at once on receipt of the melancholy intelligence. Constantine begged his brother to return instantly to St. Petersburg and repeat his declaration of renunciation of the succession. The Grand Duke Michael crossed the deputation sent from St. Petersburg. At the same time that he reached the capital with his brother's fresh repudiation, Labanoff arrived at Warsaw with documents stating that Constantine had been chosen, and containing the oaths of fealty of the army, and the people's address to him bearing a hundred thousand signatures. Every one had been required to affix his signature, on the previous Sunday, on leaving the churches; such as could not write had their hands guided. But Johanna Grudzinska's power was still victorious. The sealed document bore the inscription, " To His Imperial Majesty."

" I know the contents," said Constantine. " I am to separate from my wife and espouse the imperial throne. Much obliged! This document is not addressed to me; I am no ' Imperial Majesty.' Take it back to those who sent it."

And with seals unbroken he sent back the documents.

The Grand Duke Michael's mission met with similar success. The letter of Constantine was addressed to Czar Nicholas. He would not receive it. Constantine had already been elected; the army had sworn allegiance to him; the people had signed an address; important state papers were being prepared in his name. It was unalterable.

Michael had to return once more to Warsaw and endeavor to move Constantine. This time he met the returning deputation at Dorpat, taking back the bull with seals unbroken.

Thus Russia had no Czar. The republicans said: "All right. If they can't settle with one, let them try two."

Suddenly came news in St. Petersburg that a seditious rising had been detected in the Southern Army.

Now neither party could hesitate any longer. Pestel

and ten leaders of battalions were arrested ; but this, far from suppressing the insurrection, only hurried it on.

Late in the evening of the 25th of December Nicholas decided to accept the crown. ·This brought things to a crisis.

The manifesto of his accession was drawn up at two o'clock in the morning, thus could not be made public then and there. On the following morning the regiments were to swear the oath to the new Czar, without knowing what had happened to the one to whom they pledged allegiance but a fortnight before. The conspirators passed the night deliberating what should be done.

"All is ready for the war of freedom," said enthusiastic Ryleieff.

"But one thing is wanting," answered Zeneida Ilmarinen ; "and that is that the people do not know what freedom is."

"True !" said Ghedimin. "The people do not understand our views. We ought to have begun by teaching them what is freedom."

"We must begin by freeing the people from their tyrants," broke in Jakuskin, "then they will soon learn the meaning of freedom."

War was declared. The conspirators, going back to their regiments, took possession, with their mutinous troops, of the square in front of the Winter Palace in the mist of early morning. Their watchword was "Derevaski daloi" (throw away your touchwood). In ordinary gun practice touchwood was used. Now all hastened to change this for steel and flint. Then came the cry, "Hurrah, Constantine !" Only Constantine then; and no word of freedom ? But that had been provided for. The mutinous soldiers set up the shout,

"Long live the Constitution!" They had been made to believe that "Constitucia" *was the wife of Grand Duke Constantine*, and thus waxed enthusiastic for freedom as the Czar's wife.

Freedom itself lay deep, deep under the snow like a buried acorn, needing the rays of the sun to awaken it to vitality. On the morning of his accession, the first day of his rule, the Czar was greeted by the tumult of a revolution. They were the household troops, the crack regiments, that rose against him. Their hurrahs resounded from Czar Peter's Platz to the Winter Palace, which Nicholas had exchanged for the little, quiet, old-fashioned Anikof Palace, where he formerly resided. Pale with terror, his generals rushed up to tell him of the danger of the rebellion. Nicholas had seen one like it before, five-and-twenty years ago. Then, a little boy, he was sleeping peacefully in his bed, when his mother, suddenly rushing into the room, snatched him up in her arms, and ran the length of the dark apartments crying for help. One of the doors she was passing opened, and a pale man emerged from it. From a neighboring room came the sounds of a furious struggle—some one within was fighting for his life. That some one was his father. The pale man, Count Pahlen, tore the mother and her trembling burden away from the scene of terror. This episode Nicholas had never forgotten. He, too, now had a little son, still slumbering in his bed. And he, too, snatching up the child in his arms, dashed with it down the stairs of the palace. But before handing over his son to the soldiers he took his wife into the chapel. There, kneeling side by side, they swore to die in a manner worthy of rulers of the empire. That moment of terror gave the Czarina a palsied movement of the head which she never lost in after-life. Then the Czar, taking his son up in his arms, went out with him into the courtyard. The battalion on guard at the Winter Palace chanced to be of a Finnish regiment. Kalevaines, despised as Tschuds by the Suomalai tribes—they were no Russians—what interest had they in Rurik's empire?

The new Czar, going up to them, his son in his arms, tore open his uniform, and, presenting his bare breast to the bayonets, said:

"If you have cause against me, fire at my defenceless breast!"

And Pushkin was right.

The feeling of humanity is stronger than the thirst for freedom. It protects the serf when the Czar persecutes him, and protects the Czar when persecuted by the serf.

"Fear not. We will protect you!" cried Zeneida's countrymen.

"*Then to you I intrust my child; take care of him. If I fall, he is your future Czar.*" And he threw his pale little successor, Alexander II., into the arms of the most heavily oppressed of all his subjects.

He knew the hearts of men. By this action he had turned their weapons from his own bosom upon his assailants.

That one Finnish battalion defended the Winter Palace from the morning to the evening against the whole revolutionary force.

Nicholas, however, springing on his horse, dashed through the gates, followed by his generals.

In front of the palace surged a dense mass of the lowest of the low, roaring out *The Song of the Knife*—its harvest-time had come. Riding into their very midst, Nicholas said:

"What are you doing here, dear children? This is no place for you."

The people looked at one another.

"Eh! He is a kind man! He calls us his dear children, and tells us so kindly to go away from here. Let's go home!"

And they dispersed.

Outside the Admiralty he was received by some well-affected battalions. At their head he marched to the vast Czar Peter's Platz, where was the insurgents' camp. One-half of the square was occupied by them; the other half by the troops loyal to him. Betwixt the opposing armies was the colossal statue on its granite pedestal, with hands outstretched, no one knows whether to command or bless. One party of insurgents stormed the castle on the other side of the frozen Neva; the other pressed on towards the gates of the Winter Palace, Nicholas wandering, meanwhile, undecidedly up and down the great square, weighing on which cast of the die hung the fate of his imperial house and empire. He had first endeavored by every means in his power to avoid the conflict—had sent the most popular leader of the army, General Miloradovics, to parley with the insurgents and move them to submission. A ball had struck him from his horse before he could speak ; it was Kakhowsky who had shot him. The heroic general died in the Czar's arms. Then he had sent the highest Church dignitary of the country, the metropolitan Seraphim, in full canonicals, to parley with his enemies.

What cared they now for priests? Seizing the venerable man by his snow-white beard, they had roared in his ears :

"If you are a priest, read your breviary, and don't meddle to your hurt in military matters!"

The insurgents received unexpected support. The marines and half the grenadier regiments joined them.

Their numbers grew and grew; the square echoed with the cry, "Long live the Constitution!"

Then the Czar himself rode up to them. The rebels saw him coming. It was a temptation to them to see him ride up unattended. A cavalry officer galloped up to him, a loaded pistol in his hand.

"What is your business?" the Czar asked, threateningly, as he came near. There was such a spell in his cold look that the foolhardy man, hiding his face, turned away his head and galloped back.

It was only by force that his followers could tear the Czar away from the scene of revolt.

It began to grow dusk.

The armies of Gog and Magog went on ever increasing, and darkness added its terrors to the rest. With night, axe and knife would begin their work; seventy thousand mujiks would decide who should be Russia's future ruler!

The generals entreated the Czar to give the signal to attack. He still hesitated. First, he tried to disperse the insurgents by means of a feigned attack upon the square of the enemy, and gave the Horse Guards orders to this effect. They were received by a salvo of artillery, and the Horse Guards retreated decimated. At that critical moment drums beating to attack were heard advancing from Morskoje Street, and Grand Duke Michael appeared at the head of the Moscow regiment. He had just returned from Moscow, and, hastily summoning those of his own regiment who had remained faithful to him, advanced against the rebels, and the fight began.

The noisiest of the insurgents, the heroes of the Bear's Paw, cleared out of the square at the first volley; the soldiers alone stood fire. The heroes of freedom fought heroically. The poor soldier, however, who fell without knowing why or wherefore, perhaps learned in his death-agony that she for whom he had fallen was a living goddess, who in some future time would make his de-scendants happy—the goddess of Freedom.

Until late in the night they held the square and re-pulsed the attacks of the imperial troops.

Then, in the deep darkness, a division of artillery sud-denly approached up Nevski Prospect. This broad, radial street opens in such a manner on to the great square, which lies between the Admiralty, the Winter Palace, and Isaac Cathedral, that it commands both sides of the square.

The fire of the approaching cannon might as easily be directed against the Czar's army as against the rebels' camp; and nearly all the officers in the artillery were in league with the insurgents! They were received by the latter with cheers as they unlimbered their guns at the corner of the street. Of course, they had come to the aid of the rebel army! At that critical moment Grand Duke Michael, dashing up to the foremost gun, snatched the fuse from the gunner's hand, sighted on to the mass of the insurgents, and the first thunder of cannon belched forth into their ranks a fire of destructive grape.

That first cannon-shot decided the fate of the day and of the epoch. Others followed. The whole division turned their destroying force upon the insurgent army.

CHAPTER LI

THE NAMELESS WIFE OF A NAMELESS MAN

But, meanwhile, what had become of the Dictator—the leader—the active spirit of the whole movement? He had been seeking all day for a man he could not find—himself.

How should he find him, when he was running away from himself?

The task he had undertaken was neither suited to him physically nor morally. At the very first step he had become conscious of the awful chasm into which the whole affair he had undertaken must ·drag himself and all concerned in it.

Instead of an enthusiastic people, excited to heroic resolves by the baptism of fire, he found a mob of soldiers, fooled by the pretext that their leaders wanted to steal away from them their former Czar, whom, by-the-way, they hated, but to whom they had sworn allegiance; a senseless band of soldiery clamoring for "Constitucia," whom they believed to be the wife of the Czar! What would be the consequence did they gain the victory to-day? To-morrow some new lie must be fabricated for them, that they might not find out that it was Freedom for which they had fought. What was Hecuba to them, they to Hecuba? What had Freedom and Life Guards in common with each other? How would "Constitucia" better their condition?

True, their commanding officers had promised them
that "Constitucia" would double their monthly pay;
but the people must be doubly taxed if the soldiers were
to get double pay. Is that freedom? And what would
ensue if he for whom they had been fighting, Constantine, were to come among them? Might he not come
from Warsaw at the head of the army he had brought
with him, and say, "You wanted me; here I am. The
constitution I bring with me is not my wife, but a stout
stick!" What would follow then?

And the people? These poor wretches, resigned to
rags and misery, working day by day to keep body and
soul together. Seventy thousand mujiks, representatives
of the oppressed of the four corners of the earth—not
the Russian people, but the dregs of all imaginable Slav
races—Finnish, Lithuanian, Lapp, and Wallachian—who
do not speak each other's tongues, who are only united
by their common misery. And their leaders? A set of
runaway French adventurers. What do they understand
by Freedom? The wrecking of a brandy-store or plundering palaces and shops. A mutinous word sets them
on fire like straw, and a charge of grape-shot scatters
them like chaff before the wind.

His soul could find no guiding thought. He went
hither and thither, and could rest on no single idea. In
the course of his wanderings he came upon Ryleieff, in
whose face were reflected his own feelings. The poet
sadly grasped his hand.

"The time was not ripe," he whispered in his ear, and
hurried away.

In another street he met Colonel Bulatoff in mufti.
Bulatoff had been chosen as military leader of the rebellion, and here was he, going abroad in frock-coat and
tall hat. They did not wish to recognize each other, so

passed hurriedly by, one on one side, the other on the opposite side of the street.

Less than all had he the courage to go to Zeneida's palace. He dreaded more to look into her face than into the mouth of a cannon. She defied danger, while he, who had dragged her into it, fled from it. At last, however, he could no longer delay seeking her. He must cross Moika bridge. But the toll-keepers would see him ; the canal was frozen, so, descending the steps of the stone quay, Ghedimin prepared to cross the ice in order to reach the other side.

Scarce had he gone two steps before he heard his name whispered behind him. Startled, he turned. From under one of the arches peeped a well-known face—that of Duke Odojefski, a bloodthirsty braggart, who but that morning would have mown men down right and left; now all his courage had oozed out, and he was hiding under the arch of a bridge !

"Don't venture near Zeneida's ! Her palace is surrounded !" whispered he, and crept back into his hiding-place again.

What a sight ! Odojefski in hiding ! The colonel, whose battalion is even now fighting on Isaacsplatz; the duke, whose palace is among the grandest of the capital, whose family name is renowned in history, who himself has claimed a place between Brutus and Riego—in hiding behind a snow-drift ! And what is he about there? Scarring his face with a stick of caustic to render himself unrecognizable.

Ghedimin lost his head completely. Turning back by the other bank, he hurried home. There arrived, he wrote on a visiting-card, " I entreat you, for Heaven's sake, to come across to my grandmother's house. I have important secrets to confide to you. "

This card he sent up by his house-porter to Korynthia.   He himself then repaired to his grandmother's.
It was his last refuge.

Without it was already night.   The roar of cannon did
not cease.   The watch-fires were the only lights in the
imperial capital.

Good old Anna Feodorovna was still alive among her
fortune-telling cards, her purring cats, and her faithful
Ihnasko, with whom she counted the days still remaining
before the New-year.

"Another New-year!   What will it bring with it?
Who will live through it?"

It is the day after Christmas day.   If two tapers of
equal length are lighted on that evening, one can tell
who will die first, the husband or the wife, by seeing
whose taper is the first to burn out.

This time it was the wife's taper.

"Well, God's will be done," sighed the old woman,
"if I must go first.   And it is time; I have lived long
enough!   But I cannot but pity the poor old man, whose
life will be so lonely without me.   He must not be told
that I am dead.   Let him think I am still alive.   And see
that every birthday and name-day he gets one of the red
nightcaps I always give him.   Do you hear, Ihnasko?"

"Oh, don't keep on talking so much about dying,
your Highness," ejaculated the old man, with chattering
teeth.   "All my bones are shaking, without that, from
the thunder of those cannons."

"Because you are a coward, and because you have
never been a soldier.   The idea of being frightened at
the sound of cannon that are only inviting people to join
the great Christmas procession!   The Czar is now giving a gala banquet to the court and a display of fireworks

to the people. Do you hear those reports? They are
rockets. Now the great set piece is going off! And
when six such volleys are fired, one after another, it
means that the Czar is raising his glass for a toast.
Oho! how often have I attended such festivities! Not
one took place without me. Ah, I was beautiful as a
young woman, and my voice was musical as silver.
Czar Paul was constantly asking me to sing him his
favorite song— *When by Evening's Latest Rays.* It is a
pretty song still. But I have no one now to sing it to."

At that very moment came some one who liked to listen to the "pretty" song.

"Blessed be the Lord of all!" cried Anna Feodorovna, clapping her hands. "Has her nest-bird remembered his old grandmother? What? You have left the
Czar's brilliant banquet in the lurch, to come and pay a
visit to your poor old grandam on this second Christmas
day? Now that is really very good of you, Ivan Maximovitch. But you must be going back. Don't on my
account do anything to excite the Czar's displeasure.
For the favor of the Czar is like a virgin's innocence;
there must not be a breath upon it. If he has happened
to notice that you have left before the time, seek an audience with him. Confess to him that you came away
early in order to visit your old grandmother. He knows
me, and used to be very fond of me as a little boy.
Ah! I was quite a young woman then!"

The old lady was talking of Czar Alexander, only
twenty-seven years younger than herself.

"How often have I hushed him on my lap when, to
please his father, I sang the song he was so fond of—
When by Evening's Latest Rays. Don't you know it?
Come; I will sing it. Sit down on my footstool and
rest your head on my hands."

Ivan sat at his grandmother's feet. How restful it was to be a child once more! And the old lady began her song. True, her voice sounded like some old harpsichord hidden away and forgotten in some king's palace for five-and-twenty years, out of tune, and with some of the strings broken; but, all the same, she sang to her grandson:

> "'When by evening's latest rays
> Thou art resting 'neath the trees,   .
> And a silent peaceful form
> Wakes thee out of sweetest dreams,
> Thy true friend it is who nears—
> Seek, oh, seek, not to avoid him;
> For he thinks of you and brings
> Joy, true joy, upon his wings.'"

Ivan kissed his grandmother's hand for her sweet song.

"But you are so sad to-day, Ivan! Tell me, what is troubling you? Are you going, perhaps, on some journey —a long, far journey?"

"A very far journey."

"Ah, I can guess whither!" she said, laughing. "You are going to see your father, my beloved Maxim."

She had guessed truly!

"You are right, dear granny. That is where I am going." (To the other world.)

"Then take him these kisses—and a hundred more! See, I cannot cry. Old eyes are forever weeping—that is, when one does not want to weep; when one fain would, there are no tears to shed."

Ivan Maximovitch wept in her stead. He was such an "affectionate boy."

"Now, you see, you are going away and leaving me here. And going without having married, without being able to leave me your wife here in your stead."

30

"But I have married, granny dear," returned Ivan. "And I came purposely to-night to present my wife to you."

"Oh, what a happy day! You are married—you have a little wife! A dear, charming little angel of a wife! And I shall see her soon? That I call indeed a Christmas present!"

But then the old lady must needs temper the joyful news with a little reproach.

"But why have you kept this to yourself until after your wedding, when I have so often told you that I specially wished that your wife should receive her bridal tiara from my hands? That was not right of you! I hope she is of noble blood."

"She is a Princess Narishkin."

"I suppose you sought the Czar's permission to your marriage?"

"He granted it, grandmother."

"Then I cannot guess why you should have kept it secret from me. Perhaps she did not know Russian when you married, and you were obliged to teach it her first, that she might be able to speak to me, for I know no other language—I am a Muscovite."

Ivan let her suppose that to have been the reason. It was nothing unusual. The St. Petersburg princesses know but little Russian—as little as, at that period, the great ladies of Hungary knew Hungarian.

The sound of the bell at the outer door interrupted their talk. The rustle of a silk dress was heard in the adjoining room. Then Korynthia had fulfilled her husband's wish; she had come, at his entreaty, to meet him at his grandmother's. There were good reasons why Ivan had not gone to her instead of begging her to come here to him — reasons his wife knew well. In society

they were to be seen, she leaning on his arm, all affection. But did the husband knock at his wife's door
the answer was "You cannot come in." So it had
been ever since the night of the 21st of June. Korynthia was unusually pale; her expression cold and
resolute.

"Thank you for coming," said her husband to her, in
a whisper; and, taking her hand, led her to his grandmother. "My wife, grandmother."

Korynthia bent one knee to Anna Feodorovna, then
presented her cheek to the kiss of the "mummy." To-
day she was bent on doing all that was required of her.
Even the old lady's hand—that hand so withered and
parchment-like—she kissed.

The good old woman was beside herself with happiness.

"What a splendid creature! How charming, how
lovely she is! How beautifully brought up! And
what an exquisite ball-dress she is wearing. It is easy
to see that she has come from the Czar's ball."

Good old lady! She took Korynthia's gown for a
ball-dress. In her day silk dresses, trimmed with the
delicate lace Korynthia wore upon her dressing-gown,
were only worn at court balls. The grandmother had
not seen a fashion-book or interviewed a dressmaker for
the past five-and-twenty years. So she thought it was a
ball-dress.

"I do not know how the tiara I have been keeping
for you will suit that dress. Ihnasko, bring me my
jewel-case."

The old lady looked out the antique ornament set
with pearls and brilliants, almost worth an earl's ran-
som, and was in sore perplexity how to place it upon
Korynthia's giraffe-like mode of wearing her hair, not

arranged to support it. Yet she must, at any price, see it worn.

Korynthia suffered herself to be adorned.

"Ah! now you are handsomer than ever! Wearing that tiara, you can well take her back to the Czar's ball, to be the envy of all."

"No, grandmother, we are not going back," said Ivan. "If you will allow us we will stay with you and pass our Christmas evening here."

"But what will the Czar say to that?"

"He knows that we are here, and has given us permission to remain."

"Oh, if you have his permission, that is quite another thing, and I shall be glad to have you here. But how can I amuse you? Can your wife play ombre?"

"Oh yes."

"But my cards I play with every day are soiled. I should be ashamed to bring them out."

"My wife will see about getting a fresh pack. Give me permission to tell her where she will find some."

"Of course, dear boy. Ihnasko, you meanwhile can be getting the card-table ready. Dear me! How long it is since I had a game of ombre! Never since the little dark duchess and the general's wife have been unable to mount the stairs. Then put out tea and cakes. Now some logs on the fire. We will see who will be the first to get sleepy when once we have warmed to our game. I know I shall not!"

Meanwhile Ivan began speaking in French to his wife, constraining his face to wear as calm an expression as though he were merely explaining whereabouts in his room she would find the cards.

"I am lost. The insurrection which has broken out to-day, and which, I believe, is already quelled, was secretly instigated by me.   Prince Trubetzkoi was the *nominal* Dictator; in reality it was I.   I was the guiding hand, he only the mask.   Trubetzkoi has already washed his hands of it; he has been to the commander-in-chief and taken the oath of allegiance to the Czar.   This leaves me alonè in the post of danger.   The leadership falls upon me.   Nor would I put it back upon his shoulders. The poor fellow has a young wife who is devotedly fond of him.   That I have taken no part in to-day's revolt helps me not in the slightest, for, all the same, I was Dictator.   If the papers connected with this movement are discovered I am irrevocably lost, and with me thousands of the highest in the land whose names are inscribed in a book we call ' the green book.'   This book must be destroyed !"

"Will you intrust that to me ?"

"To whom else?   All that I have I possess in common with you.   My name, my wealth, my rank are yours; my honor, too, is yours.   All this is now at stake ; and you can help me—none other."

" Command what shall I do."

" Oh, do not speak so !   It is not command, but entreaty.   For what I now ask of you I crave as ardently as a man craves forgiveness from his Maker for his sins. That book is in Zeneida Ilmarinen's keeping."

" Ah !"

" I know that you hate her; but without reason, I swear to you !   But of what value is the oath of a desperate man ?   No feeling has ever bound me to that lady that could in any way hurt your woman's pride.   It was another tie—far more dangerous to me—but innocuous to you.   But you do not believe me.   Nor do I ask it. What I do implore is that in this hour of supreme danger you should show yourself magnanimous.   If you have had cause of anger against me, forget it for the sake of the honor of the Ghedimin escutcheon, and lose no time in going to Fräulein Ilmarinen's house with this key, which unlocks the hiding-place. I well know the sacrifice I ask of you in begging you to cross that threshold. But I dare not go myself, for were I to be seen in the vicinity of that house I should be at once arrested. But no one will suspect you. See Fräulein Ilmarinen without delay, and tell her of the imminence of the danger, of which she may know nothing. She may have been informed, and, in that case, would certainly have destroyed 'the green book' were it not locked away in a place of safety, only to be broken open with great strength and much loss of time. Throw the book on the fire, and wait until you have seen it reduced to ashes; then hasten back to rescue me from my desperate situation!"

"I will act as beseems a Princess Ghedimin."

"My life and honor I give into your hands."

"I know it." And, taking the key, Korynthia hurried away. .

"What a hurry the child is in!" said the old lady.

"She will soon be back."

"With the cards?"

"Yes; with the cards."

"Then, meanwhile, I will make myself smart, that she does not find me looking so untidy."

The smartness consisted in the old lady's having her new cap—fashioned in 1807 — brought to her with its large yellow ostrich feather. This she duly put on, and with it her two false curls. Her hair was white, the curls black.

A full hour went slowly by.

"What a long time the child is finding the cards! She will be changing her dress, taking off her grand ball-dress, and slipping into a cotton morning-wrapper. Wait a minute; it will be such fun. How it will make her laugh! I will sing the Matrimonial Ditty. It is really very pretty. Bring me my guitar, Ihnasko. Ah, how well I used to play it!"

And the good matron took the ancient instrument, and, encouraged by her previous success, set about amusing her little nest-bird with a cheery old song—he sitting there, the drops of cold perspiration on his brow.

"Listen—

> " 'It is a good wife's part
>   To honor and obey,
> In gossiping and dress
>   Time ne'er to pass away.
> By daybreak she is up,
>   His breakfast to prepare ;
> Then a good roast and wine
>   With him at noon to share.'

Isn't it pretty? This is the second verse :

> " 'A husband's part it is
>   With her wishes to comply,
> And whatsoe'er she ask
>   In no case to deny.
> Through fire itself to go,
>   If but her hand to kiss,
> And ever to be slow
>   To mark what's done amiss.'

Ha, ha, ha !" laughed the good old grandmother, in praise of her own merry ditty, and quite disposed, had Ivan expressed but the slightest word of entreaty, to repeat it for his benefit. " I only hope your little wife will soon come back to hear it."

But Ivan was no longer paying attention to her—a sound was audible from without. There had been time

for Korynthia to have gone to Zeneida's and to have returned.   He hurriedly opened the door.

But it was not the expected Korynthia who entered,
but one whom of all others he desired least to meet with
in this sublunary world—Galban.

The Chevalier was not alone ; four grenadiers of the
Finnish regiment stood behind him.

The Chevalier, without taking off his hat in presence
of the lady of the house, or in any way saluting her into
whose apartment he was thus forcing an entrance, exclaimed :

"Ivan Maximovitch Ghedimin, you are my prisoner !
Surrender your sword !"

Without a word, Ivan, unbuckling his sword, handed
it to him.

Anna Feodorovna was furious.

"What does this fellow mean by breaking into my
apartment and presuming to take away my grandson's
sword, the sword of a Duke Ghedimin?   Who is this
gentleman ?"

"Who I am, madame, it is absolutely unnecessary
for you to know; but I will tell you who your grandson
is.   He is the *Dictator of yonder mutinous rebels* who attempted to murder the Czar and have been defeated."

"Ihnasko ! Ihnasko !" shrieked the matron, "come
here, and laugh instead of me !   I cannot; help me to
laugh.   Look at this carnival buffoon who is performing here.   He says that my nest-bird is the Dictator of
the rebels !   Where have you crept to ?   Laugh—laugh !"

Ivan said in a low voice, and in French, to Galban,
"I can exculpate myself to the Czar.   There is no proof
against me."

"How about ' the green book ?' "

"I know nothing of it."

"Do not build up vain hopes, Ivan Maximovitch! You are thoroughly undone. Your wife has betrayed you. No sooner did you give over into her hands a certain key which, as you are aware, opens a certain roulette-bank at Fräulein Zeneida's than she went directly to the President of Police and placed that key in his hands. 'The green book' is now in good keeping."

Ghedimin felt his knees totter at these words, as though the stars had fallen from the skies upon his head. His head sank upon his breast. Horror so illimitable numbed his power of thought. The next moment, however, the blood within him took fire; he trembled with rage and indignation.

"No, no! It is impossible that a woman should betray her own husband, and sacrifice her honor, her means, by so doing! Such a monster the world has never known! Nor have I ever committed such grave sins as to demand such sore punishment at God's hands!"

"You have a short memory, Ivan Maximovitch," whispered Galban in his ear. "Remember the night on which you conveyed to Korynthia the news of Sophie Narishkin's death, and with it the news of Bethsaba's flight with Pushkin. Did you not know that Sophie Narishkin was her daughter, and that even then she was awaiting Pushkin and not you?"

This disclosure was a heavier blow to Ghedimin than even his disgrace. With rigid, wide-open mouth he gasped for breath; his hands convulsively grasped at some invisible phantom, his heart was nigh to bursting.

"But do not disturb yourself with jealousy, either on account of Pushkin or of your wife. Pushkin will have a ball through his head when and wherever he is found. Your wife will receive back her wealth and rank, and husband also, in compensation. You will perform your little walk to the scaffold; but your fine possessions and titles—most probably your wife into the bargain—will be inherited by one who knows better how to value them than you have done—possibly by Chevalier Galban!"

At these words Ivan's arms sank helplessly to his side. He saw and heard no further.   Chevalier Galban's next duty was to finish the condemned man's "toilet."

First he tore the orders from his breast, then the epaulettes from his shoulders; finally cut off every regimental button bearing the imperial arms.

The grandmother did not understand the subject of their talk, but when she saw her grandson being stripped of every vestige of his military and civil rank, and of all his orders, she found herself endowed with strength, if not to rush to his assistance, still to rise from her chair, and, supporting herself by the table, to cry to the audacious intruders:

"You murderer! Godless man! how dare you assail my grandson? Stop! Insult him no further.   Your accusations are lies! I will go myself to the Czar; he will hear me.   He has ever been gracious to me.   Ihnasko, give me my mantle; I will go myself to the Czar! Leave off your mutilations, you executioner! You shall not put a convict's dress upon my grandson, my Ivan! A convict's dress! Before my very eyes! You varlets! And cut off his hair! Where is the Czar? I will go to the Czar—to Czar Alexander, to implore mercy!"

Her strength of will worked miracles.   Her infirm, paralyzed body seemed to be galvanized into life like a walking ghost.   She succeeded in staggering up to where Galban stood, and seized his hands.

"To Czar Alexander," she breathed, "for pardon!"

"He has already gone to heaven," said the Chevalier, brutally.

" Then I will go after him," sighed the venerable lady, and fell where she stood. She had said truly.

She had gone after him—thither where even the Czars of All the Russias do not grant, but must entreat, pardon.

The last locks of hair were severed from the head of Ghedimin, no longer a prince. This is the tonsure of those condemned to death. He stood alone. He had no one to mourn his fate. The old servant, concealed behind the stove, sobbed uninterruptedly over the shameful operation.

Ivan was not even permitted to raise his dead grandmother from the ground. A condemned rebel has henceforth no family either among the living or the dead.

They fettered him hand and foot with the heavy iron fetters, of which the Counsellor of Enlightenment was wont to say, " Never you fear, you won't have to pay for them !" And, being an officer of high rank, he had received as distinction a heavy ball fastened to the end of his chain, which he was compelled to drag along at every step.

" Now, shoulder arms ! The prisoner in the middle ! Forward—march !"

But in the doorway their advance was hindered by some one with the words :

" In the name of the Czar !"

It was Zeneida Ilmarinen.

Chevalier Galban looked at her in astonishment.

" Ah, Fräulein, you still at large ?"

" As you see. I come from the Czar."

" How could you get to him ?"

" Did not my countrymen, the Kalevaines, take the son, mother, and wife of the Czar under their protection to-day ?"

" I see; it was they who gave you admission to the
Czar. And then?"

" The Czar has pardoned Ivan Maximovitch Ghedimin. Here is his pardon."

" Ah! you have saved Ivan Ghedimin from the scaffold?"

" And also from the mines. The Czar is graciously
pleased to exile him to Tobolsk among the sable-hunt-
ers, whither he will go at once."

" On foot, it is to be hoped."

" Not so—in his own sledge, and alone!"

" And all this has been effected by your dark eyes,
fair lady? But allow me, an instant. At the time that
the Czar signed this pardon he was not aware that 'the
green book' had been discovered."

" What 'green book?' "

" Ah, my charming *diva*, you are playing the unconscious innocent! But the part does not suit you. This
time I fear I shall have to,hiss. Do you not know that
the key to your secret roulette-bank is in the hands of
the police?"

" I know; and then?"

" And this time the police will not be fooled as I
once was, when Michael Turgenieff said, *'Je suis un président sans phrase. Messieurs, faites vos jeux.'* 'The green
book' has been found!"

" As far as I know a *yellow* book has been found."

" And in it the conspirators had signed their names
to the Constitution, and the several schemes of rebellion were traced."

" In it were the names of those gentlemen who remained debtors to the banker of the roulette-table and
those whose debts of honor were unredeemed."

" You act comedy well, exceedingly well, Fräulein; but,

all the same, you will be hissed off the stage. *Written characters* must witness against you."

" They will witness against no one. Knowing that roulette is a forbidden game, being unable to open the safe, I took the precaution to pour aquafortis through the keyhole; and they into whose hands the 'yellow' book has fallen have not found a single name inscribed upon its pages, for they are all effaced. I was present when it was produced; there was no writing to be seen."

At these words there was a loud clanking of chains, Ivan striking together those which fettered his hands.

Chevalier Galban was wild with rage.

"You are truly an imp of Satan, Zeneida Ilmarinen. By this demoniacal act you have deprived Siberia and the scaffold of ten thousand conspirators!"

" Let us add their families, and reckon it at a hundred thousand."

"Only a woman could be capable of such an abomination. And you dare to tell it to me?"

"What have I to fear from you? I have in my possession a letter from the Czar, authorizing me to leave this unhappy country and to go wherever I like."

Chevalier Galban, seeing that she was thus outside the pale of his castigation, wished to return to his tone of studied French courtesy.

" The world of St. Petersburg, madame, will deeply regret its loss after this 'farewell' performance of yours to-day. And where may you be going, if I may take the liberty of asking, that I may instruct the police to allow you to pass unmolested?"

" Where else than where my *master* leads—to Tobolsk?"

" What! You are going with Ghedimin to Siberia?"

"Why not? I am not his wife, to separate from him
when misfortune overtakes him. I am only his friend;
I cannot desert him." And, going to the chained prisoner, she took the heavy ball hanging to his feet in
her hands; it was her bridal dowry. "We can go now,
master."

At this moment Ivan proudly raised his head, a glow
upon his face. The attitude of the shaven head was
what it should have been before—that of a hero—the
statuesque head of one fighting for his country's freedom. With his fettered hands he raised Zeneida's to
his lips and cried, in the full metallic tones of his manly
voice:

"I thank thee, O my God! Thou hast made me richer
now than ever I was before!"

Zeneida, nestling up to him, put her arms about him.

"Now you may hiss to your heart's content, Chevalier Galban. The play is over!"

But Galban had no desire to do so. Even his des-
picable heart was touched by so much nobility of spirit.
The four grenadiers, too, stood with sunken heads,
against all military discipline.

"But, Fräulein," stammered the Chevalier, "only consider what is in store for you if you seriously carry out
this tremendous determination."

Zeneida looked at Ivan Maximovitch, her whole soul
in that look.

"I will be a *nameless wife* to this *nameless man*. Let
us go."

The heavy chains clanked at each step. In the deserted room the only sound now heard was the sobbing
of the faithful old serving-man; but on the face of the
dead, stretched upon the floor, all lines had been smoothed
away. She smiled.

Similar figures, sketched in with equally grand lines, were abundant in that great historic epoch. Thus the young wife of Trubetzkoi, the nominal Dictator, accompanied him to Siberia; so did the wives of the two Muravieffs and Narishkins. Ryleieff's widow haughtily refused to accept the pension assigned her by the Czar. A young governess, who had had the strength to shut up within her own heart her love for a Russian prince while his rank raised him so high above her, confessed her feelings for him to his parents when he was degraded and sentenced to serfdom in Siberia. She became his wife and went with him into exile.

But the dark side of the picture stood out also in grewsome detail. The Prince Odojefski, who hid himself under the bridge, was betrayed by his own relatives; and one might form a long list of those who, on the same melancholy day that their people were setting out for Siberia, crossed hands with Korynthia Ghedimin in a country-dance at the Winter Palace.

EPISODES

THE RESCUED POET

THE revolution was entirely suppressed. The last body of insurgents, under the leadership of Jakuskin, had thrown themselves into a palace and defended it with the heroism of despair until it had been attacked on all sides. This ended the St. Petersburg attempt.

Equally disastrous was the Southern insurrection. The two brothers Muravieff Apostol,* being taken prison-

* Apostol was the family name.

ers, were rescued by some officers belonging to the republican "League of United Serfs." Then, placing
themselves at the head of the Southern Army, they proclaimed a republic in Vasilkov, its priest blessing their
arms. But the blessing bore no fruit. The soldiers had
nothing to urge against a republic; but *who would be its*
Czar? For a republic must necessarily have a Czar!
Upon the hills of Ustinoskai they lie buried, where they
were shot down in whole companies and trodden under
the horses' feet. Upon the grave which covers their
remains a gallows has been erected as their memorial.

The dead of the Northern Union did not even receive
a memorial such as that. From the beginning of the
fight they were hustled under the ice of the Neva, and
the Neva retains its coating of ice for five whole months.
Jakuskin was taken prisoner; but in his prison he dashed
his brains out against the stone walls of his cell.

Pushkin was miraculously saved. The hearts of two
women accomplished the miracle — two women who
united so perfectly in their love for him that to both,
equally, he owed his life.

The digression he had made in going first to Galban's
delayed his arrival on time at St. Petersburg on the
eventful day. Before he had even reached Czarskoje
Zelo his horses had broken down under the strain of the
long journey, on the road he met Battenkoff, fleeing from
the St. Petersburg slaughter, and learned from him that
all was lost, that Prince Ghedimin was exiled to Siberia,
whither Zeneida was voluntarily accompanying him.

Pushkin was free to turn back to his wife. There
was no longer an Eleutheria. She was dead and buried.

There was no one to accuse him of having belonged
to the League of the Partisans of Freedom. His name
had been inscribed among that ten thousand whom the

"demoniacal" whim of an actress had saved from the scaffold and from banishment to Siberia.

After that came enough of the hard times beloved by Pushkin's muse.

And, that he might belong entirely to his muse, Bethsaba, too, forsook him.

She went—to rejoin Sophie. She could no longer endure this cold prison-world of ours. And Pushkin then remained alone in his desolate castle, with no other confidante than old Helenka. To her he read his verses.

In the spring of the following year he received a command from Czar Nicholas to present himself at St. Petersburg.

His imprisoned friends at that time were to be executed.

That, too, was a tragic episode! It would need the pen of a Victor Hugo to describe how, at the very moment of execution, the whole bloody holocaust broke down, and condemned, executioners, and officers of justice were alike buried beneath it.

It was then that the Czar commanded Pushkin in audience before him. Pushkin was wearing mourning.

"For whom do you mourn?" the Czar asked.

"For my wife, sire."

"So, not for your dead friends? Now, confess. *On which side would you have stood had you been here in St. Petersburg?*"

Pushkin felt the cold edge of the executioner's sword at his throat. Dare one answer such a question with a lie? According to the world's ethics, one may—one does. The conspirator is not in duty bound to accuse himself, to make confession of what cannot be proved against him, is not required to open out the secrets of his heart. And yet Pushkin could not bring a lie to

31

his lips.   Reason dictated it, but his proud heart went counter to it.

"*Had I been present,*" he answered the Czar, "*I should have taken my place by the side of my friends.*"

" I am glad that you have answered me thus," returned the Czar.   " I am about to have the period of Peter the Great written, and seek a man for the purpose who can poetize, but who cannot lie.   That man I have found! I commit the writing of that epoch to you.   Go back to your home and begin ; and to all that you from hence-forth write I will myself be censor."

Thus did one of Russia's greatest poets and personal-ities escape the fatal catastrophe.

At the Bear's Paw they certainly proscribed him as a traitor ; for although all other secret societies had paid for their opinions with their blood, that of the Bear's Paw still existed, and did not cease even then to thirst for Freedom.

GHEDIMIN AND ZENEIDA

Ghedimin was no longer a prince, but became, in To-bolsk, the happiest of men.

Five children, all sons, were born to him there, not one of whom has become a prince.   One is a tanner, another a furrier ; but they are prosperous, and know nothing of the ancestral palace in St. Petersburg.

This, it is true, is a prosaic ending ; but we may not observe silence upon it, for it is true to history, and, moreover, no exceptional case.   How many a descend-ant of princely families tans and works the skins of that ermine once worn by his ancestors !

The eldest of the three brothers Turgenieff, Michael,

who presided at that memorable "green-book" conference, was, although absent in a foreign country at the time of the insurrection, condemned to death, and his property confiscated. The news of this sentence broke the heart of his younger brother Sergius. His other brother, Alexander, followed the condemned man into exile and shared his own fortune with him.

Such hearts as these, too, the fatherland of ice can bring forth !

THE ROMANCE OF CONSTANTINE

Krizsanowski was perfectly right when he maintained that the Poles had no reason to unite their fate with any schemes of Russian aspirants after freedom.

The Polish people needed no explanation of the meaning of " Constitution."

But this, too, is true—that to a Pole the wife of Constantine was wellnigh the equivalent. She was their Providence—turning evil into good, wrath into gentleness, remitting punishments — a Providence bringing blessings in its train.

The famous *Nie pozwolim!* ("I will not have it!") had certainly never so often swayed the wills of the kings of Poland as had the gentle " I should so like it " the will of the Viceroy.

And when time and opportunity were ripe, and the necessary strength had been attained, the whole nation rose in its might—five months after the flight of the French king, Charles X.

One night the Polish youths broke open the gates of Belvedere and pressed, armed to a man, to the Grand

Duke's bedchamber. But first they had to break into Johanna's room.

She started from sleep as the dagger was already pointed at her heart.

" Keep silence ! Not a sound !"

" What !" she cried, "a Pole turning assassin ! Infamous !" And, springing from the other side of her bed, she rushed into her husband's room, not even feeling the dagger - thrust in her back. Hastily bolting the tapestried door through which she had passed, she flew to the heavily sleeping Viceroy.

" Wake ! we are surprised !"

" What ! Assassins ?" exclaimed the Viceroy, seizing his weapons.

" Not assassins," returned his wife, proudly concealing her indignation, " but heroes of liberty ! The Polish people have risen against you. Fly !"

" What ! The Polish people risen ? And you, a daughter of Poland, not siding with your own people ? You protecting me ? Is it a miracle ?"

" Husband, I love you ! I will save you !"

And with these words, pressing a spring in a corner of the room, she disclosed the secret passage by which the veteran Krizsanowski had come to her, and of which Constantine knew nothing.

" We must be quick ! These stairs lead down to the garden gate."

The tapestried door was backed with iron ; the assailants could not force it. Johanna threw a cloak about her, not mentioning her wound, and seizing her husband's hand led him hurriedly through the familiar passage until they had reached the gate of the subterranean way under the garden.

᾿ They were saved. But only for a brief period. From

the adjacent city of Warsaw resounded the clang of alarm-bells: the insurrection had triumphed.

Outside the walls of Lazienska they met with a mounted lancer. Calling to him, the Viceroy bade him dismount and give him his horse, and, springing on to it, he lifted Johanna behind him and galloped away.

But the lancer making haste to inform the insurgents of the Viceroy's flight, he was quickly followed.

A division of lancers reached the fugitives in the forest of Bjelograd. The double burden was too much for the horse. The leader of the troops was Krizsanowski himself.

As they came up to her husband Johanna encircled him with her arms.

"Only through my body do you reach his!"

Krizsanowski replaced his sword in its scabbard.

"Good! So let it be! There's not a man who could injure *your* husband! We will form Constantine's escort."

And the troop of Polish cavalry gave escort to the fugitive Viceroy until he had reached the encampment just assembled for manœuvres.

An enemy protecting a fugitive!

Magnanimity is sometimes contagious, not always; but occasionally people are carried away by it.

It was only in camp that Constantine knew that Johanna, in saving his life, had been wounded. It touched him to the heart. Only such deep emotion as he then experienced makes it intelligible that a Russian Grand Duke, viceroy and field-marshal, could rise to the unexampled magnanimity of uttering in camp such words as these to the troops ranged before him in battle-array:

"He who is a Pole, and loves his fatherland more

than he does me, may step forth from the ranks and go free."

And, with arms and banners, he suffered every Polish regiment under his command to march out, and then with his remaining Russian troops withdrew from Poland, and, at their head, returned to Russian territory.

Could such immense magnanimity be forgiven?

Never!

Upon arrival at Minsk the Grand Duke Constantine died suddenly.

By whose hand?

No other than that of *the man with the green eyes.* Only that this time it was not he of the Tsatir Dagh, but he of the banks of the Ganges—cholera.

It was said, too, that he was buried—that his coffin had been lowered into the vault in the Church of Peter-Paul at St. Petersburg. But the people would not believe it.

Tradition has it that he was taken prisoner and conveyed to " Holy Island."

Not many years after there was a peasant rising, and it was rumored that their leader was Constantine. The rising was suppressed, but the leader was not captured; the people had hidden him too securely.

And to this day the belief is that Grand Duke Constantine is still alive.

The fishermen of Lapland, when at nights their boats beat about off Solowesk Monastery, often see the figure of a tall, gray-headed man wandering about the bastions. It is attended by two armed sentinels; and ever and anon the spectre raises its clasped hands to heaven, as if in supplication.

Then they whisper to one another that the mysterious prisoner of Holy Island is none other than the vanished

Constantine, though forty years have passed since his disappearance.

Snow lies deep all around—so deep that no roads are visible. A gray, leaden firmament spans the horizon. All is intense silence.

But beneath the deep snow something is still growing, and the roots of which will never die.

THE END